David Durell

Critical Remarks on the Books of Job, Proverbs, Psalms, Ecclesiastes, and Canticles

David Durell

Critical Remarks on the Books of Job, Proverbs, Psalms, Ecclesiastes, and Canticles

ISBN/EAN: 9783744781183

Printed in Europe, USA, Canada, Australia, Japan

Cover: Foto ©Andreas Hilbeck / pixelio.de

More available books at **www.hansebooks.com**

ON THE BOOKS OF

JOB, PROVERBS, PSALMS,

ECCLESIASTES, AND CANTICLES.

By D. DURELL, D.D. Principal of Hertford College,
and Prebendary of Canterbury.

OXFORD:
PRINTED AT THE CLARENDON PRESS.
M DCC LXXII.

TO THE RIGHT REVEREND

ROBERT, LORD BISHOP OF OXFORD,

THESE CRITICAL REMARKS

ON THE POETICAL BOOKS

OF THE OLD TESTAMENT,

WHICH HIS LORDSHIP HAS MOST EMINENTLY

ILLUSTRATED

IN HIS ACADEMICAL LECTURES,

ARE, WITH THE GREATEST RESPECT,

HUMBLY INSCRIBED

BY THE AUTHOR.

PREFACE.

*T*HE *Books which are here examined are all in Metre; whence some Difficulties naturally arise[a]. Besides which many great Obscurities in them owe their Being to enigmatical[b] and proverbial[c] Expressions; or to Allusions to local Usages[d] and popular[e] Sentiments. But the chief Perplexities are derived I am persuaded from the Haste and Ignorance of Transcribers, who have not given us true Copies of the original Text. To correct these Errors, has been my chief Aim; and I flatter myself that not a few Passages will be found to be restored to their primitive Genuineness[f]. To this End, a Method is frequently pursued, which seems to carry with it the strongest Conviction, viz. the Investigation of the natural Limits of each Word and Sentence. In Confirmation of these new Lections I cannot alledge the Authority of any MSS. for I have consulted none. That Trouble I thought might be spared, as Dr. Kennicott was preparing his Collations for the Press: but I doubt not but that it will be found, on the Publication of his Work, that some of his MSS. establish several of my various Lections; the same Thing having already happened in regard to The Parallel Prophecies, as the Dr. has informed me. Besides, MSS. can, at most, but give a better Sense than that which is found in the Text: but if that Text, wherever it is erroneous, can be so improved by a new Combination of the very same Letters, without the least Addition, Transposition, or Alteration whatever, from which emerge other Words perfectly clear and consistent; in that case, I say, MSS. are not very essential; for we may rationally conclude that, without their Assistance, we have attained to the* VERY TEXT.

[a] Besides that Poetry is more terse, concise, and less subject to the Rules of Grammar than Prose, it abounds more in all Kinds of Enallages and other Figures of Rhetoric; more frequently wants a Subject to the Sentence, as well as the Prepositions, the Signs of Cases, and other necessary Implements. [b] *N.B.* In all the References here adduced I shall confine myself to the XXX first Chapters that occur: Job. X. 21, 22. XIII. 14. XV. 19. XVII. 6. XXI. 33. XXIV. 18, 19. XXVI. 5. [c] VI. 16. VIII. 17. IX. 3. XIII. 25, 27. XIV. 18. XVI. 14. [d] III. 8. V. 4, 26. VI. 19. VII. 19. IX. 33. XV. 26. XXX. 4. [e] VI. 6. IX. 9. XI. 6, 12. XIV. 14. XXVII. 21. XXIX. 24. [f] IV. 19. V. 5. VI. 14. VIII. 12. IX. 11. XVII. 12, 16. XXI. 30. XXIV. 5, 6, 19.

In determining the Signification of the Words, I have made the English Version, now in Use, the Standard. In the principal Places which I judged to be faulty, I have taken the Liberty to correct it, or to prefer some of the other old English Versions. Those I have chiefly used are Arch-Bishop Parker's *Bible, generally known by the Name of the Bishop's Bible, a Folio, dated* 1568 ; *and that* 4to *Edition of the Geneva Translation, printed by* Barker *in* 1599 : *which last, it ought to be noted, is meant when I speak of the* Old Version, *without Specification. These three Versions have doubtless their peculiar Merit and Demerit ; the two latter ones especially : but which of these claims upon the whole the Preference, I shall not presume absolutely to determine. One would naturally expect that the Version now in Use begun under the Auspices of* James I. *would be entitled to this Distinction : when we find that near fifty of the most learned Men of this Kingdom were commissioned to undertake the Work* [g] ; *had, for their Encouragement, Assurances of Preferment* [h] ; *and took due Time for the Execution : " revising," as they say, " what they " had done, by bringing back to the Anvil that which they had hammered; " and, having used as great Helps as were needful, feared no Reproach " for Slowness, nor coveted Praise for Expedition* [i]." *The chief Excellency of this Version consists in being a closer Translation than any that had preceded ; in using the properest Language for popular Use, without Affectation of Sublimity, nor yet liable to the Charge of Vulgarity of Expression. It has likewise observed a due Medium between the* Genevese *and* Romish *Versions ; equally avoiding on the one Hand the Scrupulosity of the* Puritans, *who prefer their new Terms, such as* Washing *and* Congregation, *to the old ecclesiastical ones,* Baptism *and* Church ; *and on the other Hand the Obscurity of the* Papists, *in not translating such Words as* Azymes, Holocaust, Prepuce, Pasche, &c. [k] *But, notwithstanding these Concessions in it's Favour, it certainly does not exhibit in many Places the Sense of the Text so exactly as the Version of* 1599 [l]: *and mistakes it besides in an infinite Number of Instances. Frequently it expresses not the proper Subject of the Sentence* [m] : *and adheres at other Times so closely to the Letter as to translate Idioms* [n]. *It arbitrarily gives new Senses to Words* [o] ; *omits* [p] *or supplies them without Necessity* [q] : *these last are indeed distinguished by another Character ; but very unfa-*

---

[g] Lewis's Hist. of the Transf. of the Bible, P. 310.   [h] *Ibid.* P. 312.   [i] Pref. to the Bible.   [k] *Ibid.*   [l] VIII. 17, 18. IX. 7, 35. XV. 26. XXIV. 1, 18. XXX. 11   [m] IV. 5. VIII. 18. XV. 26.   [n] VIII. 17. IX. 3. XVI. 15. XXII. 8. XXIII. 14. XXVII. 11. XXX. 2. [o] VI. 6. XI. 17. XVII. 11. XX. 20. XXII. 2, 25. XXIII. 2. XXV. 5. XXIX. 4. XXX. 5, 24. [p] I. 11. II. 5. VI. 22. VIII. 12, 14. IX. 7, 11. XI. 3.   [q] III. 23. IV. 21. VI. 14. XI. 18. XII. 6. XV. 23. XVI. 5. XVIII. 2. XXII. 18. XXIV. 19. XXIX. 12. XXX. 18, 20, 31.

vourable

*vourable Inferences, either to the Genuineness of the Text, or to the Na-
ture of the Hebrew, must thence be drawn by a Reader unacquainted
with that Language. It is deficient in respect to the short explanatory
Notes' in the Margin, which abound in the last mentioned Version. The
Words are at Times so transposed as to create an* Hyperbaton '; *or are
not sufficiently varied'. And, to sum up all, it has this Fault in common
with the other, that it may justly be questioned, whether any possible
Sense can by fair Interpretation be deduced from the Words in not a
few Places".*

This Version was first published in the Year 1611; *and at the Beginning of this Century received considerable Improvements from Bishop
Lloyd, who, among other Things, added the Æra throughout in the
Margin, with Tables of Chronology, of Coins, Weights and Measures".
In the Year* 1745 Dr. *Paris at Cambridge revised the whole, with a view
to distinguish in it by other Characters the Words which were not in the
Original'. In this University we have lately gone farther, by improving
in the same respect on the Cambridge Plan, by framing a new Abstract
of each Chapter, by a new Division of the Paragraphs, and by inserting
in the Margin some new References, and the Explanation of Hebrew
Words. But notwithstanding it must still be confessed, that these and similar Improvements can be deemed at best but superficial; forasmuch as
they do not penetrate to the Substance, or strike at the Root of the Evil.
No Individual, however, nor any Society can presume to go farther, till
the great Council of these Realms shall think it expedient to delegate the
important Charge of a new Translation to Men of approved Learning
and Judgment.*

*In the meantime, hoping this very desirable Period may not be far dis-
tant, I have thought it my Duty to lay before the Public some Part of
the Materials which have lain by me for a considerable Time. My Motive
for so doing is, that they may be duly weighed in the Interval, in order
that if they meet with Approbation they may be serviceable on that Occasion; and that others, blessed with greater Abilities and Advantages,
may hereby be induced to pursue the same Course.*

*But before I quit the Subject, may I be permitted to subjoin at the Close
some few Observations, neither I hope foreign to the Purpose, nor yet*

' The following are all that occur, when there ought to be at least as many Scores, *viz.*
IV. 9. VI. 3, 29. VII. 7, 8. XII. 13. XXI. 17. XXII. 21. XXIII. 10. XXVII. 3.   ' Com-
pare XXIV. 1. and XXVII. 2, 3. 4. with the Text.   ' III. 29. XXV. 6. XXX. 11.   " V. 5.
VI. 7. VIII. 17. XII. 5. XVIII. 13, 15. XXI. 24. XXII. 30. XXVI. 5. XXVII. 11, 15. XXX. 2.
* See the Folio Bible printed 1702.   * This appears by a Series of Letters written and
communicated by Arch-Bishop Secker to the Author.

impertinent ?

impertinent? It has been asked for Instance, Whether the present Æra could furnish a proper Number of Persons better qualified for this Undertaking than the Beginning of the last Age. I do not hesitate in replying in the affirmative. There was indeed a Time, about the Middle of the last Century, when Oriental Literature very eminently flourished in these Kingdoms, and was almost carried to it's utmost Degree of Perfection by those shining Lights, the Waltons, the Pocockes, the Castles, the Clarkes, and others. These would undoubtedly have approved themselves to have been greater Masters by the Execution of the Task: but the Anarchy, which then prevailed, was not a Time favourable to the Undertaking; it was however productive of a more extensive public Good, by occasioning the Publication of the Original Text, with all the ancient Versions of the East; a Work, which has done more Credit to this Nation than any other Production of the English Press. But, to return to the Question; those who will not grant the Superiority to the present Generation, will, at least, surely allow an Equality; and must withal acknowledge, that we are possessed of Advantages, to which those of a former Age were utter Strangers. Besides the Polyglot not then existing, several old Eastern Versions not known, to say nothing of the MSS. of the Text not thought of; there have since appeared a great Number of judicious Critics in the different Parts of Europe, who either professedly writing on the Subject, or only incidentally (as Chronologers, Natural Historians, Travellers, and others,) have thrown great Light on the sacred Records. These Helps would indubitably not be contemned by the approved Translator; who, besides his more general Acquaintance with universal Science, would be free from the Shackles, which not long since confined the Opinions of all the learned (not excepting the great Pococke himself) in respect to the Integrity of the Hebrew Text.

Is it pretended that the Times will not bear a new Version? I answer by another Question. Is the Temper of the People of these Days totally different from that of their Ancestors, at the Distance of six Generations? On the Introduction of the present Version into our Churches in the Year 1611, we read of no Tumult, Clamour, nor Discontent. The same pacific Disposition prevailed in the Reign of Q. Elizabeth; when more than one new Translation received the royal Sanction. To ascend higher, would be as unnecessary, as to controvert the Axiom, that similar Causes always produce similar Effects. The godly, the learned, the ingenuous, would doubtless rejoice; the gay, the thoughtless, the voluptuous, would still continue uninterested and unaffected: but the Caviller, the Sceptic, and the Deist, would hereby find the sharpest and most trusty Arrows of their

Quiver

Quiver blunted; and the illiterate Vulgar, who always depart reluctantly from old Institutions, would soon be reconciled; when, instead of an Invasion of their Property, they experienced that the old debased Coin was only called in, in order that they might be repaid in new, of true Sterling Value.

The Minds of the People cannot hereby be unsettled. All the leading Articles of Religion will remain undisturbed; neither will the Ground of their Faith or Practice be ever so remotely affected. If there be any Foundation for this Plea, it seems to me (with due Deference to Government may I be understood to hint it!) to be derived from the Legislature itself; which, in it's Acts of perpetual Duration, does not appear to allow sufficiently for the Mutability of Human Affairs, or the Changes incident to Time: whereas were it enacted, that these Acts should all be revised at the Distance of half a Century, many of the Inconveniences complained of would no longer exist, and the almost sacred Veneration the People have for Things, which not their Merit, but Antiquity alone, has consecrated, would gradually subside, and leave no Traces in their Minds [y].

But may not the Eagerness for Reformation carry Matters to too great a Length? Innovations, it is confessed, are often dangerous; and the Spirit of Zealots, the most uncontroulable of any other: but in this Case, the Bounds would be clear and distinct; and there would be no Cause to fear, when the Commission expresly set forth the Limits of it's Extent, that cool and discreet Subjects would overleap them. But, to give the Argument it's full Scope; Would the Innovator herewith rest satisfied? Would he not desire after this a Revisal of the Liturgy, with the XXXIX Articles; and proceed from ecclesiastical, to civil, Matters? These are not necessary, perhaps not probable, Consequences: but allowing they were; what nobler Object could the Parliament, could the Convocation, have under their Contemplation, than the Petitions of serious and well disposed Men; presented, at proper Intervals, with becoming Humility; praying, not to be released (as in a late Instance) from the Bands by which Society is united, but that Means might be devised the most efficacious for quieting their conscientious Scruples, and setting them forward in the Way of religious Improvement?

Lastly; How is this Motion to be made, and who will undertake it? If the Convocation sate, it ought perhaps to originate there. But, if it

---

[y] Sir William Blackstone shews clearly the Defects in our Criminal Law; and the Inconveniences it labours under, from Want of the new Statutes being referred by the legislative Power to the learned Judges before they are enacted; and asserts that the Mischief complained of would be remedied, *were a Committee appointed but once in an hundred Years to revise them.* Comment. B. IV. C. I.

were

were not judged expedient to apply to the Sovereign to convene the Houses for that Purpose, the venerable Bench of Bishops might easily agree among themselves, to take an Opportunity in the Visitation of their respective Dioceses, to collect the Sentiments of the Clergy, (and of some of the Laity too perhaps,) on this Point: and, as the general Report (it is presumed) could not but be favourable, any one of their Lordships afterwards making the Motion, his Majesty having previously consented, an Act would most probably be obtained, without a single Division in either Part of the Senate [z].*

But to return to my Subject; (from which an honest, but perhaps too ardent Zeal has insensibly carried me too far; and for which I must again beg Leave to apologize to all concerned:) it should be here observed, once for all, that in the following Remarks it has been thought sufficient to point out perhaps only in one Instance the Sense of some particular Appellatives, as שאול; which generally signifies the Grave, *or lower Regions of the Earth, though almost constantly rendered* Hell *in our Version: that as my Design was not to appear in the Light of a professed Commentator or Paraphrast, I have seldom touched on these Provinces, but where the Reading proposed by me seemed to require it. Lastly, I doubt not but some of my Observations may have been anticipated by other Critics, as many are sufficiently obvious: but, if that be the Case, it is more than is come to my Knowledge; for I have purposely avoided having Recourse to such Authors, except perhaps in some perplexing Places, that my Remarks might be my own. Such, however as the Public is already in Possession of, have doubtless no Pretensions to Novelty: they have nevertheless the Advantage of being fresh, independent, and unbiassed Evidences in Support of Truth.*

I cannot conclude without publicly acknowledging my Obligations to my Friend, Mr. Blayney, *Fellow of Hertford College; whose Labour, Judgment, and Accuracy in the Edition of the Oxford Standard Copy of the Bible have done him great Honour. He has been so kind as to revise with close Attention my MS. Copy; and to him I am indebted for the Correction of several Mistakes, and for many important Remarks, and judicious Emendations in every Part of this Work.*

---

[z] As Dr. *Kennicott*'s Collation is said to be in great Forwardness, it may perhaps be thought convenient to wait for the Publication before any such Measure be taken.

CRITICAL REMARKS

ON THE

BOOK OF JOB.

CHAPTER I.

VERSE 5. — *and offered Burnt Offerings* according *to the Number of them all :* והעלה עלות במספר כלם] There is no Occasion to exprefs *according* in another Character ; for במספר is compounded of the Prepofition מ, which here fignifies *according*, and ספר *Number*. See Noldius' Concordance. מ. 32.

V. 11. — *and he will curfe thee to thy face.* אם לא על פניך יברכך] Our Verfion takes no Notice here of the compounded Particles אם לא, except in the Margin, where they are rendered *if not*, which is not their Senfe in this Place : they ought to be rendered TRULY, or INDEED, as they are Numb. XIV. 35. Jofhua XIV. 9. &c. *Qu.* might not this Place be tranflated thus — AND WILL HE then INDEED BLESS THEE TO THY FACE, or, BID THEE FAREWELL? See alfo Ch. II. v. 5. & 9.

V. 14. — *The Oxen were plowing,* הבקר היו חרשות] בקר is here ufed, as in fome other Places, collectively : but cannot agree with חרשות, on account of the Difcord of Number and Gender. חרשה fignifies here *A Wood*, or *Foreft*, as 1 Sam. XXIII. 15. This Place

A   therefore

therefore ought to be rendered—THE OXEN WERE in THE WOODS. What follows confirms this Senſe — *the Aſſes were feeding by the Side of them.*

V. 21. — *Naked came I out of my Mother's Womb, and naked ſhall I return thither :* ערם יצתי מבטן אמי—וערם אשוב שמה] Our old Verſion has here this Note, *viz.* " that is, into the Belly of the Earth, " which is the Mother of us all." Others, who take the Words in the Proper Senſe, ſuppoſe Job to have pointed to the Earth. But, with-out having recourſe to that Figure or this Hypotheſis, may not theſe Words, without Violence, be rendered — NAKED CAME I OUT OF MY MOTHER'S WOMB, AND NAKED SHALL I DEPART with DESOLATION ? שמה has this Senſe Iſa. XXIV. 12. and ſeems parti-cularly ſuitable here to Job after all the Diſaſters which had juſt be-fore happened to him. The Targum has here — לבית קבורתא, *to the Houſe of the Grave :* and this may probably be the Senſe here ; for Job (Ch. X. 19.) puts the *Grave* in Oppoſition to the *Womb, viz.*— " I ſhould have been carried from the Womb to the Grave."

Chap. II.

V. 5. — *and he will curſe thee to thy Face.* אם לא אל פניך יברכך] See Ch. I. v. 11.

V. 9. — *curſe God, and die.* ברך אלהים ומת] The Verb ברך in Chaldee, and in Arabic, is uſed for *taking Leave* or *bidding Farewell* ; and ought I think to be thus rendered here.

V. 12. — *and ſprinkled Duſt upon their Heads toward Heaven.* ויזרקו עפר על ראשיהם השמימה :] This Place would be more intelligible, were it rendered, AND THREW DUST THROUGH THE AIR UPON THEIR HEADS. See Acts XXII. 23. where this Cuſtom is alluded to.

Chap. III.

V. 3. — *and the Night in which it was ſaid, There is a Man Child conceived.* והלילה אמר הרה נבר :] *Qu.* ought not the Text to be read thus — והליל האמר — AND THE NIGHT WHICH SAID, A MAN CHILD IS BROUGHT FORTH ? For ליל is of the Maſculine Gender ; and ה is here more neceſſary, conſidered as articular and relative, than as paragogic.

paragogic. If it be objected that it is too bold a Figure to make the Night ſpeak, I anſwer that it is not bolder than to wiſh the Day to periſh; which ſtrictly ſpeaking it can no more do, than the Night ſpeak.

V. 5. — *let the Blackneſs of the Day terrify it.* יבעתהו כמרירי יום] Our Verſion does not expreſs the Senſe of the Original: and indeed it is no wonder; for this is a very obſcure Place; and the ancient Verſions give us but little Light. However, from the LXX and Vulgate we may perhaps collect the true Reading of כמרירי, by ſuppoſing that the Word כמרירי is defective for מאירי or מארות, and that כ has crept into the Place of ב; Inſtances of both which Miſtakes are not unfrequent. If this Reading be admitted, the Words before us may be rendered --- LET THEM DISTURB IT WITH CURSES CONTINUALLY. See יום thus uſed, Pſ. LX. 8. &c. The 8th Verſe ſeems to confirm this Senſe.

V. 8. — *who are ready to raiſe up their Mourning.* העתידים ערר לויתן] Rather --- WHO ARE READY TO RAISE UP THE LEVIATHAN: (whether by this Word be meant the CROCODILE with Bochart, or a great SERPENT with Schultens:) For it is certain that we have no other Authority for the Signification of *Mourning* here given to this Word, than that of the Rabbi's, which has no Weight. On the other Hand, it is well known that the ancients were ſkilled in the Methods of *charming* Serpents, (ſee Pſ. LVIII. 4, 5.) ſo that Job may reaſonably be ſuppoſed to be wiſhing here, that theſe Inchanters might practiſe their Arts, to add to the Horrors of that terrible Night, againſt which Evil is here ſo ſolemnly imprecated.

V. 9. — *neither let it ſee the Dawning of the Day.* ואל יראה בעפעפי שחר] *Qu.* might not the literal Verſion of theſe Words be here admitted, *viz.* NEITHER LET IT SEE THE EYELIDS OF THE MORNING? This beautiful Image could not I think fail of being underſtood by the Vulgar; and it is countenanced by much obſcurer enigmatical Expreſſions. It ſurpaſſes in my Opinion Homer's favourite ῥοδοδακτυλος Ηως — *roſy-finger'd Morn.*

V. 10. *Becauſe it ſhut not up the Doors of my* Mother's *Womb:* כי לא סגר דלתי בטני] We muſt here read ſimply בטן with the Vulg. and Targum; or, with the other Verſions, בטן אמי, as Ch. I. v. 21.

V. 12. *Why did the Knees prevent me? or why the Breaſts that I ſhould ſuck?* מדוע קדמוני ברכים — ומה שדים כי אינק] The Word *prevent*

prevent is here at beſt but equivocal. It generally ſignifies in our Verſion, either *to go before* as a Guide, as *thou preventeſt him with the
Bleſſings of Goodneſs*; Pſ. XXI. 3. or *to anticipate*, as *mine Eyes prevent
the Night Watches*; Pſ. CXIX. 148. But almoſt the only Senſe in which
it is now uſed is that of *hindering* or *obſtructing*. The Meaning of the
Text is evidently this — " Why did the Knees of the Midwife kindly
" aſſiſt at my Birth in preſerving my Life ? And why were the Breaſts
" of my Mother ready to give me Nouriſhment ?" I would therefore
tranſlate this Verſe thus --- WHY DID THE KNEES INTERPOSE IN
MY FAVOUR ? WHY THE BREASTS ALSO, THAT I SHOULD
SUCK ? The Verb קדם is uſed preciſely in this Senſe, Deut. XXIII. 4.
they met you not (*i. e.* DID NOT INTERPOSE) *with Bread and Water*:
ſo Job XLI. 11. Pſ. LIX. 10.

V. 19. *The ſmall and great are there:* קטן וגדול שם הוא] Rather
--- THERE THE SMALL AND GREAT are THE SAME. For that
ſeems to be the preciſe Idea of the Particle הוא in this Place. See
Lev. XXII. 30. Pſ. CII. 27.

V. 21. —— *and dig for it more than for hid Treaſures.* ויהפרהו
ממטמונים:] Rather — AND SEARCH FOR IT MORE &c. For there
ſeems to be an Incongruity in the Expreſſion of *digging for one's Death*:
and the Verb הפר is uſed for *ſearching*, Joſ. II. 2, 3. &c.

V. 22. *Which rejoice exceedingly*, and *are glad* — השמחים אלי גיל ―
ישישו] Rather — to avoid the Anticlimax — WHO ARE EXCEED-
INGLY GLAD and OVERJOYED.

V. 23. Why is Light given *to a Man whoſe Way is hid, and whom
God hath hedged in ?* לגבר אשר דרכו נסתרה — ויסך אלוה בעדו] Our
Tranſlators repeat here the four firſt Words from the 20th Verſe: but,
beſides that this is far fetched, it is unneceſſary, if we thus render the
Verſe --- YEA, THE WAY OF A MAN IS HIDDEN TO HIM-
SELF; FOR GOD HATH COVERED IT : *i. e.* the Deſigns of Pro-
vidence are unknown to a Man : God has reſerved them to Himſelf.
The words ſignify literally — *The Step of his Way is hidden to a Man.*
See אשר in this Signification, Ch. XXXI. 7. 1 Sam. XV. 20. and בעדו,
Amos IX. 10.

V. 25. *For the Thing which I greatly feared is come upon me*] ויאתני
would I think be more properly rendered here, HATH HAPPENED UNTO
ME, becauſe יבא is tranſlated by the Word *come* in the next Clauſe.

CHAP.

CHAP. IV.

V. 5. But now it is come upon thee — כי עתה תבוא אליך] There being no Subject to the Verb in the Heb. the LXX supply here πόνος, and the Vulgate *plaga :* and I think it would be better, if, in Imitation of them, we were to add in another Character the Word *Misfortune*, or *Affliction*, instead of the Pronoun *it*, to which there are no Traces of an Antecedent in the Text.

V. 6. Is not this thy Fear, thy Confidence, thy Hope, and the Uprightness of thy Ways ? הלא יראתך כסלתך — תקותך ותם דרכיך] Rather --- Is not thy Fear of God thy Confidence ? And the Uprightness of thy Ways, thine Hope ? I add the Words *of God* for the fake of Perspicuity ; that being certainly the Meaning of the Word *Fear* here, as in many other Places in Scripture, as is evident from Chapter I. v. 1. from the whole Scope of this Book, and from the Words — *the Uprightness of thy Ways*, which are exegetical of this Word, as the other Words *Hope* and *Confidence* are of each other.

V. 10. The Roaring of the Lion, and the Voice of the fierce Lion, and the Teeth of the young Lions are broken. שאגת אריה וקול שחל — ושני כפירים נתעו :] As there is only one Verb in this Verse, which affects every Member of it, it ought if possible to be so rendered, as to be applicable to each Part. Now the Verb *broken* suits only the latter Clause : but that of *frustrated*, which נתע may equally signify, will answer that Purpose. The Sense is — The Strength and Terror of the Mighty are rendered useless.

V. 19. — which are crushed before the Moth. ידכאום לפני עש] This Word as it is now read is the 3d P. pl. of the Fut. Pih. or Hithp. and signifies, *they shall crush them :* but doubtless the Text is here corrupt, and ought to be read thus — ידכאו מלפני עש — Which are crushed by the Moth.

V. 20. — they perish for ever without any regarding it. מבלי משים : לנצח יאבדו] The Verb שום simply is never used in Scripture for *laying to Heart*, or regarding : the Word לב or על לב are constantly added. I therefore think מבלי ought to be read מלבו, and the Construction will then be this --- They perish for ever so that none lays it to Heart. See the Prep. מ thus used Mic. III. 6. and the Note Isa. LVI. 11.

V. 21. *Doth*

V. 21. *Doth not their Excellency* which is *in them go away?* הלא
נסע יתרם בם] Rather — DOTH NOT THEIR EXCELLENCY GO
AWAY WITH THEM?

CHAP. V.

V. 3. *I have seen the foolish taking Root : but suddenly I cursed his
Habitation.* אני ראיתי אייל מישריש — ואקוב נוהו פתאם] The LXX,
Syriac and Arabic Versions seem to have read ואבד instead of ואקוב;
for they all render the Verse thus — I HAVE SEEN THE FOOLISH
TAKING ROOT, AND HIS HABITATION SUDDENLY PERISHED.

V. 5. — *and taketh it even out of the Thorns,* ואל מצנים יקחהו]
Not one of the ancient Versions seems to have read the Text as we now
do : and the Sense given to it, though but indifferent, is rather forced.
I have no doubt that the two first Words were originally written either
ואיל מצנים, or ואלם צנים; both which will convey nearly the same
Sense, *viz.* AND A MIGHTY MAN WITH ARMS WILL TAKE IT,
or A TROOP WITH ARMS &c. The Targum reads here ופולמוסין במני
זינא ידברוניד — *and armed Men with warlike Arms will take it :*
Aquila's Version is αυτοι δε προς οπλων αρθησονται : and the Vulgate —
et ipsum rapiet armatus. These Evidences seem to be sufficient Authority to restore the Text by either of the Methods here proposed.

—— *and the Robber swalloweth up their Substance.* ושאף צמים
חילם] This Word צמים occurs only here and Chap. XVIII. 9. and,
what is remarkable, though it has a plural Form, is really singular, as
we may judge by the Verbs in both Places. Our Translators give it
the Signification of *Robber,* on the Authority of Aben Ezra, but that
of CALAMITY from the Chaldee and Arabic, or of SWORD from the
Syriac, may be more proper.

V. 9. — *marvellous Things without Number.* נפלאתו עד אין מספר]
All the ancient Versions instead of נפלאתו HIS *marvellous Things,* read
ונפלאת, AND MARVELLOUS &c. which doubtless is the true Reading.

V. 15. *But he saveth the poor from the Sword, from their Mouth,
and from the Hand of the mighty.* וישע מחרב מפיהם — ומיד חזק אביון]
I consider מחרב as the Participle Hophal of חרב, as Ezek. XXIX. 12.
and render the Verse thus — BUT HE SAVETH THE OPPRESSED (or
wasted)

waſted) FROM THEIR MOUTH; AND THE POOR FROM THE HAND OF THE MIGHTY. It is remarkable that the Vulgate here, and in ſome other Places, gives מהרב both Senſes; *viz. Porro ſalvum faciet* EGE-NUM A GLADIO *oris eorum.*

V. 24. *And thou ſhalt know that thy Tabernacle* ſhall be *in Peace:* וידעת כי שלום אהלך [שלום is not here a Subſtantive, but the In-finitive. This Hemiſtic ought therefore to be rendered — AND THOU SHALT PERCEIVE THAT THY TABERNACLE IS SAFE.

—— *and thou ſhalt viſit thy Habitation, and ſhalt not ſin.* ופקרת נוך ולא תחטא] Rather — AND THOU SHALT GO TO SEE THY HABITATION, AND SHALT NOT MISS THE MARK. See the Verb חטא thus uſed Judg. XX. 16. and Note, Ch. XLI. 25. That this is the true Senſe of this Hemiſtic, is I think evident from the foregoing one.

V. 26. *Thou ſhalt come to thy Grave in a full Age, like as a Shock of Corn cometh in in his Seaſon.* תבוא בכלח אלי קבר — כעלות גדיש בעתו] Rather —— THOU SHALT COME TO THE GRAVE IN FULL AGE, LIKE THE OFFERING OF A SHOCK OF CORN IN ITS SEASON. Though ſome Interpreters are of Opinion that there is no Alluſion to the Moſaic Inſtitution in this Book; yet I think this Verſe has a plain Reference to the *waving the Sheaf* of the firſt Fruits at the Time of Harveſt. See Lev. XXIII. 10, 11.

C H A P. VI.

V. 2. — *and my Calamity laid in the Balances together!* והיתי במאזנים ישאו יחד: [והיתי is marked by the Maſſora as erroneouſly written for והות: but I think it is more probable that the true Lec-tion is והוות as in v. 30. or that it is contracted, the ו formative of the Plural being omitted. The LXX and Targum have here that Number, and the Verb which agrees with it plainly ſhews that it ought to be thus conſtrued.

V 6. — *or is there any Taſte in the White of an Egg?* אם יש טעם בריר חלמות: [Rather — IS THERE any TASTE IN THE SLAVER OF DREAMERS? To this Effect the LXX, *viz.* ει δε ϗ εςι γευμα εν ρημασι κενοις; חלמות properly ſignifies *Dreams,* but ſeems here uſed by a Metonymy for *Dreamers.* Terence uſes the Word *Somnium* precisely

in

in the fame Senſe. — *Tu quantus quantus, nihil niſi ſapientia es: Ille,* SOMNIUM———. *Adelphi* Act. III. Sc. 3. V. 40. See Schultens and Taylor.

V. 7. — are *as my ſorrowful Meat.* כדוי להמי] The Vulgate ſeems to have read here בדוי ; which makes a much better Senſe ; *viz.* "are "MY MEAT IN MY SORROW." Our Verſion is indeed ſcarcely intelligible in this Place.

V. 10. — *yea, I would harden myſelf in Sorrow : let him not ſpare ;* ואסלדה בחילה לא יהמול] This is only one Hemiſtic, and ought I think to be thus rendered — YEA, LET HIM NOT SPARE, I SHALL DANCE WITH ACTIVITY : That is, I ſhould be overjoyed if God would put an End to my Life. The Verb סלד occurs only in this Place : and the Signification here given to it is borrowed from the Arabic Verb صلب, *in ſaltu pedum terram pedibus percuſſit ;* and from the Chaldee, Syriac, Arabic, and LXX Verſions, which are all to the ſame Effect. I can find no Authority to confirm the Senſe of our Verſion.

V. 14. *To him that is afflicted Pity* ſhould be ſhewed *from his Friend; but he forſaketh the Fear of the Almighty.* — למס מרעהו חסד — ויראת : שדי יעזוב] Inſtead of חסד ויראת, I read הסדו יראת; and render the Verſe thus --- As FOR HIM THAT IS EXHAUSTED OF (or, FAILETH IN) HIS COMPASSION FOR HIS FRIEND, HE FORSAKETH THE FEAR OF THE ALMIGHTY. Or --- THE FEAR OF THE ALMIGHTY FORSAKETH HIM. The ל is uſed in this Senſe, 1 Sam. IX. 20. Pſ. XVII. 4. Ezek. X. 13. See alſo Iſai. XVI. 7. and Ch. IX. 19. And this is the Senſe given by the Targum, the Vulgate, the Syriac and Arabic Verſions. I think it cannot be doubted that the Verb מסס has the Signification here given it.

V. 16. *Which are blackiſh by Reaſon of the Ice,* — הקדרים מני קרח] As the Verb קדר has no Signification which is ſuitable to this Place, (for it is contrary to Fact to ſay that Ice makes Water *black*) we may reaſonably ſuppoſe that there is ſome Error in it. And what is more probable, than that the Word ought to be written הקרדים, WHICH STAND STILL ? The Verb قرّ ſignifies *to be quiet,* and قرّ *to remain fixed* in a Place.

V. 18. *The*

V. 18. *The Paths of their Way are turned aside*; ילפתו ארחות דרכם] It would be more agreeable to the Rules of Grammar, and to the Context, to render --- THEY PERVERT THE PATHS OF THEIR WAYS.

V. 21. *For now ye are nothing*; — כי עתה הייתם לא] It is very doubtful whether thefe Words will bear that Senfe. לא is marked in the Maffora for לו; and accordingly we read in the Margin of our Bibles — *For now ye are like unto them.* Heb. *to it.* But it feems more probable to me, that the true Lection is כן and לי; for כן is the Particle which ufually correfponds to כ; and would be particularly fuitable here after a Comparifon, which continues for fix Verfes. And the Syriac, LXX, and Arabic, feem to have read the Pronoun as here propofed. If this Reading be admitted, the Senfe will be — THUS ARE YE NOW TO ME.

—— *ye fee my cafting down.*] Inftead of חתת the LXX and Vulgate read חתתי.

V. 22. *Did I fay* — הכי אמרתי] DID I INDEED SAY? for כי has that Force here.

V. 26. *Do ye imagine to reprove Words, and the Speeches of one that is defperate, which are as Wind?* הלהוכח מלים תחשבו — ולרוח אמרי נואש] Rather — DO YE IMAGINE TO REPROVE WORDS, AND TO PUT AWAY THE SPEECHES (COMPLAINTS) OF HIM THAT IS DESPERATE? That לרוח is here a Verb, may be concluded from the preceding Hemiftic; and that it has the Signification contended for, or of *difperfing* and *fcattering with a Blaft*, cannot I think be doubted from the Ufe of the Noun.

V. 29. *Return, I pray you, let it not be Iniquity; yea, return again, my Righteoufnefs is in it.* שבו נא אל תהי עולה — ושבו עוד צדקי בה] Rather, I think --- RETURN, I PRAY YOU, LEST IT BE INIQUITY: YEA, RETURN AGAIN TO JUSTIFY ME IN THIS. In this Book the Infinitive with the Affix is ufed precifely in this Form, *viz.* צדקו, *to juftify him*, and צדקך *to juftify thee*, Ch. XXXII. 2. XXXIII. 32.

CHAP. VII.

V. 2. — *and as an Hireling looketh for the Reward of his Work.* וכשכיר יקוה פעלו] Rather — AND AS AN HIRELING LOOKETH FOR HIS WAGES. See פעל thus rendered Lev. XIX. 13.

B

V. 8. — *thine*

V. 8. — *thine Eyes* are *upon me, and I am not.* : עיניך בי ואינני]
As the preceding Hemiſtic is expreſſed in the future, ſo I think this
ſhould alſo be — *viz.* THINE EYES ſhall be UPON ME : BUT I ſhall
NOT be. It is ſo rendered in the laſt Verſe of this Chapter ; and for
the ſame Reaſon.

CHAP. VIII.

V. 6. — *ſurely now he would awake for thee,* — כי עתה יעיר עליך]
Would not the Verb יעיר be here more properly rendered, HE WOULD
STIR, as in other Places in this Book, and elſewhere ?

V. 11. — *can the Flag grow without Water ?* ישגה אחו בלי מים:]
ישגה is here corruptly written for ישגא : and it would be more properly rendered, INCREASE, becauſe יגאה is tranſlated in the preceding
Hemiſtic, *grow up.*

V. 12. *Whilſt it is yet in his Greenneſs,* and *not cut down,* — עדנו
באבו לא יקטף] Rather — SHALL IT NOT BE CUT DOWN, WHILST
IT IS YET IN ITS GREENNESS ? The Interrogation being ſupplied,
and continued, from the preceding Verſe. Or the Text may be thus
read, עדנו באב ולא יקטף — WHILST IT IS YET IN GREENNESS,
AND NOT CUT DOWN. The LXX read it ſo.

—— *it withereth before any* other *Herb.* : ולפני כל הציר ייבש]
Rather—AND WITHER &c. Our Verſion omits the Copulative Particle.

V. 14. *Whoſe Hope ſhall be cut off,*—אשר יקוט כסלו] The Senſe here
given is a good one : but the Words of the Text will not bear it.
The following is certainly nearer the Original, *viz.* WHO WILL DE-
TEST HIS OWN EXPECTATION.

V. 17. *His Roots are wrapped about the Heap,* — על גל שרשיו יסבכו]
Rather — ABOUT A FOUNTAIN, as in the old Verſion. גלה ſignifies
a Fountain, Joſ. XV. 19.

—— and *ſeeth the Place of Stones.* בית אבנים יחזה:] Theſe
Words are ſo obſcure, that the Integrity of the Text may reaſonably
be queſtioned. There is no Doubt that the LXX and Vulgate read
here בין and יחיה ; from which ſlight Alteration a better Senſe may be
deduced, *viz.* HE LIVETH BETWEEN THE STONES.

V. 18. *If he deſtroy him* — אם יבלענו] Rather, with our old Verſion, IF any DESTROY HIM : for *God* is at too great a Diſtance to
ſuppoſe that He is the Antecedent. CHAP.

CHAP. IX.

V. 3. — *he cannot anfwer him one of a thoufand.* לא יעננו אחת מני
אלף] As אחת is here feminine, which anfwers to the neuter in
other Languages, it would be better expreffed here by ONE THING,
as in the old Verfion ; or adverbially, as ONCE IN A THOUSAND
TIMES.

V. 7. — *and fealeth up the Stars.* ובעד כוכבים יחתם :] The Verfion now in Ufe takes no Notice of the Word בעד. The old Verfion
confiders it as compounded of the Prepofition ב and עד *a Witnefs,* and
renders it — as UNDER A SIGNET.

V. 11. *Lo, he goeth by me, and I fee* him *not : he paffeth on alfo,* &c.
הן יעבר עלי ולא אראה—ויחלף וגו] The Words ויהלף אראה ought
I think to be read thus — אראהו — יחלף ; for the Pronoun is here
wanting, and not the Copulative Particle ; as is apparent from our
Verfion, which fupplies the one, and omits the other.

V. 19. *If* I *fpeak of Strength, lo, he is ftrong :*— אם לכח אמיץ הנה]
As the Particle הנה is always put firft in a Sentence ; it is probable
that it is here a Miftake for הוה or הוא, which are generally ufed in
fimilar Cafes. The Particle ל feems to fignify here IN RESPECT TO,
OR IN REGARD OF ; and אם may be conftrued TRULY, as Pf.CXXXIX.
19. Prov. XXIII. 18. *et paffim.* Thus moft of the ancient Verfions
confidered them.

V. 27. — *I will leave off my Heavinefs :* אעזברה פני] I cannot find
that פני ever fignifies *Heavinefs :* it is ufed for ANGER, Lam. IV. 16.
which Senfe might be here adopted.

V. 29. If *I be wicked,* אנכי ארשע ******] Here are manifeftly
fome Words wanting to complete the Hemiftic : and none will be
more fuitable than thofe, with which the 27th Verfe begins — אם אמרי
—IF I SAY.

V. 35. — *but* it is *not fo with me.* כי לא כן אנכי עמדי :] Rather,
with the old Verfion — but BECAUSE I am NOT SO, I HOLD ME
STILL. עמדי being there confidered as the Participle with the י paragogic, or as the Infinitive with the Affix of the firft Perfon.

C H A P. X.

V. 15. — and if I be righteous, yet will I not lift up my Head וצדקתי לא אשא ראשי] Rather—AND IF I BE RIGHTEOUS, SHALL I NOT LIFT UP MY HEAD?

—— *I am full of Confusion; therefore see thou mine Affliction.* שבע קלון וראה עני:] I would connect this Clause with the preceding one, and suppose אתה understood after ראה; in this Sense — though I be FULL OF CONFUSION, AND THOU SEE MINE AFFLICTION.

V. 16. For it increaseth: Thou huntest me as a fierce Lion: ויגאה כשחל הצורני] The Hemistic seems to require that these Words should be connected; which may perhaps be best done thus —While IT (*viz.* MINE AFFLICTION) INCREASETH, THOU HUNTEST ME &c. The Syriac seems to have read אם אגאה, *If I exalt myself.*

V. 22. A Land of Darkness, as Darkness itself; and of the Shadow of Death, -- ארץ עפתה כמו אפל צלמות] Rather — A LAND OF DARKNESS, AS THE DARKNESS OF THE SHADOW OF DEATH.

C H A P. XI.

V. 3. — and when thou mockest, shall no Man make thee ashamed? — ותלעג ואין מכלם] The Words signify literally — AND SHALT THOU MOCK, AND NO MAN MAKE THEE ASHAMED?

V. 6. —— God exacteth of thee less than thine Iniquity deserveth. ישה לך אלוה מעונך:] These Words seem rather to signify — GOD COVERETH (literally *maketh to be forgotten*) A PART OF THINE INIQUITY. Thus — *Blessed is he whose Sin is* COVERED. Pf. XXXII. 1. and LXXXV. 2. *Thou hast* COVERED *all their Sin.* See also Prov. X. 12.

V. 17. —— thou shalt shine forth, thou shalt be as the Morning. תעפה כבקר תהיה:] How our Version came to give תעפה a Sense directly contrary to that which the Verb עוף, from which it is derived, constantly has, I cannot imagine. This particular Word occurs no where else: but by its Form must be *a Noun,* and signify DARKNESS: There can therefore be no Doubt, that this Hemistic ought thus to be
rendered

rendered --- THE DARKNESS SHALL BE AS THE MORNING : That is, "thine Affliction fhall be converted into Joy."

V. 18. —— *yea, thou fhalt dig* about thee, and *thou fhalt take thy Reft in Safety,* : והפרת לבטה תשכב] Rather, I think —— AND THOU SHALT SEARCH FOR SAFETY, and BE AT REST. Thus הפר is rendered Ch. III. 21. Deut. I. 22. Jofh. II. 2, 3.

CHAP. XII.

V. 5. *He that is ready to flip with* his *Feet,* is as *a Lamp defpifed in the Thought of him that is at Eafe.* —— לפיד בוז לעשתורת שאנן : נכון למועדי רגל] לפיד is here confidered as compounded of the Prepofition ל and פיד *a Misfortune:* I would therefore render literally thus --- TO CALAMITY IS CONTEMPT, IN THE THOUGHTS OF HIM THAT IS AT EASE, PREPARED FOR THE SLIPPING FOOT; which may be thus paraphrafed — " Calamity generally meets with " Contempt from the profperous Man, whofe Self-Conceit makes him " ready to attribute the Misfortunes of others to Want of Prudence or " Conduct." This was exactly Job's Cafe with his Friends.

V. 6. —*and they that provoke God are fecure;* — ובטחות למרגיזי אל] Thefe Words fignify literally — AND there is SECURITY TO THEM THAT PROVOKE GOD.

—— *into whofe Hand God bringeth* abundantly. לאשר הביא אלוה בירו :] There is no Occafion to fupply any Word in the Verfion, for לאשר expreffes the Idea, which is fuppofed to be wanting to complete the Senfe; אשר fignifying *Profperity.* See Inftances of the ל prefixed to the Accufative Cafe in Noldius. Thefe Words may therefore be rendered --- INTO WHOSE HAND GOD BRINGETH PROSPERITY.

V. 17. *He leadeth Counfellors away fpoiled,* מוליך יועצים שולל] It would be more accurate to render --- HE LEADETH COUNSELLORS TO BE SPOILED. For שולל is here the Supine, fo likewife V. 19.

V. 18. *He loofeth the Bond of Kings, and girdeth their Loins with a Girdle.* מוסר מלכים פתח—ויאסר אור במהניהם :] Qu. ought not this Verfe to be thus rendered --- HE CHASTISETH KINGS; HE LOOSETH AND GIRDETH THE ROPE UPON THEIR LOINS? For the

the same Mode of Expreſſion (*viz.* the Participle) is uſed ſix Times in the foregoing and ſubſequent Verſes. Or thus (in order to preſerve the Uniformity of the Hemiſtics) --- HE LOOSETH THE BOND OF KINGS, AND GIRDETH THE GIRDLE UPON THEIR LOINS. By *loofing the Bond,* or *Band,* may be meant " depriving them of their " Strength ;" *a Girdle* being uſed figuratively to denote STRENGTH, and ſo tranſlated at the 21ſt Verſe (where what is rendered, *weakeneth the Strength,* is literally, *loofeth the Girdle*) and Iſa. XXIII. 10. and the *not having the Girdle of their Loins loofed* (Iſa. V. 27.) is deſcriptive of " Perſons in full Vigour and Strength." According to this Interpretation, when it is ſaid, as an Inſtance of GOD's Power, that *he loofeth the Band of Kings,* it may be meant thereby, " that he taketh " away their mighty Power ;" which the next Hemiſtic may be underſtood to intimate was " His original Gift."

CHAP. XIII.

V. 12. *Your Remembrances* are *like unto Aſhes, your Bodies to Bodies of Clay.* : זכרניכם משלי אפר — לגבי חמר גביכם] Rather---YOUR REPETITIONS OF WISE SAYINGS are as ASHES, YOUR SUBLIME Things AS HEAPS OF CLAY. The ל in לגבי is here comparative, as Joſ. VII. 5. 1 Sam. XXV. 37. And משלי muſt have the Senſe here given it ; for it is never uſed but in Niphal to denote *Likeneſs.*

V. 13. *Held your Peace, let me alone,* החרישו ממני] The Words ſignify literally --- HOLD YOUR TONGUES FROM ME, viz. *do not interrupt me.*

V. 14. — *and put my Life in mine Hand?* : ונפשי אשים בכפי] This Phraſe occurs in ſeveral Parts of Scripture ; and always ſignifies *to expoſe one's Life to imminent Danger.* The Ground of it ſeems to me to be this ; that, as יד *the Hand* is often uſed by a Metaphor for *Power,* a Perſon is ſaid *to put his Life in his Hand,* when he is " re- " duced ſolely to his own Power, or Agency, for the Preſervation of it." Or *the putting of any Thing valuable into one's Hand* may ſignify, *expoſing it to Danger;* on this Account, becauſe it is then ready to be ſnatched away by any one that is ſtronger ; whereas a Treaſure locked up, and kept in a retired Place, is not ſo eaſy to be come at, nor affords the like Temptation. This Expreſſion has been thought to be an Hebraiſm : but

but it is found, and used in the same Sense, in the best Greek Writers; thus Titus addresses the Jews — ω ταλαιπωροι, τινι πεποιθοτες; ȣ νεκρος μεν υμων ο δημος, οιχεται δε ο ναος, υπ᾽ εμει δε η πολις, EN XEΡΣI ΔE TAIΣ HMAIΣ EXETE TAΣ ΨΥXAΣ, ειϑ᾽ ὑπολαμβανετε δεξαν ανδρειας τε θανατων; *Joseph. de bello Jud. Lib.*VI. *Cap.*VI. Hudf. p.1285. It is also found in a Fragment of Xenarchus the Poet, preserved by Athenæus, *Lib.* XIII; where, speaking of those who courted the Athenian Matrons, he says ——

As ȣτ᾽ ιδειν εσ᾽, ȣϑ᾽ ερανϑ᾽ ιδειν σαφως,
Aει δε τι τερμαινοντα και Φιθυμιειν
Δυδιετα, EN TH XEIPI THN ΨΥXAN EXON-
TA, &c.

V. 18. *Behold now I have ordered my Cause:* הנה נא ערכתי משפט] The LXX, Syriac, and Arabic, seem to have read משפטי MY CAUSE. The next Word beginning with a י might occasion the Omission.

V. 19. — *for now, if I hold my Tongue, I shall give up the Ghost.* כי עתה אהריש ואגוע:] Rather — FOR SHALL I NOW HOLD MY TONGUE, AND GIVE UP THE GHOST ? *i. e.* "die without clear-" ing my Character." כי here seems to be interrogative (as well as cau-sal) as Prov. XXX. 4. Isa. XXIX. 16.

V. 27. — *thou settest a Print upon the Heels of my Feet.* על שרשי רגלי תתחקה:] Rather — THOU ENGRAVEST UPON THE SOLES OF MY FEET, viz. *the Marks of thy Displeasure.* Alluding perhaps to the Custom of beating Slaves upon the Soles of the Feet. See Taylor.

V. 28. *And he as a rotten Thing consumeth,* &c.] As this Verse is quite unconnected with what precedes, and the Pronoun has no Ante-cedent, I cannot but suspect that it has, by the Negligence of the Transcribers, got out of its Place, and ought to have come after the next Verse, *i. e.* the first Verse of the next Chapter, where it would suit admirably well.

CHAP. XIV.

V. 6. — *till he shall accomplish, as an Hireling, his Day.* עד ירצה כשכיר יומו:] Rather — TILL HE SHALL BE SATISFIED, LIKE AN HIRELING, with his DAY. For רצה never signifies *to accomplish.*

Or

Or might not עד be rendered, *so far as*, thus — TURN FROM HIM THAT HE MAY REST, SO FAR at least AS TO BE SATISFIED, LIKE AN HIRELING, WITH HIS DAY, or CONDITION; though it be none of the best?

V. 21. — *but he perceiveth* it *not of them*.   ולא יבין למו:] Rather BUT HE DOTH NOT ATTEND TO THEM.

CHAP. XV.

V. 20. — *and the Number of his Days is hidden to the Oppressor*.] Here and in the preceding Verse seem to be plain Allusions to the Sanctions of the Mosaic Law. For no other Institution ever insured Long Life, and other temporal Blessings, to the Observers of it. See Ch. V. v. 26.

V. 23. *He wandereth abroad for Bread*, saying, *Where* is it? נדד הוא ללחם איה] Rather — HE WANDERETH ABROAD FOR BREAD WHEREVER it is; viz. *to be found*.

V. 26. *He runneth upon him*, even *on* his *Neck*; — ירוץ אליו בצואר] In our present Version it is not clear whether God, or the Wicked Man, is here the Aggressor: from the Construction the latter might seem most probable; but from Reason, it must be the former. I would therefore, with our old Version, supply — *Therefore God*, and thus render the other Words --- WILL ATTACK HIM ON THE NECK.

V. 28. *And he dwelleth in desolate Cities*, — וישכן ערים נכחדות] This Verse ought I think to be expressed by the future Tense, as the two following Verses are; being rather a Judgment denounced against the wicked Man, than a Description of the State he is in.

V. 32. *It shall be accomplished before his Time*: — בלא יומו תמלא] If the next Hemistic be construed first, the Sense will be clearer, and there will be a proper Antecedent to תמלא: thus —— AND HIS BRANCH SHALL NOT BE GREEN: IT SHALL HAVE AN END BEFORE ITS TIME.

CHAP. XVI.

V. 5. — *and the moving of my Lips should affwage* your Grief. וניד
שפתי יחשך :] Rather — OR THE MOVING OF MY LIPS SHOULD
BE STOPPED. Job seems here to intimate to his Friends, that, if they
were in his Case, he would plead on their Behalf, and administer what
Comfort he could; or, at least, sympathise with them in Silence.

V. 8. *And thou hast filled me with Wrinkles,* ותקמטני] This Word
occurs only in another Place, *viz.* Ch.XXII.16. The Idea of *Wrinkles*
is deduced from the Chaldee and Syriac: but the Arabic Verb كفت signifies *to tie Neck and Heels*; which Sense, used as a Metaphor for IG-
NOMINIOUS TREATMENT, will I think best suit this Place, as well as
the other referred to.

——— *and my Leanness rising up in me beareth Witness to my Face.*
ויקם בי כחשי בפני יענה :] Rather — AND HE THAT DEALETH
DECEITFULLY WITH ME RISETH UP AGAINST ME, and CON-
TENDETH TO MY FACE. Thus Symmachus — και ανεςη μοι καταψευ-
δομενος κατα προσωπον με αντιλεγων μοι· and the Vulgate ——— *Suscitatur*
falsiloquus adversus faciem meam, contradicens mihi.

V. 9. *He teareth* me *in his Wrath, who hateth me:* אפו טרף
— וישטמני] The natural Construction of these Words is ——— HIS
WRATH TEARETH AND WITHSTANDETH ME.

V. 15. — *and defiled my Horn in the Dust.* ועללתי בעפר קרני :]
Would not the Figurative, be more suitable here than the Proper,
Sense: either STRENGTH, POWER, or HONOUR? In that Case
this Verse would be nearly parallel to Pf.VII.5. — *Let him tread down*
my Life upon the Earth, and lay MINE HONOUR IN THE DUST.

V. 17. *Not for any Injustice in mine Hands: also my Prayer* is *pure.*
על לא חמס בכפי — ותפלתי זכה :] Rather — THOUGH there were
NO INJUSTICE IN MINE HANDS, AND MY PRAYER were PURE.
See these two Particles thus used Isa. LIII. 9.

V. 21. *O that* one *might plead for a Man with God, as a Man* plead-
eth *for his Neighbour!* ויוכח לגבר עם אלוה — ובן אדם לרעהו]
Rather, I think --- O THAT one MIGHT PLEAD FOR A MAN
WITH GOD! AND THE SON OF MAN FOR HIS NEIGHBOUR, or
FRIEND! The latter Hemistic exegetical of the former.

C   CHAP.

C H A P. XVII.

V. 2. — and doth not mine Eye continue in their Provocation?
ובהמרותם תלן עיני׃] Rather—Doth not mine Eye abide upon
their Provocations ?

V. 3. Lay down now, put me in a Surety with thee ; שימה נא ערבני
עמך] The Terms here are evidently *forenfic*, and refer to the Forms
of commencing a Law Suit, where the Parties were bound in a Surety
to abide the Iffue. *Refpondere vadatus.* Hor. *Serm.* Lib. I. S. 9. V. 36.
In Lev. VI. 2. we find the Words — בתשומת יד, which are rendered
in our Verfion — *in Fellowſhip*, but literally, in putting the Hand,
viz. *by way of Engagement*, or *Pledge :* accordingly I would propofe
to render שימה, Put forth now (*viz.* the Hand) bind me in a
Surety with thee ; and render כי at the Beginning of the next
Verfe — Surely. We find this Cuftom *of ſhaking*, or *joining Hands*
upon folemn Occafions, by way of Ratification, prevailed very univerfally. Thus Xenophon (*Anab.* Lib. II. & *paſſim*) Οιδα μεν ημιν ορκες γεγε-
νομενες, και ΔΕΞΙΑΣ ΔΕΔΟΜΕΝΑΣ· fo Virgil, *Æneid.* III. v. 610.

Ipfe pater DEXTRAM *Anchifes, haud multa moratus,*
DAT *juveni, atque animum* PRÆSENTI PIGNORE FIRMAT.

Quint. Curtius alfo introduces Darius fpeaking before his Death to Po-
lyftratus, *Alexandro hoc fidei regiæ unicum* DEXTRÆ PIGNUS *pro me*
DABIS. *Hæc dicentem,* ACCEPTA *Polyftrati* MANU, *vita deftituit.* Lib. I.
And we read in Valerius (VI *Argon.* 339.) JUNGERE DEXTRAM AD
FOEDERA.

V. 5. He that ſpeaketh Flattery to his Friends, even the Eyes of his
Children ſhall fail : לחלק יגיד רעים — ועיני בניו תכלינה] Rather —
He that exhorteth the wicked to plunder, or exhort-
eth to be a Partner with the wicked &c. Thus is the
Verb חלק ufed in the firft Senfe, 2 Chron. XXVIII. 21. and implies the
Guilt of *Sacrilege ;* and in the latter, Prov. XVII. 2. XXIX. 24. The
different Conftruction of רעים folely depends upon the Maffioretical
Points. The Senfe here propofed feems more agreeable to the Con-
text, to the general Scope of this Book, and to the Proceedings of
God's particular Providence in the Adminiftration of human Affairs,
particularly the *Jewiſh.* For it muft be allowed, that he who perfuadeth
another

another to commit an Act of Impiety is as guilty as the Perpetrator; and that God in the second Commandment declares, " he will visit " the Iniquity of the Fathers upon the Children;" which I apprehend is implied in these Words, *the Eyes of his Children shall fail,* or they shall suffer some temporal Evil. But the Case is different in respect to using *flattering Words:* and Job surely never seems to have thought that his Friends were chargeable with that Sin. On the contrary, he may rather be thought to intimate here that they were privy to the Plunder of the Sabeans, or Chaldeans, Ch. I. v. 15, 17. Or the Words may possibly admit of this Sense, HE THAT SPEAKETH SMOOTHLY TO EVIL-DOERS, *i.e.* encourageth them by Flattery to proceed in their Wickedness. Or, Job may be understood to make an Apology for himself, for speaking so freely of his Friends, by saying that he durst not flatter, because &c. If either of these last Interpretations be admitted, the ו at the Beginning of the next Verse ought to be translated, *But.*

V. 6. *He hath made me also a Byword of the People; and aforetime I was as a Tabret.*] The latter Hemistic, *viz.* ותפת לפנים אהיה, is not properly translated: it should be thus — I HAVE BEEN AS A TABRET TO THE BEHOLDERS, or THOSE WHO LOOKED on me. As 1 Kings VII. 25. The Marginal Lection is *before them:* but in that Case the Hebrew ought to be לפניהם.

V. 10. *But as for you all, do ye return, and come now: for I cannot find* one *wise* Man *among you.* ואלם כלם תשובו ובאו נא — ולא אמצא בכם חכם:] Rather — BUT WHEREFORE DO YE ALL RETURN AND COME NOW, SEEING I CANNOT, &c. See the Particles thus used, אלם Ch. XXXIII. 1. and ו Gen. XV. 2. Ruth. I. 21.

V. 11. — *my Purposes are broken off,* even *the Thoughts of my Heart.* וזמתי נתקו מורשי לבבי:] The Word מורשי is here rendered *Thoughts* without any Authority. It would therefore be better to translate this Place thus --- MY PURPOSES, THE POSSESSIONS OF MY HEART, ARE BROKEN OFF. Thus the Law of Moses is called the *Inheritance,* or *Possession* of the Israelites. Deut. XXXIII. 4.

V. 12. *They change the Night into Day: the Light* is *short because of Darkness.* לילה ליום ישימו — אור קרוב מפני השך:] Rather — Which CHANGE THE NIGHT INTO DAY: and THE APPROACHING LIGHT is DARKNESS BEFORE ME. As the Text is now

read

read, ביורשי muſt I think be the Antecedent to the Verb : for which
Reaſon I add the Relative for the Connection. But if we read ישים
ואור, the Conſtruction will be — HE (viz. *God*, who is often underſtood in the poetical Books) CHANGETH NIGHT INTO DAY : AND
&c. That is —— I am kept waking the whole Night as in the Day ;
and the Morning Light is as gloomy to me as the Darkneſs of Night.
So Bildad underſtood Job, as appears by his Reply in the next Chapter,
V. 5 & 6.

V. 13. *If I wait, the Grave is mine Houſe ;* — אם אקוה שאול ביתי]
Rather --- SURELY I WAIT FOR THE GRAVE, which is MY
HOUSE ; or --- FOR MY HOUSE, THE GRAVE. The two Sub-
ſtantives ſeem here put in Appoſition.

V. 16. *They ſhall go down to the Bars of the Pit,* — בדי שאל תרדנה]
Theſe Words ought I think to be rendered — IT SHALL GO DOWN
with WAILING INTO THE GRAVE. I ſeparate נד from הרד, making
תקותי the Subject of the Verb, which in our Verſion is wanted ; and
conſider בדי as a Prepoſition, of which there is alſo need in this Place.
Laſtly, I make נד a Subſtantive, as Ezek. VII. 11. from the Verb
נהה *to lament.*

—— *when our Reſt together is in the Duſt.* אם יחד על עפר נחת :]
Rather, I think --- SURELY IT SHALL DESCEND ALTOGETHER
INTO THE DUST ; this Hemiſtic being conſidered as exegetical of the
foregoing.

CHAP. XVIII.

V. 2. *How long* will it be ere *ye make an End of Words ?* עד אנה]
תשימון קנצי למלין] Rather — WHEN, I PRAY YOU, WILL YE
MAKE AN END &c.

V. 4. *He teareth himſelf in his Anger :* — טרף נפשו באפו] Our old
Verſion here adds — *Thou art as one* that teareth &c. which connects
better with the Context.

V. 6. — *and his Candle ſhall be put out with him.* ונרו עליו ידעך :]
Rather --- AND HIS CANDLE that is BY HIM SHALL BE EXTIN-
GUISHED. So על is uſed Judg. III. 19. *& paſſim.*

V. 7. *The Steps of his Strength ſhall be ſtraitened :* — יצרו צעדי אונו]
Would not און be more properly rendered here POWER ?

V. 11. — *and*

V. 11. — *and shall drive him to his Feet.* : והפצהו לרגליו] Rather
--- AND SHALL DASH HIM TO PIECES IN HIS GOINGS ; *i. e.*
shall bring him to Destruction when he falls into the Snare. Or thus
— AND SHALL SCATTER HIM (according to the Sense of this Word
in the Margin of our Version) IN HIS GOINGS ; *i. e.* shall drive him
from Place to Place, till at length he fall into the Toils of his Enemies.
See נפץ and פון. לרגל is used precisely in this Sense, Gen. XXXIII.
14. where, in the Margin, we read *according to the Foot :* but it
ought to be rendered GOINGS there, as well as here.

V. 13. *It shall devour the Strength of his Skin:* — יאכל ברי עורו]
In the Margin we find, *Heb.* BARS. But neither the Proper, nor the
Figurative, Sense can here be admitted. The chief Mistake lies in the
Construction of ברי ; which, instead of being considered as a Substantive, is really nothing more than the Preposition ב with the *adjec-*
tive Particle רי, which is used with the following Letters ב, כ, ל, מ.
This Hemistic ought therefore to be rendered—HIS SKIN ABOUT (or
UPON) HIM SHALL BE CONSUMED : The Affix ו having I suppose dropt
out, and the Word being originally written בריו, as in the next Hemistic,
and Ch. XLI. 12. See ברי thus construed Ch. XVII. 16. The Preposition
ב is here used as in this Instance, וישם שק במתניו — *and he put Sack-*
cloth about, or upon, his Loins. Gen. XXXVII. 34. This Particle is
of Chaldee Origin, and is found only in this Book, Daniel, and Ezra.
—— even *the first - born of Death shall devour his Strength.*
: יאכל ברי בכור מות] *The first-born of Death* is a Phrase that conveys no Idea ; and the Allegations of Critics in Support of it are forced and unnatural. I would therefore consider בכור as compounded of
the Preposition ב, and כור *a Furnace* ; and render this Place thus —
DEATH SHALL CONSUME HIM IN THE FURNACE. It is well
known that *Furnace* is used metaphorically for the greatest Oppression,
see Deut. IV. 20. Isa. XLVIII. 10. &c.

V. 15. *It shall dwell in his Tabernacle, because* it is *none of his :*
Brimstone shall be scattered upon his Habitation. — תשכון באהלו מבלי לו
: יזרה על נוהו גפרית] According to our present Version the Antecedent to *it* ought to be *Confidence,* mentioned in the preceding Verse.
But this cannot be ; as that Sense would be contradictory both to the
Assertion there, as well as to Fact. If it be *Destruction,* fetched from
the 13th Verse ; this is contrary to the Rules of sound Interpretation,
when no less than eight different Substantives have intervened. In the
old Version (the Translators being aware of these Inconveniences) the
Word

Word *Fear* is added in another Character: but this is too arbitrary, when it can be avoided. The Correction here wanted may be made without the least Alteration of the Text, excepting the Division of the Words, thus — — תשכין באהלו כבליל — וזרה וגו — CONFUSION SHALL DWELL IN HIS TABERNACLE, AND BRIMSTONE &c. The Root of כבליל is בלל *to confound*. It does not indeed occur in that precise Form: but that is no material Objection, as numberless ἅπαξ λεγομενα are found in this Book. By this Interpretation we also get rid of that Incongruity, *his House which* is *none of his*.

CHAP. XIX.

V. 17. — *though I intreated for the Children's* Sake *of mine own Body.* והנתי לבני בטני:] Rather — AND I INTREATED THE CHILDREN OF MINE OWN BODY.

V. 18. *Yea, young Children despised me* ; — — [גם עולים מאסו בי גם ought here I think to be rendered — BUT, or YET.

V. 25. *For I know* that *my Redeemer liveth, and* that *he shall stand at the latter* Day *upon the Earth.* ואני ידעתי גאלי חי — ואחרון על עפר יקום:] Rather — FOR I KNOW that MY DELIVERER LIVETH, AND SHALL STAND UP FOR me HEREAFTER ABOVE THE DUST. As I think it will appear that there is no Allusion to Christ, or the Resurrection of the Body, in this Passage, it seems better to substitute a Word instead of Redeemer, which may not mislead our Ideas. For the same Reason I would avoid using the Expression of *the latter* Day, and either render it adverbially, or make *Time* the Substantive, as, *in after* Time. The Verb קום frequently signifies *to stand up for*, or *side with* a Person See Exod. II. 17. Ps. CIV. 16. עפר על *above the Dust* signifies *on this Side the Grave*, as *in* or *under the Dust* does *after Death.*

V. 26. *And though after my Skin* Worms *destroy this* Body, *yet in my Flesh shall I see God.* ואחר עורי נקפו זאת — ומבשרי אחזה אלוה:] The Words, *though, Worms, Body*, are arbitrary, and not found in the Text, which may literally be rendered thus --- AND AFTER THAT THEY HAVE TORN THIS MY SKIN, EVEN FROM MY FLESH, I SHALL SEE GOD. The Subject to the Verb נקפו is *his Friends*, of whom he had just said, v. 22. that *they were not satisfied with his Flesh*.

V. 27. *Whom I shall see for myself, and mine Eyes shall behold, and not another.* אשר אני אחזה לי — ועיני ראו ולא זר:] Rather, WHOM I
SHALL

SHALL SEE, AND MY EYES SHALL BEHOLD, ON MY SIDE, AND
NOT A STRANGER, OR ENEMY. The ל is uſed exactly in this Senſe
Pſ. CXXIV. 1. —לילי יהוה שהיה לנו—*If it had not been the Lord who was
on our Side.* The Verb זור, from whence זר is derived, ſignifies to
be *alienated* or *eſtranged from*; and זר לא is by a Negation exegetical of
לי *on my Side,* as if it had been rendered in Latin, *amicum, non alienum.*
—— though *my Reins be conſumed within me.* ‏[‏ כלו כליתי בהקי :
Theſe Words I think ſhould be read thus —‏ כל וכליתי בהקי, and carried to the Beginning of the next Verſe, where they may be thus
tranſlated, WHEN I SHALL HAVE FULFILLED, or, SHALL BE COMPLETE
IN, ALL THAT IS APPOINTED FOR ME. The Verb כלה hath this Signification, and is accordingly here rendered by the LXX συντετελεςαι. חקי
is rendered *the Thing appointed for me,* Ch. XXIII. 14. and comes from
חקק, to *preſcribe* or *aſſign* a Man *his Lot* or *Taſk.* See Exod. V. 14.
where כליתם חקכם ſignifies *performed the Taſk aſſigned you.*

V. 28. *But ye ſhould ſay, Why perſecute we him, ſeeing the Root of the
Matter is found in me?* ‏[‏ כי תאמרו מה נרדף לו —ושרש דבר נמצא בי :
The LXX and other Verſions ſeem to have read בו *in him,* and ſo the
Senſe evidently requires. The rendering ſhould be, SHALL YE NOT
(or SURELY YE SHALL) SAY, WHY HAVE WE PERSECUTED HIM?
HATH ANY GROUND OF THE CHARGE BEEN FOUND IN HIM?
That is, *he is not found guilty of any Thing laid to his Charge.* דבר
ſignifies *the Matter that was alledged.* The Sentiment ſeems to be the
ſame with Wiſd. V. 1, 2. &c.

V. 29. *Be ye afraid of the Sword; for Wrath* bringeth *the Puniſhments of the Sword, that ye may know* there is *a Judgment.* גורו לכם
‏[‏ מפני חרב —כי חמה עונות חרב —למען תדעון שדין : I ſtrongly
ſuſpect that inſtead of לכם *for yourſelves,* the Word was originally
לכן, the illative particle *therefore;* and the LXX favours the Suppoſition by reading here δι και. The Senſe is indeed the ſame according
to the preſent Text, but the Connexion is more ſtrongly marked by
the Particle, which draws the Inference. The Verſe then may be
rendered thus; FEAR YE THEREFORE THE VISITATION OF
THE SWORD; FOR WRATH BRINGETH RUIN UPON INIQUI-
TOUS PROCEEDINGS, TO THE INTENT THAT YE MAY LEARN
WHAT IS JUST. מפני ſignifies *from before,* and may properly be
rendered *the Approach* or *Viſitation;* עונות ſignifies *Iniquities,* from עוה
to act perverſely; and the ſecond חרב in this Verſe is a Verb, which
properly ſignifies *to deſolate* or *lay Waſte.* The LXX here tranſlates,
θυμος

Θυμος επ' ανομοις επελευσεται. The concluding Sentiment brings to mind a similar one, Ifai. XXVI. 9. *when thy Judgments are in the Earth, the Inhabitants of the World will learn Righteousness.*

By taking the whole Paffage together from Ver. 23. we fhall fee a very confiftent Senfe fairly, and without the leaft Violence, deduced from it, on the Notion of Job's expecting a temporal Deliverance only. In the midft of his Exclamations on his own Mifery and the Cruelty of his Friends, a Ray of Light and Hope feems to be juft breaking in upon him from the Confideration of the Divine Juftice and Goodnefs, which makes him cry out—Ver. 23, 24. "Oh that my Words, which "I now utter in Juftification of myfelf, were recorded, fo as to remain "uneffaced till the Event fhall verify them! V. 25. For I know that "I have yet a Deliverer left, who will hereafter efpoufe my Caufe, "even on this Side the Grave; V. 26. and that after thefe Men fhall "have exercifed their Cruelty upon me, which I compare to flaying "me alive, I fhall at length fee God; V. 27. whom I fhall fee, and "my Eyes fhall behold, declaring himfelf in my Favour, and no lon- "ger alienated from me, as he feems at prefent. Then when I fhall "have accomplifhed my Fate, V. 28. fhall ye not begin to fay among "yourfelves, Why have we perfecuted him in fuch a Manner? Hath "not the Event proved him guiltlefs of the Crimes alledged againft "him? Beware therefore of drawing down God's Judgments upon you, "for his Vengeance will feverely vifit all unrighteous Doings, fo as to "teach you to deal more candidly with your Neighbour for the time "to come." As for the Interpretation which converts the Paffage into a Prophecy of the Refurrection of the Body, befides that it implies a Degree of Light ill correfponding with the Times in which either Job is fuppofed to have lived, or this Book to have been written; it re- quires fuch Interpolation of new Words, and forced Conftruction of thofe found in the Text, that I am fully perfuaded, with the Allow- ance of fuch Liberties, an ingenious Conjecturer may make almoft any Text in Scripture depofe in Favour of this or of any other Doctrine. The beft Commentators have therefore juftly exploded it. Nor let it be imagined that we are undermining the Foundations of our Faith, by withdrawing a Support that does not belong to it. It remains firmly fixed on the Bafis of Truth, which cannot be moved, and wants no Affiftance from Falfhood and Error. But neither are we in any wife allowed *to handle the Word of God deceitfully,* from an Ap- prehenfion of the ill Ufe which unftable or wicked Men may make of a right Interpretation of it, at the Hazard of their own Salvation.

C H A P.

CHAP. XX.

V. 10. *His Children shall seek to please the poor*,—בניו ירצו דלים [Here the marginal Lection, *viz.* THE POOR SHALL OPPRESS HIS CHILDREN, seems more agreeable to the Context.

. V. 11. *His Bones are full of the Sin of his Youth*, עצמותיו מלאו עלומו [Rather—HIS BONES ARE FULL OF SECRET Sin. So is עלום rendered Pf. XC. 8.

V. 17. *He shall not see the Rivers, the Floods*,—אל ירא בפלגות נהרי [Rather---HE SHALL NOT SEE THE STREAMS OF THE RIVERS: or---IN THE STREAMS RIVERS [and BROOKS OF HONEY AND BUTTER.]

V. 20. *Surely he shall not feel Quietness in his Belly:* כי לא ידע שלו שלו [בבטנו is no where used as a Substantive ; and, allowing it were, the Sense of it does not seem very suitable to this Place. But if we confider this Word as compounded of the Relatif ש and the Pronoun לו in the Dative Cafe; the Meaning will then be——SURELY HE SHALL NOT FEEL IN HIS BODY that WHICH belonged TO HIM. The two next Hemistics, and V. 23. add great Weight to this Interpretation. See a long Note on the above combined Particles in the Parallel Prophecies of Jacob and Mofes, Gen. XLIX. 10.

V. 26. *All Darkness* shall be *hid in his secret Places*; כל השך טמון לצפוניו [Rather—A TOTAL DARKNESS shall be RESERVED FOR HIS TREASURES : that is, " he shall for ever be as much deprived of " them, as if they were still buried in the Bowels of the Earth." See V. 21.

V. 28. — and his Goods *shall flow away in the Day of his Wrath.* נגרות ביום אפו : [Rather perhaps — and there shall be DRAININGS IN THE DAY OF HIS WRATH ; *viz.* of his *Family*, (including Relations, Domestics, and Slaves;) as may be inferred from the Context : for it is said before, that he had lost the Rest of his Goods. See V. 21.

CHAP. XXI.

V. 4. *As for me,* האנכי] *Qu.* is not this Word compounded of the ה interrogative, the Adverb אן contractedly written (as it sometimes is)

for

for אנה, *I pray you*, and of the Conjunction כי, *truly, indeed*; in this Senſe --- Is, I PRAY YOU, INDEED &c?

V. 11. *They ſend forth their little ones like a Flock :* ישלחו כצאן עויליהם] Rather — THEY INCREASE (or BREED) THEIR LITTLE ONES LIKE SHEEP.

V. 13. *They ſpend their Days in Wealth ;—* יבלו בטוב ימיהם] *Marg.* or, *in Mirth.* If by *Wealth* in this Place be meant HAPPINESS, it ought to be ſo rendered. For in the other Places, where Job uſes the Word טוב, it has that Senſe. Ch. VII. 7. XXX. 26.

V. 24. *His Breaſts are full of Milk,—* עטיניו מלאו חלב] עטין is an ἁπαξ λεγομενον, the Signification of which cannot be determined from the kindred Dialects. The LXX render the Word by τα εγκατα αυτε, and the Vulgate, to the ſame Effect, by *viſcera ejus.* The Syriac and Arabic have another Senſe, *viz.* ܟܒܘܣ and جوانب HIS SIDES. Either of theſe Senſes would better ſuit with the Context, particularly if we render חלב FAT. As to the Senſe of *Breaſts*, it is not countenanced by any Authority, and can ſcarcely be juſtified by Fact : and the marginal Lection, *his Milk-Pails,* has only the Targum to ſupport it.

V. 29. — *and do ye not know their Tokens ?* ואתחם לא תנכרו :] Rather, I think — THEIR MONUMENTS. Coccejus makes the Word to ſignify here *a Sepulchre.* Theſe it is well known were placed by the *Way* Side. Thus Lycidas the Shepherd ſays to his fellow Traveller Mœris :

> *Hinc adeo media eſt nobis via ; namque ſepulchrum*
> *Incipit apparere Bianoris.* —— Virg. Ecl. IX. 59.

V. 30. — *they ſhall be brought forth to the Day of Wrath.* ליום עברות יובל :] The Context, both before and after this Sentence, runs in the Singular, and ſo this would, if we ſeparate the ו final from יובל, and join it to מי, at the Beginning of the next Verſe ; where it will be very ſuitable.

V. 33. — *and every Man ſhall draw after him, as there are innumerable before him.* ואחריו כל אדם ימשוך — ולפניו אין מספר :] Rather --- AND EVERY MAN SHALL GO AFTER HIM, AS they have gone WITHOUT NUMBER BEFORE HIM. The Verb משך, *to draw,* is never I believe uſed intranſitively, except in the Senſe of *approaching,*

proaching, or *receding*, with some Particles, such as *toward*, *near*, *back*, added to it. It is used intransitively only in two other Places besides this, *viz*. Judg. IV. 6. and XX. 37. and in both signifies properly *to go, march*, or *advance*. In the former Instance the true Sense is disguised by the Preposition ב which follows being rendered *toward*; as if Barak had been directed only *to approach near* to Mount Tabor; and not, as appears to have been the Case, TO GO UP TO it, and collect his Forces upon the Mount; see V. 12, 14. In the latter Instance the Translation runs, *and the Liers in wait drew* themselves *along*, instead of THEY MARCHED UP, AND &c.

CHAP. XXII.

V. 2. — *as he that is wise may be profitable unto himself?* כי יסכן כי] עלימו משכיל: is never used as a Particle of Comparison: it ought to be rendered here BECAUSE.

V. 8. But as for *the mighty Man, he had the Earth:* ואיש זרוע לו הראץ] Three Words might here be spared in our Version, if we render --- BUT THE MIGHTY MAN HAD THE EARTH.

V. 9. — *and the Arms of the fatherless have been broken.* וזרעות יתמים ידכא:] The Verb is here corrupt. If the Sense given to it in our Version be right, it ought then to have been נדכאו: but it is more than probable that תדכא is the true Lection, for the Difference is slighter, it suits with the preceding Hemistic, and has the Countenance of all the ancient Interpreters; with whom therefore I would render --- AND THOU HAST BROKEN THE ARMS OF THE FATHERLESS.

V. 16. *Which were cut down out of Time;* — אשר קמטו ולא עת] Rather --- WHO WERE AFFLICTED BEFORE their TIME. This Verb occurs no where else except Ch. XVI. 8. which see.

V. 17. *Which said unto God, Depart from us: and what can the Almighty do for them?* האמרים לאל סור ממנו — ומה יפעל שדי למו] The LXX, Syriac, and Arabic, read here (instead of למו *for them*) לנו FOR US; which the Sense seems to require.

V. 20. *Whereas our Substance is not cut down;* — אם לא נכחד קימנו] Instead of קימנו, all the ancient Versions read here קמהו, or קמו; which doubtless is the true Reading. For the Word קים, as a Substantive, is not to be found; and the Pronoun of the first Person is foreign to

the

the Subject. קמה fignifies *ftanding Corn*, and the ו has here the Force of כ, as in numberlefs Places. The true Tranflation therefore feems to be --- IS NOT THEIR STANDING CORN CUT DOWN? [AND DOTH NOT THE FIRE CONSUME WHAT REMAINETH TO THEM?]

V. 24. *Then fhalt thou lay up Gold as the Duft, and* the Gold *of Ophir as the Stones of the Brooks.* ושית על עפר בצר — בצור נחלים אופיר] Rather — THEN SHALT THOU PUT THY GOLD UPON THE EARTH, AND the GOLD OF OPHIR ON THE ROCKS OF THE VALLEYS. Becaufe על is never ufed as a Particle of Comparifon; as was obferved on V. 2. neither has ב ever that Force; for the Inftances adduced by Noldius are evident Miftakes for כ. I tranflate עפר EARTH, a Signification it frequently has in this Book; fee Ch. XIX. 25. XXX. 6. &c. particularly as it is oppofed to VALLEYS (as in the laft Place referred to) which is as genuine a Senfe of נחלים as that of *Brooks*. In this Verfe is a double *Paronomafia*. The Senfe of Eliphaz, as here explained, feems to be this — " *If thou return to the Almighty* &c. " thou wilt fo utterly difregard Gold, and whatever is efteemed " precious, as to throw them in the Highways; for thy fole Delight, " Comfort, and Support will be in Him."

V. 25. — *and thou fhalt have Plenty of Silver.* וכסף תועפות לך] The marginal Reading is — *Silver of Strength*. But would it not be better to render thefe Words — AND THY STRENGTH, SILVER: the Verb underftood from the foregoing Claufe? The firft Senfe has no Authority to fupport it; the fecond is harfh: but the latter feems liable to no Exception, and correfponds exactly with the preceding Hemiftic; if בצר be rendered GOLD, as it certainly ought to be: for it never fignifies *Defence* without fome of the *Heemantic* Letters. And it may be obferved that the Word תועפות, which occurs but thrice, is twice applied to *God*; fo that it may well be confidered in this Place as equivalent to צור *a Rock*, a Name, or Attribute, frequently afcribed to Him. Or thus, FOR THE ALMIGHTY SHALL BE THY CHOICEST GOLD, (fo בצר properly fignifies) AND SILVER OF WEIGHT (or, *the fineft Silver*) TO THEE. The Finenefs of Silver being in Proportion to its Weight. For the Verb יעף fignifies *to be weary*; and hence its Derivative תועפות may not improperly be confidered as fignifying *a Load*, or *Weight*, which *fatigues* the Perfon who carries it.

V. 29. — *and he fhall fave the humble Perfon.* ושח עינים יושע] Rather --- AND THE HUMBLE PERSON SHALL BE SAVED: for
the

the Verb is in Hophal. By this Conftruction the Enallage of Perfons is alfo avoided.

V. 30. *He fhall deliver the Ifland of the innocent;* — ‏ימלט אי נקי‎] ‏אי‎ in this Place does not feem to be a Subftantive, but an Adverb, as Ch. XV. 23. I would therefore render it with the Syriac and Arabic — THE INNOCENT, WHEREVER he is, WILL ESCAPE, or DELIVER HIMSELF; and this is alfo the Senfe of the LXX and Vulgate, though they omit this Particle. There is befides an Inconfiftency in making with our Verfion *God* and *Job employed together in delivering an Ifland.*
—— *and it is delivered by the Purenefs of thine Hands.* ‏ונמלט בבר‎ ‏כפיך‎] If the preceding Emendation be admitted, ‏נמלט‎ muft be conftrued imperfonally, *viz.* AND DELIVERANCE SHALL BE to thee BY THE PURITY OF THINE HANDS: or elfe we muft read ‏תמלט‎, THOU SHALT BE DELIVERED, with the LXX; or change the ‏ך‎ into a ‏ו‎ after ‏כפי‎, with the Syriac and Arabic, and render --- BY THE PURITY OF HIS HANDS.

C H A P. XXIII.

V. 2. — *my Stroke is heavier than my Groaning.* ‏ידי כברה על אנחתי‎ :] I would here adopt the Lection of the LXX, Syriac, and Arabic, ‏ירו‎ HIS HAND, *viz.* God's, fo often underftood, and fo lately mentioned. A *Stroke*, fay the Critics, is derived from ‏יד‎ *the Hand*; becaufe it is inftrumental to it. But, by Parity of Reafon, it might fignify ten thoufand other Things which are performed by its Agency. Befides, do not Strokes owe their Exiftence to a Million of other Caufes? Nay, were the Suppofition allowed to be probable, ‏ידי‎ *my Stroke* would, but be equivocal, at beft; either active or paffive; either *the Stroke that I inflicted*, or *the Stroke that I received.* In refpect to the Places commonly referred to in Support of this Senfe, a fatisfactory Reafon may be given in every Inftance, fo as to invalidate the Application in this Paffage.

V. 3. *O that I knew where I might find him!* that *I might come even to his Seat!* ‏כי יתן ידעתי ואמצאהו‎—‏אבוא עד הכונתו‎ :] Or— O THAT I KNEW WHERE I MIGHT FIND HIM; I WOULD even GO TO HIS SEAT!

V. 6. — *No; but he would put Strength in me.* ‏לא אך הוא ישם בי‎] There is a great Difficulty in accounting for the Meaning of ‏ישם בי‎.
I cannot

I cannot think that we have Authority to fupply here a Subftantive to compleat the Senfe; but am perfuaded that this Hemiftic ought to be rendered --- No; BUT HE WOULD BE ASTONISHED, OR BE SILENT, BEFORE ME; that is, "He would have Nothing to object to mine "Apology." See the fame Verb שמם, not שום, thus ufed Ch. XXI. 5.

V.7. *There the righteous might difpute with him :*—שם ישר נוכח עמו] The fame Words occur Ch. XIII. 3. and are there rendered *to reafon with him.* The Meaning of Job in both Places was, that he would *prove his Innocence before God.*

V. 9. *On the left Hand, where he doth work, but I cannot behold* him :—שמאל בעשתו ולא אחז] The Verb אהלך *I go forward,* at the Beginning of the preceding Verfe, is fuppofed to extend to this Hemiftic: but I doubt whether fo extenfive an Influence can be admitted. We have here a Verb, which at prefent is ufelefs, to fay the leaft of it, when applied to God. This fame Verb with the Arabic Signification given to it, and a Change of Perfons, would exactly fuit this Place. عشا fignifies ADIIT *eum;* ADIIT *eum fpe alicujus boni;* RECESSIT *ab eo ad alium.* The Senfe would then be — WHEN I TURN TO THE LEFT, THERE I CANNOT BEHOLD HIM. The Syriac reads --- حصمحا حدحال *I fought at my left Hand,* and the Arabic —— عن شمالي طلبت — *to the fame Effect.* And it cannot appear extraordinary that Job, who is allowed to have been an Arab, fhould occafionally ufe an Arabic Idiom. It is univerfally agreed, that in this Book we have many other Words borrowed from that Language and the Chaldee.

V. 12. — *I have efteemed the Words of his Mouth more than my neceffary* Food. :מחקי צפנתי אמרי פיו] Rather —I HAVE LAID UP THE WORDS OF HIS MOUTH WITHIN MY BOSOM. So render the LXX and Vulgate. For the Verb צפן never fignifies *to efteem,* and the Senfe given חקי is forced. Note חיק *a Bofom* is fometimes found without the י, as Prov. XVII. 23. &c.

V. 13. *But he is in one* Mind, *and who can turn him?* והוא באחד ומי ישיבנו] Rather — THOUGH HE be ALONE, YET WHO CAN TURN HIM? The ב here, prefixed to the Nominative Cafe, in אחד is redundant; as 1 Kings XIII. 34. Hof. XIII. 9. &c.

V. 14. *For*

V. 14. *For he performeth* the Thing that is *appointed for me:* כי
ישׁלים חקי] Rather—YEA, HE WILL RESTORE ME MY DUE. Thus
is the Word rendered, Lev. X. 13, 14. Or—MY PORTION, as Gen.
XLVII. 22.

—— *and many such Things* are *with him.* וכהנה רבות עמו :]
The Words — are *with him*, are too idiomatic; fit only for the Margin: in the Text they ought to be rendered — are IN HIS POWER.

CHAP. XXIV.

V. 1. *Why, seeing Times are not hidden from the Almighty, do they
that know him not see his Days?* מדוע משׁדי לא נצפנו עתים — וידעו
לא חזו ימיו :] The Authors of our present Version, in order I suppose
to put the most favourable Construction on Job's Words, are here
chargeable with a violent Transposition; besides confounding the Hemistics. The old Version seems to give this Verse its genuine Meaning,
and the proper Explanation, *viz.* HOW SHOULD NOT THE TIMES
BE HID FROM THE ALMIGHTY, SEEING THAT THEY WHICH
KNOW HIM SEE NOT HIS DAYS? " Thus Job speaketh in his
" Passions, and after the Judgment of the Flesh: that is, that he
" seeth not the Things that are done at Times; neither yet hath a
" peculiar Care over all, because he punisheth not the wicked, nor
" revengeth the godly." The Note upon *Days* is also pertinent, *viz.*
" when he punisheth the wicked, and rewardeth the good."

V. 5. — *rising betimes for a Prey: the Wilderness* yieldeth *Food for
them* and *for their Children.* משׁחרי לטרף ערבה — לו להם לנערים :]
Qu. ought not the Words לו--ערבה to be thus divided, ער--בהלו,
and the two Hemistics rendered --- RISING BETIMES TO PLUNDER
THE ENEMY; THEY GET HASTILY (*i.e.* BY RAPINE) FOOD
FOR THEIR CHILDREN? See this Verb thus used, Esth. II. 9. and
Prov. XX. 21.

V. 6. *They reap* every one *his Corn in the Field;*—בשׁדה בלילו יקצורו]
The LXX, Chaldee, and Vulgate, seem to have read בלין or בליהם,
for they thus render this Place — *They reap in a Field which is not
their own.* The true Lection, however, seems to be בליל ויקצורו, and
this the Sense --- AND THEY REAP THE FIELDS IN THE NIGHT,
viz. of the oppressed, mentioned in the next Hemistic. This Interpretation
will

will be found perfectly confiſtent with the whole Context; whereas the Senſe of our Verſion ſeems at Variance with it.

—— *and they gather the Vintage of the wicked.* : יכרם רשע ילקשׁו]
Rather — of THE TROUBLED, or OPPRESSED. So רשׁע is uſed Ch. XXXIV. 29. Thus alſo the Vulgate — *vineam ejus, quem vi oppreſſe-rint, vindemiant.*

V. 7. —— *that* they have *no Covering in the Cold.* : ואין כסות בקרה]
Rather --- AND WITHOUT COVERING IN THE COLD.

V. 12. *Men groan from out of the City, and the Soul of the wounded crieth out :* — מעיר מתים ינאקו — ונפש חללים תשׁוע] The Words מתים and חללים are here equivalent ; the *dead* and the *ſlain :* If the literal Verſion be thought too bold, *viz.* THE DEAD GROAN OUT OF THE CITY, AND THE SOUL OF THE SLAIN CRIETH OUT ; theſe Participles may perhaps be conſidered as the Participles in *rus* of the Latins, which the Hebrews want.

V. 17. —— *if* one *know* them, they are in *the Terrors of the Shadow of Death.* : כי יכיר בלהות צלמות] A Subject is here wanting for the Verb יכיר, for which I take *the Morning* from the preceding He-miſtic, and render --- SURELY IT DISCOVERETH THE TERRORS OF THE SHADOW OF DEATH, *viz.* in their Countenances for Fear of being known.

V. 18. *He is ſwift as the Waters ;* — קל הוא על פני מים] Rather --- HE IS SWIFT UPON THE SURFACE OF THE WATERS : על being never uſed as a Particle of Compariſon. So the old Verſion.
—— *their Portion is curſed in the Earth.* — תקלל חלקתם בארץ] This and the next Hemiſtic would perhaps be better rendered by the future Tenſe, as they are in the old Verſion : for this ſeems mentioned as a Judgment upon the Oppreſſor.

V. 19. —— ſo doth *the Grave* thoſe which *have ſinned.* : שׁאול חטאו]
The ו in חטאו ſeems to belong to the Beginning of the next Word : without it theſe Words will ſignify —— ſo doth THE GRAVE THE SINNER. So the old Verſion.

V. 20. *The Womb ſhall forget him,* — ישׁכחהו רחם] Rather —— TENDER PITY, or COMPASSION —— ; for Womb, without adding the Words — *which bore him,* does not ſeem ſufficiently clear.

V. 22. — *he*

V. 22. — *he rifeth up, and no* Man *is fure of Life.* יקום ולא יאמין
בהיין׃] There feems to be fuch a Confufion of Perfons according to
the prefent Reading, that it is difficult to make out any confiftent Senfe in
this Verfe, and the two following ones, according to the Rules of grammatical Interpretation, I would therefore read — יקומו לא — and render
--- HE DRAWETH THE MIGHTY ALSO WITH HIS POWER: THEY
RISE UP; HE TRUSTETH NOT IN LIFE. (V. 23.) IT IS GIVEN
HIM to be IN SAFETY, AND HE RESTETH THEREON; AND
HIS EYES are UPON THEIR WAYS. (V. 24.) THEY HOLD
THEMSELVES HIGH FOR A LITTLE WHILE, BUT ARE NOT, &c.
The Meaning of which I conceive to be this; in Verfe 21, is fhewn
how the wicked Man oppreffes the weak and friendlefs. This, how-
ever, is not all; for V. 22. it is added — *he draweth* (*viz.* to their
Deftruction, as the Word feems to fignify Pf. XXVIII. 3. and
Ezek. XXXII. 20. as well as here) *the mighty alfo with his Power:*
but as the Word *draw* feems to imply, that he could not make fuch
fhort Work here as in the Cafe before mentioned, but that the
Bufinefs required Time and Management; fo in the latter Hemiftic
of this Verfe the Reafon is affigned why he did fo; becaufe, *if the
mighty rofe up* to oppofe him, he might run the Rifk of his Life.
Therefore, as it follows (V. 23.) he contrives to live upon Terms of
Security and Confidence with them; וישען, and upon this Ground he
proceeds, or he refts himfelf here, and lies upon the Watch for an
Opportunity to do them a Mifchief. Then follows the Confequence,
(V. 24.) They enjoy their Greatnefs for a little while, but are at
length reduced and brought to nought by his Artifices, fharing herein
the common Fate of all other.

CHAP. XXV.

V. 5. *Behold even to the Moon, and it fhineth not;* — הן עד ירח ולא
יאהיל] The Verb אהיל fignifies no where, either in Heb. or any of
the Sifter Languages, *to fhine:* that Signification has been given to it
from the fuppofed *exigentia loci*, or from fome of the Verfions. The
Words I think ought to be tranflated --- BEHOLD HE WILL NOT
INDEED PITCH HIS TENT NEAR THE MOON, *viz.* as not worthy
of his Habitation.

6. *How much less Man, that is a Worm? and the Son of Man, which is a Worm?* :אף כי אנוש רמה —ובן אדם תולעה] As there are here in the Hebrew two different Words to express *Man* and *Worm*, would not one of each be better rendered by MORTAL and REPTILE?

CHAP. XXVI.

V. 2. *How hast thou helped* him that is *without Power?* מה עזרת ללא כח] Rather — WHOM HAST THOU HELPED WHO HAD NO POWER? So in the next Verse, *mutatis mutandis*.

V. 3. — *and how hast thou plentifully declared the Thing as it is?* ותושיה לרב הודעת:] *Qu.* ought not these Words to be rendered — AND HAST THOU SHEWN KNOWLEDGE TO THE MULTITUDE?

V. 4. — *and whose Spirit came from thee?* ונשמת מי יצאה ממך:] Rather, I think ---AND WHOSE INSPIRATION CAME FROM THEE? as Ch. XXXII. 8.

V. 5. *Dead* Things *are formed under the Waters, and the Inhabitants thereof.* הרפאים יחוללו מתחת —מים ושכניהם:] By this our Translators understood *Mines* and *Metals* formed in the Bowels of the Earth. See the Note in the old Version. But the Word רפאים is never used in this Sense, nor do I see a sufficient Reason for giving it such an Interpretation. The Passage has ever been considered as very dark and difficult; but I flatter myself that I have at last hit upon its true Meaning. By רפאים I understand no other than the *Manes mortuorum, the Spirits of deceased Persons*, confined in שאול, commonly translated *Hell*, but more properly to be stiled the *Place*, or *Mansion, of the dead*, the same as ὁ Ἄδης in Greek, and *Orcus* in Latin. Whoever will take the Trouble of considering attentively the following Texts, where the Word רפאים occurs, Ps. LXXXVIII. 10. Prov. II. 18. — IX. 18. — XXI. 16. Isa. XIV. 9. — XXVI. 14, 19. will see Reason to conclude the Use of it in all those Places to be exactly as here represented. As the Point is curious, tending to throw some Light upon the Notions of the ancient Jews concerning the State of departed Souls, I may be allowed to consider two or three of these Passages at large. In Isa. XXVI. 13. it is said, *Other Lords besides thee have had Dominion over us*, viz. *the Gods of the Heathen* — But V. 14. it follows, these are no other than *dead* Men, מתים, (see Wisd. XIV.

15.)

15.) in Oppofition to the *living* God; they are רפאים, *departed Spirits*, who have not Power to ftir from their Place of Confinement, *they cannot rife*. Again V. 19. the מתיך, *thy dead Men who fhould live and rife again*, the שכני עפר, *the Inhabitants of the Duft*, who are called *to awake and fing*, and the רפאים, *the dead, to be caft out by the Earth*, are all the fame Individuals. In that beautiful *Profopopæia*, Ifai. XIV. 9. שאול *Hell* (to which is added *from beneath*, מתחת, the very Word ufed in the Paffage before us) is poetically defcribed as ftirring up her Inhabitants, רפאים, *the dead, the Spirits of departed Captains and Kings*, reprefented as fitting there upon their Thrones, to meet with Taunting and Infult the haughty Tyrant of Babylon, on his being brought down to thofe infernal Shades. But the Paffage, Pf. LXXXVIII. 10, &c. not only illuftrates the Signification of רפאים in the prefent Text, but both the Senfe and Terms fo aptly correfpond in both Places, that I can hardly fuppofe one written without Allufion to the other. There it is faid, *Wilt thou fhew Wonders to the dead*, למתים? *Shall the dead*, רפאים, (which for the Sake of Variation I would tranflate, *the deceafed*,) *arife and praife thee? Shall thy loving Kindnefs be declared in the Grave?* (קבר, the fame as שאול) *or thy Faithfulnefs in Deftruction?* (אבדון in both Places) *Shall thy Wonders be known in the dark*, rather, *the Place of Darknefs? and thy Righteoufnefs in the Land of Oblivion?* Thus much may fuffice to afcertain the general Import of רפאים; let us now attend to the Connection of the Verfe before us. In Ch. XXV. Bildad had fpoken of God's Majefty, and Man's Impurity in refpect of him. To which Job replies, and farcaftically afks, V. 4. whether he thought the Perfon he fpoke to did not know as much as himfelf; and how he came by his Knowledge? *whofe Spirit*, or rather *Infpiration* (as the Word נשמה is rendered Ch. XXXII. 8.) *came from thee?* Did (fays he, V. 5.) the רפאים, ANY DEPARTED SPIRITS BRING it THEE FROM BENEATH? (the Place of their Abode under Ground) or FROM THE SEA AND ITS INHABITANTS? The ה prefixed marks the Interrogation; and יחוללו is the Preter Pihel from חול, which admits of that Senfe. See Prov. XXV. 23. Margin. It deferves Notice, that Ch. IV. 15, &c. Eliphaz had faid, that a Communication of the fame Import had been made to him by a *Spirit* or *Ghoft* in the Vifions of the Night; to which I cannot but think Job alludes, afking Bildad if he too, as well as his Friend, had been favoured with fuch an extraordinary Vifitant. Not that he thought the Thing impoffible in itfelf, though perhaps he doubted of it in the prefent Inftance. On the contrary, the Poffibility of its happening by God's fpecial Direction and

Appoint-

Appointment feems ftrongly intimated in the next Verfe; where, as if
he had faid from the before cited Pfalm, that the רפאים could not of
themfelves rife up again to tell of God's Wonders and Righteoufnefs,
he fubjoins, that God himfelf had Power, if he pleafed, to fend them on
fuch an Errand; for fuch, I think, is the Connection of שאול being
naked before him, and אבדין (a Word of the fame Import) being *without
a Covering*, or *Cover*, *i. e.* the Gates of the lower Regions were always
open to his Command. And this he confirms by fhewing how all other
Things in Nature were difpofed to obey the Divine Power. That the
Jews had a Notion of the feparate Exiftence of the Souls of the dead,
and the Poffibility of their revifiting the Earth, is evident from Saul's
Application to the Witch of Endor, and particularly from the Parable
of the rich Man and Lazarus, Luk. XVI. 24. where the rich Man
requefts Abraham to fend Lazarus to admonifh his Brethren. But
Abraham replies, that what he afked was impoffible, meaning doubtlefs without exprefs Commiffion from God, becaufe the dead were
not otherwife allowed to pafs the Gulph fixed between them and the
Earth. As to the latter Hemiftic, which I render *from the Sea and
its Inhabitants*, the Meaning is fufficiently clear from Rev. XX. 13.
where at the general Refurrection it is faid, *The Sea gave up the dead
which were in it, and Death and Hell delivered up the dead which were
in them*; as if thofe who were drowned or buried in the Sea had their
Place under the Waters, as thofe who were buried on dry Land had
their's under Ground. It is not however impoffible that by *the Sea*
might be meant *the Sea of Sodom*, or *the Lake Afphaltites*, which bordered upon *Idumea*, the Scene of Action, the Waters of which were
faid to be of fuch a peftilential Quality, as to kill the Birds that at-
tempted to pafs over it; whence perhaps it was called the *Dead Sea*.
And I fubmit it to Confideration, whether the Notion, that prevails
among the Vulgar, of Ghofts being laid or confined in the Red Sea
(miftaken perhaps for *the Dead Sea* on Account of its fimilar Sound,
the one Name being alfo more familiar to the common People than the
other) might not have arifen from fome fanciful Tradition concerning
the Habitation of departed Spirits in that Place of Horror.

V. 6. *Hell is naked before him :* — עָרוֹם שְׁאוֹל נֶגְדּוֹ] The Word
שאול fignifies here and Ch. XI. 8. THE NETHER RECESSES or
LOWER PARTS OF THE EARTH. It has a very extenfive Signification
which is to be determined by the Context; as for Inftance, when Jonah
faid that *he cried out of* שאול, the Word certainly means THE
WHALE'S BELLY, wherein he was then confined; and fhould not be
rendered

rendered *Hell*, as in our Verſion. (Ch. II. 2.) Its moſt general Senſe
is *the Grave*, or common Receptacle of the dead. It can I think ſignify the Region of the damned but in two Places, *viz.* Pſ. IX. 17.
Prov. XV. 24. if it does ſo there.

V. 9. *He holdeth back the Face of his Throne, and ſpreadeth*, &c.
"מאחז פני כסה — פרשז וגו] Rather — HE BARRETH THE FRONT
OF his THRONE, SPREADING &c. Thus Ch. XXII. 14. *Thick Clouds
are a Covering to him.* So alſo Pſalms XVIII. 11. *He made Darkneſs
his ſecret Place ; his Pavilion round about him were dark Waters, and
thick Clouds of the Skies.* And XCVII. 2. *Clouds and Darkneſs* are
round about him.

V. 12. *He divideth the Sea with his Power, and by his Underſtanding
he ſmiteth through the Proud.* : בכחו רגע הים —ובתבונתו מחץ רהב]
Were it not for a ſeeming Incongruity in introducing an Act of God's
particular Providence among the other Inſtances of Almighty Power,
which are general ones, I ſhould be apt to think that there was a plain
Alluſion here to the miraculous Paſſage of the Iſraelites through the
Red Sea, and that the Word רהב was uſed not as an Appellative, but
as a Proper Name for *Egypt*, as Pſ. LXXXVII. 4. Iſa. LI. 9. and particularly Pſ. LXXXIX. 10; which laſt might be conſidered as a parallel
Place to this. But though it might appear allowable in the favoured
Nation, eſpecially in their Songs of Praiſe, to break out of the common Road, in order to commemorate ſo ſignal a Deliverance ; it may
be thought a Violation of Character in an Alien, an Idumean, as Job
was, one in no wiſe particularly intereſted in the Event. If there be
any Force in this Objection, we may in the former Hemiſtic give to
רגע the Signification it ſometimes has of *reſting* or *cauſing to reſt*, and
render it --- HE STILLETH THE SEA BY HIS POWER. The old
Verſion reads, *The Sea is calm by his Power.* As to the latter Hemiſtic,
we may render רהב *ſpacious* or *wide*, (in which Senſe it is applied to
the Sea, Pſ. CIV. 25.) ſupplying after it the Word *Ocean*, to render it
more intelligible ; or with the ſame Addition may continue to it the
Signification we find in our preſent Verſion, *the proud*, which Epithet
is alſo applied to the ſwelling Waves, Ch. XXXVIII. 11. Thus ——
HE SMITETH, or SUBDUETH BY HIS UNDERSTANDING THE
WIDE, (or PROUD) Ocean. The Sentiment will then correſpond with
what is ſaid of God's Power and Wiſdom, Pſ. LXXXIX. 9. *Thou ruleſt
the Raging of the Sea ; when the Waves thereof ariſe, thou ſtilleſt them.*
But as the Verſion ſtands at preſent, it ſeems in this latter Clauſe to
denote

denote an Act of God's Moral Government in bringing down *proud* or *lofty* Men, which, how true foever, would be unfuitable to the Context.

V. 13. *By his Spirit he hath garnished the Heavens:* — ברוחו שמים שפרה] Rather — BY HIS SPIRIT THE HEAVENS are BRIGHT-NESS; for שפרה feems rather to be a Noun than a Verb.

— *his Hand hath formed the crooked Serpent.* : חללה ידו נחש ברח] Bochart makes this Animal to be the *Zygæna*, fo called becaufe it has a ζυγον, or *tranfverfe Bar*, in the Forehead : but allows that it may be properly confidered here (as many Rabbi's have done) for the Conftellation of DRACO. The Evolutions and Diftortions of this Animal are well defcribed by Virgil, Geo. *Lib.* I. V. 244.

> *Maximus hic flexu finuofo elabitur Anguis,*
> *Circum perque duas, in morem fluminis, Arctos.*

CHAP. XXVII

V. 2. As *God liveth, who hath taken away my Judgment*; — הי אל הסיר משפטי] Our Verfion adds three Particles in this Verfe, and omits two other Particles in the two following Verfes. For this there feems to be no Neceffity; as the whole Paffage will be equally clear, if literally rendered thus --- THE LIVING GOD HATH TAKEN AWAY MY JUDGMENT; AND THE ALMIGHTY HATH IMBITTERED MY SOUL: BUT ALL THE WHILE MY BREATH IS IN ME, AND THE SPIRIT OF GOD IS IN MY NOSTRILS: SURELY MY LIPS SHALL NOT SPEAK WICKEDNESS, NOR MY TONGUE UTTER DECEIT.

V. 11. *I will teach you by the Hand of God*; — אורה אתכם ביד אל] Rather --- I WILL INSTRUCT YOU IN THE POWER OF GOD. See ביד thus rendered Prov. XVIII. 21.

V. 15. *Thofe that remain of him fhall be buried in Death:* — שרידיו במות יקברו] Ought not this Place to be rendered — SUCH OF HIS WHO HAVE ESCAPED FROM DEATH SHALL BE BURIED? that is, thofe who have efcaped a violent Death (fee V. 14.) fhall neverthelefs furvive but a fhort Time.

V. 18. — *and as a Booth that the Keeper maketh.* : וכסכה עשה נצר] Rather --- AND HE MAKETH A BRANCH IN THE FORM OF A BOOTH; that is, " whatever he builds will be of very fhort Duration."

V. 19. *The*

V. 19. *The rich Man shall lie down, but shall not be gathered:* — עשיר ישכב ולא יאסף] Rather — THE RICH LIETH DOWN, AND NOTHING IS TAKEN AWAY. Thus אסף is rendered, Isa. XVI. 10. and LVII. 1.

—— *he openeth his Eyes, and he is not.* עיניו פקח ואיננו :] Rather --- HE OPENETH HIS EYES, AND there is NOTHING left.

CHAP. XXVIII.

V. 3. *He setteth an End to Darkness, and searcheth out all Perfection; the Stones of Darkness and the Shadow of Death.* קץ שם להשך ולכל תכלית — הוא חוקר אבן אפל וצלמות :] This Verse in our Version does not seem to be rightly divided. There appear only two Hemistics, *viz.* Man SETTETH AN END TO DARKNESS AND TO EVERY PURPOSE; HE SEARCHETH OUT THE STONES OF DARKNESS, AND THE SHADOW OF DEATH; *i. e.* the Stones buried under Ground.

V. 4. *The Flood breaketh out from the Inhabitant;* — פרץ נחל מעם גר] Rather — FROM THE SPRING; for גר is not derived from גור, but from נגר *to pour down.*

V. 8. *The Lion's Whelps have not trodden it:* — לא הדריכהו בני שחץ] Rather — THE WHELPS OF THE WILD BEAST &c. For שחץ, according to Bochart, is only a generic Name, denoting any large, fierce, and untameable Beast.

V. 17. — *and the Exchange of it shall be for Jewels of fine Gold.* ותמורתה כלי פז :] Rather — NOR are VESSELS OF FINE GOLD IT'S RECOMPENSE. So is תמורה used Ch. XV. 31.

V. 27. *Then did he see it, and declare it; he prepared it, yea, and he searched it out.* אז ראה ויספרה — הכינה וגם חקרה :] Rather — THEN DID HE SEE IT, AND SHEWED IT FORTH; HE ESTABLISHED IT, FOR SURELY HE HAD FOUND IT OUT. For otherwise there seems to be an Anticlimax.

CHAP. XXIX.

V. 4. *As I was in the Days of my Youth:* — כאשר הייתי בימי חרפי] חרף never signifies *Youth:* in that Sense it can have no Connection with

with the Root, which, among other Senſes, ſignifies to *pluck* or *ſtrip off Fruit:* hence AUTUMN, the Seaſon when Fruits are *plucked.* See Iſa. XVIII. 6. MY AUTUMN here means "that Part of my Life "when my Body was vigorous, and I enjoyed Proſperity."

—— *When the Secret of God* was *upon my Tabernacle;* — בסוד אלוה עלי אהלי׃] Rather — WHEN GOD was SECRETLY UPON MY TA-BERNACLE.

V. 12. *Becauſe I delivered the poor that cried, and the fatherleſs, and* him that had *none to help him.*] This latter Hemiſtic, *viz.* ויתום ולא עזר לו׃, might be rendered with more Exactneſs, thus —— AND THE FATHERLESS WHO HAD NO HELPER.

V. 18. *Then I ſaid, I ſhall die in my Neſt;* — ואמר עם קני אגוע] The Word קן is uſed for A CELL, A ROOM, or APARTMENT, Gen. VI. 14.

V. 24. — *and the Light of my Countenance they caſt not down.* ואור פני לא יפילון׃] Or — NEITHER DID THEY SUFFER THE LIGHT OF MY COUNTENANCE TO FALL. The *Countenance falls* when the Marks of Chagrin, Uneaſineſs or Shame appear on it. See Gen. IV. 5. In this Place either the Particle ו or לא might ſeem redundant: but ſee a ſimilar Inſtance Exod. XX. 4.

CHAP. XXX.

V. 2. — *in whom old Age was periſhed.* עלימו אבד כלח׃] By this obſcure Phraſe our Tranſlators ſeem to have underſtood, "That "their Fathers died for Famine before they came to Age;" as appears by a Note in the old Verſion. But it is moſt probable that the printed Text is corrupt in this Place; for כלח is not acknowledged by any of the ancient Verſions, except one of the Targums; and the LXX, Syriac, Arabic, and Symmachus read כלה, which makes an excellent Senſe when connected with the preceding Part of the Verſe; thus — *Yea, what* was *the Strength of their Hands to me,* when THE WHOLE OF IT WAS SPENT UPON THEMSELVES. However, if this Lection be not admitted, I would at leaſt render the Text, as it is now read, thus --- WHOSE OLD AGE WAS WITHERED. See the Verb אבד thus uſed, Jon. IV. 10.

V. 3. — *fleeing*

V. 3. — *fleeing into the Wilderneſs in former Time deſolate and waſte.*
הערקים ציה אמש שואה ומשאה:] Theſe Words would be clearer,
were they rendered thus --- FLEEING LATELY INTO THE WIL-
DERNESS, which is DESOLATE AND WASTE: or --- INTO THE
WILDERNESS, UNTO DESOLATION AND DESTRUCTION.

V. 4. *Who cut up Mallows by the Buſhes ;* — הקטפים מלוח עלי שיח]
That *Mallows* were uſed for Food appears from Horace, *viz.*

———————— *me paſcunt olivæ*
Me cichoreæ, leveſque MALVÆ. Lib. I. Ode 31.

Again ———————— *aut gravi*
MALVÆ *ſalubres corpori.* Epod. II.

So alſo Martial —— *Utere lactucis, et mollibus utere* MALVIS.
Lib. III. Epig. 88.

—— *and Juniper Roots for their Meat.* ושרש רתמים לחמם:]
Out of the Root of the רתם grew an Excreſcence, which alſo ſome-
times ſerved for Food to the pooreſt People. See Bochart *Hierob.*
P. II. P. 246.

V 5. *They were driven from among* Men : מן גו ינרשו] The Word
גו never ſignifies any Thing elſe than a *Carcaſe, Body,* or *Back.* None
of which Senſes can be here applicable. I would therefore read the
Text thus — מן גוי נרשו — and render it — THEY WERE DRIVEN
FORTH FROM THE PEOPLE.

V. 7. — *under the Nettles they were gathered together.* תחת חרול
יספחו:] Rather — UNDER THE SHRUBS. For חרול properly ſignifies
the *Paliurus,* a THORNY SHRUB, according to Bochart. See *Hierobot.*

V. 8. They were *Children of Fools,* — בני נבל] Rather, I think
— They were a CONTEMPTIBLE GENERATION for נבל in Scrip-
ture generally ſignifies *one who has no Reputation* ; or who is deſtitute
of Wiſdom, Goodneſs, and every Principle of Virtue. The Words
which immediately follow ſeem to determine for this Senſe.
—— *yea, Children of baſe Men :* גם בני בלי שם] I ſee no Reaſon for departing from the Proper Senſe of the Words ; for CHILD-
REN OF NO NAME, or OF NO ACCOUNT, is a Phraſe univerſally underſtood. We uſe it in Proſe, as well as Verſe. Thus Bacon ſays ; " Viſit
" eminent Perſons of great *Name* abroad :" And Shakeſpear —" What
" Men of *Name* reſort to him." So in Latin, *magnum* NOMEN *in ora-*
toribus

F

toribus habuerunt. Cic. and *homo* NULLIUS NOMINIS fignifies *a low de-fpicable Fellow.* So alfo in Greek — απο γαρ της μαχης το τετε ONOMA μεγιςεν ηυξετο˙ Philoſtr. *ap.* Steph.

V. 11. *Becauſe he hath looſed my Cord,* — כי יהרי פתח] The Subject to the Verb is fuppoſed to be *God*; and is fupplied in the old Verſion. But the Verb is in Pyhal, and ought to be tranſlated IS RELAXED; be-cauſe שלח is rendered in the next Hemiſtic by *letting looſe.* This ſeems to be an Alluſion to *the ſtretched Cords* by which Job's *Tent* was fixed to the Ground.

—— *they have alſo let looſe the Bridle before me.* : ורסן מפני שלחו] Our Verſion is here not very intelligible. Either the Words ought to be rendered in the figurative Senſe, *viz.* THEY HAVE CAST OFF RE-STRAINT BEFORE ME: or a Note to that Effect ought to be added in the Margin, as in the old Verſion.

V. 12. *Upon* my *right* Hand *riſe the youth:* — על ימין פרחח יקומו] The laſt Letter in פרחח is fuſpicious, as we meet with few *quadrilite-ral* radical words: but פרח with its Affixes is common. The Targum read here evidently פרחם THEIR YOUTH.

V. 13. — *they* have no *helper.* : לא עזר למו] Rather, I think — there is NO HELPER AMONG THEM, that is, *none ready to aſſiſt me.* This Senſe the whole Scope of the Place ſeems evidently to require: and that this Conſtruction may be admitted, ſee Exod. XII. 2. Numb. III. 40, &c.

V. 14. *They came* upon me *as a wide Breaking in* of Waters: *in the Deſolation they rolled themſelves* upon me. כפרץ רהב יאתיו — תהת שאה התגלגלו :] Rather — THEY CAME AS A WIDE TORRENT; THEY ROLLED THEMSELVES IN ORDER TO DESTROY. The Verb פרץ is applied to Waters *breaking out violently,* and I think the Noun may be uſed fimply to denote *a violent Irruption,* or *Torrent.* See the Prepoſition תחת in fuch a Senſe, 1 Sam. II. 20. 2 Sam. XIX. 21.

V. 15. *Terrors are turned upon me:* — ההפך עלי בלהות] This ap-parent Soleciſm would be removed by rendering — TERRORS are AN OVERTHROW TO ME. הפך has here the ה *demonſtrative:* it is thus uſed, Iſa. XXIX. 16.

—— *they purſue my Soul as the Wind;* — תרדף כרוח נדבתי] Rather --- MY SPIRIT IS AGITATED AS THE WIND: for the Reaſon juſt mentioned. The Verb is here in *Pyhal,* as Iſa. XVII. 13.

V. 17. *My*

V. 17. *My Bones are pierced in me in the Night Seafon*; לילה עצמי נקר מעלי] Here again, for the fame Reafon, I render — MY BODY IS PIERCED &c. עצם has this Senfe, Exod. XXIV. 10. Ch. VII. 15, and Lam. IV. 7. Or — IT HATH PIERCED MY BONES ; viz. *Affliction*, mentioned immediately before.

V. 18. *By the great Force of my Difeafe is my Garment changed*; ברב כח יתחפש לבושי] Rather — WITH GREAT FORCE IS MY GARMENT CHANGED. That is, on Account of his Weaknefs, which his Sufferings had brought upon him, " he was not able to change his " Clothes, and draw them off from his Body," as the next Hemiftic feems to fhew.

V. 20. — *I ftand up, and thou regardeft me* not. עמדתי ותתבנן בי] The negative Particle is not here wanting : the ו has that Force, being juft before preceded by לא. The true Verfion therefore is —— I STAND UP ; NEITHER REGARDEST THOU ME.

V. 24. *Howbeit, he will not ftretch out his Hand to the Grave*; אך לא בעי ישלח יד] Rather — HOWBEIT, UPON INTREATY HE WILL NOT STRETCH OUT THE HAND. בעי comes from בעה *to afk*; not from עיר, which fignifies only *an Heap*; and is not to the Purpofe, as the next Hemiftic fhews.
—— *though they cry in his Deftruction.* : אם בפידו להן שוע] Rather --- IF THEY CRY WHEN HE DESTROYETH. להן is put here for להם. Many fuch Chaldee Terminations of Plurals occur in this Book.

V. 27. —— *the Days of Affliction prevented me.* : קדמני ימי עני] Rather — RUSHED IN UPON ME. See this Word explained Ch. III. v. 12.

V. 31. *My Harp alfo is* turned *to Mourning,* — ויהו לאבל כנרי] Rather --- MY HARP ALSO IS BECOME MOURNFUL. The Abftract for the Concrete ; than which Nothing is more common in the Eaftern Poetry. ל is here prefixed either to the Nominative, according to Noldius, as יהיו לבשר אחד — *and they fhall be one Flefh.* Gen. II. 24. והייתי לכם לאלהים — *and I will be to you a God,* Exod. VI. 7. Or it is an oblique Cafe ufed for the Nominative, as, URBEM *quam ftatuo* — in Virgil ; and EXITIO *eft avidis mare nautis* ; or it may be a Prepofition fignifying *for,* or *in the Place of.*

CHAP.

V. 3. — *and a strange* Punishment *to the Workers of Iniquity.* ונכר
לפעלי און] *Qu.* ought not נכר to be here rendered A DISOWNING
or DISAVOWAL ? It is used precisely in the same Sense, and conjoined
with *Destruction*, as here, Obad. V. 12.

V. 11. — *it is an Iniquity* to be punished by *the Judges.* הוא עון
פלילים:] Rather—IT IS AN HEINOUS (or ARBITRATORY) CRIME,
i. e. an Iniquity which any Arbitrator, even the Criminal himself,
would condemn. See Taylor, Schultens, and Gusset.

V. 20. *If his Loins have not blessed me, and if he were* not *warmed
with the Fleece of my Sheep.* : אם לא ברכוני חלצו—וכנז כבשי יתחמם]
The latter Hemistic ought doubtless to be rendered — NOR WERE HE
WARMED &c. See the last Ch. V. 20.

V. 24. — *or have said to fine Gold,* Thou art *my Confidence.* ולכהם
אברתי מבטהי:] Rather—— OR HAVE CALLED FINE GOLD MY
CONFIDENCE. Thus אמר is rendered, Isa. V. 20.

V. 27. — *or my Mouth hath kissed my Hand.* ותשק ידי לפי] In this
and the preceding Verse are evident Allusions to the superstitious Rites
of Idolaters. The Custom of *kissing the Hand*, in Token of Adoration, is very ancient, as well as universal. The Ground of it appears
to me to be Awe or Respect : thus Job, when he determines to be silent before God says, *I will lay my Hand upon my Mouth.* Ch. XL. 4.
Pliny, where he enumerates strange Customs, (that of bowing when
another sneezes is, by the by, not omitted) says ; *In adorando dextram
ad osculum referimus, totumque corpus circumagimus ; quod in lævum,
Galliæ religiosius credunt.* Nat. Hist. B. XXVIII. C. 2. Apuleius observes, that "many of his Countrymen applied *their right Hand to
their Mouths, the first Finger being upon the Thumb erect, in order
" that they might perform due Adoration to the Goddess Venus." *De
Asin.* L. IV. And, in another Place, he takes Notice of a Person,
who thought it a Crime *to kiss his Hand*, when he passed by a Temple.
Apol. I. Lucian also remarks, that the poor, who had Nothing to offer in Sacrifice but *the kissing of their Hands*, were not excluded. *Dial.
de Sacrif.* Lastly, it may not be improper to observe in this Place,
that the Syrians to this Day, when they receive the holy Sacrament, are
said

said to *kiss* the Bread and Cup before they partake of them.   *Vie de Monf. De Chateuil.*

V. 31. *If the Men of my Tabernacle said not,* אם לא אמרו מתי — אהלי] This cannot be the Senfe of the Place: it ought to be rendered --- SURELY THE MEN OF MY TABERNACLE SAID --- See אם לא thus rendered Numb. XIV. 35. Jofh. XIV. 9. and V. 36.

V. 40. *The Words of Job are ended.* : תמו דברי איוב] As this is doubtlefs a marginal Glofs, which has unwarrantably crept into the Text; ought it not to be diftinguifhed by other Characters? In the old Verfion thefe Words are written in capital Letters

CHAP. XXXII.

V. 16, 17. *When I had waited, (for they fpake not, 'but flood ftill, and anfwered no more.) I faid, I will alfo anfwer my Part; &c.* ——— [והוחלתי כי לא ידברו — כי עמדו לא ענו עוד : אענה אף אנו הלקי ונו " The Parenthefis might be here omitted, and the two Verfes rendered without Addition --- AND I WAITED, BUT THEY SPAKE NOT; BUT STOOD STILL, WITHOUT ANSWERING MORE: SO I WILL SPEAK MY PART; &c. See אף thus conftrued Ch. XXXVI. 16.

CHAP. XXXIII.

V. 5. —*fet thy Words in Order before me, ftand up.* ערכה לפני התיצבר:] Rather — PREPARE THYSELF, STAND BEFORE ME. As Numb. XXIII. 4. Pf. XXIII. 5.

V. 19. —*and the Multitude of his Bones with ftrong* Pain. ורוב עצמיו אתן :] Some Copies read here וריב, which makes a better Senfe, *viz.* AND there is A STRONG CONTENTION IN HIS BONES: agreeably to the Phrafe we meet Pf. XXXVIII. 4. אין שלום בעצמי, *there is no Peace in my Bones*: or — XXII. 4. — *all my Bones are out of Joint.*

V. 20. *So that his Life abhorreth Bread:* והמיתו חיתו לחם] Rather---So THAT HIS APPETITE MAKETH HIM TO ABHOR MEAT. See חיה fo rendered Ch. XXXVIII. 39. This Verb זהם occurs only here; the Signification is properly derived from the Arabic رغم *Pingue-dine guedine illitum fuit*, item *fætuit.* I give it a tranfitive Senfe (which many Verbs have, though not in *Hiph.*) becaufe of the Affix.

V. 21. — *and his Bones* that *were not feen ftick out.* ושפו עצמתיו לא ראו] Rather — AND HIS BONES ARE BROKEN, that they CANNOT BE PERCEIVED. This Verb alfo occurs only in this Place; and I give it the Chaldee Signification, as the moft warrantable of any; which the Arabic alfo countenances.

V. 27. *He looketh upon Men, and if any fay, I have finned:* ישר על אנשים ויאמר חטאתי] The marginal Lection ought I think to be here admitted, *viz.* HE WILL LOOK UPON MEN, AND SAY, I HAVE SINNED.

V. 28. *He will deliver his Soul* — פדה נפשי] There feems to be no Reafon for adopting the Mafforetical Lection. The prefent Text is, at leaft, as clear; and is countenanced by more of the ancient Verfions. I would therefore render — HE WILL DELIVER MY SOUL; and prefently after — והיתי AND MY LIFE &c.

C H A P. XXXIV.

V. 1. *Furthermore, Elihu anfwered and faid.* ויען אליהוא ויאמר] Rather — SPAKE AND SAID: as Ch. III. 2. and XXXV. 1. for none had replied to Elihu.

V. 6. *Should I lie againft my Right?* — על משפטי אכוב] Rather, I think --- I AM DISAPPOINTED (or FRUSTRATED) OF MY RIGHT. See כוב thus ufed Ch. XLI. 9, &c.

—— *my Wound is incurable without Tranfgreffion.* אנוש הצי בלי פשע] Our Tranflators here ufe a very bold Figure; by making הצי, the conftant Senfe of which is AN ARROW, to fignify *a Wound.* I cannot deny that Inftances of fuch Metonymies, of Caufe for Effect, and the like, occur in the beft Writers: but here there is no Neceffity to depart from the Proper Senfe of the Words; which may be rendered --- I AM DESPERATELY PIERCED THROUGH by ARROWS &c. אנוש is here confidered as the firft Perfon of the Future, as Pf. LXIX. 20. and הצי ufed fpecially, as in Abundance of Places, for הצים. See what was obferved on ידי Ch. XXIII. 2. which adds Weight to this Interpretation.

V. 10. — *far*

V. 10. —*far be it from God* that he fhould do *Wickednefs; and* from *the Almighty*, that he fhould commit *Iniquity*. הללה לאל
מרשע — ושרי מעול :] The Analyfis of this Idiom feems to me to be this — *Profanenefs would be to God in doing Wickednefs, and to the Almighty in committing Iniquity;* for both the Verbs are in the Infinitive; as in thefe Inftances — ירא מהביט אל אלהים, *he was afraid to look* (literally *in looking*) *upon God*; Exod. III. 6. and ויכלו מחלק את הארץ, *and they made an End of dividing* (literally *in* or *from dividing*) *the Earth*; Jofh. XIX. 51. I would therefore render — FAR BE IT FROM GOD TO DO WICKEDNESS, AND FROM THE ALMIGHTY TO COMMIT INIQUITY.

V. 14. *If he fet his Heart upon Man, if he gather* &c.— אם ישים
אליו לבו — וגו"] Rather — IF HE SET HIS HEART AGAINST HIM, HE WILL GATHER &c.

V. 16. *If thou haft Underftanding, hear this:* — ואם בינה שמעה]
בינה is here not a Subftantive, but a Verb in the Imperative, with the ה paragogic, as Pf. V. 1. and ought to be rendered —— BUT, I PRAY THEE, UNDERSTAND, HEAR THIS.

V. 17. *Shall even he that hateth Right govern?* האף שונא משפט
יחבוש] Rather — YEA, SHALL HE THAT HATETH JUSTICE RECTIFY? for חבש never fignifies *to govern*.

—— *and wilt thou condemn him that is moft juft?* ואם צדיק כביר
הרשיע :] Rather —— AND WILT THOU GREATLY VEX THE RIGHTEOUS? The Conftruction of our Verfion feems contrary to the Genius of the Hebrew. כביר is here confidered as an Adverb, as Ch. XV. 10. XXXI. 25. and the Verb is ufed as 1 Sam. XIV. 47. or as V. 29.

V. 18. *Is it fit to fay to a King*, Thou art *wicked?* האמר למלך
בליעל] Rather — SHALL WICKEDNESS BE ATTRIBUTED TO (OR PUBLISHED OF, or CONCERNING) THE KING; and UNGOD-LINESS, OF PRINCES? This Conftruction feems eafy; whereas the other is repugnant to the Rules of Grammar.

V. 19. How much lefs to him *that accepteth not the Perfons of Princes:* — אשר לא נשא פני שרים] This Sentence will not be defective, if we render אשר BEHOLD, HE ACCEPTETH &c. as it ought to be, 2 Sam. II. 4. — XIV. 15. That Particle, in this Senfe, is properly introduced, when the Admiration is to be raifed, or a Contraft is intended to be exhibited. V. 20. — *and*

V. 20. — *and the mighty shall be taken away without Hand.* ויסירו
אביר לא ביד :] Rather — AND THEY SHALL TAKE AWAY THE
MIGHTY WITHOUT FORCE : *i. e.* he will be so feeble, that Force,
used against him, will be unnecessary.

V. 22. There is *no Darkness, nor Shadow of Death, where the
workers of Iniquity may hide themselves.* אין חשך ואין צלמות — להסתר
שם פעלי און :] Rather — NEITHER DARKNESS, NOR THE SHA-
DOW OF DEATH WILL HIDE THERE THE WORKERS OF INIQUITY:
the Infinitive for the Preter.

V. 23. *For he will not lay upon Man more* than right ; כי לא על
איש ישים עוד] *Qu.* ought not this Hemistic to be rendered — FOR
NEITHER YET WILL HE DECREE (or ORDAIN) IN RESPECT TO
MAN ? See ישים thus used, Isa. LXI. 3. and Hab. I. 12. and in respect
to the על, see Numb. VIII. 22. 1 Kings XXII. 8.

V. 30. *That the Hypocrite reign not, lest the People be ensnared.*
ממלך אדם חנף — ממקשי עם :] Rather —— THE HYPOCRITE IS
MADE TO REIGN, ON ACCOUNT OF THE SNARES OF THE PEOPLE.
The Verb is here considered as the Participle *Pahul*, and the Preposition,
as Exod. VI. 9. Deut. VII. 7. See the same Sentiment, Isa. III. 4, 5, &c.

V. 31. *Surely it is meet to be said unto God, I have borne* Chastise-
ment, *I will not offend* any more. כי אל אל האמר — נשאתי לא אחבל :]
Rather, I think --- SURELY IT MAY BE SAID UNTO GOD, I
HAVE BEEN DECEIVED ; I WILL NOT ACT CORRUPTLY.

CHAP. XXXV.

V. 3. *For thou saidst, What Advantage will it be unto thee ?* and,
What Profit shall I have if I be cleansed from my Sin ? כי האמר מה
יסכן לך — מה אעיל מחטאתי :] Rather — FOR THOU SAIDST, WHAT
ADVANTAGE WILL THERE BE UNTO THEE, and WHAT PROFIT
SHALL I HAVE, FROM MY LOSS, or SUFFERING ? Thus is
חטא rendered Gen. XXXI. 39. and ought to be — XLIII. 9.

V. 8. *Thy Wickedness* may hurt *a Man as thou* art : *and thy Righteousness* may profit *the Son of Man.* לאיש כמוך רשע — לבן אדם
צדקתך :] The Sense I think is sufficiently clear without any other Addition

dition than the Verb Subſtantive, thus — THY WICKEDNESS IS FOR A MAN AS THYSELF; AND THY RIGHTEOUSNESS FOR THE SON OF MAN.

V. 9. *By Reaſon of the Multitude of Oppreſſions they make* the oppreſſed *to cry:* — כרוב עשוקים יזעיקו] The Verb ישועו, *they cry out,* which immediately follows, ſeems to determine that יזעיקו is here to be conſidered as in the firſt Conjugation, as it frequently is; ſo that this Place might be rendered — THEY BEWAIL BY REASON OF THE MULTITUDE OF OPPRESSIONS.

V. 14. *Although thou ſayeſt thou ſhalt not ſee him, yet Judgment is before him, therefore truſt thou in him.* אף כי תאמר לא תשורנו — דין לפניו ותחולל לו :] Rather — NOTWITHSTANDING THOU HAST SAID THOU SHALT NOT SEE HIM; EXECUTE JUDGMENT BEFORE HIM, AND THOU MAYEST WAIT FOR HIM.

V. 15. *But now, becauſe* it is *not ſo, he hath viſited in his Anger; yet he knoweth* it *not in great Extremity.* ועתה כי אין פקד אפו — ולא ידע בפש מאר :] Our Tranſlators make God the Subject of the firſt Hemiſtic, and Job of the latter; as appears by the Margin; which is harſh. They next derive פש from פוש; which is ſurely unjuſtifiable. And, to compleat all, after having coined a new Word, they give it an arbitrary Senſe, which has not the moſt diſtant Connection with the Root. There is the ſtrongeſt Evidence that this Word is defective in the printed Text; that, inſtead of בפש, it ought to be written בפשע: for the LXX render it παραπτωμα, ſo does Theodotion; Symmachus παραπτωματα, and the Vulgate *Scelus:* and the Syriac and Arabic evidently countenance this Lection. The Chaldee is corrupt. On the Authority therefore of all theſe diſtinct Witneſſes, we cannot heſitate to admit this Reading, and render the Verſe thus — BUT NOW, BECAUSE HIS ANGER HATH NOT VISITED, AND HE HATH NOT REGARDED TRANSGRESSION GREATLY &c.

CHAP. XXXVI.

V. 4. — *he that is perfect in Knowledge is with thee.* תמים דעות עמך :] Rather, I think — but PERFECT KNOWLEDGE (literally *the Perfection,* or *the Oracle, of Knowledge*) ſhall be WITH THEE.

V. 5. *Behold God is mighty and deſpiſeth not any:* he is *mighty in Strength and Wiſdom.* הן אל כביר ולא ימאם — כביר כח לב :] Our Verſion

G

Verfion fupplies here the Prepofition and copulative Particle, that the laft Hemiftic may bear the Senfe given to it. But, if without thefe Additions, a Senfe, better in itfelf, and more agreeable to the Context, can be deduced from the fame Letters, in the very fame Order, is it not to be admitted ? And this is done by bringing clofer the four laft Letters ; or making one Word out of two. כחלב will then have the ufual Particle of Comparifon prefixed, and חלב will fignify *a Suckling*, as 1 Sam. VII. 9. thus — Though God be MIGHTY, YET HE DESPISETH NOT : though MIGHTY, yet AS A SUCKLING : *i. e.* gentle. The Particle הן is thus ufed Jer. II. 10. The Antithefis of the next Verfe favours alfo this Interpretation. The Syriac and Arabic evidently read the Text, as is here propofed : but miftook the Senfe.

V. 16. *Even fo would he have removed thee out of the ftrait* into *a broad Place, where* there is *no Straitnefs.* ואף הסיתך כפי צר — רחב לא מוצק תחתיד :] In the Hebrew each of thefe Hemiftics contains a diftinct Sentiment ; which may not improperly be thus rendered — EVEN SO WOULD HE HAVE RESCUED THEE FROM THE JAWS OF THE OPPRESSOR ; HE WOULD HAVE GIVEN thee ROOM INSTEAD OF STRAITNESS ; (or --- LARGE, NOT STRAIT fhould have been THY PLACE.) For תחת is ufed fubftantively for a Man's *Place,* Exod. X. 23. 1 Sam. XIV. 9. 2 Sam. II. 23. See V. 20.

V. 18. *Becaufe* there is *Wrath,* beware *left he take thee away with* his *Stroke :* — כי חמה פן יסיתך בשפק] Rather — FORASMUCH AS there is WRATH, BE THOU NOT MOVED TO SELF-CONFIDENCE, (or SELF-COMPLACENCY ;) which is the Senfe of שפק ; fee Taylor. The Verb is imperfonal, and implies the Senfe here given to it. The Fault which Elihu finds with Job is his thinking too well of himfelf, and not humbling himfelf fufficiently under the Divine Chaftifement.

V. 19. — *not Gold, nor all the Forces of Strength.* לא בצר וכל מאמצי כח :] Thefe Words would be more intelligible were they rendered, as they certainly may be — NOT GOLD, NOR ALL THE POWERS OF WEALTH. See Ch. VI. 22. Prov. V. 10. &c.

V. 20. *Defire not the Night, when People are cut off in their Place.* אל תשאף הלילה — לעלות עמים תחתם :] Rather — DESIRE NOT THE NIGHT, IN ORDER TO DESTROY THE PEOPLE, WHOM

THOU

THOU HAST TAKEN; (or — IN THEIR PLACE, *i.e.* murder them in their Houses.) I give the Verb עלה, the Senfe it has, Pf. CII. 24.

V. 23. *Who hath enjoined him his Way?* — מי פקד עליו דרכו] The Verb פקד, when it has the Prepofition על or עליו after it, fignifies *To animadvert upon, to correct* or *punifh.* This Place ought therefore to be rendered — WHO CAN CHARGE HIM WITH HIS WAY? or --- WHO CAN ANIMADVERT UPON HIM FOR HIS WAY? And this Senfe will perfectly agree with the next Hemiftic.

V. 25. *Every Man* — כל אדם] Rather — EVERY ONE, becaufe אנוש, *Man,* follows immediately after.

V. 27. *For he maketh fmall the Drops of Water: they pour down Rain according to the Vapour thereof.* כי ינרע נטפי מים — יזקו מטר לאדו:] Neither the Verb, nor the Pronoun, of the laft Hemiftic. feems to have any Antecedent, as they are rendered in our Verfion. Thefe Faults however are not to be charged on the Text; for it may be rendered — FOR HE MAKETH SMALL THE DROPS OF THE WATER, which POURETH DOWN RAIN THROUGH HIS VAPOUR: Or --- FOR HE RESTRAINETH THE DROPS OF THE WATERS, which POUR DOWN RAIN THROUGH THE VAPOUR; (V. 28.) AND WHICH THE CLOUDS &c.

V. 29. *Alfo can any underftand the Spreadings of the Clouds,* — אף אם יבין מפרשי עב] The natural Conftruction of the Words, ab-ftractedly confidered, the Syntax, and the Context, confpire to make God the Subject of this Verfe; which ought to be rendered — YEA, VERILY HE UNDERSTANDETH THE EXPANSIONS OF THE CLOUD, &c.

—— *or the Noife of his Tabernacle?* תשאות כסתו:] Rather — THE THUNDER WITHIN, viz. *within the Cloud;* or THE THUNDER OF HIS HABITATION; viz. *God's;* for God is faid to make the Clouds the Place of his Refidence. See Pf. XVIII. 11. XCVII. 2. The old Verfions render תשאות *Thunder,* and the Context evidently points out that particular Senfe.

V. 32. *With Clouds he covereth the Light:* — על כפים כסה אור] The Word כף fignifies no where *Clouds.* It is therefore better to ren-der this Place thus —— WITH his HANDS HE COVERETH THE LIGHT.

G 2

——and

—— *and commandeth it* not to fhine *by the Cloud that cometh be-twixt.* :ויצו עליה במפגיע] Rather --- AND COMMANDETH THE UPPER REGION BY THAT WHICH IS INTERPOSED ; *i. e.* by fuch Interpofition He as it were iffues His Orders to the upper Regions above the Clouds, that their Radiance fhould not vifit the Earth. עליה is not here a Prepofition with the affix Pronoun, becaufe it cannot agree with אור, its fuppofed Antecedent ; but feems to be ufed for *an upper Chamber* ; a Term not unufual in Scripture to denote *Regions :* thus Ch. IX. 9. *the Chambers of the South* ; and Ch. XXXVII. 9. *Out of the Chamber cometh the Whirlwind* ; and Pf. CIV. 2. 13. *He layeth the Beams of his Chambers in the Waters. — He watereth the Hills from his Chambers.* And, not to mention more Inftances, we meet with *Chambers of Death,* Prov. Ch. VII. 27.

V. 33. — *the Cattle alfo concerning the Vapour.* :מקנה אף על עולה] Thefe very obfcure Words, which have fo much perplexed the Critics, may, I think, without Violence admit of this Conftruction, *viz.* IT IS RED HOT WITH INDIGNATION, THEREFORE IT BURNETH. מקנה is here confidered as the Part. fing. m. *Hiph.* for מקנא, as Ezek. VIII. 3. Now the Verb קנא in Arabic, fo alfo in Hebrew pri-marily, fignifies *to be red hot, to be inflamed* ; whence is derived its moft ufual Signification, *to be moved with Zeal.* The Prepofition על is ufed in the like Manner as it is here, Gen. XLI. 32 ; and the Verb עלה has the Senfe of *burning,* Exod. XXVII. 20. Numb. VIII. 3. &c. Or על עולה may be conftrued by the Gerund, *viz.* IN ASCENDING, or *all the way upwards.* The Words thus explained will perfectly agree with the three preceding Hemiftics, which clearly defcribe the Rife, Progrefs, and Effect of Thunder and Lightning. Thefe Symp-toms here defcribed might well ftrike Elihu with Awe and Trembling ; after which, as the Storm increafeth, he goes on to defcribe the loud Burfts of Thunder, and the Flafhes of the Lightning.

C H A P. XXXVII.

V. 2. *Hear attentively the Noife of his Voice,* —— שמעו שמוע ברגז קולו] Rather --- HEAR ATTENTIVELY HIS VOICE, WITH TREMBLING : or ---HEAR ATTENTIVELY THE RATTLING (or CONCUSSION) OF HIS VOICE.

V. 4. — *He thundereth with the Voice of his Excellency* ; —— ירעם בקול גאונו] Would not — WITH HIS MAJESTIC VOICE — be better ? —— *and*

—— *and he will not stay them, when his Voice is heard.* ולא יעקבם
כי ישמע קולו] As there is no Antecedent to the plural Affix; ought
not there to be a marginal Note, as in the old Version, *viz.* That is,
Rains and Thunders? Or — might not the Text be read — יעקב מכי
--- and thus rendered --- A N D H E W I L L N O T R E S T R A I N T H E
S T R O K E S when H I S V O I C E I S H E A R D? *i. e.* " the Effects of his
" Thunderbolts." The very fame Word, and fame Conftruction occur
Jer. XVIII. 21.

V. 6. — *likewife to the fmall Rain, and to the great Rain of his*
Strength. ונשם מטר ונשם מטרות עזו] Rather — L I K E W I S E T O
T H E S H O W E R O F R A I N, E V E N T H E S H O W E R O F T H E R A I N S O F
H I S S T R E N G T H: *i. e.* even to the Showers of the moft violent Rain.

V. 7. *He fealeth up the Hand of every Man:* — ביד כל אדם יחתום]
Rather, 1 think — B Y M E A N S of them (*viz.* the violent Rains juft
mentioned) H E S H U T T E T H U P E V E R Y M A N. ביד fignifies here
through the Agency or Inftrumentality. There may perhaps appear a
Sort of Catachrefis in attributing *Hands to Clouds,* or *to the Tongue;*
as Prov. XVIII. 21. &c. but in all thefe Cafes, where the Head, Hand,
Heart, Feet, or other Parts of Body, are ufed with reference to inanimate Matter, the Etymology is not fo much to be attended to as
the Analogy.

V. 8. — *and remain in their Places.* ובמעונותיה תשכן] Rather
— I N T H E I R C A V E R N S; *exegetical* of D E N S in the preceding Hemiftic.

V. 9. *Out of the South cometh the Whirlwind, and Cold out of the*
North. מן החדר תבוא סופרה — ממזרים קרה] What the precife
Idea conveyed by thefe Words, חדר and מזרים, is, cannot be determined with Certainty. Our Tranflators give the firft the Senfe of *South,*
becaufe that Word is joined to it Ch. IX. 9. and of courfe, by a Sort of
Analogy, founded on Experience, make the other Word to fignify *the*
North. This, it muft be acknowledged, is but a weak Foundation to
build upon: a better Ground, however, in my Opinion might be found,
were we to render ההדר T H E U P P E R R E G I O N S; for it fignifies a
Chamber, a Recefs, or *Repofitory,* as Ch. IX. 9. Pf. CXXXV. 7. In
regard to the other correfponding Word, it appears to me to be a
Miftake for אצרים or אצרות, a Word of the fame Import as its Relative, and ufed in a Parallel Place in the next Chap. V. 22. But I lay
no Strefs on this Conjecture; and would therefore render מזרים T H E

CONSTEL-

Constellations, a generic Name, to which it has an indubitable Right.

V. 11. *Also by watering he wearieth the thick Cloud:*—[אף ברי יטריח עב] Rather --- ALSO WITH FAIR WIND HE DRIVETH AWAY THE THICK CLOUD. This doubtlefs is the true Senfe of ברי in this Place, from the Verb ברר *To make clean, clear, and bright.* But where our Tranflators got the Idea of *watering,* I cannot find. As the Verb טרח occurs only in this Place, I give it the Signification of the Arabic طرح, *Longe removit, amandavit.*

—— *he fcattereth his bright Cloud.* [יפיץ ענן אורו :] Rather—— HE SCATTERETH THE CLOUD BY HIS LIGHT (or BRIGHTNESS.)

V. 12. — *upon the Face of the World in the Earth.* [על פני תבל ארצה:] The old Verfion feems here preferable, *viz.* UPON THE FACE OF THE WHOLE WORLD; which correfponds to the *Orbis terrarum* of the Latins.

V. 13. *He caufeth it to come, whether for Correction, or for his Land, or for Mercy.* [אם לשבט אם לארצו — אם לחסד ימצאהו :] It is not improbable that אם is repeated before לארץ by the Miftake of an ignorant Tranfcriber, who finding the ל prefixed might think it neceffary to add the אם too, as in the other Inftances. Without it the Senfe would be complete and proper — HE CAUSETH IT TO COME UPON HIS LAND, WHETHER FOR CORRECTION, OR FOR MERCY.

V. 15. — *and caufed the Light of his Cloud to fhine.* [יהפיע אור עננו :] Rather --- AND CAUSED THE LIGHT TO ILLUMINATE THE CLOUD.

V. 16. *Doft thou know* &c. [והתדע וגו] AND DOST THOU KNOW — ? I add the ו from the laft Word; imagining it more neceffary in this Place than there.

V. 18. — which is *ftrong,* and *as a molten looking Glafs ?* [חזקים כראי מוצק:] Rather — which is SOLID LIKE A MOLTEN MIRROUR. Our Tranflators, not feeing the Connection between Strength and a Looking Clafs, make of each of thofe Ideas feparate Articles. But it ought to be remembered, that the Inftruments originally ufed for the Purpofe of reflecting the Light were Plates of polifhed Metal; than which a more apt Simile could not be ufed in refpect to the Sky.

V. 19. — for

V. 19. —— for *we cannot order* our Speech *by reaſon of Darkneſs.* : לא נערך מפני חשך] Rather — WE CANNOT BE PREPARED BY REASON OF DARKNESS. See Ch. XXXIII. 5.

V. 20. *Shall it be told him that I ſpeak? if a Man ſpeak, ſurely he ſhall be ſwallowed up.* : אם אמר איש כי יבלע —היספר לו כי אדבר] Rather --- SHALL IT BE SAID TO HIM, BUT (or SURELY) I WILL SPEAK? IF ANY ONE SAY SO, HE SHALL BE SWALLOWED UP. Our Tranſlators make the firſt Hemiſtic to have reference to God's Omniſcience: but the Context directly oppoſes that Senſe. It ſeems more probable that this alludes to Job's great Preſumption, in wiſhing to be able to find God in order to diſpute with him. Ch. XXIII. 3, 4. See alſo XVI. 21.

V. 21. *And now* Men *ſee not the bright Light, which is in the Clouds: but the Wind paſſeth and cleanſeth them.* —וערה לא ראו אור : ורוח עברה ותטהרם —בהיר הוא בשהקים] Rather — AND NOW Men SEE NOT THE LIGHT, WHICH IS BRIGHT ABOVE (or WITHIN) THE CLOUDS, TILL THE WIND &c. See ב thus uſed, Numb. XIV. 10. Deut. XXXI. 15. Exod. XX. 10. and ו Gen. XVIII. 5. 1 Sam. XIV. 24.

V. 22. — *with God is terrible Majeſty.* : על אלוה נורא הוד] Rather --- ABOVE is GOD OF TREMENDOUS MAJESTY. See the Prepoſition thus conſtrued, Lev. XV 25.

V. 23. Touching *the Almighty, we cannot find him out:* שדי לא מצאנהו] The Affix Pronoun might with Propriety be paſſed over unnoticed, as being an *Hebraiſm*; thus — WE CANNOT FIND OUT THE ALMIGHTY.
—— *and in Plenty of Juſtice,* ורב צדקה] Rather — AND PLENTEOUS IN RIGHTEOUSNESS. As Exod. XXXIV. 6. &c.

CHAP. XXXVIII.

V. 8. — *when it brake forth, as if it had iſſued out of the Womb.* : בגיהו מרחם יצא] Simply thus —— WHEN IT BRAKE FORTH, ISSUING OUT OF THE WOMB.

V. 10. — *and brake up for it my decreed Place:* : ואשבר עליו הקי] In the Margin we read — *and eſtabliſhed my Decree upon it;* which is

a

a much better Senſe: The old Verſion is to the ſame Effect: but שבר does no where elſe ſignify *to eſtabliſh.* This Signification may however I think be juſtified from the Arabic Verb شبر *Spithamis di-menſus fuit. Donavit. Præbuit.*

V. 12. — *and cauſed the Dayſpring to know it's Place.* ידעה שחר מקומו] Here the maſſoretical Lection ought doubtleſs to be inſerted into the Text; *viz.* ידעת השחר.

V. 14. *It is turned as Clay to the Seal, and they ſtand as a Garment.* תתהפך כחמר חותם — ויתיצבו כמו לבוש :] The Connection of this Verſe, as it is now read in our Verſion, is not obvious. The Tranſlation of it ought I think to be this — IT IS CHANGED AS CLAY by AN IMPRESSION; AND THEY ARE MADE TO STAND FORTH AS A GARMENT upon it, that is, covering the Earth with their Light. So God is ſaid *to cover Himſelf with Light as with a Garment.* Pſ. CIV. 2. The Antecedent to the ſingular Pronoun is *the Earth*; and the plural Pronoun has *the Morning and the Dayſpring* for its Antecedent. The Senſe of the former Hemiſtic ſeems to be — " The Earth, after the " Gloom of the Night is paſt, is as much changed in its external Ap- " pearance, as the rude Maſs of Clay is by the Form it receives from Art."

V. 15. — *and the high Arm ſhall be broken.* וזרוע רמה תשבר :] Rather --- AND THE ARM OF THE DECEIVER SHALL BE BROKEN. For רמה, is not derived from רום; but is the Participle of רמה, *To hurt in an unexpected perfidious Way.*

V. 21. — *or becauſe the Number of thy Days is great.* ומספר ימיך ספר] cannot poſſibly agree with רבים, and מ is here a Pre-poſition ſignifying *on account of.* It would therefore be more accurate to render --- OR ON ACCOUNT OF THE NUMBER OF THY MANY DAYS.

V. 24. which *ſcattereth the Eaſt Wind upon the Earth.* יפץ קדים עלי ארץ] Rather — AND THE EAST WIND SCATTERED UPON THE EARTH; אי זה הדרך, *by what Way*, being repeated from the preceding Hemiſtic.

V. 26. — *wherein there is no Man.* לא אדם בו :] Rather — WHEREIN there is NO ONE, or NO INHABITANT; becauſe איש is rendered *Man* in the preceding Hemiſtic.

V. 30. The

V. 30. *The Waters are hid as* with *a Stone*; — ‏כאבן מים יתחבאו‏]
Moſt of the ancient Verſions give ‏חבא‏ the Signification of *growing
hard*; which I think is the Senſe of it in this Place; for though this
Verb ſignifies only *to hide*, yet by Analogy it may ſurely be extended
ſo as to convey the Idea of *Congelation*, as is done in reſpect to the
Verb in the next Hemiſtic. The Poverty of the Hebrew in point of
Copiouſneſs is well known: and in this Caſe, where the Language
does not furniſh a Proper Word, what can be more natural than to
expreſs that Sentiment by the Phraſe — *the Waters hide themſelves,*
when they are no longer fluid? I would therefore render —— THE
WATERS ARE CONGEALED LIKE A STONE.

V. 31. *Canſt thou bind the ſweet Influences of Pleiades, or looſe the
Bands of Orion?* &c. ‏התקשר מערנות כימה — או משכות כסיל תפתח : ונ‏]
Rather — CANST THOU RESTRAIN — ? Thus Homer in deſcribing
Achilles's Shield, takes Notice of the very ſame Stars, which is very
remarkable, Iliad Σ. v. 485.

> Εν δε τα τειρεα παντα, τα τ᾽ ꭒρανος εϛεφανωται,
> Πληιαδας Ꝯ᾽ Ἱαδας τε, το τε Ꝯενος Ὡριωνος,
> Αρκτον Ꝯ᾽, ην και αμαξαν επικλησιν καλꭒσιν.

V. 36. — *or who hath given Underſtanding to the Heart?* ‏או מי נתן‏
‏לשכוי בינה :‏] This ſtrange Word ‏לשכוי‏ cannot I think but be a
Miſtake for ‏לשכירת‏ or ‏לשכיות‏, as it is written in other Places. It
ought, however, to be rendered — (not *to the Heart*, but) — TO THE
IMAGINATION.

CHAP. XXXIX.

V. 1. — *or, canſt thou mark when the Hinds do calve?* ‏חלל אילות‏
‏תשמר :‏] Rather --- HAST THOU OBSERVED THE TRAVAIL OF
THE HINDS? For this is not only the more uſual Senſe of ‏חלל‏. but
the Tautology of our Verſion in the next Verſe is hereby avoided. It
is moreover obſerved by Bochart, and others, that Hinds bring forth
their young with great Difficulty.

V. 3. — *they caſt out their Sorrows.* ‏חבליהם תשלחנה :‏] As the
Verb ‏חבל‏, among other Significations, ſignifies to *travail* or *bring
forth a young one*, the Derivative may well be ſuppoſed to ſignify AN
OFFSPRING, or YOUNG; and ſhould I think be ſo rendered here as it
is in the LXX.

H

V. 5. Who hath sent out the wild Ass free? — [מי שלח פרא חפשי
If the פרא and the ערוד are really the same Creature (as Bochart asserts, but does not prove;) I would still give the Latin Name to the first, *viz.* THE ONAGER; to avoid Tautology. Thus we retain the foreign Name of foreign wild Beasts, as *Hyæna, Rhinoceros, Hippopotamus* &c. This Animal seems to have no Affinity with the common Ass, but in the Name; for it is beautiful, excessively swift, and wild. *Hieroz.* B. III. C. 16.

V. 8. The Range of the Mountains is his Pasture: — [יתור הרים מרעהו
Rather --- THE EXCELLENCY (or THE ABUNDANCE) OF THE MOUNTAINS &c. *i. e.* " He chuses for his Food whatever is most " excellent among their Produce." I derive this Word from יתר; which is more agreeable to Rule than to make it a Root, as some Lexicographers do; or to deduce it from הור *exploravit.*

V. 13. Gavest thou *the goodly Wings unto the Peacocks?* כנף רננים
נעלסה] Rather — THE WING OF OSTRICHES VIBRATES WITH EXULTATION; or (more probably) --- CARRIES THEM IN THEIR COURSE. The first is the Sense of the Verb עלס, the latter of غلس.
—— *or Wings and Feathers unto the Ostrich?* אם אברה חסידה
ונצה:] Rather — So do THE WING AND FEATHERS, THE STORK. This ought to be considered as a *Parenthesis;* because what follows has reference to the Ostrich.

V. 18. What Time she lifteth up herself on high; — כעת במרום
תמריא] Rather — AT THE TIME SHE HAUGHTILY ASSUMES COURAGE: for the Ostrich cannot *soar,* as other Birds: besides the Verb מרא occurs only in this Place, and in Arabic it signifies in the 5th Conj. *fortitudinem præ se tulit, vel simulavit: et ejus gloriam captavit per vituperium.*

V. 19. — *hast thou clothed his Neck with Thunder?* התלביש צוארו
רעמה:] Rather — HAST THOU CLOTHED HIS NECK WITH PRIDE? for רעמה has that Sense in Chaldee, which seems more suitable than that of Thunder.

V. 20. — *the Glory of his Nostrils is terrible.* הוד נחרו אימה:]
Rather --- THE VIOLENCE OF HIS SNORTING IS TERRIBLE. So Jer. VIII. 16. See Bochart. *Hieroz. Cap.* VIII.

V. 21. He

V. 21. *He paweth in the Valley,* — יחפרו בעמק] The ו has here doubtlefs crept into the Text; it not being acknowledged by the old Verfions. Thus Virgil — Æn. VIII. 596.

Quadrupedante putrem fonitu quatit ungula campum.

CHAP. XL.

V. 2. *Shall he that contendeth with the Almighty, inftruct him?* —— הרב עם שדי יסור] Rather — Is THERE ENOUGH OF INSTRUCTION WITH THE ALMIGHTY? *i. e.* has He faid enough to fhew thee thy Prefumption? LET HIM THAT REPROVETH (or pretendeth to FIND FAULT WITH) GOD ANSWER IT, *i. e.* what has been already advanced. Or, DOTH CONTENTION WITH THE ALMIGHTY INSTRUCT? If fo, LET HIM THAT REPROVETH GOD REPLY TO IT. The firft Interpretation feems the better.

V. 12. — *and tread down the wicked in their Place.* והדך רשעים תחתם :] Or — AND TREAD DOWN THE WICKED, and BREAK THEM TO PIECES. The Lexicographers make הדך an *απαξ λεγομενον,* and confider it as a *Radix:* but can any Thing be more obvious, than that it is the Imperative of דכך in *Hiphil* with the *Apocope* of ה, which is not uncommon to Verbs of that Termination? See Deut. IX. 14. &c.

V. 13. — *and bind their Faces in fecret.* פניהם הבוש בטמון :] Rather, IN THE GRAVE; for בטמון may fignify the Grave from טמן to hide by burying under Ground. The Senfe is —— " confine them " clofe Prifoners in the Grave."

V. 15. *Behold now Behemoth which I made with thee:* — הנה נא בהמות אשר עשיתי עמך] Rather ——— BEHOLD NOW THE HIPPOPOTAMUS, WHICH I MADE NEAR THEE; that is, " in the Nile, " bordering on Arabia, thy Country." *The Behemoth* in this Place can I think poffibly mean no other Animal than this amphibious one defcribed by Bochart, B. V. C. 15. See alfo B. I. C. 7. &c. The Word בהם is a very generic Appellative; the Senfe of which is in general to be reftrained by the Word in Oppofition. It fometimes fignifies *the whole Brute Creation,* as Pf. XXVI. 6. at other times *tame, domeftic Animals,* as Gen. I. 25. &c. But here it is confined to one particular Species; and, though the plural be ufed, this is to be confidered as

H 2

an

an Hebraism, (or rather an Idiom common to many Languages) to denote *Magnitude, Excellence,* or some other transcendent Quality : thus in Greek — α πεϱ Σολωνα, for *Solon :* in Latin, English, French, Italian, &c. a King speaks of himself *in the plural,* and eminent Personages are addressed, or spoken of, *in that Number.* St. Paul often speaks of himself in that Style. 2 Cor. I. ;—14.

V. 17. *He moveth his Tail like a Cedar :* — יחפץ זנבו במו ארן] Rather --- HE MOVETH HIS TAIL which is LIKE A CEDAR.

— *the Sinews of his Stones* &c. גידי פחדו ישרגו [פחד is an απαξ λεγ. which Bochart has shewed ought to be rendered from the Arabic فاخذ THIGHS, and not from the Chaldee, as in our Version. *Loc. cit.*

V. 18. *His Bones are as strong Pieces of Brass ; his Bones are like Bars of Iron.* עצמיו אפיקי נחשה — גרמיו כמטיל ברזל :] Rather — HIS SMALL BONES &c. HIS LARGE BONES &c. In this Sense are Horses called *brazen footed,* χαλκιποδις, by Homer. Iliad. VIII. V. 41. so Virgil — ÆRIPEDEM *cervam* — Æn. VI. V. 802.

V. 19. *He is the chief of the Ways of God :* — הוא ראשית דרכי אל] Ought not this to be a little qualified, and rendered --- HE is among THE CHIEF OF GOD's PRODUCTIONS ? Thus Amalek is called *the first of the Nations,* for a principal one, Numb. XXIV. 20. I give דרכי the Sense of the Syriac Verb ودﺟﺭ, *genuit, peperit.*

—— *he that made him can make his Sword approach* unto him. העשו יגש הרבו :] Rather --- HIS MAKER PRESENTED HIM WITH HIS TOOTH. Bochart *loc. cit.* has proved from very good Authorities that the Word הרב is of Phœnician Origin, and signifies here *a Tooth,* whence the Greek αϱπη, which the Poets attribute to *the Hippopotamus* --- thus Nicander *Theriacwn,* V. 566.

Η ιππη, τον Νειλοιο ϋπεϱ Σαιν αιϑαλοεσαν
Βοσκει, αϱϱρηγιν δε κακλω επιϐαλλειη ΑΡΠΗΝ.

Upon which the Scholiast observes, Αρπη δε σημκινει μεν δϱεπανην. νυν δε τας εδονιας λεγει δεικνυς οτι ελας τας ευχυας τρωγει See also *Nonnus* in B. XXVI. of his Διννυσιακων to the same Effect. Not that I see any Necessity of having Recourse to foreign Authorities ; since the Ground of giving to הרב the Signification of *Sword* is no other than its being an Instrument of Ravage and Desolation, from the Verb הרב *to lay waste and desolate.* There is the same Reason for interpreting it *Tooth,* when applied to this Beast. And it is very properly introduced in the Description of his Parts, that his Maker has furnished him with a Weapon

pon

pon fo eminently offenfive. I give here to the Verb נגש the Signification it has in *Hiphil*, as Jud. VI. 19.

V. 22. *The fhady Trees cover him* with *their Shadow: the Willows*
&c. צלל — יסבהו וגו — יסכהו צאלים צללו] I read the Text thus — צלל
— וייבבהו — and render — THE SHADY TREES COVER HIM with
SHADE, AND THE WILLOWS —. For the Singular Affix Pronoun
cannot agree with the plural Noun, and the copulative Particle is
wanted to connect the Hemiftics.

V. 23. *Behold he drinketh up a River*, and *hafteth not* : — הן יעשק
נהר לא יחפוז] The Verb עשק cannot I think poffibly fignify *to drink up*,
and the Senfe merely of *hafting* given to חפז feems foreign to the Purpose.
I would therefore render --- BEHOLD A RIVER RISETH VIOLENTLY
UPON him; yet HE RUNNETH NOT AWAY THROUGH FEAR.

—— *he trufteth that he can draw up Jordan into his Mouth.* יבטח
כי יגיח ירדן אל פיהו :] Rather I think (without the Hyperbole) thus
--- HE IS UNCONCERNED, THOUGH THE RIVER WERE TO OVER-
FLOW UP TO HIS MOUTH. I render ירדן *a River*, confidering it as an
Appellative, rather than as a Proper Name. It is derived from ירד *to
defcend*, the moft common Property of all Rivers; which for the moft
part have only fome Common Name, that in Time becomes appropriate, as *Avon* with us; by which Name we have no lefs than five or
fix Rivers in this Kingdom called; and it is well known this is only the
generic Appellation in Saxon. The fame holds in regard to BOURN, a
Rivulet. By the Word thus interpreted *the Nile* may be underftood to
be meant, which is more likely than *Jordan*; becaufe the Hippopo-
tamos is a Stranger to this latter River, as was Job himself probably.
I cannot find that the Verb גוח has any where the Senfe which our
Verfion gives it: it is here conftrued as Ch. XXXVIII. 8.

V. 24. *He taketh it with his Eyes:* — בעיניו יקחנו] What Senfe our
Tranflators affixed to thefe Words, I know not; I connect them however with the preceding Hemiftic thus — Though one TAKE HIM IN
HIS GINS &c. I give עיניו this Senfe from the Arabic مشك *Laqueolus
in extremitate nervi*, which its *correlate* in the next Hemiftic points
out. Bochart's Interpretation appears to me forced, viz. *in oculis ejus,
i. e. aperta vi et manifefta, fine machinis et dolo.* This Animal is not
to be taken in Snares according to *Achilles Tatius*, for he fays — επει περι
γε το καρτερειν, ουδεις αν αυτω κρατησειεν βια· τα γαρ αλλα εστιν αλκιμωτατος, και
το δερμα φερει τραχυ, και εκ εθελει πειθεσθαι σιδηρου τραυματι, αλλ' εστιν, ως
ειπειν,

ειπειν, ελεφας Αιγυπτιος· και γαρ επιδὑτερα φερε] εις αλκην ελεφαντος Ινδῶ· B. IV. Or --- though one SEIZE HIM in a Trap BY HIS EYES, or VISAGE: YET HIS NOSE FORCETH ITSELF THROUGH THE SNARES; which agrees very well with what is said above of his vaſt Force, and the Impenetrability of his Skin by Iron.

CHAP. XLI.

V. 1. *Canſt thou draw out Leviathan with an Hook?* — תמשך לויתן [בהכבר] לויתן is another generic Name for a Beaſt of an enormous Size: thus it is uſed for *a Whale*, Pſal. CIV. 26; for *a Serpent*, Iſa. XXVII. 1; and, by a *Metaphor*, it ſignifies in general *a Tyrant*, XXVII. 1, and *Pharaoh* in particular, Pſ. LXXIV. 14. But it is probable that the Cauſe of the Appropriation of this Name to an oppreſſive Monarch is in its Origin deduced from the Cruelty of that *Pharaoh* (for even this Name is in Coptic only a common Appellative for *a King*) who kept the Children of Iſrael in Bondage; becauſe *the Leviathan*, or CROCODILE, is both unfriendly to Man, and an Inhabitant of Egypt. And that this is the Animal here meant, is I think, from its Characteriſtics, ſufficiently clear. See Bochart, *Hieroz.* B. I. C. 7. Ælian ſays it may be tamed; B. VIII. C. 4.

—— *or his Tongue with a Cord* which *thou letteſt down?* ובהבל [תשקיע לשונו]: Rather — OR TIE HIS TONGUE WITH A CORD: for קṣṃ in Samaritan ſignifies the ſame as הבש, viz. *Ligavit, Cinxit.*

V. 2. *Canſt thou put an Hook into his Noſe?* — [החשים אגמן באפו] Rather --- CANST THOU PUT A ROPE ABOUT HIS NOSE? for אגמן here ſignifies properly *a Rope made of Reeds.*

—— *or bore his Jaw through with a Thorn?* [ובחוה תקב לחיו]: חוח ſignifies, among other Things, A FISHER'S HOOK, and ought to be rendered here HOOK. It is probable that in Job's Time the Method of taking the Crocodile was not known. For Herodotus informs us that, when he was in Egypt, this was attended with no Difficulty; for he ſays — αγραι δε σφεων (κροκοδειλων) πολλαι κατεςεατι, και παντοιαι· η δε μοι δοκιει αξιωτατη απηγησιος ειναι, ταυτην γραφω· επεαν νωτον συος διλεαση περι ΑΓΚΙΣΤΡΟΝ, μετιει εις μεσον τον ποταμον· αυτος δε πει τα χειλεα τα ποταμε εχων δελφακα ζωην, ταυτην τυπτει επικρους δε της φωνης ο κροκοδειλος, ιεται κατα την φωνην· εντυχων δε τω νωτω, καταπινει. οι δε ελκυσι· επεαν δε εξελκυσθη ες γην, πρωτον απαντων ο θηρευτηρ πηλω κατ ων επλασε αυτω τας οφθαλμους.

Θαλμσς. τουτο δε ποιησας, καρτα ευπετιως τα λοιπα χειρουται μη ποιησας δε τουτο, συν πονω. *Euterpe. Cap. LXX.*

V. 6. *Shall thy Companions make a Banquet of him?* — יכרו עליו חברים] Some Egyptians, Ælian informs us, eat the Crocodile, when he was in that Country; while others, more superstitious, rejoiced, if by Chance their Children were devoured by that Animal, which they worshipped as a God. B. X. C. 21.

V. 7. *Canst thou fill his Skin with barbed Irons?* — התמלא בשכות עורו] The Skin of his Back is said to be impenetrable. Οἱ δε Κροκοδειλοι εχουσι — δερμα αρρηκτον Φολιδωτον Aristotle Nat. Hist. B. II. C. 10. So Pliny — *Unguibus hic armatus est, contra omnes ictus cute inviclâ.* Nat. Hist. B. VIII. C. 25.

V. 8. *Lay thine Hand upon him, remember the Battle, do no more.* שים עליו כפך—זכר מלחמה אל תוסף:] The last Hemistic would be clearer, were it rendered --- but REMEMBER THOU SHALT HAVE NO OTHER CONFLICT: for this is doubtless the Sense. The Note in the old Version is, —— " If thou once consider the Danger, thou " wilt not meddle with him."

V. 11. *Who hath prevented me, that I should repay* him? מי הקדימני ואשלם] Rather — WHO HATH BENEFITED ME &c? *i. e. who hath first done me a Kindness,* and laid me under an Obligation *to repay him?* So this Verb signifies, Deut. XXIII. 4. Isa. XXI. 14. See Rom XI. 35.

V. 12. *I will not conceal his Parts, nor his Power,* — לא אחריש בדיו ודבר גבורות] Rather --- I WILL NOT CONCEAL IN HIM NEITHER ANY THING OF HIS POWER &c. for that seems to be the precise Meaning of דבר in this Place: and in respect to בדיו, I cannot find that it ever signifies either *Parts, Limbs,* or *Strength.* See Ch. XVIII. 13.

—— *nor his comely Proportion.* וחין ערכו:] Rather — NOR THE ADVANTAGE OF HIS STRUCTURE.

V. 13. *Who can discover the Face of his Garment?* —מי גלה פני לבושו] Rather --- WHO CAN UNCOVER THE FACE OF HIS GARMENT? For *the Face of his Garment* would by a common Hebraism signify the upper or external Garment.

V. 14. — *his*

V. 14. — *his Teeth* are *terrible round about*. סביבות שני אימה]
Rather perhaps --- THE ROWS OF HIS TEETH are TERRIBLE.
His Mouth is faid to be fo large, that it can take in a whole Sheep;
and he has thirty fix fharp pointed Teeth in each Jaw.

V. 15. His *Scales* are his *Pride*; — גאור אפיקי מגנים] That is
doubtlefs the Senfe of this Place: but notwithftanding ought not the
Words to be literally rendered --- THE STRENGTH OF BUCKLERS
is his PRIDE?

———— *fhut up together* as with *a clofe Seal*. סנור הותם צר] The
Participle here cannot agree with either of the Nouns in the foregoing
Hemiftic. This Claufe ought therefore to be rendered — HE IS SHUT
UP CLOSE as with A SEAL.

V. 18. — *and his Eyes* are *like the Eyelids of the Morning*. ועיניו
כעפעפי שהר] *Hebetes oculos hoc animal dicitur habere in aqua, extra*
ACERRIMI VISUS. Plin. B. II. C. 25.

V. 22. — *and Sorrow is turned into Joy before him.* ולפניו תדוץ
דאבה] Rather, I think — AND SORROW GOETH BEFORE HIM:
i. e. " he caufes Sorrow wherever he goes." In our old Verfion we
read — *and Labour is rejected before him:* that is, " Nothing is hard
" or painful unto him." But the Words cannot bear that Interpretation: and that which is given in our prefent Verfion does not feem
pertinent. The Verb דוץ has the Signification there adopted from the
Chaldee (for it occurs only in this Place:) but I derive it from the Arabic دوس *ex alto deorfum defcendit.* This Animal, it is well known,
occafions great Ravages in a Country. See V. 25.

V. 23. *The Flakes of his Flefh are joined together;* מפלי בשרו דבקו]
--- THE RIBS (or BONES) OF HIS BODY CLEAVE FAST TO-
GETHER: for either Senfe may I think be juftified from the Arabic
خلل *caro in cava parte, five latere coxæ.*

———— *they are firm in themfelves, they cannot be moved.* יצוק עליו
בל ימוט] Rather — HE IS COMPACT IN HIMSELF that HE CAN-
NOT BE MOVED. See V. 15.

V. 24. — *yea, as hard as a Piece of the nether* Milftone. ויצוק כפלח
תחתית] Rather, I think — YEA, AS HARD AS THE COULTER
OF THE PLOW: literally, *the lower Part.* As there is nothing faid of
Milftone,

Milſtone, and פלח has no Senſe ſuitable in Hebrew, I borrow from the Arabic the Signification of فلخ *Aratrum, Vomer*.

V. 25. *When he raiſeth himſelf, the mighty are afraid: by reaſon of Breakings they purify themſelves.* [משתו יגורו אלים—משברים יתחטאו:] Our Verſion is not very intelligible in the latter Hemiſtic: the old one is; but the Words cannot admit of that Conſtruction, *viz.* and *for Fear they faint in themſelves.* The Verſe ought to be thus rendered --- BY REASON OF HIS GREATNESS (his enormous Bulk) THE MIGHTY ARE AFRAID: THEY WHO BRUISE HIM (endeavour ſo to do) MISS THEIR AIM. משתו is here conſtrued as Ch. XXXI. 23. and תחטאו, as Judg. XX. 16. and Ch. V. 24. This is very appoſite to the Context.

V. 30. *Sharp Stones* are *under him: he ſpreadeth ſharp pointed Things upon the Mire.* [תחתיו חדודי חרש — ירפד חרוץ עלי טיט:] Rather---UNDER HIM IS A SHARP PLOUGHSHARE: HE MAKETH HIS BED upon HARROWS IN THE MIRE. חדודי ſignifies literally *Sharpneſſes.* חרש is the ſame Word without the *Heemantics* as מחרשה, 1 Sam. XIII. 20. רפד is uſed *for making a Bed*, Ch. XVII. 13; and for *ſupporting one's ſelf*, Cant. II. 5; and חרוץ is an *Harrow*, 2 Sam. XII. 31. and 1 Chron. XX. 3.

V. 32. — one *would think the Deep* to be *hoary.* יחשב תהום [לשיבה:] Rather — HE CAUSETH THE DEEP TO BE THOUGHT HOARY: for יחשב is in *Hophal*.

V. 34. *He beholdeth all high* Things:— [את כל נבה יראה:] Rather ---HE LOOKETH UPON EVERY THING with HAUGHTINESS. This Senſe the next Hemiſtic ſeems to confirm.

CHAP. XLII.

V. 8. — *leſt I deal with you* after your *Folly*; לבלתי עשות עמכם [נבלה:] Rather — THAT I MAY NOT REQUITE YOUR FOLLY, as 2 Sam. II. 6.

V. 14. *And he called the Name of the firſt Jemima* &c. ויקרא שם [האחת ימימה וגו'] That is — A TURTLE, or DOVE; from يمام *Turtur, Columba ſylveſtris: Keſſia*, or rather — CASSIA, from قصيعة,

I   the

the aromatic Shrub so called ; and *Keren-Happuch*, i. e. THE BOSOM OF DELIGHT : for ڬرﻦ signifies *a Bosom*, and the Verb ﻜﺤﺺ, *festi-vus, jocosus, urbanus fuit*.   I make the Arabic the Fountain of all these Names, because it was Job's vernacular Dialect.   Why their Names are particularly mentioned more than those of their Brethren seems to be for these two Reasons, *viz.* because they were remarkably beautiful ; and because they were peculiarly favoured in being allowed to divide their Father's Inheritance with their Brethren : a Favour greater than that which was conferred on the Daughters of Zelophehad; each of whom has also her Name recorded, Numb. XXVII. 1. &c.

V. 16. *After this Job lived an hundred and forty Years.*]   From this *Datum* we may fix the Æra in which Job may be supposed to have lived ; *viz.* about the Time of Abraham.   For most of the Patriarchs, whose Ages are recorded by Moses, lived in that Period to about this Age.   See this Point discussed on Pf. XC. 10.

BEFORE I conclude my Remarks on this Book, it may perhaps be expected that I should deliver my Sentiments in regard to the leading Subject, as well as the Object, of it ; and touch upon the Nature of this Composition, the Author, and the Time, when it may be supposed to have been written.

I shall therefore speak to each of these Points briefly, except the last, on which I shall beg Leave to enlarge ; as I think it will be incontestably proved by a long Induction of Particulars, that the Book could not have been written till about the Time of the Babylonish Captivity.   The Texts I shall bring in Confirmation of this Point have been collected by a late ingenious Clergyman, whose MS. was obligingly communicated by a Friend some Time after these Sheets had gone to the Press.   To this I shall subjoin some of the Remarks and Classical Illustrations of the same learned Man, which I flatter myself will also be no disagreeable Present to the Public.

WHETHER such a Personage as Job ever existed, is a Matter of very doubtful Disputation.   The affirmative Side of the Question appears probable, when we find him ranked by Ezekiel with Noah and Daniel, and referred to by St. James.   But on the other Hand, the Silence of Moses and all succeeding Historians concerning him is apt to induce the contrary Opinion.   The Prophet might perhaps chuse to mention Job preferably to Abraham, or any other righteous Man, because the Book had lately been published, and particularly because Job is there

represented

reprefented as having obtained his Deliverance (as the two others had done, one from the Flood, the other from the Den of Lions) by his Righteoufnefs. This fuited the Prophet's Argument; and the Inftance would equally ferve his Purpofe, whether the Character were real or fictitious. The fame holds likewife in regard to St. James; who, wanting to recommend Patience by an Example, would naturally refer his Countrymen to this Book. But had there ever been fuch a Perfon as Job, it has been fhewn in the laft Note that he muft have been in all Probability a contemporary with Abraham; and as he is faid to have been an Idumean, (or an Inhabitant of Arabia deferta, which bordered upon Canaan,) it might be expected that there would have been fome Intercourfe between thefe great and good Men; that Abraham in his Journeys to Egypt would have taken an Opportunity of doing him Honour, as he did to Melchifedec, or that Job would gladly have embraced any Opportunity of making himfelf known to *the Father of the Faithful.* The fame may be faid in regard to the fucceeding Patriarchs, if he be fuppofed to have lived later. But if we bring him down to the Time of Mofes, (which is the lateft Period that can be affigned) it will appear ftill more extraordinary, that he, who lived in Sight of Mount Sinai, fhould have continued to walk ftill by the Light of Nature only, when he muft have had fenfible Demonftration of God's Revelation of his Will, and might have put himfelf under the more immediate Direction of Jehovah. Befides, what would make Job's Character ftill more extraordinary is, that he fhould always have retained his Integrity amidft the Contagion of bad Example; for the Wild Arabs, from the Days of Ifhmael to thefe Days, have uniformly been Rovers and Freebooters, as was predicted of them. Gen. XVI. 12.

Whereas if we fuppofe this Poem to be merely of the Dramatic Kind, (the effential Requifites of which it has) it would anfwer the Author's Purpofe beft to create a Subject, that Hiftoric Truth might not embarrafs him in any Circumftance conducing to the End he propofed.

Now if we fuppofe the Author to have been a Jew, and that he wrote his Book with a Defign of comforting his captive Brethren, the Book will be found perfectly confiftent with this Hypothefis; which is to fhew, that temporal Evils are not always intended by Providence as Punifhments for paft Crimes, but alfo for Trials of Virtue, and for the Benefit of inftructive Example to others; and that Patience and Submiffion to the Will of Heaven is both the indifpenfable Duty of

Perfons

Perfons under Affliction, and the moft probable Means of procuring them Deliverance and Reftoration. This exactly quadrates with the Cafe of the Jews. They were carried to Babylon, not merely for the punifhment of their Idolatries and Wickednefs; but alfo that they might be tried *in the Furnace of Affliction*, which *thoroughly purified them* from idolatrous Practices at leaft; and with this farther View likewife, that the moft confpicuous Part of the then known World might be more acquainted with their Hiftory and their facred Books, which contained both the paft Difpenfations of God's particular Providence, and his future Defigns with refpect to Mankind. They were alfo taught by their Prophets to look for a Reftoration after a ftated Period, and exhorted to wait patiently and quietly till the Change fhould come.

It is furprizing that the Name of the Author of fo excellent a Compofition fhould always have been concealed from the World. What his Motives for fuch Concealment were, and who he was, it would be loft Time to inquire, as it is now perhaps impoffible to difcover. That he wrote about the Time of the Captivity appears to me clearly from the many Chaldee Words, and Chaldee Termination of Hebrew Words, throughout the Book: but a ftill more forcible Argument is the frequent indirect Allufion to the Pentateuch and other Books of the Jewifh Canon; whereby the Author inadvertently betrays himfelf; of which fee the following Lift.

Passages in the Book of JOB, which have a Reference to other Parts of the Sacred Writings.

Chapter I. 5. — *Have curfed God in their Hearts.* 1 Kings XXI. 10. "Thou didft blafpheme God and the King." V. 6. *The Sons of God came to prefent themfelves.* Here the Angels are called *Sons of God.* The Expreffion is particular: but we find it ufed in Daniel, Ch. III. v. 25. *viz.* "the Form of the fourth is like *the Son of God.*" What Daniel meant by that Expreffion appears from V. 28. "Bleffed "be God who hath fent his *Angel.*" So that *Angel* and *Son of God* here fignify the fame Thing. V. 21. *Naked came I out of my Mother's Womb &c.* This anfwers to Ecclef. V. 15. "As he came forth of his "Mother's Womb, naked fhall he return to go as he came." *The Land of Uz* is mentioned Lam. IV. 21. "O Daughter of Edom, that "dwelleft *in the Land of Uz.*" The Edomites fettled in Arabia; and Uz, as it appears from this Paffage, was a Part of that Country: thus the Place was called at the Time of the Captivity.

Ch. III. 3.

Ch. III. 3. *Let the Day perish, wherein I was born.* Jer. XX. 14.
" Cursed be the Day, wherein I was born." V. 5. — *the Shadow of
Death.* The same Expression, Ps. XXIII. 4. V. 16. *As an hidden un-
timely Birth, I had not been; as Infants* which *never saw the Light.* This
seems to be an Improvement upon Ps. LVIII. 8. " As the untimely
" Fruit of a Woman, let them not see the Sun." נפל, *untimely Fruit,*
is the Word in both Places. V. 23. *Whom God hath hedged in.* So
Lam. III. 7. " He hath hedged me about, that I cannot get out."

Ch. IV. 4. *Thou hast strengthened the feeble Knees.* So Isa. XXXV. 3.
" Strengthen the weak Hands, and confirm the feeble Knees." V. 8.
They that plow Iniquity, and sow Wickedness, reap the same. Hos. X. 13.
" Ye have plowed Wickedness, ye have reaped Iniquity." V. 9. *By
the Blast of God they perish, and by the Breath of his Nostrils are they
consumed.* This seems to be borrowed from Exod. XV. 8. " With the
" Blast of thy Nostrils the Waters were gathered together." V. 19. *Which
are crushed before the Moth.* This Image is frequently used in Scripture.
Ps. XXXIX. 11. " As the Moth, thou makest his Beauty to consume
" away." Hos. V. 12. " I will be to Ephraim as a Moth." Isa. L. 9.
" The Moth shall eat them up."

Ch. V. 4. *They are crushed in the Gate.* So Prov. XXII. 22.
" Neither oppress the afflicted in the Gate." Gate is used in both
Places to signify a Court of Justice. V. 14. *And grope in the Noon-
Day as in the Night.* So Deut. XXVIII. 29. " And thou shalt grope
" at Noon-Day, as the blind gropeth in Darkness." V. 18. *He maketh
sore, and bindeth up: he woundeth, and his Hands make whole.* Hos.
VI. 1. " He hath smitten, and he will bind us up." And Deut. XXXII.
39. " I wound, and I heal." V. 23. *The Beasts of the Field shall be
at Peace with thee.* So Hos. II. 18. " I will make a Covenant for
" them with the Beasts of the Field."

Ch. VI. 3. *Heavier than the Sand of the Sea.* Perhaps this may be
taken from Prov. XXVII. 3. " The Sand is weighty." V. 4. *The Arrows of the Almighty are within me.* Ps. XXXVIII. 2. " Thine Arrows
" stick fast in me." V. 20. Job speaking of the Caravans, which come
to the Springs in Arabia, and find no Water, says, *They were confounded, because they had hoped: they came thither, and were ashamed.* Jer.
XIV. 3. says upon the same Occasion, " They returned with their
" Vessels empty; they were ashamed and confounded, and covered
" their Heads." The Thought is the same: but in Job the Manner
of expressing it is more poetical.

Ch.

Ch. VII. 2. As the Hireling expecteth his Wages. The Law of Moses says, " the Wages of the Hireling, (פעלת שכיר, the Words " are the same,) shall not abide with thee." *V.* 10. *Neither shall his Place know him any more.* Pf. CIII. 16. has exactly the same Words, *viz.* ולא יכירנו עוד מקמו. *V.* 20. *Why hast thou set me as a Mark against thee.* So Lam. III. 12. " He hath set me as a Mark for the Arrow."

Ch. X. 4. *Seest thou as Man seeth.* So 1 Sam. XVI. 7. " The Lord " seeth not as Man seeth." *V.* 9. *Thou hast made me as the Clay, and wilt thou bring me into the Dust again?* which seems to be an Allu-fion to these Words, " Dust thou art, and to Dust shalt thou return." *V.* 20, 21. *Let me alone, that I may take Comfort a little, before I go whence I shall not return.* So Pf. XXXIX. 13. " Spare me, that I " may recover Strength, before I go hence, and be no more."

Ch. XI. 19. *Thou shalt lie down, and none shall make thee afraid.* This seems to be taken from Lev. XXVI. 6. " Ye shall lie down, and " none shall make you afraid."

Ch. XII. 14. *He shutteth up a Man, and there can be no opening :* taken probably from Isai. XXII. 22. " He shall shut, and none shall " open." *V.* 16. *The deceived and deceiver are his* — probably alludes to the History of the Fall. *V.* 22. *He discovereth deep Things out of Darkness.* So Dan. II. 22. " He revealeth the deep and secret Things ; " he knoweth what is in the Darkness." *V.* 24. *He taketh away the Heart of the chief of the People of the Earth, and causeth them to wander in the Wilderness,* where there *is no Way.* So Pf. CVII. 40. " And causeth them " to wander in the Wilderness, where there is no way." The Words of the Pfalm are allowed to refer to the wandering of the Children of Israel in the Wilderness.

Ch. XIII. 5. *O that you would altogether hold your Peace, and it should be your Wisdom :* alluding perhaps to Prov. XVII. 28. " Even a " Fool, when he holdeth his Peace, is counted wife." *V.* 14. *And put my Life in my Hand.* The Expression is remarkable, and seems to be taken from 1 Sam. XXVIII. 21. " I have put my Life in my Hand;" *i. e.* I have exposed myself to the utmost Danger We have it too, Pf. CXIX. 109. " My Soul is alway in my Hand." *V.* 24. *Wherefore hidest thou thy Face?* So Pf. XIII. 1. " How long wilt thou hide thy Face " from me."

Ch. XV. 14. *What is Man that he should be clean?* So Prov. XX. 9. " Who can say I have made my Heart clean?" *V.* 16. *Drinketh Ini-*
quity

quity like Water. So Prov. XIX. 28. "The Mouth of the wicked de-
"voureth Iniquity." V. 23. *He wandreth abroad for Bread,* faying,
where is it? So Pf. LIX. 15. "Let them wander up and down for
"Meat." V. 27. *He covereth his Face with his Fatnefs.* Pf. XVII. 10.
"They cover themfelves with their Fatnefs"

Ch. XVI. 10. *They have fmitten me upon the Cheek reproachfully.* So
Lam. III. 30. "He giveth his Cheek to him that fmiteth him : he is
"filled full with Reproach." V. 18. *O Earth, cover not thou my
Blood, and let my Cry have no Place;* which feems to allude to
Gen. IV. 10. "The Voice of thy Brother's Blood crieth out to me
"from the Ground."

Ch. XVII. 7. *Mine Eye alfo is dim by reafon of Sorrow.* So Pf. VI. 7.
"Mine Eye is confumed becaufe of Grief."

Ch. XVIII. 19. *He fhall neither have Son nor Nephew.* This appears
clearly to be taken from Ifaiah XIV. 22. "I will cut off from Babylon,
"faith God, both the Son and the Nephew," וְנִין וָנֶכֶד. The Author
of the Book of Job ufes the fame Words, defcribing the Judgments of
God in the Punifhment of a wicked Man, and makes a Sentence of
them, לֹא נִין לוֹ וְלֹא נֶכֶד.

Ch. XIX. 7, 8. *Behold, I cry out of Wrong, but I am not heard; I
cry aloud, but there is no Judgment. He hath fenced up my Way, that
I cannot pafs, and he hath fet Darknefs in my Paths.* Here is a very
near Refemblance to Lam. III. 8, 9. "When I cry and fhout, he
"fhutteth out my Prayer : he hath inclofed my Ways with hewn
"Stone; he hath made my Paths crooked." V. 13. *He hath put my
Brethren far from me, and mine Acquaintance are verily eftranged from
me.* So Pf. LXXXVIII. 8. "Thou haft put away mine Acquaintance
"far from me."

Ch. XX. 6. *Though his Excellency mount up to the Heavens, and his
Head reach unto the Clouds.* Thus Ifa. XIII. 14. "I will afcend into
"Heaven : I will afcend above the Heights of the Clouds; I will be
"like the moft High;" where the Prophet fpeaks of Lucifer. V. 16.
He fhall fuck the Poifon of Afps. So Deut. XXXII. 33. "Their Wine
"is the Venom of Afps."

Ch. XXI. 5. *Be aftonifhed, and lay your Hand upon your Mouth.* So
Judg. XVIII. 19. "Hold thy Peace, lay thy Hand upon thy Mouth."
V. 19. *God layeth up his Iniquity for his Children.* This feems to
allude

allude to the Second Commandment; "visiting the Iniquity of the "Fathers upon the Children."

Ch. XXII. 6. *Thou haft taken a Pledge from thy Brother for nought, and haft ftripped the naked of their Clothing* This is a plain Allufion to Exod. XXII. 26, 27. "If thou at all take thy Neighbour's Raiment "to Pledge, thou fhalt deliver it to him by that the Sun goeth down, "for that is his only Covering; it is his Raiment for his Skin : wherein "fhall he fleep?" The Crime objected to Job is, that he has taken a Pledge. The Jewifh Law made this criminal. This appears only from the Jewifh Law, which fuppofes the Pledge to be the Raiment, the only Covering. V. 13. *Thou fayeft, How doth God know ?* So Pf. LXXIII. 11. "They fay, How doth God know ?" V. 19. *The right-cous fee* it, *and are glad.* So Pf. CVII. 42. "The righteous fhall fee "it, and rejoice."

Ch. XXIII. 10. *He hath tried me, I fhall come forth as Gold.* Pf. LXVI. 10. "Thou haft tried us as Silver is tried."

Ch. XXIV. 4. *The poor of the Earth hide themfelves together :* taken probably from Prov. XXVIII. 28. "When the wicked rife, Men hide "themfelves."

Ch. XXVI. 8. *He bindeth up the Waters in his thick Clouds.* This feems to be borrowed from Prov. XXX. 4. "Who hath bound the "Waters in a Garment?" In both Places the Water above the Firma-ment is underftood. Again, it is faid of the Clouds (Ch. XXXVI. 30.) that they conceal thofe Foundations which fupport the Sea. Thefe are plain Allufions to the Waters above the Firmament. Gen. I. 7.

Ch. XXVII. 7. *Let mine Enemy be as the wicked.* This Thought feems to be taken from 1 Sam. XXV. 26. "Let thine Enemies be as "Nabal." V. 14. *If his Children be multiplied, it is for the Sword.* So Hof. IX. 13. "Ephraim fhall bring forth his Children to the Murderer." V. 15. *Shall be buried in Death, and his Widows fhall not weep.* So Pf. LXXVIII. 64. "Their Priefts fell by the Sword, and their Widows "made no Lamentation." V. 17. *He may prepare* it, *but the juft fhall put* it *on.* So Prov. XXVIII. 8. "He fhall gather it for him that will "pity the poor."

Ch. XXVIII. 15. *It cannot be gotten for Gold; neither fhall Silver be weighed for the Price thereof.* So Prov. III. 14. "The Merchandife of "it

" it is better than the Merchandife of Silver, and the Gain thereof
" than fine Gold."

Ch. XXIX. 3. *By his Light I walked through Darkness.* So Pf.
XVIII. 28. " The Lord my God will enlighten my Darknefs." V. 6.
The Rock poured me out Rivers of Oil. Perhaps this may be taken out
of Deut. XXXII. 13. " He made him to fuck Honey out of the Rock,
" and Oil out of the flinty Rock." And what is very remarkable
(V. 22, 23.) *My Speech dropped upon them, And they waited for me as for
the Rain, and opened their Mouth wide as for the latter Rain,* feems
taken from the fame Chap. V. 2. " My Doctrine fhall drop as the Rain,
" my Speech fhall diftil as the Dew." V. 12. *I delivered the poor when
he cried, the fatherlefs and him that had none to help him* — taken probably from Pf. LXXII. 12. " He fhall deliver the needy, when he
" crieth, the poor alfo, and him that hath no helper." V. 14. *I put on
Righteoufnefs, and it clothed me.* So Ifa. LIX. 17. " He put on Right-
" eoufnefs as a Breaft Plate." V. 20. *My Bow renewed its Strength in
my Hand.* This feems to be taken from Gen. XLIX. 24. " His Bow
" abode in Strength."

Ch. XXX. 9. *I am their Song, and become their Byword.* So Lam.
III. 14. " I was a Derifion to all my People, and their Song all the
" Day." V. 16. *My Soul pours out itself within me.* So Pf. XLII. 4.
" I pour out my Soul within me." Job fays — נפשי תשתפך עלי : the
Pfalmift fays — אשפכה עלי נפשי. V. 30. *My Bones are burnt with
Heat.* So Pf. CII. 3. " My Bones are burnt as a Hearth."

Ch. XXXI. 4. *Doth he not fee my Ways, and count all my Steps?* So
Prov. V. 21. " The Ways of Man are before the Eyes of the Lord,
" and he pondereth all his Goings." V. 7. *Mine Heart walked after
my Eyes,* taken perhaps from Numb. XV. 39. " Seek not after your
" own Heart, and your own Eyes." V. 8. *Then let me fow, and let
another reap;* this appears to be borrowed from Lev. XXVI. 16. " Ye
" fhall fow your Seed in vain, for your Enemy fhall eat it."

Ch. XXXIII. 14. *God fpeaketh once, yea twice:* (*i.e.* often.) So
Pf. LXII. 11. " God hath fpoken once, nay twice have I heard it."
V. 30. *Light of the living.* We have the fame Expreffion, Pf. LVI. 13.

Ch. XXXIV. 11. *For the Work of a Man fhall he render unto him.* So
Pf. LXII. 12. " Thou rendereft to every Man according to his Work."

Ch. XXXV. 10. *God, who giveth Songs in the Night.* So Pf. XLII.
8. " In the Night his Song fhall be with me. V. 12. *There they cry,*

K *but*

but none giveth Answer. So Prov. I. 28. " Then fhall they call upon " me ; but I will not anfwer."

Ch. XXXVI. 7. *He withdraweth not his Eyes from the righteous.* So Pf. XXXIV. 15. " The Eyes of the Lord are upon the righteous." V. 8. *If they* (*i. e.* Kings) *be bound in Fetters—he openeth their Ear to Difcipline :— and if they obey, they fhall fpend their Days in Profperity.* This was the Cafe of Manafich, who was carried bound to Babylon, and upon his Repentance reftored to his Kingdom. Compare this with 2 Chron. XXXIII. 11, 12, 13.

Ch. XXXVIII. 1. *The Lord anfwered Job out of the Whirlwind.* So Nah. I. 3. " The Lord hath his Way in the Whirlwind." V. 4. *Where waft thou when I laid the Foundations of the Earth?* alluding probably to Prov. VIII. 29. " When he appointed the Foundations of the Earth, " then I was by him." V. 9. *When I made a Cloud to be the Garment of the Sea, and thick Darknefs it's fwaddling Band.* This may allude to Gen. I. 2. " Darknefs was upon the Face of the Deep." V. 15. *The wicked fhall be deprived of their Light,* may perhaps allude to the Egyptian Darknefs. *The high Arm fhall be broken.* So Pf. X. 15. " Break thou the Arm of the wicked."

Ch. XLI. 4. *Wilt thou take him for a Servant for ever?* Exod. XXI. 6. " He fhall ferve him for ever." The Expreffion is very particular, and fignifies in both Places, to be a Part of the Family. Ch. XXXI. 33. we have thefe Words, *If I have covered my Tranfgreffion as Adam.* Ch. XXXVI. 14. there feems to be an Allufion to the Deftruction of Sodom ; Ch. XL. 12, 13. to the Punifhment of Corah, Dathan, and Abiram. Idolatry was punifhed by the Jewifh Law, and no other, with Death, and Job. XXXI. 28. fays, *This were an Iniquity to be punifhed by the Judge.*

[Ch. XXXVIII. 22, 23. *Haft thou feen the Treafures of the Hail, which I have referved againft the Time of Trouble, againft the Day of Battle and War?* This probably alludes to the Deftruction of the five Kings of the Amorites at Bethhoron by Jofhua, when the Lord deftroyed their Armies with Hailftones. X. 11. *Heath.*

Ch. XX. 17. *The Brooks of Honey and Butter,* probably taken from thofe Paffages in Exodus, Ch. III. 8. — XIII. 5. " A Land flowing " with Milk and Honey." Bp. *Warburton.*

Ch.

Ch. XXII. 22. *Receive the Law from his Mouth*, alluding probably to the verbal Delivery of the Law from Mount Sinai. *Idem.*

Ch. XXIX. 4. *O that I were as in the Days of my Youth, when the Secret of God was upon my Tabernacle!* This feems to allude to the Refidence of the Divine Prefence on the Ark. *Idem.*

Ch. IX. 7. *Who commandeth the Sun, and it rifeth not, and fealeth up the Stars*, may perhaps allude to the Egyptian Darknefs, and the Sun ftanding ftill in the Days of Jofhua. *Idem.*

Ch. XXVI. 12. *By his Strength he quieteth the Sea, and by his Underftanding fmiteth it's Pride.* Bp. *Warburton* applies this to the dividing of the Sea, and the drowning of Pharoah and his Hoft.]

FROM what has been faid I think it clear that the Author of this Book was a Jew; and that he lived after the Time of Mofes. There are other Paffages in this Book, which agree with other Parts of SS. but whether they are taken from thence, or thofe Parts of SS. taken from Job, is not fo certain. I fhall mention the moft remarkable of them. Ch. V. 19. it is faid, *He fhall deliver thee in fix Troubles; yea, in feven there fhall no Evil touch thee.* So Prov. VI. 16. " Thefe " fix Things doth the Lord hate, yea, feven, &c." V. 10. God is called the *Holy One.* The Prophets call Him " *the Holy One* of Ifrael." But Job being not reprefented as a Jew, the Word *Ifrael* is omitted. Ch. XIV. 17. We have thefe Words, *My Tranfgreffion is fealed up in a Bag; and thou foweft up my Iniquity.* So Hof. XIII. 12. " The " Iniquity of Ephraim is bound up in a Bag, his Sin is hid." In both Places there is an Allufion to the Cuftom of fealing up Records in a Bag. Ch. XV. 7. *Waft thou made before the Hills?* are the fame Words that are ufed, Prov. VIII. 25. לפני גבעות חוללתי. In the laft Verfe of the fame Ch. *To conceive Mifchief, and bring forth Vanity* are almoft the fame Words with Pf. VIII. 15. הרה עמל וילד שקר; and Ifa. LIX. 4. הרו עמל והוליד און. Ch. XVI. 13. *He poureth out my Gall upon the Ground.* So Lam. II. 11. " My Liver is poured " upon the Earth." Ch. XVII. 3. *Give me a Surety for thy Appearance: who is it that will ftrike Hands with me?* agrees with Prov. VI. 1. " My Son, if thou be Surety for thy Friend, if thou haft ftricken " thy Hand with a Stranger." The Surety was to ftrike Hands with the Perfon to whom the Security was given. The fame Cuftom is alluded to, and the fame Word, תקע is ufed in both Places. Ch. XVIII. 7. *The Steps of his Strength fhall be ftraitened*, are the fame

Words

Words with Prov. IV. 12. לא יצרו צעדיך, "Thy Steps fhall not be
"ſtraitened." The Expreſſions are remarkable : and in Job *the
Steps of his Strength* ſeem to be an Improvement upon *Thy Steps.*
V. 15. *Brimſtone ſhall be ſcattered upon his Habitation.* So Pſ. XI. 16.
"He ſhall rain upon the wicked Fire and Brimſtone." Brimſtone is
uſed in both Places for Lightning.   Ch. XIX. 20 *My Bone cleaveth
to my Skin and my Fleſh,* are the ſame Words with Pſ. CII. 6. דבקה
עצמי לבשרי, "My Bone cleaveth to my Fleſh,"—and are a particular
Way of expreſſing the ſame Thing ; that there was no Fat between
the Bone and the Fleſh.   Ch. XX. 8. *He ſhall fly away as a Dream ;
he ſhall be chaſed away as a Viſion of the Night.* The ſame Words are
in Iſa. XXIX. 7. כהלום הוון לילה, "as a Dream, the Viſion of the
"Night." The Addition of the two Verbs in the Paſſage, as it ſtands
in Job, may perhaps be thought an Improvement upon Iſaiah.   V. 23.
*God ſhall caſt upon him the Fury of his Wrath ; and it ſhall rain upon
him in the Midſt of his Food.* So Pſ. XI. 6. "Upon the wicked he
"ſhall rain Fire and Brimſtone, and a ſtrong Tempeſt ſhall be the
"Portion of their Cup." Ch. XXI. 18. *They are as Stubble before the
Wind, and as Chaff which the Storm ſuddenly ſweeps away,* ſeems to
be an Improvement upon Pſ. I. 4. " Like Chaff which the Wind
"driveth away."   Ch. XXIV. 4. *They drive the poor out of the Way*
—— are the ſame Words with Amos II. 7. דרך ענוים יטו.   Ch.
XXVI. 6. *Hell is naked before him, and Deſtruction hath no Covering.*
This looks like an Improvement upon Prov. XV. 11. " Hell and De-
"ſtruction are before him." The ſame Words too are uſed, נגד —
אברון—שאל. There is one Obſervation, which I make by the Way ;
that this Likeneſs of Expreſſion adds great Authority to the Books of
SS. If the Author of the Book of Job borrowed from the other SS.
they were certainly eſteemed as ſacred Books in his Time, and could not
be compoſed by Ezra, as Lord Bolingbroke inſinuates. If they borrowed from Job, then it follows that the Book of Job was delivered
down under the ſame Character among the Jews. But to return : V
13. *His Hand hath formed the crooked Serpent,* נחש ברח. See Iſa.
XXVII. 1. where the ſame Words are uſed, and Leviathan is ſaid to
be " the crooked Serpent." But this Paſſage being well known, there
was no Occaſion for the Author of this Book to be ſo explicit.   Ch.
XXVIII. 28. *The Fear of the Lord, that is Wiſdom ; and to depart from
Evil is Underſtanding.* So Prov. IX. 10. "The Fear of the Lord is
"the Beginning of Wiſdom, and the Knowledge of the Holy is Underſtanding."   Ch. XXIX. 16. *I was a Father to the poor, and the Cauſe*
that

that I knew not I searched out. So Prov. XXIX. 7. "The righteous
"considereth the Cause of the poor: but the wicked regardeth not to
"know it." V. 25. *I dwelt as a King in an Army, as one who comforteth Mourners,* seems to be taken from Isa. LXI. 1, 2. "He hath sent
"me to proclaim Liberty to the Captives, to comfort all that mourn."
לנחם כל אבלים. The Words are the same, and agree better with
the Context in Isaiah than in Job.   Ch. XXX. 29. *I am a Brother
to Dragons, and a Companion to Ostriches.* So Mic. I. 8. "I will make
"a Wailing as the Dragons, and Mourning as the Ostriches." I observe that Job says, he is a Brother and a Companion to these Animals; but why? It wants to be explained. The Reason is expressed in
Micah. It is because of their Mourning. So that probably that Passage in Micah being well known, the Author of Job thought it enough
to say, He was a Brother and a Companion of them.   Ch.
XXXIV. 14. *If he should withdraw to himself his Spirit and his Breath,
all Flesh would expire together, and Man would return to Dust.* So
Ps. CIV. 29. "Thou takest away their Breath; they die and return to
"their Dust."   Ch. XXXVIII. 10, 11. *And determined my Decree
upon it,* and *set Bars and Doors; and said, Hitherto shalt thou go, and
no farther,* &c. So Prov. VIII. 29. "When he gave to the Sea his
"Decree, that the Waters should not pass his Commandment." V. 41.
*Who provideth for the Raven his Food, when his young ones cry to God,
and wander for Lack of Meat?* So Ps. CXLVII. 9. "He feedeth the
"young Ravens that call upon him." But this Psalm seems to have
been composed after the Captivity, and therefore the Author of it
perhaps borrowed from Job.   Ch. XXXIX. 1. *Knowest thou the
Time when the wild Goats bring forth &c?* alludes to a common Notion that Goats and Deer have a Difficulty in bringing forth their
young, and that they are assisted in it by Thunder. This is expressed
Ps. XXIX. 9. "The Voice of the Lord maketh the Hinds to bring
"forth young."   That the Book of Job was written after the Time
of Hezekiah, appears probable from Ch. XXXIII. where the Case of
Hezekiah recovering from his Sickness seems plainly to be alluded to
from V. 23 to 29. *If there be a Messenger, an Interpreter, one of a
Thousand, to declare to Man his right Way,* this seems to be Isaiah,
sent to Hezekiah with a Message from God: Mr. Heath says it is
hardly possible to apply it otherwise. See Bp. Warburton, Vol. V. P. 37.
It follows in Job, *If any Man say, I have sinned, and perverted that
which was right, and it profited me not; he will deliver his Soul from
going into the Pit, and his Life shall see the Light.* Hezekiah says,
"Thou

"Thou haſt in Love to my Soul delivered it from the Pit of Corrup-
"tion; for thou haſt caſt all my Sins behind thy Back."   There is
one Paſſage, Pſ. CVII. 40. which is certainly borrowed from Job; becauſe the Words being the ſame, their Conſtruction agrees better with
the Context in Job, than they do in the Pſalm; and from hence we
have a Proof, that the Book of Job was written before that Pſalm.
But that Pſalm ſeems not to have been compoſed till after the Captivity. The Words are theſe, " He poureth Contempt upon Princes, and
" cauſeth them to wander in the Wilderneſs, where there is no Way."
They are taken from the 21ſt and 24th Verſes of Ch. XII.   In the
ſame Pſalm we have, " Iniquity ſhall ſtop it's Mouth," taken from
Job. V. 16.   Another Proof that the Book of Job was written before the Return of the Jews from their Captivity is taken from Ezekiel, Ch. XIV. *Though theſe three Men, Noah, Daniel, and Job, were
in it, they ſhould deliver but their own Souls by their Righteouſneſs.* It
is obſervable that Job is joined with Noah and Daniel: from whence
it appears that this Book was eſteemed by the Jews at that Time as
one of their ſacred Books.   Mr. Pen obſerves, I think, very juſtly
from theſe Words, Ch. VIII. 6. *If thou wert pure and upright, ſurely
now he would awake for thee, and make the Habitation of thy Righteouſneſs proſperous;* that they probably relate to Jeruſalem, and the Temple
there, which then lay in Ruins. The Words, THE HABITATION
OF THY RIGHTEOUSNESS, are very remarkable.

A D D E N D A.

Ch. I. V. 20. *Then Job aroſe and rent his Mantle, and ſhaved his
Head.*] Thus Homer,

Δακρυα θερμα χεον Δαναοι, κειροντο τε χαιτας·

Ch. II. 8. — *and he ſat down among the Aſhes.*] Homer ſays of
Ulyſſes in his low Eſtate,

Εζετ επ εσχαρη εν κονιησι ——

V. 12. — *and they rent every one his Mantle, and ſprinkled Duſt
upon their Heads toward Heaven.*]

Αμφοτερησι δε χερσιν ελων κονιν αιθαλοεσσαν
Χευατο κακκεφαλης, χαριεν δ' ησχυνε προσωπον,
Νεκταρεωδε χιτωνι μελαιν αμφιζανε τεφρη.   Iliad. XVIII. 22.

Ch.

Ch. III. 3. *Let that Day perish* &c.] So Statius,

> *Excidat illa dies ævo, ne poftera credent*
> *Sæcula.* ——

> *Converte, Titan clare, anhelantes equos,*
> *Emitte noctem, pereat hic mundo dies.* Hercules in Seneca.

—— *There is a Man Child conceived.*] — BROUGHT FORTH: for הרה is *to bring forth* as well as *to conceive*

V. 9. — *the Eyelids of the Morning.*] So Sophocles in Antigone,

> Εφανθης ποτ' ω χρυσεης
> Αμερας βλεφαρον

V. 15. *Or with Princes that had Gold,* &c.] It was ufual to bury a great Deal of Wealth with Princes in their Sepulchres. Thus Cyrus and Semiramis are faid to have been buried. See an Account of fuch a Sepulchre of a Woman buried with many Jewels; Pocock's Not. ad Spec. Hift. Arab. P. 156.

V. 19. *The fmall and great are there;*] שם הוא *are* THERE THE SAME. So Pf. CII.

Ch. V. 23. *For thou fhalt be in League with the Stones of the Field.*]

> *Quin votis lapidofa tuis, ceu fœdere pacto,*
> *Refpondebit humus, neque lætum differet uber.*

Ch. VI. 4. *For the Arrows of the Almighty are within me,* &c.] See Tully's II. Tufculan.

> *Hæc me irretivit vefte furiali infcium,*
> *Quæ lateri adhærens morfu lacerat vifcera,*
> *Urgenfque graviter, pulmonum haurit fpiritus.*

V. 7. — *are as my forrowful Meat.*] — IS NOW, IN MY DISTRESS, BECOME MY FOOD. I have taken the Liberty to read ברוי, inftead of כרוי. St. Jerom feems to have read it thus.

Ch. VII. 12. *Am I a Sea.*] So Arabsjad calls Tamerlane, *a vaft Sea fwallowing up every Thing.*

V. 19. — *nor let me alone till I fwallow down my Spittle.*] It is now a proverbial Expreffion among the Arabs, and fignifies the fame, as *Give me Time to breathe,* Dr. Hunt's Præl.

Ch. IX. 8. — *and treadeth upon the Waves of the Sea.*]
> —————— *præruptus aquæ mons.* Virgil.
> —————— τιναστομενης αλις ακρας. Homer.

> *Atque rotis fummas levibus perlabitur undas.* Virgil.

V. 9. *Which maketh Arcturus* &c.] N.B. There is here the fame Quotation from Homer, as I have inferted in the Note on Ch. XXXVIII. 31.

Ch.

Ch. XIII. 9. — *the Hand of the Lord*] יהוד. Therefore written by a Jew, after the Time of Moſes.

V. 27. — *and lookeſt narrowly unto all my Paths* &c.] So Sophocles, in his Ajax, Line 2. —— μετρουμενον
Ιχνη τα κεινε νεοχαρακθ᾽ —.

V. 28. *And he*] The Man ; *i. e.* I myſelf. So Euripedes,
—— ε γαρ τωθ᾽ ιτ᾽ εις τετο εεγες.
Go not with this Man, that is, *with me* Some think that this Verſe ſhould follow the 1ſt of the next Chapter.

Ch. XV. 10. *With us are both the grey-headed, and very aged Men*] ישיש, hence comes the Word *Iſis*, as Diodorus Sic. ſays — τεθειμενης της πρεσηγοριας απο της αιδιε και παλαιας γενεσεως.

Ch. XVI. 16. — *on my Eyelids is the Shadow of Death.*] Homer,
— θανατε νεφος εσ᾽ εκαλυψε.

Ch. XVII. 7. — *and all my Members are as a Shadow.*] Eurip. And.
Σκια γαρ αντιςοιχος ως, φωνην εχεις
Αδυνατος εδεν αλλε, πλην λεγειν μονεν.

Ch. XVIII. 6. — *and his Candle ſhall be put out.*] The Egyptians always have Lamps burning in their Houſes ; ſo that the Want of Light implies Deſolation.

V. 15. — *Brimſtone ſhall be ſcattered upon his Habitation*] So Lucretius, —— *graves exhalant ſulfuris auras.*

V. 17. — *and he ſhall have no Name in the Street.*] Perhaps alluding to the Cuſtom of placing monumental Inſcriptions near the Roads.

V. 19. *He ſhall neither have Son nor Nephew.*] So Silius Ital.
Æthereo ramos populantur ſulfure flammæ,
Donec victa Deo late procumbit, et omnem
Collabens operit ſpatioſo ſtipite prolem.

Ch. XIX. 24. — *with an Iron Pen and Lead.*] The Uſe of Lead was to fill up the Letters cut in Stone. So Bochart underſtands it. Perhaps upon Lead.

V. 25. is thus tranſlated, For I know that the Avenger of my Cause liveth, and that he at length shall appear upon Earth. Or perhaps, *he ſhall riſe in Judgment for Man,* who *is Duſt :* for קום is certainly uſed in a judicial Senſe, and על may ſignify *for.* Theſe Words are to prepare us for the final Cataſtrophe of the Drama.

V. 26.

V. 26. AND AFTER THIS MY SKIN IS CONSUMED, THEN FROM MY FLESH SHALL I SEE GOD: (V. 27.) WHOM I SHALL SEE MY FRIEND, (OR MY OWN) AND MINE EYES SHALL BEHOLD, AS NOT AN ALIEN. Job often refers his Caufe to God, and is now confident that he will appear in his Behalf. This agrees with the Defign of the whole; *viz.* That good Men fometimes fuffer, but that it is only by Way of Trial, and God will deliver them. F. Simon approves of this. See Bibliotheque choifie, Tom. III. P. 461.

Ch. XX. 17. — *the Brooks of Honey and Butter.*] So Ovid,
Flumina jam lactis, jam flumina nectaris ibant.

Ch. XXII. 11. — *and Abundance of Water cover thee.*] So Æfch. Prom. Οις σε χειμων και κακων
Τριχυμια επεισ' αφυκτες.

Ch. XXIV. 5. *Behold as wild Affes in the Defert, go they forth.*] Bochart obferves that a Robber can be compared to a wild Afs in no other refpect, than as he lives in the Defert: for a wild Afs is not a rapacious Animal. So Oppian,
Χιλιν εδει, Φερβει μιν αδην πεεσιτρεφος αιει,
Αλλ' αυτος κρατεροις αγαθη βεσις επλετο θηρσι'
And Ecclef. XIII. 19. "As the Wild Afs is the Lion's Prey, fo the "rich eat up the poor."
V. 25. *They are exalted for a little while, but are gone*]
——— *Jam non ad culmina rerum*
Injuftos creviffe queror, tolluntur in altum
Ut lapfu graviore ruant. [Claud. *in Rufin.* I. 21.]

Ch. XXVI. 10. *He hath compaffed the Waters with Bounds &c.*] The Ancients thought the Earth to be furrounded by the Sea. So Herodotus, Ωκεανντε ρεοντα γραφωσι περιξ: and they thought the Southern Hemifphere to be Darknefs: So Virgil, [*Georg. Lib.* I. 247.]
Illic ut perhibent, aut intempefta filet nox
Semper, et obtenta denfantur nocte tenebræ,
Aut redit a nobis Aurora. ———

Ch. XXVII. 1. — *his Parable*] משל fignifies any Thing written in a loftier and more concife Style than Hiftory. Hence the Proverbs of Solomon are called *Parables.* It is ufed in the Pfalms in this Senfe, LXXVIII. 2. XLIX. 4. Numb. XXIII. 7, 18. and XXIV. 19, 20, 21, 23. &c. *Balaam took up his Parable,* was tranfported with a Prophetic Spirit.

L

V. 6. — *my Heart shall not reproach* me] MY HEART SHALL NOT BE REPROACHED. An Impersonal, which makes the Sense clear.

V. 18. — *and as a Booth* that *the Keeper maketh*.] AND AS THE TENT which THE SPIDER MAKETH. בצר, *the Watcher*: the LXX translates it, *Spider*: It is certainly some Insect.

V. 19. — *but he shall not be gathered*.] לא יאסף, *non illi additur*, impersonally: HE SHALL HAVE NO MORE.

V. 21. *The East Wind carrieth him away*] Thevenot describes an East Wind which had terrible Effects in those Parts. It is scorching, and stifles Men; and in an Instant makes their Flesh slack. He says that 4000 Men died by it at Bassora in one Month.

Ch. XXVIII. 7. There is *a Path which no Fowl knoweth, and which the Vulture's Eye hath not seen*, &c.] Man in hunting after his Prey is more rapacious than the Eagle, more quicksighted than the Hawk, (איה, *the Merlin Hawk*, Bochart) more ravenous than the Lion.

V. 9. *He putteth forth his Hand upon the Rock*;] So Pliny, *Cuniculis per magna spatia actis, cavantur montes, ad lucernarum lumina. Occursant silices; hos igni et aceto rumpunt. Nihil durius putant. Auri fames durissima est. Mons fractus cadit ab sese longe, fragore qui concipi humana mente non possit: spectant victores ruinam naturæ.*

V. 10. *He cutteth out Rivers among the Rocks*;] Either to drain off the Water, or to wash away the Dirt from the Oar. These Things have not the Appearance of that Antiquity, which Some ascribe to this Book.

V. 11. *He bindeth the Floods from overflowing*;] HE BINDETH UP STREAMS FROM WEEPING.

> *In saxis ac speluncis permanat aquarum*
> *Liquidus humor, et uberibus flent omnia guttis.* [Lucret. *Lib.* I. 349.]

V. 16. *It cannot be valued with the Gold of Ophir*,] There are here four different Words to signify different Sorts of Gold: which does not agree with the Simplicity of the first Ages of the World.

Ch. XXIX. 2. *O that I were as in the Months past*, &c.] Thus Catullus,

> *Ego gymnasii fui flos, ego eram decus olei,*
> *Mihi januæ frequentes, mihi limina tepida,*
> *Mihi floridis corollis redimita domus erat,*
> *Linquendum ubi esset orto sole cubiculum.*

V. 8. *The young Men saw me, and hid themselves*;] Οδων υποχωρουντας, και καθ' οδας υπεξισαμενος. Plutarch, *de moribus Lacædemoniorum.*

—— and

—— *and the aged arose*, and *flood up.*] *Si Emir ingrediatur, omnes confurgunt, nec unquam fedent, donec qui poftremus venit, adfederit prior.* Laurent. D'Arvieux *de moribus Arabum.*

Ch. XXX. 4. *Who cut up Mallows by the Bushes, and Juniper Roots* for *their Meat.*] מלוח, a Kind of *Bramble*, without Thorns. Dioscorides writes thus; *Halimum, quod populus Syriæ* MALUCH *vocant, est arbustum, ex quo fiunt sepes, Rhamno simile, nisi quod caret spinis. Folium ejus coquitur et comeditur.* Εν τη χαραδρα τρωγεντες αλιμα, και κακα τοιαυτα συλλεγοντες, says Antiphanes speaking of the Pythagoreans. Galen says that the Tops, when young, are eaten : Serapio writes that they are cried about the Streets of Bagdad.

V. 10. —— *and spare not to spit in my Face.*] Πτυειν αυτιον αισχρον εςι. Herodotus of the Medes. Αισχρον εςι Περσαις το αποπluειν, says Xenophon. Observe that the Author is a Chaldean. The Arabians never spit before a Person, whom they reverence. See Raphelius.

V. 12. —— *and they raise up against me the Ways of Destruction.*] The Metaphor is taken from a Siege, " They raise up their Bulwarks."

V. 13. *They mar my Path*] MY WAY, *viz.* from receiving Succour.
—— *they* have *no helper.*] I have NO HELPER (למו, perhaps) AGAINST THEM. Noldius. So the Vulgate.

V. 15. *Terrors are turned upon me.*] There is AN OVERTHROW : TERRORS are UPON ME. The Verb is impersonal.
—— *they pursue my Soul as the Wind :*] A Verb singular with a Nominat. plural. נדבתי, MY NOBLE PRINCIPLE, my Soul.

V. 28. *I went mourning without the Sun :*] I am BLACK, BUT NOT BY REASON OF THE SUN. קדר the proper Colour of the Arabians. Hence *the Tents of Kedar* are " the Tents of the Arabs." This is a proverbial Expression : *blacker than if burnt by the Sun.* So the Arabians say; *wise, but not as wise as Lochman, i.e.* WISER : *rich, but not as rich as Korah*, that is, RICHER.

V. 29. *I am a Brother to Dragons, and a Companion to Owls.*] So Mic. I. 8. *I will make a Wailing as the Dragons, and Mourning as the Ostriches.* Bochart supposes that this refers to the dreadful Kind of Hiss of these Serpents. He says too that the Word תנים may perhaps be derived from תנה *plangere*, as יענה, the Name of the Ostrich, implies *Wailing*. He proves that the latter is not *the Owl*, but *the Ostrich*, which has a loud melancholy Cry.

Ch. XXXI. 10. *Then let my Wife grind unto another, and let others bow down upon her.*]

Alienas

— *Alienas Permolere uxores* —. Horace. [*Sat. Lib.* I. ii.]

———— το γεγενησεν η ρ́ ετι μυλλει

Τηκαν ταν κυανοφρυν εζωτιδα; Theocritus. *Idyl.* Δ. 40.
So Bochart underſtands it; טהן and جَبٌ have the ſame Senſe.

V. 27. — *or my Mouth hath kiſſed my Hand.*] *Oſcula jacere*, is a well known Phraſe. *Inter adorandum dextram ad oſculum referimus*, ſays Pliny. *Cæcilius, ſimulachro Serapidis viſo, ut vulgus ſolet, manum ori admovens, labiis impreſſit*, ſays Minutius Felix. Ημεις την χειρα κυσαντες ηγημεθα εντελη ημιν ειναι την ευχην, ſays Lucian. The Mohammedans, when they ſhew Veneration to an unſeen Being, *kiſs their Hand*, and put it to their Forehead.

Ch. XXXIII. 19. — *and the Multitude of his Bones with ſtrong* Pain.] THE DISORDER OF HIS BONES IS STRONG. ריב, *Lis, Diſſidium,* Diſorder. So in Arabic رِب, *adverſa Fortuna, malum.*

Ch. XXXIV. 36. *My Deſire is that Job may be tried*] I PROPOSE &c. אבי, for אביא. So Mic. I. 15. 1 Kings XXI. 21, 29. Jer. XIX. 15. — XXXIX. 16.

Ch. XXXVI. 22. *Behold God exalteth by his Power: who teacheth like him?*] BEHOLD it is GOD THAT EXALTETH BY HIS POWER, WHO IS LORD LIKE HIM? מורד in the Chaldee Language ſignifies *Lord.*

Ch. XXXVII. 4. — *and he will not ſtay them*] AND THERE IS NO DELAY; *the Stroke is given.* The Verb is imperſonal.

Ch. XXXVIII. 7. *When the Morning Stars ſang together, and all the Sons of God ſhouted for Joy.*] Perhaps this may refer to an Opinion, that the Stars are under the Direction of Guardian Angels. But why *the Morning Stars?* Becauſe it was at the Time of the Creation, *the Morning of the firſt Day.*

V. 32. *Canſt thou bring forth Mazzaroth in his Seaſon, or canſt thou guide Arcturus with his Sons?*] CANST THOU BRING FORTH THE ZODIACK IN IT'S SEASON, OR LEAD THE NORTHERN CONSTELLATIONS WITH IT'S SONS? מזרות. We have 2 Kings XXIII. 5. מזלות, which is tranſlated *Planets.* The Words are — *To the Sun, and to the Moon, and to the Planets, and to all the Hoſt of Heaven.* Hence the Word here is ſuppoſed to mean *the Zodiack.* Note, *the Pleiades* uſhered in the Spring, and *Orion* the frozen Winter.

Ch. XXXIX. 5. *Who hath ſent out the wild Aſs free?* Varro ſays of this Animal, *E fero fit manſuetus facile.* Επει τας αγριας ονος ημεροσι, ſays fays Anatolius. So that this muſt be underſtood of their natural State: Or perhaps the Opinion concerning them was ſuch at that Time.

V. 6. *Whoſe Houſe I have made the Wilderneſs, and the barren Lands his Dwelling.*] ערבה, from whence, *Arabia.* מלחה, *Terra ſalſuginoſa.* So Virgil, [*Georg.* II. 238.]

> Salfa autem tellus, et quæ perhibetur amara,
> Frugibus infelix. ——

V. 8. —— *and he ſearcheth after every green Thing.*] So Oppian,

> Χιλον εδειν Φερβει μιν αδην ποεσιτροφες αια.

V. 9. *Will the Unicorn be willing to ſerve thee?*] THE WILD ORYX. Oppian's Deſcription of him agrees with this Paſſage.

> Εςι δε τις δρυμαισι παρεςιος, οξυκερως Θηρ,
>
> Αγριοθυμος Ορυξ, κρυερος Θηρεσσι μαλιςα,
>
> Ουδε βροτων αλεγυσιν αναιδηησι νοοιο.

V. 18. —— *ſhe ſcorneth the Horſe and his Rider.*] So Xenophon, Στρατον δε κεεις ελαβεν. οι δε διωξαντες των ιππεων ταχυ επαυοντο. πολυ γαρ απεπια αποφυγκσαι.

V. 20. —— *the Glory of his Noſtrils is terrible.*] So Silius,

> —— crebros expirat naribus ignes. [And Book XVII.]
> Collectumque premens volvit ſub naribus ignem.

V. 21. *He paweth in the Valley,*] So Virgil, [*Geo.* III. 88.]

> —————— cavatque
> Tellurem, et folido graviter fonat ungula cornu.
> Conculcatque folum, generoſo concita pulſu,
> Ungula ———————. Ovid. [*in Halieutico.*]
> Stare adeo miferum eſt, pereunt veſtigia mille
> Ante fugam, abſentemque ferit gravis ungula campum. Statius,
> [*Lib.* VI. *Theb.*]

—— *and rejoiceth in his Strength:*] Ovid. [*ibid.*]

> Nam capiunt animis palmam, gaudentque triumpho.
> Tantus amor laudum, tantæ eſt victoria curæ! Virgil, [*Geo.* III. 112.]

—— *he goeth on to meet the armed Men.*] Ovid, [*ibid.*]

> —— Adverſis infert ſua pectora telis.
> —— Tum ſi qua fonitum procul arma dedere,
> Stare loco neſcit, micat auribus, et tremit artus. Virgil, [*Geo.* III. 33.]
> —————— μαλα θαρσηντες
>
> Οπλοις αντιααν, πυκινην ρηξαι τε Φαλαγγα. Oppian. [*Lib.* I. *Cyneg.*]

V 23. *The Quiver rattleth againſt him, the glittering Spear and the Shield.*]

> Aurataeque vomunt ſtridentia tela pharetræ. Statius, [*Lib.* X. *Theb.*]
> Και χαλκον σελαγευντα, και αςραπτοντα σιδηρον. Oppian, [*loc. cit.*]

Primus

Primus equi labor est, animos atque arma videre
Bellantum ————. Virgil, [*Geo.* III. 132]
V. 24. *He swalloweth the Ground with Fierceness and Rage :*]
————— *Latumque fuga consumere campum.* [*Nemesianus.*]
————— *acri*
Carpere prata fuga ————. Virg. [*Georg. Lib.* III.]
Cum rapuere, pedum frustra vestigia quæras. Silius, [*Lib.* III.]
Viam vorare. Plautus.
———— *neither believeth he that it is the Sound of the Trumpet.*] AND
STANDETH NOT STILL WHEN THERE IS THE SOUND OF THE
TRUMPET. This Sense agrees best with the former Part of the Verse.
Stare loco nescit ————. Virg. [*Georg. Lib.* III.]
Ut fremit acer equus, cum bellicus ære canoro
Signa dedit tubicen, pugnæque assumit amorem. Ovid. [*Met. Lib.* III.]
————— *Motus clangore tubarum*
Saxa quatit pulsu, rigidos vexantia frænos
Ora terens, spargitque jubas, et surrigit aures,
Incertoque pedum pugnat non stare tumultu. Lucan, [*Lib.* IV.]
V. 25. *He saith among the Trumpets, Ha! Ha!*]
———— *Ad lituos hilarem, intrepidumque tubarum*
Prospiciebat equum ————. Statius.
———— *and he smelleth the Battle afar off:*]
Tum si qua sonitum procul arma dedere, &c.
V. 29. *From thence she* (the Eagle) *seeketh the Prey, and her Eyes*
behold afar off.] *Inde cuncta despiciens,* ———— *circum tuetur, et quærit,*
quorsum potissimum in superne sese ruat. Apuleius.
————— ον ρα τε φασιν
Οξυτατον δερκεσθαι επερανιων πετεηνων. Homer.

Ch. XL. 23. *Behold, he drinketh up a River,* and *hasteth not : he*
trusteth that he can draw up Jordan into his Mouth.] BEHOLD, LET
A RIVER PRESS UPON HIM, HE WILL NOT BE IN HASTE TO
FLY : HE WILL BE SECURE, THOUGH JORDAN SHOULD BREAK
OUT EVEN UP TO HIS MOUTH. So Ælian. Ει καλυπτοιτο ὑπο τε ρευ-
ματος, αντεχοσι μεντοι τας προβοσκιδας υπερ το υδωρ. The same is mentioned
by Polybius in Hannibal's passing the Rhone. But what Wonder is it,
for the River Horse not to be afraid of a River? Or what has an
Animal living in the Nile to do with Jordan? [See my Note on this
Word. An Argument may hence be drawn from the mention of Jordan against the high Antiquity of this Book; and that the Author
was a Jew.]

Ch.

Ch. XLI. 1. *Canst thou draw out Leviathan with a Hook? or his Tongue with a Cord —?*] Purchas says, *Aristoteles Crocodilos negat habere linguam; at ego in omnibus linguam reperi, sed brevem, tenuem, et latam.* Ezekiel calls the King of Egypt THE GREAT LEVIATHAN, *that lieth in the midst of his Rivers;* that is, the Crocodile. If it be objected, that the Crocodile may be taken, so may *the Whale.* This is to be understood of the great Difficulty of it. Plutarch calls him αμικροτατον, και θηριοτατον. Hasselquist confirms this, P. 216. 440. It bites off all fishing Tackle.

V. 13. — OR WHO CAN ENTER INTO HIS DOUBLE BIT ? His Jaws are called, *duplex frænum lupatum.*

V. 14. *Who can open the Doors of his Face?*] Οταν χαιη προς τας αχρας, ολος σομα γινη). Achilles Tatius.

V. 18. — *and his Eyes are like the Eyelids of the Morning.*] Ανατολην λεγοντες, δυο εφθαλμυς κροκοδειλυ ζωγραφυσιν, επειδη προ παντος σωματος ζωα οι οφθαλμοι εκ τυ βυθυ αναφαινονται. Horus of Hieroglyphics.

V. 19. *Out of his Mouth go burning Lamps;*] So Achilles Tatius of *the Hippopotamus,* πνεων πυρωδη καπνον, ως απο πηγης πυρος. So Ovid of *the Boar;*

      Fulmen ab ore venit, frondesque afflatibus ardent.

So Silius Italicus of *the Serpent;*

      Et Stygios æstus fumanti exsibilat ore,
      Terribilis gemino de lumine fulminat ignis.

V. 22. --- AND SORROW GOETH BOUNDING BEFORE HIM.]
      Insultare solo, et gressus glomerare superbos.
      ——— παρα δε δειμος τε Φοβος τε
      Εςαταν, ιεμενοι πολεμον καταδυμεναι ανδρων. Hesiod.

V. 23. *The Flakes of his Flesh are joined together* &c.] So Theoc.
      Σαρκι σιδαρειη, σφυρηλατες οια Κολοσσος.

V. 26. — *the Habergeon*] JAVELIN, שריה, سىو, *Jaculum.*

V. 29. *Darts are counted as Stubble,*] CLUBS, תותח, جۇ, *fustis.*

V. 32. *One would think the Deep to be hoary*] So Catullus,
      Tortaque remigio spumis incanuit unda.

N.B. The Texts which differ from the English Version are of the anonymous Author's own Translation: and the Verses here produced in the Description of the Horse are borrowed from Bochart's *Hieroz. Lib.* II. *Cap.* VIII.

CRITICAL REMARKS

ON THE

BOOK OF PSALMS.

PSALM I.

VERSE 6. — *but the Way of the ungodly shall perish.*] ורדך
רשעים תאבד [Rather — SHALL FAIL, as Pf. CXLII. 4. &c.

PSALM II.

V. 7. *I will declare the Decree: the Lord hath said unto me,* אספרה
אל חק יהוה [Rather — I WILL DECLARE THE
— אמר אלי וגו
DECREE OF THE LORD : HE SAID UNTO ME &c. This Conftruction the Hemiftics point out.

—— *Thou* art *my Son, this Day have I begotten thee.* בני אתה אני
היום ילדתיך [That this Paffage was prophetic of the Meffiah we
have the higheft Authority for believing. Acts XIII. 33. where it is
applied to Chrift's Refurrection. But if the Inquiry be, in what Senfe
David could be fuppofed to fpeak this of himfelf, the Anfwer is, from
the fpecial, and as it were paternal, Care, which God promifed to take
of him : the Time of making which Promife may be fairly faid to be
the Day of God's having *begotten* or *adopted* him for his Son ; which
was an Act of *begetting* in a civil Senfe. In like manner God promifes
to take Solomon under his peculiar Protection. 2 Sam. VII. 14. *I will
be to him a Father, and he fhall be to me a Son.* And in this Senfe it
is ufed of David, Pf. LXXIX. 26. *He fhall cry unto me, Thou* art *my
Father* ; and V. 27. *Alfo I will make him my firft-born, higher than the
Kings*

Kings of the Earth, as is evident from the Context. Kings in general are also said to be *Children of the most High*, (Pf. XXXII. 6.) as being Objects of his more immediate Concern, on account of the general Interest: from which Notion among the Heathens we often find them called Διογενεις.

V. 11. — *and rejoice with Trembling.* ויגילו ברעדה] Rather — WITH AWE, as Pf. IV. 4.

V. 12. *Kiss the Son left he be angry,* — נשקו בר פן יאנף] בר in the Sense of *Son* is of Chaldee Origin. *To kiss* implies in this Place *to reverence*; thus, *All the Knees which have not bowed unto Baal, and every Mouth which hath not* KISSED *him.* 1 Kings XIX. 18. So again, *Let the Men that sacrifice* KISS *the Calves.* Hof. XIII. 2. See what was observed on Job. XXXI. 27. To which I would add, that Demosthenes being carried into a Temple is said (though I cannot now cite the Place) *to have kissed his Hand*, in token of Adoration. Thus we kiss the King's Hand; and it is customary now in many Countries to kiss the Garment of a superior, out of Respect.

—— *and ye perish* from *the Way* — והאברו דרך] Rather — AND YE FAIL in (or, as to) THE WAY. The Words are here the same as Pf. I. 6. only the Construction is a little varied.

PSALM IV.

V. 2. *O ye Sons of Men, how long* will ye turn *my Glory into Shame?* בני איש עד מה כבודי לכלאה] Rather — O YE SONS OF MEN, HOW LONG shall MY GLORY be A DISHONOUR?.

V. 4. *Stand in Awe, and sin not:* — רגזו ואל תחטאו] That is, " Let this strike you with Awe, and beware of offending God." The Version of the LXX is, Οργιζεσθε, και μη αμαρτανετε, which St. Paul quotes: but he only uses such Words as suited his Purpose, without regarding the Original.

V. 6. There be *many that say, Who will shew us any Good? Lord, lift thou up* &c. "נסה וגו׳ — רבים אמרים מי יראנו טוב] Rather — Since MANY SAY, WHO WILL SHEW US ANY GOOD? LORD &c.

PSALM V.

V. 2. *Hearken unto the Voice of my Cry, my King, and my God: for unto thee will I pray.* הקשיבה לקול שועי מלכי—ואלהי כי אליך אתפלל]

Thus

Thus I think ought the Hemiftics to be divided, and rendered ——
HEARKEN UNTO THE SOUND OF MY CRY, O MY KING: FOR
SURELY UNTO THEE, O MY GOD, WILL I PRAY. See Pf. XXVIII.
1. and XXXVIII. 21.

V. 3. — *in the Morning will I direct my Prayer unto thee, and will
look up.* : בקר אערך לך ואצפה] Rather — IN THE MORNING
WILL I PREPARE myfelf FOR (or DIRECT myfelf UNTO) THEE,
AND WILL LOOK UP. As if he had faid, " I will addrefs both my
" Mind and Eyes to thee." See Job. XXXII. 14. and Prov. XVI. 1.

PSALM VI.

V. 3. *My Soul is alfo vexed: but thou, O Lord, how long?* — ונפשי
: נבהלה מאד — ואת יהוה עד מתי שובה] The laft Verfion is here
very obfcure : that which is bound up with our Common Prayer is
more intelligible, by the Addition of thefe Words — *wilt thou punifh
me:* the Edition of 1599 has here — *wilt thou delay;* and others
add — *wilt thou be angry.* But there is no Neceffity to add any Thing
to the Text to complete the Senfe. All that is wanting is to remove
the Stop from after עד מתי to the next Word, שובה. The Conftruction then will be this --- MY SOUL IS ALSO VEXED: BUT WHEN
will there be A RETURNING OF THE LORD? (or --- WITH THE
LORD.) See the fame Words thus conftrued, Pf. XC. 13. CXXVI. 4.

V. 4. *Return, O Lord, deliver my Soul:* — [שובה] יהוה חלצה נפשי
According to the Interpretation juft given of the preceding Verfe, this
Hemiftic muft be rendered fimply — O LORD, DELIVER MY SOUL:
which moreover will exactly correfpond in Number of Words to the
next Hemiftic.

PSALM VII.

V. 1. ——*fave me from all them that perfecute me, and deliver me.*
: הושיעני מכל רדפי והצילני] Rather — FROM EVERY ONE THAT
PERSECUTETH ME &c. Which Verfion, befides that it is more accurate, points out the Subject of the fingular Verbs in the next Hemiftic.

V. 4. *If I have rewarded Evil unto him that was at Peace with me:
(yea, I have delivered him that without Caufe is mine Enemy:)* This
Parenthefis

Parenthefis might be fpared, if the latter Hemiftic, *viz.* ואחלצה
צוררי ריקם, were rendered thus — OR HAVE TAKEN UP ARMS
WITHOUT CAUSE AGAINST MINE ENEMY. See חלץ thus ufed,
Numb. XXXI. 3. — XXXII. 17, 20. I Chron. XII. 23, 24. *Qu.* ought
not the Text to be read — ואחלץ הצוררי? For though the Future
fometimes admits the ה *paragogic*; yet it may be more properly confidered in this Place as *articular*; and that, either as demonftrative,
which may imply *my greateft Enemy*; or as indefinite, *any one of mine
Enemies*.

V. 6. —— *and awake for me to the Judgment* that *thou haft commanded*. ועורה אלי משפט צוית:] Rather — AND AWAKE; feeing THOU HAST COMMANDED JUDGMENT FOR ME.

V. 7. —*for their Sakes therefore return thou on high.* עליה למרום שובה:]
Rather --- AND RETURN UNTO IT (viz. *the Congregation*) FROM ON
HIGH, or FROM ABOVE. The Senfe of our Verfion feems directly contrary to the Intent of the Pfalmift: for if God be *below*, why fhould
He be entreated to afcend up *on high* in order to affift the faithful?
JEHOVAH is not furely, as the Syrians pretended, *a God of the Hills,
but not of the Valleys?* I Kings XX. 18. The Pfalmift plainly alludes
to the *Shechinah*, or Symbol of God's Prefence under the more immediate *Theocracy*, which difappeared for ever upon the full Eftablifh-
ment of the Jewifh State. לרום is here conftrued as — העלו מסביב
למישכן קרח — *Get you up* FROM *about the Tabernacle of Korah*, Numb.
XVI. 24. See alfo Prov. XIV. 20. &c.

V. 8. — *judge me, O Lord, according to my Righteoufnefs, and according to mine Integrity* that is *in me*. שפטני יהוה כצדקי — ובתמי עלי:]
The latter Claufe ought to be rendered — AND SET ME UP ACCORD-
ING TO MINE INTEGRITY. עלי is here the Imperative of עלה, which
fuffers an *Apocope* on account of the Affix. I render it as Ezek. XIV. 7.

V. 10. *My Defence is of God*, — מגני על אלהים] Rather — MY
BUCKLER IS THE MOST HIGH GOD; for על is thus rendered, Hof.
XI. 7. and ought to be fo, 2 Sam. XXIII. 1.

V. 11. *God judgeth the righteous : and God is angry* with the wicked
every Day. אלהים שופט צדיק — ואל זעם בכל יום] Rather —
GOD JUDGETH THE RIGHTEOUS : BUT IS NOT ANGRY ALL
THE DAY LONG: as Pf. CXL. 2. &c.

V. 17. *I will praise the Lord according to his Righteousness:* אודה
יהוה כצדקו] Rather— BECAUSE OF HIS RIGHTEOUSNESS: or,
ON ACCOUNT OF. See Pſ. XII. 8. XXV. 7. &c.

PSALM VIII.

V. 8. — *and whatſoever paſſeth through the Paths of the Seas.* עבר
ארחות ימים:] Rather, I think — AND THE PASSAGE THROUGH
THE PATHS OF THE SEAS, *i. e.* " Navigation." For עבר cannot
agree with דני; and if it could, this Sentence would then be a mere
Pleonaſm. Whereas nothing appears more natural than to ſuppoſe the
Pſalmiſt meant, (after he had mentioned in general and in Detail the
whole of the Creation, whether animate or inanimate) to ſum up all
by touching on the amazing Power God had given Man over the boi-
ſterous Element.

PSALM IX.

V. 18. — *the Expectation of the poor ſhall* not *periſh for ever.*
תקות עניים תאבד לעד:] As this Hemiſtic plainly requires ſome
negative Particle, which we find in all the ancient Verſions, it is moſt
probable that the original Reading was ותקות; in which Caſe the ו
would have a negative Force, as it is preceded by a Negative: Or
the Hemiſtic may be thus rendered interrogatively —— SHALL THE
EXPECTATION OF THE POOR FAIL FOR EVER? See Pſ. I. 6. II. 12.

PSALM X.

V. 2. *The wicked in* his *Pride doth perſecute the poor:* —— בגאות
רשע ידלק עני] Rather — THROUGH PRIDE THE WICKED PER-
SECUTETH THE POOR; or, DOTH PROUDLY PERSECUTE ---- :
as the Word is rendered, Pſ. XVII. 10. Our Tranſlators thought,
either that the Affix ו had dropped out of בגאות, or that it was *in
regimine*; but neither is the Caſe: the Word is in the Plural, to denote *Abundance,* or merely to ſerve as *an Adverb,* as it frequently
happens.

V. 4. *The wicked, through the Pride of his Countenance, will not ſeek*
after God: רשע בגברה אפו בל ידרש] Rather —— THE WICKED
                                    THROUGH

THROUGH PRIDE WILL NOT SEEK HIS FACE, viz. *the Lord's*; mentioned immediately before.

—— *God is not in all his Thoughts.* : אין אלהים כל מזמותיו [Rather (with the Margin) ALL HIS THOUGHTS are, There is NO GOD: agreeably to Pf. XIV. 1. and LIII. 1.

V. 5. *His Ways are always grievous*; — יחילו דרכו בכל עת [The Text is doubtlefs here corrupt. According to our Verfion, it ought to be יחילו דרכיו : but the Lection of the Arabic Verfion feems preferable, as it approaches nearer to the Text, *viz.* יחיל דרכו — HE HATH POLLUTED HIS WAY. See חלל.

— as for *all his Enemies, he puffeth at them.* : כל צורריו יפיח בהם [Simply thus — HE ENSNARETH ALL HIS ENEMIES. A common *Hebraifm.* The fame Idiom is properly rendered, Pf. XI. 4.

V. 6. *He hath faid in his Heart, I fhall not be moved: for* I fhall *never* be *in Adverfity.* : אמר בלבו בל אמוט — לדר ודר אשר לא ברע [Rather — HE HATH SAID IN HIS HEART, I SHALL NOT BE MOVED; NEITHER SHALL I SEE ADVERSITY. אשר is here confidered as contractedly written for אישור, the future of שור, which fignifies *to fee,* Job. XXXV. 5.

V. 7. — *under his Tongue is Mifchief and Vanity.* תחת לשונו עמל ואון: [Rather — HIS TONGUE STICKETH UPON MISCHIEF AND INIQUITY, as Pf. XXXVIII. 2. or — SETTLETH UPON — as LXV. 10. *i.e.* " is continually uttering." לשון is of the common Gender; but more frequently feminine. תחת is here defective, as Prov. XVII. 10. (where it fignifies *entreth into*) for הנחת.

V. 8. — *his Eyes are privily fet againft the poor.* : עיניו לחלכה יצפנו [Rather — HIS EYES PRIVILY LURK FOR THE POOR: as Prov. I. 11.

V. 9. *He lieth in wait fecretly, as a Lion in his Den: he lieth in wait to catch the poor: he doth catch the poor when he draweth him into his Net.* יארב במסתר כאריה בסכה — יארב לחטוף עני — יחטף עני במשכו : ברשתו [The Repetitions are here very ftriking: in them are united the *Anaphora,* and *Anadiplofis.*

V. 10. *He croucheth and humbleth himfelf, that the poor may fall by his ftrong ones.* : ודכה ישח — ונפל בעצומיו חלכאים [Rather perhaps thus — THE OPPRESSED IS CAST DOWN; AND THE WHOLE BAND

BAND OF THE AFFLICTED FALLETH, WHEN HE PREVAILETH
OVER THEM. The Maſſora reads ירכה : but there ſeems to be no
Occaſion for an Alteration. I conſider ורכה with Aquila, as having
the ה *paragogic*, as להלכה, V. 8. ישח as the Future *Niphal*, from שחה,
as Iſa. II. 11,17. I read בעצומי, with the LXX, Arabic, Æthiopic, and
Vulgate, making it the Infinitive : and laſtly, I conſtrue that ſtrange
Word, הלכאים, as compounded of היל *an Army*, and כאה *to make ſad*.

V. 11. — *he hideth his Face ; he will never ſee it.* הסתיר פניו בל
ראה לנצח] Rather — HE HIDETH HIS FACE ; HE WILL NOT
ALWAYS LOOK ON ; or, HE WILL NOT FOR EVER BEHOLD.

V. 12. *Ariſe, O Lord ; O God, lift up thine Hand :* — קומה יהוה אל
נשא ידך] Perhaps better thus — ARISE, O LORD GOD, LIFT UP
THINE HAND.

V. 14. *Thou haſt ſeen it, for thou beholdeſt Miſchief and Spite to re-
quite it with thy Hand :* — ראתה כי אתה עמל—וכעס תביט לתת בידך]
Each Hemiſtic ought to be conſidered ſeparately thus — BUT THOU
HAST SEEN MISCHIEF, AND BEHOLDEST PROVOCATION TO RE-
QUITE &c.

PSALM XI.

V. 1. *Flee as a Bird to your Mountain.* נודו הרכם צפור :] The
Maſſora reads here נודי ; which, as it agrees with נפשי, is preferable.
That Lection is beſides countenanced by all the ancient Verſions. It
is alſo probable that the other two Words are wrongly divided ; for the
Affix Pronoun ſeems here unneceſſary, and a Particle of Similitude is
wanting ; thus נודי הר כמצפור — FLY THOU AS A BIRD TO THE
MOUNTAIN. The Particle כ being not unfrequently prefixed to the
Nominative, and all other Caſes : ſee Noldius 44.

V. 3. *If the Foundations be deſtroyed,* כי השתות יהרסון] The Word
שתות occurs only in another Place, (*viz.* Iſa. XIX. 10.) and there it
has a different Senſe. The Signification here given to it, either in the
Proper or Figurative Senſe, ſeems arbitrary, and not very ſuitable to
this Place. The LXX, Syriac, Arabic, and Vulgate read השתת
2. m. ſing. Pret. *Kal* with ה relative prefixed : which Lection is doubtleſs preferable, *viz.* WHEN THEY DESTROY WHAT THOU HAST
ESTABLISHED &c.

V. 4.

V. 4. — *his Eyes behold, his Eyelids try the Children of Men.* יהוז
עפעפיו — יבחנו בני אדם:] Rather — HIS EYES BEHOLD, HIS EYE-
LIDS INSPECT —. Hence comes בחון, *a Tower*, or Place of *Inspection*.

V. 6. *Upon the wicked he shall rain Snares, Fire and Brimstone,* —
ימטר אל רשעים פחים אש] Rather ——— UPON THE WICKED HE
WILL POUR DOWN QUICK BURNING COALS : as in the Margin.

——— *and an horrible Tempest :* this shall be *the Portion of their Cup.*
 וגפרית ורוח זלעפות מנת כוסם:] Rather — AND BRIMSTONE AND
A SCORCHING TEMPEST shall be THE PORTION OF THEIR CUP:
in order to avoid the Repetition of *burning* twice in the same Verse.

P S A L M   XII.

V. 5. — *I will set* him *in Safety* from him that *puffeth at him.* אשית
בישע יפיח לו:] Rather — from him that ENSNARETH HIM. See Pſ. X. 5.

V. 6. — as *Silver tried in a Furnace of Earth,* — בסף צרוף בעליל
לארץ] The Word עליל is not uſed for *a Furnace* in any other Place;
neither has it the leaſt Connection with the Root. This Senſe has
been given to it from the Targum and from the *Exigentia loci.* In the
many other Places where this *Simile* occurs, *a Furnace* is always expreſſed by כור; whence I conclude that it has not this Signification;
and would therefore either read בליל, and render — as SILVER PU-
RIFIED FROM THE MIXTURE OF EARTH; or, retaining the preſent Lection, conſtrue it thus --- as SILVER PURIFIED FROM THE
REMNANTS OF EARTH. See בלל *to mix Things together,* and עלל
to glean Grapes or Corn, after a Vintage or Harveſt. This Verb is uſed
figuratively for *picking up Stragglers;* and why may not its Derivative
be uſed for *any ſcattered Particle,* or *Remnant of any Thing?*

V. 8. *The wicked walk on every Side, when the vileſt Men are exalted.*
סביב רשעים יתהלכון — כרום זלות לבני אדם:] I would render the
latter Hemiſtic thus — THAT THEY MAY EXALT THE REFUSE OF
THE SONS OF MEN : *i. e.* "the wicked ſpare no Pains in order to pro-
" mote ſuch vile Wretches as will countenance their Deſigns." Or thus
--- WHEN THE REFUSE OF MANKIND ARE EXALTED, WICKED
MEN GO ABOUT (*viz.* ABOUND) ON EVERY SIDE : *graſſantur
impii undequaque.* "Vice prevails when impious Men bear Sway."
Perhaps the Pſalmiſt might allude to ſome ſuch Perſon as Doeg having
Influence at the Court of Saul, to the Oppreſſion of the Righteous.

PSALM XIII

V. 1. *How long wilt thou forget me, O Lord, for ever?* — עד אנה

יהוה תשכחני נצח] Rather — How LONG WILT THOU TOTALLY
FORGET ME? See Pſ. LXXXIX. 46. Iſa. XXV. 8.

V. 2. *How long ſhall I take Counſel in my Soul?* עד אנה אשית

עצות בנפשי] Rather perhaps — FOR MY LIFE? *i. e.* "for preſer-
" ving it." The Prepoſition is thus uſed, Gen. XVIII. 28. &c.

V. 3. — *leſt I ſleep the Sleep of Death.* : פן אישן המות] The ה
articular is here equivalent to the ה *local*, as העיר, *into the City*; Joſ.
VIII. 19. &c. הבית *into the Houſe*; 2 Sam. XIX. 6. The old Verſion
ſeems therefore more exact, *viz.* THAT I SLEEP NOT IN DEATH.

V. 4. *Leſt mine Enemy ſay, I have prevailed againſt him;* and *thoſe
that* &c. פן יאמר איבי יכלתיו צרי—וגו] It is highly probable that
the original Reading here was — יכלתי וצרי — thus — LEST MINE
ENEMY SAY, I HAVE PREVAILED: AND THOSE &c: for the
Verb יכל, when uſed in the Senſe of *prevailing againſt*, is always conſtrued with a ל after it: See Gen. XXXII. 25. Jer. XX. 10. &c. beſides
that the copulative Particle is here wanted.

—— *when I am moved.* : כי אמוט] Rather — WHEN I FALL; as
Prov. XXV. 26; or, as in the old Verſion, WHEN I SLIDE.

PSALM XIV.

V. 2. — *to ſee if there were any that did underſtand,* and *ſeek God.*
: דרש את אלהים—היש משכיל] Rather — THAT DID UNDER-
STAND, SEEKING GOD.

V. 3. — *there is none that doeth good, no not one.*] St. Paul quotes theſe
three Verſes, (Rom. III. 10, 11, 12.) and immediately after adds ſix
more Verſes, which at preſent do not appear in the Heb. Copies, nor in
any of the old Verſions, except the LXX, Arabic, Æthiopic, and Vulgate. In the Vatican Copy of the LXX, F. Montfaucon informs us,
that from theſe Words ταφος ανεωγμενος ο λαρυγξ αυτων to απεναντι των οφ-
θαλμων αυτων, the whole is inſerted in the Margin, and that there is
added this Note, εδαμε κεινται των ψαλμων, ποθεν δε ο αποςολος ειληφεν
αυτες

αυτας εχτιεν. I cannot think with the anonymous Annotator, that it is difficult to find the Place, from whence the Apostle borrowed these Verses: that they were in the LXX, and in this Place, when St. Paul cited them, appears to me evident: (for it seems not probable, that they have been inserted since out of Compliment to him) and that they were in the Hebrew Copies, from which the LXX made their Version, I make no doubt. The same may be presumed in regard to the Copies used by Jerom, and the other two Interpreters. But besides these five Authorities, which together are sufficient to establish this Point, I may add that St. Paul, who calls himself *an Hebrew of the Hebrews*, and had more critical Skill *than any of the other Apostles*, would not have alledged this Passage, if there had been the least Doubt of it's Authenticity, or if it had been wanting in most of the Hebrew Copies in his Time. But how came it to be omitted in our present Copies, in the Targum, and in the Syriac? And that no Traces of it are to be found in Aquila, Symmachus, or Theodotion? The Reason seems clearly to be this; that this Omission is to be laid to the Charge of some hasty Transcriber in the middle Ages, whose MS, or a Copy of it, the Academy of Jews at Tiberias might have used for a Standard, when they collated their various Copies, in which it is probable they expunged whatever was not found in it. The Rest of the Jews would naturally follow the Example: and the same Reason I imagine is to be assigned for the Omission of several Verses in different Parts of the Book of Proverbs. In respect to the Targum, it is certain that it has been tampered with by the Jews in various Places, that it might harmonize with their Hebrew MSS: and some pious Fraud, I am apprehensive, has suggested the total Omission of this Passage in the Syriac Version, for the same Reason. As to the Silence of the other three Greek Versions, it has no Weight; it being well known that unfortunately we have only Fragments of them. Upon the whole, I think this Passage ought to be restored in our Version, and considered as authentic, as it is in our oldest Version of the Psalms.

V. 5. *There were they in great Fear:* שם פחדו פחד] Rather — THEN &c. See Prov. VIII. 27. Isa. XLVIII. 16.

—— *for God is in the Generation of the righteous.* כי אלהים בדור צדיק:] Rather —— BUT GOD IS IN THE DWELLING OF THE RIGHTEOUS. See Ps. LXXXIV. 10.

V. 6. *Ye have shamed the Counsel of the poor;* —— עצת עני תבישו] Rather — YE HAVE DISAPPOINTED ——. See Job. VI. 20. Ps. XXII. 5.

N

Zech.

Zech. IX. 5. Rom. V. 5. and compare Rom. IX. 33. with Ifa. XXVIII. 16. where poffibly the LXX (after whofe Reading the New Teftament Writers feem to cite their Authorities) might have read יביש, inftead of יהיש.

PSALM XV.

V. 4. He that *fweareth to* his own *Hurt, and changeth not.* נשבע :להרע ולא ימר [להרע feems to be Infinitive *Hiphil* of רעה, with the Apocope of the ה final; and ought to be rendered ――― TO DO A FRIENDLY ACT, or TO BE A FRIEND; as Judg. XIV. 20. Prov. XXII. 24. The Word is generally derived from the Verb רוע, *to do Mifchief:* but furely to do this can never be a Part of the upright Man's Character; and there is no Authority for adding any Thing in this Place to the Text.

PSALM XVI.

V. 2. O my Soul, *thou haft faid unto the Lord,* ――― אמרת ליהוה[אמרת is clearly a Miftake for אמרתי; for all the ancient Verfions, the Chaldee excepted, read fo. This Place ought therefore to be rendered without Hefitation --- I HAVE SAID UNTO THE LORD.

――― *my Goodnefs* extendeth *not to thee.* טובתי בל עליך :[Rather --- MY GOOD DEEDS are NOTHING UNTO THEE: *i. e.* cannot profit thee. See Neh. VI. 19.

V. 4. *Their Sorrows fhall be multiplied* that *haften after another* God. ירבו עצבותם אהר מהרו[Rather ― LET THEIR IDOLS BE MUL-TIPLIED that ARE CARRIED ALONG BACKWARD. אחר is here confidered (with the ancient Verfions) as an Adverb, contractedly writ-ten for אחור; and אחר מהרו means, I apprehend, the fame as נזרו אחור ―*they are alienated backward,* or *are gone away backward*; as Ifa. I. 4. &c. All which Phrafes imply a Revolt from the Worfhip of the one true God.

V. 5. *The Lord* is *the Portion of mine Inheritance, and of my Cup:* יהוה מנת חלקי וכוסי[This Hemiftic ought I think to be conftrued in the Vocative Cafe, thus ― O LORD, thou PORTION &c. becaufe in the next the fecond Perfon is ufed. *Cup* feems here to denote *an Houfhold,* or *Family:* becaufe the feveral Perfons who compofe a Fa-mily *drink of the fame Cup,* and generally fare alike. Thus is our Lord to be underftood, Matt. XX. 22, 23.

V. 6. *The*

V. 6. *The Lines* — הבלים] Rather — THE MEASURING LINES. These are put by a Metonymy for *Lands*, which were parcelled out by *Lines*, after the Rods had been fixed. So Amos, *Thy Land shall be divided by Line*. Ch. VII. 17. Hence this Word is sometimes used for *a Region*, see Deut. III. 4. This Custom was not peculiar to the Jews; for we find in Herodotus this Expression, καλον πεδιον σχοινω δια μετρησαν.

V. 7. — *my Reins also instruct me in the Night-Seasons.* אף לילות יסרוני כליותי :] The Word כליות signifies primarily *the Kidneys*, or *Reins*; the innermost Part of the human Constitution: but it is as frequently used figuratively, for *the Thoughts*, and *inmost Counsels of the Mind*, as *the Heart* is for *the Seat of the Affections*. See Pf. LXXIII. 21. Jer. XI. 20. Ought not therefore the Word in this Place to be rendered, MY THOUGHTS?

PSALM XVII.

V. 1. *Hear the right, O Lord,* — שמעה יהוה צדק] Rather — HEAR, O JUST LORD — for צדק is used sometimes as an Adjective.

V. 3. — *thou hast tried me,* and *shalt find nothing : I am purposed* that *my Mouth shall not transgress.* :צרפתני בל תמצא זמתי בל יעבר פי] Rather --- THOU HAST TRIED ME, but SHALT FIND NO WICKED THOUGHT (or CRIME) IN ME : MY MOUTH SHALL NOT OF- FEND. זמה has either of the Senses here given to it : I consider it as *in Regimine* with the Affix, and as equivalent to זמה בי, a Con- struction not unfrequent in the poetical Books. See Pf. VII. 4. XIII. 4. or it may be construed as we say in English — NO CRIME OF MINE. Whereas the Verb זמם never signifies *To purpose*, but only *To think :* and if this Sense, viz. *thou shalt find nothing* had been meant to be ex- pressed, the Words would most probably have been תמצא אין.

V. 4. *Concerning the Works of Men, by the Words of thy Lips,* —— לפעלות אדם בדבר שפתיך] As these Words in our Version are quite unconnected with what follows in this Verse, I would render them thus --- IN RESPECT TO THE DEEDS OF MEN AGAINST THE WORD OF THY LIPS. See Note Job. IX. 19. The Meaning is, " that " he had kept his Eye upon the Paths of the Destroyer, with respect " to those Deeds which ungodly Men commit against the Law of God, " in order to avoid them."

V. 7.

V. 7. Shew thy marvellous Lovingkindness, O thou that savest by thy right Hand them which put their Trust in thee from those that rise up against them. ‏הפלה חסדיך מושיע חוסים — ממתקוממים בימינך׃‏ Rather --- SEVER THY LOVINGKINDNESS, O SAVIOUR OF THE FAITHFUL, FROM THEM THAT RISE UP AGAINST THY RIGHT HAND. In this Place there is in our Version a remarkable *Hyperbaton*.

V. 8. Keep me as the Apple of the Eye: — ‏שמרני כאישון בת עין‏] Rather --- AS THE PUPIL &c.

V. 9. — from *my deadly Enemies, who compass me about.* ‏איבי בנפש יקיפו עלי׃‏] Rather — MINE ENEMIES FOR PLEASURE (or SPORT) COMPASS ME ABOUT. See ‏נפש‏ thus used, Ps. CV. 22. Jer. II. 24. It is also applied to all the Faculties and Affections of the Soul; and might be used in this Place for HATRED.

V. 10. They are inclosed in *their own Fat:* — ‏חלבמו סגרו‏] The Words of the Text cannot I think admit of this Sense; for the Verb is active, and the Noun seems not to be in the Ablative Case. What other Sense can be deduced from the present Lection, I know not: but am inclined to suspect that — ‏הלבמו‏ is the true Reading, thus — THEY SHUT UP THEIR HEART, *i. e.* "they are hardened against "all Compassion." So Ps. LXXVII. 9. *Hath he in Anger* SHUT UP HIS TENDER MERCIES?

V. 11. — *they have set their Eyes bowing down to the Earth.* ‏עיניהם ישיתו לנטות בארץ׃‏] Rather, with the old Version — THEY HAVE SET THEIR EYES TO BRING DOWN TO THE EARTH.

V. 12. Like as a Lion that is greedy of his Prey; ‏דמינו כאריה יכסוף לטרף‏] ‏דמין‏ occurs no where else: it is generally derived from ‏דמה‏, and said to signify *Likeness:* but even then, it must be allowed to be an unnecessary Expletive. The LXX, Arabic, Vulgate, and Æthiopic, point out the original Reading, *viz.* ‏דכוני‏ — THEY DESTROY ME AS A LION &c.

V. 13. Deliver my Soul from the wicked, which is *thy Sword.* ‏פלטה נפשי מרשע חרבך׃‏] *Qu.* is not the old Version in this Place preferable, *viz.* DELIVER MY SOUL FROM THE WICKED BY THY SWORD? This is also the marginal Lection.

V. 14. From the Men which are *thy Hand,* ‏ממתים ידך‏] So also --- FROM THE MEN by THY HAND; or as in the Margin.

——— *and*

—— *and whose Belly thou fillest with thy hid* Treasure: וצפינך תמלא בטנם] Rather — AND WHOSE BELLY THOU FILLEST WITH THY TREASURE. For צפן *signifies to lay up in Store as a Treasure.*

—— *they are full of Children,* ישבעו בנים] Rather, I think, with the Margin — their CHILDREN ARE FULL. For the Words certainly will bear this Sense : but I much question the other.

—— *and leave the rest of their* Substance *to their Babes.* והניחו יתרם לעולליהם:] Rather — AND LEAVE THEIR RICHES TO THEIR INFANTS ; *i. e.* to their Children's Children. See יתר thus rendered, Jer. XLVIII. 36.

V. 15. —— *I shall be satisfied, when I awake, with thy Likeness.* אשבעה בהקיץ תמונתך:] Rather, I think — I SHALL BE SATIS-FIED WHEN THY GLORY SHALL APPEAR, or BE ROUSED. By comparing this Place with Num. XII. 8. it will appear that תמונה is the same as the *Shechinah,* or the Symbol of God's Presence, which resided upon the Ark.

PSALM XVIII.

V. 2. —— *my God, my Strength, in whom I will trust* : אלי צורי אחסה בו] These Words are obscurely rendered in our Version both here and 2 Sam. XXII. 3. where we read — *The God of my Rock ; in him will I trust.* Whereas if the Verb substantive were repeated from the pre-ceding Clause, this Sentence would be clear, thus — MY GOD IS MY ROCK ; IN HIM WILL I TRUST.

—— *and the Horn of my Salvation, and my high Tower.* וקרן ישעי משגבי] Rather — AND THE HORN OF MY SALVATION PROTECT-ING ME : for as there is no copulative Particle before משגבי, it seems more natural to construe it as the Participle *Pihel* than as a Substantive.

V. 3. *I will call upon the Lord,* who is *worthy to be praised* : מהלל אקרא יהוה.] Rather (I think) I WILL CALL UPON THE LORD with PRAISE.

V. 4. *The Sorrows of Death compassed me* : אפפוני חבלי מות] In the parallel Place we read משברי מות — THE WAVES OF DEATH &c. which seems to have been the original Lection ; because it answers better to נחלי, *Floods,* in the next Hemistic ; and because חבלי occurs immediately after. This Verb signifying, *to compass about,* or *to attack with Violence and Terror,* seems much more applicable to *Waves* than *Sorrows.* See Taylor.

V. 5.

V. 5. *The Sorrows of Hell compaſſed me about*; — [הבלי שאול סבבוני]
Rather --- THE CORDS (or BANDAGES) OF THE GRAVE INCLO-
SED, or GIRT ME IN. הבלי is rendered *Cords* in the Margin, which
Senſe it bears with reference to *Nets* or *Snares* in ſeveral Places, ſee
Pſ. CXL. 5. Job. XVIII. 10. Prov. V. 22. And, to avoid the Repeti-
tion of *compaſſed* in two contiguous Verſes, where the Hebrew uſes two
diſtinct Words, I vary the Expreſſion.

V. 6. — *and my Cry came before him*, even *into his Ears*. ושועתי
[לפניו תבא באזניו] Rather — AND MY CRY TO HIM ENTERED
INTO HIS EARS: for לפניו is here a pleonaſtic Form for the Dative
לו. See Nold. 13. In the parallel Place this and the next Word תבא
have been omitted through Negligence.

V. 7. — *the Foundations of the Hills* — [מוסרי הרים] In the parallel
Place we read — מוסרות השמים — *The Foundations of the Heavens*:
but this appears to be the true Reading, when compared with the
Verſions in both Places.

V. 10. — *yea, he did fly upon the Wings of the Wind*. וירא על כנפי
[רוח:] Inſtead of וירא we have in the parallel Place וירא — *and he
was ſeen*. But the Reading in this Place appears to be the true one;
becauſe it is more immediately connected with the Context, and more
countenanced by the Verſions.

V. 11. *He made Darkneſs his ſecret Place*; — [ישת חשך סתרו] The
parallel Place is very corrupt; for סתרו is there omitted; סכתו is written סכו, and inſtead of השכת you find הישרת, a Word which exiſts
only there. The Hemiſtics do not ſeem to be rightly divided in our
Verſion, for סביבותיו belongs to the firſt; which I would thus render
--- HE MADE HIS COVERT DARK ROUND ABOUT HIM.

—— *his Pavilion round about him* were *dark Waters*, and *thick
Clouds of the Skies*. [סכתו חשכת כים עבי שהקים:] Thus — HIS
PAVILION DARK WATERS, THE THICK CLOUDS OF THE SKIES.
For the latter Clauſe is not a diſtinct Idea; but is in Appoſition, or
exegetical.

V. 12. *At the Brightneſs that was before him his thick Clouds paſſed*,
Hail-ſtones *and Coals of Fire* [מנגה נגדו עביו עברו — ברד וגחלי אש:]
The parallel Place is ſimply thus --- THROUGH THE BRIGHTNESS
THAT WAS BEFORE HIM WERE COALS OF FIRE KINDLED;
which

which is doubtlefs clearer : but as the Hemiftics are deficient by the Omiffion of the Words עבֿיו עבֿרו, I would retain them, and adopt the other Reading, *viz.* — בערו גחלי אש — and thus render the Verfe in both Places — AT THE BRIGHTNESS BEFORE HIM HIS BLACK CLOUDS SWEPT ALONG ; BOLTS OF FIRE WERE KIND- LED. For the Verb עבֿר implies *a conftant progreffive Motion without ftopping*, which does not feem fufficiently expreffed by the Word *paffed :* and as רשף is fometimes rendered *Coals*, and fometimes *Thunderbolts*, why may not the fame be done by נחל here, and Pf. CXL. 10 ?

V. 13. — *and the Higheft gave his Voice*, ועליון יתן קולו] Rather --- PUT FORTH &c.

—— *Hail-*ftones *and Coals of Fire.* ברד ונחלי אש :] Thefe Words feem to have been copied by Miftake from the preceding Verfe : for they are, at beft, but redundant : they are not found in the parallel Place ; and the LXX, Æthiopic, and Arabic, omit them.

V. 21. — *and have not wickedly departed from my God.* ולא רשעתי מאלהי :] Rather — AND HAVE NOT ACTED WICKEDLY AGAINST MY GOD. For רשע never fignifies *to depart.* Our Tranflators feem to have been led into this Miftake, from not attending to the Force of the Prepofition. See Lev. IV. 2. Deut. XXXIII. 7. Jer. LI. 5. &c. The old Verfion is to the fame Effect.

V. 22. — *and did not put away his Statutes from me.* וחקתיו לא אסיר מני :] The parallel Place — וחקתיו לא אסור ממנה — ought to be corrected from this ; for there is in it a very great Solecifm.

V. 30. As for *God, his Way is perfect :* האל תמים דרכו] Rather --- GOD is PERFECT in HIS WAY.

V. 39. *Thou haft girded me* — ותאזרני] In Sam. ותזרני, the א is dropped by Negligence.

V. 42. — *I did caft them out as the Dirt in the Streets.* כטיט חוצות אריקם :] אריקם feems to be a Miftake for אדיקם, for דקק fignifies *to pound* as in a Mortar. In the parallel Place we have אדקם, but this alfo wants the י in the middle. And we alfo find there the Word ארקעם, which the Metre, as well as the Senfe, fhews to be redundant. 2 Sam. XXII. 43.

V. 43. — *a People* whom *I have not known shall serve me.* עם לא
ידעתי יעבדוני :] As in this Psalm of Thanksgiving the Future has been
throughout translated by the preterperfect, it should I think so continue here, and in the two following Verses; there being no Reason
for an Alteration.

V. 45. *The Strangers shall fade away :* בני נכר יבלו] Or ——
HAVE DECAYED : for the Root may be בלה, as well as נבל.
—— *and be afraid out of their close Places.* ויחרנו ממסגרותיהם :]
Rather --- AND HAVE BEEN AFRAID IN THEIR PRIVY CHAM-
BERS, (as in the old Version) or IN THEIR PLACES OF RETREAT.
In the parallel Place we read ויחגרו, the Letters being transposed : but
this Lection is preferable.

V. 47. It is *God that avengeth me, and subdueth the People under me.*
האל הנותן נקמות לי — וידבר עמים תחתי :] Rather — THE GOD
WHO HATH AVENGED ME, AND HATH SUBDUED THE PEOPLE
UNDER ME. This Verse seems put in Apposition to the latter Part of
the preceding one; at the End of which the Punctuation should be
altered.

V. 48. *He delivereth me from mine Enemies : yea, thou liftest me up
above those that rise up against me.* מפלטי מאיבי — אף מן קמי תרוממני]
Rather --- MY DELIVERER FROM MINE ENEMIES, SURELY
THOU WILT EXALT ME &c.

PSALM XIX.

V. 2. *Day unto Day uttereth Speech, and Night unto Night sheweth
Knowledge.* יום ליום יביע אמר — ולילה ללילה יהוה דעת :] That is,
" by observing and contemplating on the Heavens, whether by Day or
" by Night, the Wisdom of God, who made them, will become daily
" more manifest; each Day adding to the Instruction of the former."

V. 3. There is *no Speech or Language,* where *their Voice is not heard.*
אין אמר ואין דברים — בלי נשמע קולם :] Rather — Though they
have NO SPEECH NOR LANGUAGE, YET THEIR VOICE IS HEARD.
So Noldius, who gives this Sense to the Verse, and it is truly a sublime
one : for whether we consider the Heavens as the Seat of the Meteors,
whose awful Sound is often heard; or confine the Idea to their ad-
mirable

mirable Structure; which will draw forth Praise and Admiration from him that contemplates on them, the Thought is truly poetical.

V. 4. *Their Line is gone out through all the Earth*, בכל הארץ יצא קום] If קום is not a Mistake for קולם, it should, at least, have the Arabic Signification given to it, *viz.* THEIR SOUND; from قوّ, *To cry out :* thus all the ancient Versions, excepting the Chaldee, render the Word. What farther confirms this Sense is the Expression, *their Words*, in the next Hemistic.

V. 5. *Which is as a Bridegroom coming out of his Chamber*; and *rejoiceth as a strong Man to run a Race.* ישיש — מחפתו יצא כחתן והוא כגבור לרוץ ארח:] Rather —— HE GOETH FORTH AS A BRIDEGROOM OUT OF HIS CHAMBER; HE REJOICETH &c. Among the Jews it seems to have been customary on the Marriage Day for the Company, who were assembled on that Occasion, to receive the Bridegroom with Flambeaus, Songs, and other Demonstrations of Joy, when he brought forth the Bride towards Midnight. Matth. XXV. 6. The Comparison therefore of the Sun rejoicing to perform his daily Task, (conscious as it were of the Blessings he diffuses around him) to the Bridegroom is very apposite: neither is it less so, in respect to a tried Racer, who vain of former Victories, and elated with the Idea of being superior to his Antagonist, sets out with Exultation, and is received at the Goal with joyful Acclamations.

V. 8. *The Commandment of the Lord* is *pure, enlightening the Eyes.* מצות יהוה ברה מאירת עינים:] Rather — IS CLEAR, (PLAIN, or MANIFEST,) "so has it Power of teaching Men true Wisdom."

V. 9. *The Fear of the Lord* is *clean*; יראת יהוה טהורה] Rather — is PURE: "free from all baser Mixture of corrupt Affections," and when it is such, "it will assuredly stand the Test, and *endure for ever.*"

V. 12. *Who can understand his Errors?* — מי יבין שגיאות] This Word seems corruptly written for שגיות or שגיגות: see the Roots שגה and שגג.
—— *cleanse thou me from secret Faults.* מנסתרות נקני:] Rather — FROM DISGUISES; that is, *from false Appearances*, or *Hypocrisy.* See Job. XXIV. 15.

13. *Keep back thy Servant also from presumptuous Sins :* גם מזרים חשך עבדך] Rather — FROM THE PROUD, or PRESUMPTUOUS: which is the constant Signification of this Word.

O

—— and

—— *and I shall be innocent from the great Transgreſſion.* ותקיתי
[מפשע רב : Rather — AND I SHALL BE EXEMPTED FROM SIN-
NING GREATLY : for פשע ſeems to be the Gerund, as Iſa. LIX. 13.
and רב an Adverb.

PSALM XX.

V. 3. — *and accept thy Burnt-ſacrifice.* [ועולתך ידשנה : Our Verſion by Accident gives דשן its proper Signification in this Place ; for it
refers to the Margin for the received Senſes, viz. *turn to Aſhes,* or
make fat. But تشن ſignifies *to give,* and *to receive,* whence comes
تشن in Arabic, and داشن in Perſic, *a Gift, an Offering upon the Al-
tar.* דשנא in Chaldee, and بعس, in Syriac have the ſame Signification.

V. 6. —— *he will hear him from his holy Heaven, with the ſaving
Strength of his right Hand.* [יענהו משמי קדשו — בנבורות ישע ימינו :
Each of theſe Hemiſtics conveys a different Sentiment, and ought I
think to be thus diſtinguiſhed --- HE WILL HEAR HIM FROM HIS
HOLY HEAVEN ; HIS RIGHT HAND SAVETH WITH GREAT
STRENGTH.

V. 7. *Some* truſt *in Chariots, and ſome in Horſes : but we will remember the Name of the Lord our God.* — אלה ברכב ואלה בסוסים
[ואנחנו בשם יהוה אלהינו נזכיר : There is no Occaſion to ſupply a
different Verb in this Place from that which occurs here. נזכר affects
every Member of the Verſe ; which ought to be thus rendered ——
SOME are mindful of CHARIOTS ; AND SOME OF HORSES : BUT
WE WILL BE MINDFUL OF THE NAME OF THE LORD OUR
GOD : *i. e.* " think of them as the only Means of Safety. The Jews
" were not allowed to uſe either Chariots or Horſes ; but, inſtead of
" them, were to truſt in Jehovah for Aſſiſtance." Deut. XX. 1. The
ſame Word, נזכר, is uſed Pſ. XXII. 27. and ſhould alſo be rendered in
the ſame Senſe.

V. 9. *Save, Lord, let the King hear us when we call.* יהוה הושיעה
[המלך — יעננו ביום קראנו : Rather — LET JEHOVAH THE KING
SAVE ; LET HIM HEAR US WHEN WE CALL. The Diviſion of
the Hemiſtics points out this Senſe ; הושיעה may as well be the 3d. P.
pret. Hiph. as the 2d. Imp. with ה paragogic ; unleſs perhaps it be a
Miſtake for הושיענו, *let him ſave us.*

PSALM

Psalm XXI

V. 4. *He aſked Life of thee*, and *thou gaveſt* it *him*, even *Length of Days for ever and ever.* ‏חיים שאל ממך נתתה לו ארך ימים עולם ועד :‎] Rather --- HE ASKED LIFE OF THEE ; THOU GAVEST HIM LENGTH OF DAYS FOR EVER AND EVER.

V. 9. *Thou ſhalt make them as a fiery Oven in the Time of thine Anger : the Lord ſhall ſwallow them in his Wrath, and the Fire ſhall devour them.* ‏תשיתמו כתנור אש — לעת פניך — באפו יבלעם ותאכלם אש :‎] Rather, I think, thus — THOU, O LORD, SHALT MAKE THEM AS A FIERY OVEN IN THE TIME OF THINE ANGER : THE FIRE IN IT'S RAGE SHALL DEVOUR THEM AND CONSUME THEM.

V. 11. — *they imagined a miſchievous Device*, which *they are not able to perform.* ‏חשבו מזמה בל יוכלו :‎] The two laſt Words ought I think to be thus rendered — but THEY HAVE NOT PREVAILED, or HAVE NOT EFFECTED it : for the Verb ‏יכל‎ has this Senſe, Gen. XXX. 8. — XXXII. 25. &c.

V. 12. *Therefore ſhalt thou make them turn their back :* ‏כי תשיתמו שכם‎] The marginal Lection is — *Thou ſhalt ſet them as a Butt.* But the Words of the Text will not I think juſtify either Senſe ; for ‏שכם‎ is never uſed as a Verb, except when it ſignifies *to riſe early* ; and there is not the leaſt Foundation for tranſlating it *a Butt*, or Mark to ſhoot at. In the two Places where that Sentiment occurs, ‏למפגע‎ or ‏למטרה,‎ are the Words, which expreſs it : (See Job. VII. 20. and XVI. 12.) Words well known, and eaſily deduced from their kindred Root. I cannot therefore but think that the ‏י‎ in ‏שכם‎ has dropped out from between the ſecond and third Letter. In that Caſe, the Senſe would be — THEREFORE SHALT THOU MAKE THEM THORNS. See ‏שכים‎ and ‏משכת,‎ Numb. XXXIII. 55. Prov. XV. 19. &c. After the wicked *had been made as a fiery Oven, whom the Fire in its Rage would conſume* ; what can be more natural, or better connected, than to ſuppoſe a Continuation of the ſame Metaphor, by rendering the Word THORNS, as a Means to that End ? Thus Iſaiah — *Wickedneſs burneth as* FIRE *it ſhall devour the* BRIERS AND THORNS. IX. 18. *And the Light of Iſrael ſhall be for a* FIRE, *and the Holy One for a* FLAME ; *and it ſhall devour his* THORNS AND BRIERS. X. 17. *And the People ſhall be as the* BURNING OF LIME ; *as* THORNS *cut up ſhall they be* BURNT IN THE FIRE. XXXIII. 12.

PSALM

V. 12. — when *thou ſhalt make ready* thine Arrows *upon thy Strings against the Face of them.* : במיתריך תכונן על־פניהם [It is evident that *Arrows* are not mentioned in the Text; and this Senſe is ſuggeſted merely from the ſuppoſed Signification of במיתריך. But, if there be no Foundation for the Senſe given to שכ־ by our Verſion in the preceding Hemiſtic, this Senſe alſo of Arrows muſt be given up, as foreign to the Purpoſe. I therefore tranſlate this Clauſe thus — THOU SHALT PREPARE THY WITHES FOR THEM. יתרים has this Senſe Judg. XVI. 7, 8, 9. It has not indeed there the *Ilœmantic:* but this is well known not to be eſſential. The Verb כון is not unfrequently conſtrued with ב ; ſee Numb. XXIII. i, 29. &c. See alſo the Prepoſition על־, Noldius 23. and פני conſidered as an expletive, Gen. XXI. 19. Jer. XVII. 16. &c. This Interpretation adds great Weight to the Senſe given to שכם or שכים, by making it nearly ſynonymous to מיתר, viz. *Thorns* and *a Bundle of Twigs* ; both intended for the ſame Purpoſe, of lighting the Fire to heat the Oven, in order to conſume God's Enemies : Or, might not the כ in שכם have been a Corruption of ב, and then if מו from the End of the preceding Word be prefixed to this, it will furniſh a well known Word, *viz.* מושבם, THEIR ABODE, or *Reſidence?* which Senſe will alſo be very ſuitable to the Context, thus --- THEREFORE THOU WILT PLACE THEIR ABODE IN THE CORDS (or NETS) which THOU HAST PREPARED FOR THEM. See Pſ. CXL. 5. Thus, *thou broughteſt us into* THE NET denotes *bringing into Calamity,* as *plucking the Feet out of the Net* does Deliverance out of it. See Pſ. LXVI. 11. — XXV. 15. And the Word מושב ſeems alſo to denote not *a tranſient,* but a permanent, Calamity. See the Notes Pſ. XXII. 3. — XXIII. 6.

PSALM XXII.

V. 1. — *why art thou ſo far from helping me,* and from *the Words of my Roaring?* : רחוק מישועתי דברי שאגתי [Rather, I think — being FAR FROM MY SALVATION, I HAVE ROARED OUT MY COMPLAINT.

V. 2. — *and in the Night-Seaſon, I am not ſilent.* : ולילה ולא דומיה לו] Rather --- AND IN THE NIGHT SEASON TRULY I AM NOT SILENT. The ו has this Senſe, Numb. XXI. 8. וראה אתו וחי — *when he looketh upon it, he ſhall* SURELY *live.* So alſo Iſa. XLIV. 8.

V. 3.

V. 3. *But thou* art *holy*, O thou *that inhabitest the Praises of Israel.*
[ואתה קדוש יושב תהלות ישראל;] The whole is rather to be rendered as a folemn Invocation, thus — BUT, O THOU HOLY ONE THAT
INHABITEST THE BOASTED Places OF ISRAEL! the Word *Place*
being feldom expreffed in Hebrew Or, if we retain the Word *Praifes,*
it muft be underftood by a Metonymy for *the Places* where God received *the Praifes* of his People, for the Mercies immediately before commemorated. There is yet a third Senfe, in which God may be faid *to*
inhabit the Praifes of Ifrael. In our own Language *to dwell,* or *abide,*
befides their primary Senfe, are ufed in a fecondary one, to denote
Permanency, or long habitual Continuance; thus our Tongue,
Thoughts, Inclinations, and Defires are faid *to dwell* upon an Object,
when they are conftantly, or frequently, turned to, or engaged upon, it.
A Perfon is alfo faid *to dwell* and *refide* in the good Graces and Affections of another, when he enjoys them for a long Time without Interruption. Thus in Scripture we are faid *to abide* in the Love, Fear, and
Favour of God, *to dwell* in God, and God and his Word *to dwell* in
us. The Hebrew Word ישב, which is here rendered *inhabit,* with
others of the fame Import, admits of the like Signification; fee Gen.
XLIX. 24. Pf. LV. 19. — LXI. 7. &c. and fo do the Verbs οικεω, ενοι
κεω, and κατοικεω in the New Teftament; fee Rom. VIII. 17, 18, 20.
Col. III. 16. Eph. III. 17. Why then may not the Text before us be
likewife fo interpreted; and by *God's inhabiting,* or *dwelling in the*
Praifes of Ifrael, be underftood *his being the conftant Theme and Object*
of thofe Praifes?

V. 6. *But I* am *a Worm, and no Man:* — [ואנכי תולעת ולא איש —]
That is, "a Creature too mean and defpicable to merit Attention."
The Antithefis between the firft Perfon and the third is finely kept up
from V. 1. and fhould be attended to.

V. 8. *He trufted on the Lord,* that *he would deliver him:* — [גל אל
יהוה יפלטהו] Rather — HE REJOICED IN THE LORD; LET HIM
DELIVER HIM: for גל is the Preter of גול *to rejoice,* not of גלל *to*
roll, as our Verfion makes it. And that this is the Senfe is moreover
evident from the next Hemiftic, where the fame Words are repeated
in an inverfe Order, viz. *let Him deliver him, feeing he delighted in*
Him: as Pf. XXVII. 14. or as Virgil, *Ecl.* VIII. 49, 50.

Crudelis mater magis, an puer improbus ille?
Improbus ille puer, crudelis tu quoque, mater:

V. 9.

V. 9. — *thou didst make me hope*, when I was *upon my Mother's Breasts.* : מבטיחי על שדי אמי] Simply thus — THOU DIDST MAKE ME HOPE UPON MY MOTHER'S BREASTS.

V. 12. *Many Bulls have compassed me: strong Bulls of Bashan have beset me round.* : סבבוני פרים רבים — אבירי בשן כתרוני] It seems rather unnecessary to repeat the Word *Bulls* in the last Clause: THE MIGHTY ONES would be sufficiently understood. Ezekiel uses the same Phrase to point out *the Princes of the Earth.* XXXIX. 18.

V. 14. — *all my Bones are out of Joint: my Heart is like melted Wax:*] Thus Ovid,

> *Sic mea perpetuis liquefiunt .pectora curis,*
> *Ignibus admotis ut nova cera folet.*

V. 17. — *they look* and *stare upon me.* : המה יביטו יראו בי] The ו before יראו has doubtless dropped out of the Text on account of the preceding Word ending with that Letter; for it is found in all the old Versions.

V. 20. — *my Darling from the Power of the Dog.* : מיד כלב יחידתי] The Word יחידתי comes from the Verb יחד, which is nearly related to אחד, *one*, and from thence borrows it's Signification of being *isolated*, or *left alone, single, unsupported:* it should accordingly be here translated *my solitary* or *friendless* one, (*Soul* being mentioned in the preceding Hemistic, to which this Word refers by an Hendyadis) in Allusion to what the Psalmist had said of his *being forsaken of God*, (V. 1.) and of *there being no Help*, (V. 11.) This Word must be taken in the same Sense, Pf. XXV. 16. XXXV. 17.

V. 21. —— *for thou hast heard me from the Horns of the Unicorns.* : ומקרני רמים עניתני] Rather --- YEA THOU HAST DELIVERED ME FROM THE HORNS OF THE MIGHTY ONES. For רמים, with the Difference of the Massoretic Points only, is thus used in several Places, 2 Sam. XXII. 28. Job. XXI. 22. &c. The Word signifying *an Unicorn* is constantly written ראם, and once רים. As for *Horns*, they are the Symbols of *Strength*, and figuratively attributed to *Men*, Pf. LXXV. 10. &c. The Change of Mood, from the Imperative to the Indicative, deserves Notice; as it seems not to be without Design, especially as it happens in the very Place where the Transition is made from the Sufferer's Complaint, to the Song of Praise and Triumph for Mercies received

received and expected. Inftead therefore of the caufal Particle, *for*, the ו is to be rendered, *yea*, or *indeed*, to mark out the Tranfition more precifely: it is fo ufed, Ifa. XLIV. 8. This Paffage, if applied to Chrift, muft denote his Refcue from the Power *of Death and the Grave*, which had haughtily tyrannifed over all Mankind.

V. 26. — *they fhall praife the Lord that feek him*; [יהללו יהוה דרשיו] Rather --- THEY SHALL PRAISE THE LORD, SEEKING HIM.

——— *your Heart fhall live for ever.* [יחי לבבכם לעד]. All the ancient Verfions read here, as the Context requires, לבבם THEIR HEART &c.

V. 29. *All they that be fat upon Earth fhall eat and worfhip:* [אכלו וישתחוו כל דשני ארץ] As the Phrafe *eating the Word of God* is ufed for digefting and underftanding it, (fee Jer. XV. 10. and Pf. XXXVII. 3.) ought not this Place to be rendered — ALL THE FAT ONES OF THE EARTH SHALL UNDERSTAND AND WORSHIP? V. 26. is alfo to be thus underftood. How elfe this can be applicable to the Calling *of the chief among all Nations* to the Gofpel of Chrift, I do not underftand.

——— *all they that go down to the Duft fhall worfhip before him:* — [לפניו יכרעו כל יורדי עפר] Rather — ALL THE DESCENDANTS OF THE DUST &c. By which Phrafe may be meant *all Mankind* fprung from Adam, to whom it was faid, DUST *thou art*; Gen. III. 9. So likewife, *All are of* THE DUST. Eccl. III. 20. After the Call of the *meek and poor* had been noticed, V. 26. then follows --- *All the Ends of the World fhall be mindful, and turn unto the Lord; and all the Families of the Nations fhall worfhip before Him.* In like manner to denote the Univerfality of Chrift's Kingdom, when *the rich* are here particularly brought into View, it follows immediately, *yea all the Sons of Adam*, defcribed by their Origin, perhaps on Purpofe to check the Pride of the wealthy, and to fhew them their Vanity without the Help of their Redeemer. Or, if we read ירדי, the Senfe will be --- ALL THE GOVERNOURS OF THE EARTH &c. and this Hemiftic will be exegetical of the foregoing one: the Prophecy may then alfo be confi-dered as having had its Completion, when Sovereigns became nurfing Fathers and nurfing Mothers to the Church of Chrift.

——— *and none can keep alive his own Soul.* [ונפשו לא חיה] The plain and natural Senfe of thefe Words as we now read them is —— *and his Soul fhall not live.* But of whofe Soul is this faid? Nay, can it be faid of any Soul? But admitting that the Verb were in *Pihel*, in which Conjugation as well as in *Hiphil*, it fignifies *to quicken*, or *pre-ferve*

ferve alive, yet would this Obfervation be unconnected with the general Scope of the Pfalm. But that the Text is here corrupt, we have almoft all poffible Evidence to prove; for the Syriac, Arabic, Ethiopic, Vulgate, LXX, Aquila, Symmachus, Theodotion, the fifth, fixth, and feventh Greek Verfions of Origen's Hexapla, all read thus ——— ונפשי לו חיה ——— MY SOUL ALSO SHALL LIVE UNTO HIM: viz. *unto His Glory and Service*: in the fame Senfe as Rom. XIV. 8. 2 Cor. V. 15. which makes an excellent Senfe, and may be confidered as an *Epiphonema*, or as a Summary of the Bleffings which the Pfalmift, with other faithful, was affured of receiving through the Merits of Chrift.

V. 30. — *it fhall be accounted to the Lord for a Generation.* יספר לאדני לדור] Rather — IT SHALL BE ACCOUNTED THE LORD'S FOR THE GENERATIONS TO COME. I connect here יבא or יבוא from the following Verfe according to all the ancient Verfions, except the Syriac.

V. 31. *They fhall come, and fhall declare his Righteoufnefs unto a People that fhall be born, that he hath done* this. — (יבא) ויגידו צדקתו לעם נילד כי עשה] Rather — AND THEY SHALL DECLARE HIS RIGHTEOUSNESS, THAT HE HATH WROUGHT, UNTO A PEOPLE THAT SHALL BE BORN.

PSALM XXIII.

V. 6. — *and I will dwell in the Houfe of the Lord for ever.* ישבתי בבית יהוה לארך ימים:] Rather — FOR A LONG SEASON, with the old Verfion.

PSALM XXIV.

V. 6. *This is the Generation of them that feek him, that feek thy Face, O Jacob.* זה דור דרשו --- מבקשי פניך יעקב:] I here read with the Maffora דרשו: but detach the ו to join it to מבקשי: and, with the LXX, Vulgate, Syriac, Arabic, and Ethiopic Verfions, fupply אלהי before יעקב. The Verfe may then be thus rendered --- THIS IS THE GENERATION OF THEM THAT SEEK, EVEN OF THEM THAT DESIRE, THY COUNTENANCE, O GOD OF JACOB.

PSALM

PSALM XXV.

V. 8. — *therefore will be teach Sinners in the Way.* עַל כֵּן יוֹרֶה הַטָּאִים בַּדֶּרֶךְ :] Rather — THEREFORE WILL HE TEACH SIN-NERS THE WAY; or INSTRUCT SINNERS IN THE WAY, viz. *of Righteousness.*

V. 11. *For thy Name's Sake, O Lord, pardon mine Iniquity.* לְמַעַן שִׁמְךָ יהוה וְסָלַחְתָּ לַעֲוֹנִי] The ו before סָלַחְתָּ seems to indicate that some Verb is wanting before it; or it ought to be rendered, I PRAY THEE; see Noldius, Art. 44.

PSALM XXVI.

V. 7. *That I may publish with the Voice of Thanksgiving,* לְשַׁמִּעַ בְּקוֹל תּוֹדָה] Rather — THAT I MAY HEAR THE VOICE OF THANKS-GIVING : for לִשְׁמֹעַ is in *Kal*, and is construed with the Preposition בְ.

PSALM XXVII.

V. 2. — *and my Foes came upon me to eat up my Flesh;*] So Xeno-phon speaking of Enemies says, ἁμᾶς καταφαγειν, *Hellen.* L. III. and ἁμον εσθιειν, *Anab.* L. IV. And Homer, Iliad IV. v. 34.

Ει δε συ γ', εισελθουσα πυλας και τειχεα μακρα,
Ωμον βεβρωθοις Πριαμον, Πριαμοιο τε παιδας,
Αλλους τε Τρωας, τοτε κεν χολον εξακεσαιο.

V. 7. *Hear, Lord, when I cry with my Voice :* שְׁמַע יהוה קוֹלִי אֶקְרָא] Rather --- HEAR MY VOICE, O LORD, when I CRY.

V. 8. *When thou saidst, Seek ye my Face : my Heart said unto thee, Thy Face, Lord, will I seek.* לְךָ אָמַר לִבִּי בַּקְּשׁוּ פָנַי — אֶת פָּנֶיךָ יהוה אֲבַקֵּשׁ :] Rather, I think thus — MY HEART SAID UNTO THEE, MY FACE WILL SEEK thee; LORD I WILL SEEK THY FACE. The ךָ seems to be omitted after בַּקְּשׁוּ. The Vulgate, LXX, Arabic, &c. read so.

V. 13. *I had fainted, unless I had believed* —— לוּלֵא הֶאֱמַנְתִּי] This Place is generally considered as eliptical, or as an *Aposiopesis:* but I

P

think

think it may not improperly be joined to the preceding Verse thus —
for false Witnesses would have risen up against me — UNLESS I HAD
BELIEVED. Or may not לולא be a Mistake for לוא, in this Sense —
Oh that I MIGHT BELIEVE TO SEE —! What makes this Conjecture
the more probable is that there is no such Particle known in Hebrew
as לולא.

V. 14. *Wait on the Lord: be of good Courage, and he shall strengthen*
thine Heart : wait, I say, on the Lord. קוה אל יהוה הזק — ויאמץ
לבך וקוה אל יהוה:] This does not seem to be precisely the same
Figure as we had Pf. XXII. 8. for here we have an *Enallage* of Moods
from the Imperative to the Future, thus — WAIT ON THE LORD ;
BE OF GOOD COURAGE : AND HE WILL STRENGTHEN THINE
HEART, AND IT WILL WAIT ON THE LORD ; *i. e.* earnestly
endeavour, and God will prosper thine Endeavours. Virg. Æn. V. 231.
—— *possunt, quia posse videntur.*

PSALM XXVIII.

V. 1. *Unto thee will I cry, O Lord my Rock, be not silent to me :* —
אליך יהוה אקרא — צורי אל תחרש ממני] Rather — UNTO THEE, O
LORD, WILL I CRY ; O MY ROCK BE NOT DEAF UNTO ME. See
Pf. V. 2.

V. 8. *The Lord is their Strength,* — יהוה עז למו] There is no
Antecedent to the Pronoun *their* (or *his,* as in the Margin) in the Text.
Our old Version will have *David's Soldiers* to be here meant : but it
is probable that, instead of למו, we ought to read לאמו, or לעמו, as in
the next Verse, and as all the ancient Versions, except the Chaldee, read
--- THE LORD IS THE STRENGTH OF HIS PEOPLE : than which
no Sense can better suit this Place.

PSALM XXIX.

V. 1. *Give unto the Lord, O ye mighty,* — הבו ליהוה בני אלים] All
the ancient Versions, the Chaldee excepted, read here אילים, RAMS,
which have no Impropriety here ; for as *the chief of the Flock* they
might by an apt Figure be put for *the Princes* of the People. Accordingly in Daniel's Vision (VIII. 20.) *the Ram with two Horns* is interpreted to be *the Kings of Media and Persia.*

V. 2.

V. 2. — *worſhip the Lord in the Beauty of Holineſs.* השתחוו ליהוה בהדרת קדש:] Rather — WITH DECENT HOLINESS, or HOLY HONOUR; the Common Prayer Verſion reads *with holy Worſhip.*

V. 9. *The Voice of the Lord maketh the Hinds to calve, and diſcovereth the Foreſts:* קול יהוה יחולל אילות — ויחשף יערות] Bochart aſſerts from this Text, that Thunder is of great Service to Hinds in bringing forth their young, as they are naturally timorous, and have great Difficulty in calving: but ſupports his Aſſertion by no other Authority. However, though the Fact were allowed, I ſee no Connection between the calving of Hinds, and making bare the Trees of a Foreſt. I would therefore render both the Members of this Sentence thus --- THE VOICE OF THE LORD SHAKETH THE OAKS, AND MAKETH BARE THE FORESTS. איל ſignifies *an Oak,* Iſa. LVII. 5. חלל has this Senſe, Verſe 8. and חשף, Iſa. LII. 10. and Joel. I. 7.

—— *and in his Temple doth every one ſpeak* of his *Glory.* ובהיכלו כלו אמר כבוד:] This Obſervation ſeems here out of Place. היכל ſignifies indeed *a Temple:* but it is alſo a Verb: בהיכלו may be the Infinitive *Hiphil,* from יכל; (which, like היטיב, does not change its firſt Radical into ו in that Conjugation) with the Prepoſition and Affix. The Senſe ariſing from this Conſtruction is — AND BY THE POWER IT HATH EVERY WHIT OF IT UTTERETH GLORY: or BY IT'S POWER IT ALTOGETHER PROCLAIMETH GLORY; *viz.* the Glory of its Author. See the Margin: and alſo this very Word, in this Voice and Form, and exactly in this Senſe, Numb. XXII. 38. There needs no Comment to ſhew how this is applicable to *Thunder,* or connected with the Context. See the like beautiful Deſcription, Job. XXXVI. and XXXVII.

PSALM XXX.

V. 5. *For his Anger* endureth but *a Moment; in his Favour* is *Life.* כי רגע באפו — חיים ברצונו] Rather — FOR HE SHAKETH WITH VIOLENCE (or BREAKETH DOWN) IN HIS ANGER; but IN HIS FAVOUR &c. See רגע thus uſed, Job. VII. 5. XXVI. 12. By this Interpretation the latter Part of the Verſe will more exactly correſpond with this Part.

V. 7. *Lord, by thy Favour thou haſt made my Mountain to ſtand ſtrong:* —— יהוה ברצונך העמדתה להררי עז] The LXX, Syriac, Vulgate, Arabic, and Ethiopic Verſions read here להדרי; for they all

render

render to this Effect --- Lord by thy Favour thou hast appointed (or added) Strength to my Glory; which seems to be the true Reading.

Psalm XXXI.

V. 9. — *mine Eye is confumed with Grief, yea, my Soul and my Belly.* עשׁשׁה בכעס עיני נפשׁי ובטני׃] Rather — mine Eye, my Soul and my Body are consumed with Grief : all the Nouns being in the Singular may admit of a Verb in that Number. Thus is בטן rendered, Deut. XXVIII. 4, 11, 18, 53. XXX. 9. Job. XIX. 17. &c.

V. 11. *I was a Reproach among all mine Enemies, but efpecially among my Neighbours, and a Fear to mine Acquaintance :* מכל צוררי הייתי הרפה — ולשׁכני מאד ופחד לידעי׃] Rather —— I was a Reproach above all mine Enemies, even to my Neighbours exceedingly, and a Terror to those that knew me.

V. 13. *For I have heard the Slander of many: Fear was on every Side :* כי שׁמעתי דבת רבים מגור מסביב] Rather—when I heard the Slander of the mighty, Fear &c.

V. 20. *Thou fhalt hide them in the Secret of thy Prefence from the Pride of Man :* תסתירם בסתר פניך מרכסי אישׁ] Rather — Thou shalt hide them under the Covert of thy Presence from the Insults (or Vexations) of Men. סתר fignifies *a Covert*, Ifa. IV. 6. XVI. 4. &c. and the Senfe of the Verb רכס is *to bind*, and *to treat roughly*.

Psalm XXXII.

V. 3. *When I kept Silence my Bones waxed old* — כי החרשׁתי בלו עצמי] Rather — were consumed: as Pf. XLIX. 14. Job. XIII. 28.

V. 8. *I will inftruct thee, and teach thee in the Way which thou fhalt go.*] The Words immediately preceding are addreffed to God ; and fo ought thefe by the general Rule of Interpretation, were it not for the Profaneneſs which would enfue. Our old Verſion has this Note, *viz.* " David promifeth to make the Reſt of God's Children " Partakers of the Benefits which he left &c." But I much doubt whether this be the Senfe. We have indeed many abrupt Tranfitions

from

from one Perſon to another in the poetical Books: but here there appears to be no Occaſion to ſuppoſe any Tranſition, if we only conſider this Verſe as a Part of *one of the Songs of Deliverance* juſt mentioned. See Job. XXXV. 10. In this Caſe God may be the Speaker with Propriety; and we need only prefix to this Verſe, as in innumerable other Places, the Word —— *ſaying.*

P s a l m XXXIV.

V. 5. — *and their Faces* —— ופניהם] Some Critics conſider the ו which begins this Hemiſtic as preſerving the regular Alphabetical Series of the Letters: but the ſecond Hemiſtic of ſeveral other Verſes in this Pſalm alſo begins with that Letter; beſides that the ה and ו, upon that Suppoſition, would have only each a Line, whereas all the other Letters have each two Lines, except the פ, which, beſides its due Number in its proper Place, has alſo two other Lines at the Cloſe of the Pſalm. Biſhop Hare thought that another Line beginning with ה immediately preceding this Hemiſtic was wanting, and another alſo ſubſequent to this beginning with ו: but does it not appear more probable that both theſe Lines belonged to ה, and that the whole Verſe beginning with ו has by ſome Accident been dropped out of the Text? becauſe thoſe are well connected; but immediately after there ſeems to be an *Hiatus.*

V. 6. *This poor Man cried* —— זה עני קרא] Rather — A Poor Man crieth. זה is not always demonſtrative; but is ſometimes uſed indefinitely, as 1 Sam. XVII. 12. it ſeems uſed here particularly on account of the Alphabetical Order.

V. 17. The righteous *cry, and the Lord heareth* ;— צעקו ויהוה שמע] Though this Verſe begins with the proper Letter, yet as there is a Nominative wanting to the Verb, and every one of the ancient Verſions read צדיקים, there can be no doubt that it ought to be reſtored to the Text. The Similarity of Letters in צעקו might occaſion the Loſs of צדיקים.

P s a l m XXXV.

V. 1. *Plead* my Cauſe, O Lord, *with them that ſtrive with me:* — ריבה יהוה את יריבי] This Hemiſtic would be rendered with more Preciſion thus --- Contend, O Lord, with them that contend

TEND WITH ME. The Context shews besides that there is here no Reference to Judicial Proceedings; but only to War.

V. 3. *Draw out also the Spear, and stop* the Way *against them that perfecute me :*——·רדפי לקראת וסגר חנית [והרק] Rather —— DRAW OUT ALSO THE SPEAR, AND STOP THE WAY OF MY PERSECU-TORS. For לקראת feems not to be an Adverb in this Place, but a Noun, as Exod. V. 20. 1 Sam. XVI. 4. or סגר may have the Chaldee Senfe, *viz.* DAGGER; thus --- DRAW OUT THE SWORD AND THE DAGGER AGAINST MY PERSECUTORS.

V. 7. *For without Caufe have they hid for me their Net* in *a Pit,* which *without Caufe they have digged for my Soul.* כי חנם טמנו לי ·לנפשי הפרו חנם רשתם — שחת [שחת] The Words שחת and רשתם cannot I think have been placed originally in the Order in which they now ftand; for it is impoffible to make Senfe of them thus placed by the plain Rules of Conftruction: whereas if we tranfpofe them, the Syntax is plain, and the Senfe excellent: thus —— FOR WITHOUT CAUSE HAVE THEY HID FOR ME THEIR NET; WITHOUT CAUSE HAVE THEY DIGGED A PIT FOR MY LIFE. Whereas as we now read them they muft be conftrued thus —— *For without Caufe have they hid for me a Pit; without Caufe have they digged for me their Net.*

V. 12. *They rewarded me evil for good,* to *the fpoiling of my Soul.* ·לנפשי שכול טובה תחת רעה [ישלמוני] I confider שכול as com-pounded of the Affix Particle and the Verb כול *to take,* and render the latter Hemiftic thus --- IN ORDER TO TAKE AWAY MY LIFE. See the Particle thus ufed, Ecc. II. 24. III. 14. and the fame Conftruc-tion in regard to ל, Gen. I. 10. This latter Claufe feems to refer to the Charges brought againft the Pfalmift by the falfe Witneffes, men-tioned immediately before the firft of thefe Hemiftics, which I confi-der as a *Parenthefis.*

V. 13. —*and my Prayer returned into mine own Bofom.* ותפלתי על חיקי תשוב [This *Hebraifm* is hardly intelligible to an Englifh Rea-der. Would it not be beft therefore to place it in the Margin, and render the Text thus --- AND I PRAYED OFTEN FROM MY HEART? *viz.* in their Behalf; which is clearly the Meaning of the Expreffion.

V. 14.

V. 14. — *I bowed down heavily, as one that mourneth* for his *Mo-ther*. :כאבל אם קדר שחותי] Rather, with the old Verfion — I BOWED DOWN MOURNING, AS ONE BEWAILING A MOTHER.

V. 15. — *they did tear* me, *and ceafed not.* :קרעו ולא דמו] Ra-ther --- THEY USED SLANDER, AND WOULD NOT BE SILENT. For though קרע properly fignifies *to tear a Thing to Pieces*, yet it is applicable figuratively to the tearing of another's Reputation.

V. 23. *Stir up thyfelf, and awake to my Judgment*, even *unto my Caufe, my God and my Lord.* העירה והקיצה למשפטי — אלהי ואדני לריבי:] Thefe Words could not poffibly, I think, have flood originally in the Order in which they now ftand, on account of the Hyperbaton. It is probable that והקיצה and אלהי have changed Places: in which Cafe the Senfe would be clear, and the Conftruction eafy, thus — STIR UP THYSELF, O GOD, TO MY JUDGMENT; AND AWAKE IN-DEED, O MY LORD, TO MY CAUSE.

V. 25. *Let them not fay in their Hearts, Ah, fo would we have it :* אל יאמרו בלבם האח נפשנו] In the Margin we read, *Ah, ah, our Soul!* which is the literal Signification of the Words : but, I think, they would be more properly rendered thus, AH, THIS IS OUR HEART's DESIRE, *q. d.* "Let them not exult as having gotten their Will "upon me." For נפש is fometimes ufed to fignify *the Defire of the Soul*, as Exod. XV. 9. Pf. XXVII. 12. Hab. II. 5. But notwithfland-ing this it feems to me more probable that the true Reading of נפשנו was נפשחנו, the 1 Perfon plural of the Future *Kal*, from the Verb פשח, with the affix Pronoun, and ought to be rendered — AH! LET US TEAR HIM IN PIECES; which Senfe would well correfpond with בלעגוהו, WE HAVE SWALLOWED HIM UP, in the next Hemiftic. See this Word thus ufed, Lam. III. 11.

PSALM XXXVI.

V. 1. *The Tranfgreffion of the wicked faith within my Heart ;* ——— נאם פשע לרשע בקרב לבי] All the ancient Verfions, except the Targum, read לבו: with them I would therefore render ——— THE TRANSGRESSOR SAITH IN HIS HEART (literally, *in the Bofom of his Heart*) THAT HE WILL DO EVIL. פשע is here confidered as the Participle, and לרשע as the Infinitive. Or perhaps it might be better

to

to render לרשע adverbially, thus—THE TRANSGRESSOR SPEAKETH WICKEDLY IN THE BOTTOM OF HIS HEART; by which is meant "that the Thoughts and Imaginations of his Heart are evil." This agrees well with what follows in the next Hemistic; as if he had said—"and no wonder, *he is not actuated by the Fear of God*," the only Principle of right Conduct.

V. 2. *For he flattereth himself in his own Eyes, until his Iniquity be found to be hateful.* כי החליק אליו בעיניו — למצא עונו לשנא :] Rather --- YET HE FLATTERETH HIMSELF IN HIS OWN EYES both WITH DISCERNING INIQUITY, AND WITH ABHORRING IT: *i. e.* "he imposes upon himself with a false Notion of the Rectitude "both of his Understanding and Will." I read למצא עון ולשנא. The Sentence, which immediately follows, seems to confirm the Sense here given, viz. *The Words of his Mouth are Iniquity and Deceit;* which is a sure Sign of a depraved Heart, and Want of right Principle. For our Saviour observes, that *out of the Abundance of the Heart the Mouth speaketh.* Matth. XII. 34.

V. 3. — *he hath left off to be wise,* and *to do good.* חדל להשכיל להיטיב :] Rather, I think — HE HATH CEASED TO JUDGE WISELY and TO DO WELL: by which the Sentiment of the second Verse is confirmed, namely, that his Notions of himself were but Self-Flattery.

V. 5. *Thy Mercy, O Lord, is in the Heavens;* and *thy Faithfulness* reacheth *unto the Clouds.* יהוה בהשמים חסדך — אמונתך עד שהקים :] Rather --- THY MERCY, O LORD, is LIKE THE HEAVENS; and THY FAITHFULNESS AS THE CLOUDS. If the ב in בהשמים is not an Error for כ, see a similar Construction of the same Letter, Isa. XLVIII. 10. Pf. XLII. 10. See also עד thus used, Nah. I. 10. 1 Chron. IV. 27. The next Verse confirms this Sense.

V. 12. *There are the workers of Iniquity fallen: they are cast down, and shall not be able to rise.* שם נפלו פעלי און — דחו ולא יכלו קום :] Rather --- THEN SHALL THE WORKERS OF INIQUITY FALL: THEY SHALL BE CAST DOWN, AND SHALL NOT BE ABLE TO RISE. As no *Place* is mentioned to which *there* can be referred, I make שם a Particle of *Inference*, as Job. XXXV. 12. Pf. XIV. 5. or make it relate to *Time*, as Job XXIII. 7. Ecc. III. 17. And though two of the Verbs be in the Preter, yet the Context seems to declare for the Future.

PSALM

PSALM XXXVII.

V. 3. — *fo fhalt thou dwell in the Land, and verily thou fhalt be fed.*
[שכן ארץ ורעה אמונה:] Rather by the Imperative — DWELL THOU
IN THE LAND, AND FEED ON TRUTH: that is, "enjoy prefent
"Bleffings, and rely for future on the God of Truth:" this Senfe the
next Verfes indicate. See Pf. XXII. 29. A fimilar Phrafe occurs Jer.
XV. 16. viz. *I did eat thy Words.* So Pf. XLII. 2. *my Soul thirfteth
for God:* and Matt. V. 6.

V. 5. *Commit thy Way unto the Lord: truft thou alfo in him, and he
fhall bring it to pafs.* [גול על יהוה דרכך—ובטה עליו והוא יעשה:]
As *it* has no Antecedent in our Verfion, ought not the laft Hemiftic to
be thus rendered --- TRUST THOU ALSO IN HIM, AND HE WILL
PREPARE it; viz. *thy Way?* See V. 23. and עשה thus ufed, Ezek.
XLV. 22. XLVI. 2.

V. 13. *The Lord fhall laugh at him:* —— [אדני ישחק לו] Here is manifeftly a Word wanted in the Text; for this is an Alphabetical Pfalm,
and the Order of the Letters points out that it muft have begun with
a ז. Now I think no Word is fo probable as the Adverb זה, NOW.
See this Particle thus ufed, Numb. XIV. 22. Judg. XVI. 15. All the ancient Verfions, excepting the Chaldee, render it by the Conjunction
But: yet I cannot find that it is ever fo ufed.

V. 17. *For the Arms of the wicked fhall be broken:*] This Verfe
begins in the Hebrew with a כ, and the next with a י; whence it may
be concluded that they have by fome Accident changed Places. If the
Verfes were tranfpofed accordingly, the Senfe would be equally good;
particularly if כי were rendered TRULY, as Jer. XXII. 22. or SURELY,
as Numb. XXII. 33.

V. 20. — *and the Enemies of the Lord fhall be as the Fat of Lambs:*
[ואיבי יהוה כיקר כרים] As יקר cannot fignify *Fat*, or make any other
convenient Senfe; *Qu.* ought not we to read יקד, and render — AND
THE ENEMIES OF THE LORD fhall be AS THE BURNING OF
LAMBS? *i. e.* "as Lambs offered up for a Burnt Offering." Ifaiah
ufes יקד in the fame Senfe, X. 16.

—— *they fhall confume; into Smoke fhell they confume away.* כלו
[בעשן כלו:] Rather — INTO SMOKE SHALL THEY ALL CONSUME
AWAY. כלו is here ufed as Exod. XIV. 7. Numb XXIII. 13 &c.

Q

V. 27.

V. 27. — *and dwell for evermore.* : וְשֹׁכֵן לְעוֹלָם] AND BE HAPPY FOR EVERMORE : as Pſ. LV. 6. or V. 3. & 29.

V. 28. —— *they are preſerved for ever* : לְעוֹלָם נִשְׁמָרוּ] Here a Word is wanting to complete the Hemiſtic ; and the Alphabetical Order of the Letters in the Pſalm ſhews that it is a Word beginning with ע. It is highly probable that עֲנָוִים is the Word, than which no other Word could be more ſuitable to the Context. It might therefore I think be ſafely reſtored to the Text, thus — THE MEEK (or POOR) ARE PRESERVED FOR EVER : and here a new Verſe ought to begin.

V. 29. *The righteous ſhall inherit the Land,*] Here we ſeem to have another Tranſpoſition ; for this Verſe begins with the Letter צ, and the next with פ, contrary to their conſtant Order : But it will be obſerved, that צ belongs to the ſecond Couplet of the reſtored ע, (in which it is immaterial what Letter is put firſt) and that the 32d. Verſe begins, as it ought, with צ

V. 31. *The Law of his God is in his Heart : none of his Steps ſhall ſlide.*] This latter Hemiſtic — לֹא תִמְעַד אֲשֻׁרָיו — ought I think to be rendered --- IT SHALL NOT SHAKE HIS STEPS. See Pſ. LXIX. 23.

V. 35. *I have ſeen the wicked in great Power :* — רָאִיתִי רָשָׁע עָרִיץ] Rather --- FORMIDABLE.

V. 38. — *the End of the wicked ſhall be cut off.* אַחֲרִית רְשָׁעִים נִכְרָתָה :] Rather, I think — THE POSTERITY &c. thus אַחֲרִית is rendered, Pſ. CIX. 13. Amos IV. 2.

V. 39. *But the Salvation* —— וּתְשׁוּעַת] The copulative Particle is certainly redundant here, as it deſtroys the Alphabetical Order ; and it is not acknowledged by the Syriac or Arabic Verſions.

PSALM XXXVIII.

V. 2, 3. *For thine Arrows ſtick faſt in me :* — *neither is there any Reſt in my Bones.*] So Ovid,

> *Non mea ſunt ſumma leviter diſtricta ſagitta*
> *Pectora, deſcendit vulnus ad oſſa meum.*

V. 4. *For mine Iniquities are gone over mine Head :* כִּי עֲוֹנֹתַי עָבְרוּ רֹאשִׁי] Rather — FOR MINE INIQUITIES ARE COME UPON MINE HEAD :

HEAD: for the Context requires this Sense, and עבר is so used, Numb. V. 14. &c.

V. 7. *For my Loins are filled with a lothsome* Disease: כי כסלי מלאו נקלה] As נקלה never signifies elsewhere *lothsome*, and there is nothing in the Text to express *Disease*, I would render this Hemistic thus --- FOR MY FLANKS ARE SATIATED WITH PURGING. The Word כסל is in every other Place rendered FLANKS, which, in Men, are *the lower Parts of the Belly*. The Verb מלא has this Sense, Eccl. I. 8. VI. 7. &c. And there being no Root in Hebrew from which נקלה can be derived, I give it the same Sense as بلل, viz. *Purgatio*, from بلّ, *Purgavit*.

V. 10. *My Heart panteth; my Strength faileth me: as for the Light of mine Eyes, it is also gone from me.* לבי סחרחר עזבני כחי — ואור עיני גם הם אין אתי:] Rather —— MY HEART PANTETH: MY STRENGTH FAILETH ME; SO DOTH THE LIGHT OF MINE EYES; FOR I HAVE NO USE OF THEM. It is evident that הם, being a a Plural Pronoun, cannot agree with אור *Light*; but the Verb with it's Affix עזבני, which is in the first Hemistic, ought to be understood in the first Clause of the second Hemistic after ואור עיני; for which Reason I add the auxiliary Verb *doth* for the Sake of Perspicuity, giving the copulative Particle the Sense it has, 2 Kings XXV. 21. Ps. CVI. 32. And as the Idiom in the last Clause could not admit of a literal Version (signifying *for they* are *not with me*) I give it's general Sense.

V. 11. *My Lovers and my Friends* &c. "אהבי ורעי וגו] Rather — MY FRIENDS AND MY COMPANIONS --- as Zech. XIII. 6.

V. 16. *For I said*, Hear me, *lest* otherwise *they should rejoice over me.* כי אמרתי פן ישמחו לי] Rather — FOR I SAID, LET THEM NOT REJOICE OVER ME.

V. 17. *For I am ready to halt:* — כי אני לצלע נכון] Rather —— FOR I AM PREPARED (or DESTINED) FOR ADVERSITY. See צלע used in this Sense, Ps. XXV. 15.

V. 20. *They also that render evil for good are mine Adversaries; because I follow* the Thing that *good* is. וישטלמי רעה תחת טובה—ישטנוני תחת רדופי טוב :] This Verse ought I think to be thus distinguished and translated --- THEY ALSO RENDER ME EVIL FOR GOOD; THEY HATE ME INSTEAD OF PROCURING ME GOOD. See רדף in this Sense, Isa. I. 23. V. 11. &c.

Q 2

Psalm XXXIX.

V. 5. —— *verily every Man at his beſt State is altogether Vanity.* אך כל הבל בל אדם נצב] I read here אכן להבל, or כי אך, or אך כי, and render --- VERILY EVERY MAN IS FIXED TO VANITY. See נצב thus uſed, Pſ. CXIX. 89. and theſe Prepoſitions in Noldius. Or this Hemiſtic may be thus read without any other Alteration than in the Diviſion of the three firſt Words, *viz.* אך כלהבל : the Senſe of which will then be --- VERILY EVERY MAN IS FIXED AS IT WERE TO VANITY : *i.e.* is naturally ſo conſtituted, for יצב has that Senſe, Iſa. XXXI. 8.

Psalm XL.

V. 2. *He brought me up alſo out of an horrible Pit*] בור שאון ſignifies A SOLITARY PIT ; or A PIT OF DESOLATION : (See Job XXX. 3. — XXXVIII. 27.) not *a Pit of Noiſe*, as in the Margin of our Bible.

V. 4. — *nor ſuch as turn aſide to Lies.* ושטי כזב :] Theſe Words might as well be rendered --- NOR SUCH AS RUN ABOUT with LIES.

V. 6. — *mine Ears haſt thou opened :* אזנים כרית לי] That is, "I "am become thy Servant for Life ;" agreeably to the Law, Exod. XXI. 8. &c. Juvenal alludes to this Cuſtom, Sat. I.

> *Cur timeam, dubitemve locum defendere, quamvis*
> *Natus ad Euphratem, molles quod in aure feneſtræ*
> *Arguerint, licet ipſe negem.*

So Petronius — *Circumcide nos, ut Judæi videamur, et pertunde aures, ut imitemur Arabes.*

V. 17. *But I am poor and needy, yet the Lord thinketh on me :* ואני עני ואביון אדני יהשב לי] Rather —— THOUGH I be POOR AND NEEDY, THE LORD &c. as 2 Sam. XVIII. 12.

Psalm XLI.

V. 8. *An evil Diſeaſe*, ſay they, *cleaveth faſt unto him : and now that he lieth, he ſhall riſe up no more.* דבר בליעל יצוק בו — ואשר שכב לא יוסיף לקום :] Rather —— LET A CURSE BE POURED OUT UPON

(or

(OR STICK FAST TO) HIM; AND WHEN HE LIETH DOWN, LET HIM RISE UP NO MORE. דבר בליעל seems in general to signify rather a *Curse* than a *Difeafe*: however, the Verb and Pronoun here ufed are more applicable to the former than the latter. The Verfe may alfo be thus rendered --- LET THIS CURSE BE POURED OUT UPON HIM, (*viz.*) THAT WHEN HE LIETH DOWN, HE MAY RISE UP NO MORE.

V. 9. — *hath lift up* his *Heel againſt me.* הגדיל עלי עקב] This is fuppofed to be a Metaphor taken from Brutes, or perhaps from Wreftlers: but this Phrafe occurs no where elfe, except where our Lord quotes it, *viz.* John XIII. 18. There it is tranflated as in our Verfion — Ο τρωγων μετ' εμε τον αρτον επηρεν επ' εμε την πτερναν αυτου. It is probable this was the Verfion of the LXX, though different from that which we now have under that Name; for there we read — ο εσθιων αρτες με εμεγαλυνεν επ' εμε πθερνισμον Our Lord repeated the original Text: but the Evangelift made ufe of fuch a Verfion as the Profelytes had, which differs effentially in many Places from the Hebrew. Here I think the Words will hardly bear that Senfe; for הגדיל is never ufed elfewhere for *lifting up*, and עקב feems capable of a better Turn, *viz.* HE HATH AT LAST BECOME GREAT (OR BEHAVED WITH HAUGHTINESS) TOWARD ME; as Dan. VIII. 8. or --- HATH BOASTED AGAINST ME; as Ezek. XXXV. 13. עקב is an Adverb, and thus ufed, Gen. XLIX. 19. See the fame Words, *viz.* הגדיל עלי in the fame Senfe, Pf. LV. 12.

PSALM XLII.

V. 2. — *when ſhall I come and appear before God?* מתי אבוא ואראה ואראה [פני אלהים: , without the Vowel-points, may as conveniently be rendered by the Future *Kal* as well as *Niphal*; thus —— WHEN SHALL I COME AND SEE THE FACE OF GOD?

V. 3. *My Tears have been my Meat* —— היתה לי דמעתי לחם [So Pf. LXX. 8. *Thou feedeſt them with the Bread of Tears, and giveſt them Tears to drink.* And Ovid to the fame Effect, *Metam.*
Cura, dolorque animi, lacrymæque alimenta fuere.

V. 4. — *for I had gone with the Multitude, I went with them to the Houſe of God:* עד בית אלהים—עד בית אלהים [כי אעבר בסך אדדם [סך nowhere fignifies *a Multitude*; neither has it the leaft Affinity in that Senfe with it's fuppofed Roots סוך or ככך. אדדם appears to be erroneoufly written

ten for אדרה, or for אדדה. I would therefore adopt either of these Readings with all the ancient Versions, and render — BUT I WILL GO TO THE GLORIOUS TABERNACLE, even TO THE HOUSE OF THE LORD; or, BUT I WILL GO UNDER A GLORIOUS PROTECTION TO THE HOUSE OF THE LORD: or, lastly, according to the last Reading --- BUT I WILL GO TO THE TABERNACLE; I WILL WALK TO THE HOUSE OF THE LORD.

—— *with the Voice of Joy and Praise, with a Multitude that kept Holyday.*] This latter Clause, *viz.* המון חוגג, ought I think to be rendered — with THE NOISE OF ONE REJOICING: for, as the Word המון signifies either *a Multitude*, or *a Noise*, this latter Sense seems better connected with the Context.

V. 5. — *for I shall yet praise him* for *the Help of his Countenance.* כי עוד אודנו ישועות פני ואלהי:] The two last Words seem to be put in Apposition, thus --- FOR I SHALL YET PRAISE HIM, THE HELP OF MY COUNTENANCE AND MY GOD: as Verse 11.

V. 8. — *and in the Night his Song* shall be *with me, and my Prayer unto the God of my Life.* ובלילה שירה עמי — תפלה לאל חיי:] Rather --- AND IN THE NIGHT A SONG shall be WITH ME, even A PRAYER UNTO &c. for there is no Affix Pronoun to either of the Substantives.

V. 9. *I will say unto God my Rock,* &c. אומרה לאל סלעי וגו"] Rather— I WILL SAY UNTO GOD, O MY ROCK, WHY HAST THOU FORGOTTEN ME?

V. 10. As *with a Sword in my Bones* ——— ברצח בעצמותי] רצח signifies nowhere else *a Sword.* I would therefore consider it as the Infinitive, or Preter, and render—WHILE THEY DESTROY MY BONES; MINE ENEMIES REPROACH ME &c.

PSALM XLIII.

V. 4. — *unto God, my exceeding Joy:* אל אל שמחת גילי] Rather perhaps --- UNTO THE GOD OF MY EXCEEDING JOY.

PSALM XLIV.

V. 10. — *and they which hate us spoil for themselves.* ומשנאינו שסו למו:] As למו seems rather foreign to the Subject, I read למוח, borrowing

rowing one of the ת's from the next Word (which may be spared) and render --- AND THEY WHO HATE US SPOIL US UNTO DEATH: or one of the ת's may well be supposed to have dropt, if three concurred. The next Verse and V. 22. seem to prove this to be the true Lection.

V. 11. *Thou hast given us like Sheep* appointed *for Meat:* תתננו כצאן מאכל] Being now reduced to read תננו, the Imperative, the Construction must be — MAKE US then MEAT LIKE SHEEP. The Sense is hereby more emphatical; and is exactly parallel to that Passage in Hosea, where he says — GIVE THEM *(O Lord) a miscarrying Womb, and dry Breasts.* IX. 14. with only this Difference; that the Imperative is here used for the Preter, and there for the Future. This Place may also be considered as ironical; like that well known Sarcasm in Eccl. XI. 9. *Rejoice, O young Man*, &c.

— *and hast scattered us among the Heathen.* ובגוים זריתנו:] Rather --- SINCE THOU HAST CAST US AWAY AMONG THE HEATHEN. The copulative Particle is here used as Gen. XV. 2. Ruth. I. 21. and the Verb as Isa. XXX. 22.

V. 12. *Thou sellest thy People for nought*] בלא הון WITHOUT GAIN. —— *and dost not increase* thy Wealth *by their Price.* ולא רבית במחיריהם:] Rather — AND DOST NOT PROFIT BY &c.

V. 16. *For the Voice* —— מקול] Rather — BY REASON OF — as in the next Period.

V. 23. — *cast* us *not off for ever.* אל תזנח לנצח:] Rather —— TURN NOT AWAY FOR EVER: as Isa. XIX. 6.

V. 25. — *our Belly cleaveth unto the Earth.* דבקה לארץ בטננו:] Rather — OUR BODY ——. See the Note, Pf. XXXI. 9.

V. 26. *Arise for our Help:* קומה עזרתה לנו] Rather — ARISE, BE THOU OUR HELP: for the second Person of the Preter admits of the ה paragogic.

PSALM XLV.

V. 1. *My Heart is inditing a good Matter;* — רחש לבי דבר טוב] Rather, I think --- MY HEART MEDITATES A GOOD SUBJECT: for דבר has a very extensive Signification. This Psalm seems to be an *Epithalamium*

Epithalamium on Solomon's Marriage with the Egyptian Princeſs. Thus
Claudian,   *Junonis thalamos audaci promere cantu*
　　　　　　Mens congeſta jubet. ———

——— *I ſpeak of the Things which I have made touching the King :*
אמר אני מעשי למלך] Rather perhaps — I WILL ADDRESS MY COM-
POSITION TO THE KING.

——— *my Tongue is the Pen* — לשוני עט] Rather — as THE PEN.

V. 3. *Gird thy Sword upon* thy *Thigh, O moſt mighty, with thy
Glory and thy Majeſty.*] This latter Hemiſtic — נבור הורך והדרך —
ought I think to be thus rendered — O thou MIGHTY IN THY GLORY
AND THY MAJESTY.

V. 4. — *becauſe of Truth, and Meekneſs,* and *Righteouſneſs :* על
דבר אמת וענורה צדק] A Perſon not acquainted with the Genius of
the Hebrew would doubtleſs conclude that the copulative Particle before the laſt Word had been omitted by the Negligence of Tranſcri-
bers. But when we find innumerable Paſſages, where, when three
Words are united in a Sentence as in this Place and V. 8, the *Copula*
is conſtantly affixed to the ſecond, inſtead of the third, what other
Concluſion can be drawn, but that this is an Idiom ? *Qu.* therefore,
whether in all ſuch Caſes the Particle might not properly be removed
in a Verſion from the ſecond to the third Place ?

V. 5. *Thine Arrows* are *ſharp in the Heart of the King's Enemies :
whereby the People fall under thee.* — ילפו — חצך שנונים עמים תחתיך
בלב אויבי המלך :] There is no Paſſage in Scripture that can juſtify
ſuch an extraordinary Tranſpoſition of the Words as that which we
have before us in our Verſion. All the ancient Verſions read as we
now do : and each Hemiſtic ſeparately conveys a clear and diſtinct
Senſe, thus --- THINE ARROWS PENETRATE INTO THE PEOPLE
UNDER THEE : THE KING'S ENEMIES FAIL IN HEART. See
שנן in this Senſe, Deut. VI. 7, 8. and the ſame Phraſe, 1 Sam. XVII. 32.
אל יפל לב אדם — *Let no Man's Heart fail :* ſee alſo Neh. VI. 16.

V. 8. *All thy Garments* ſmell *of Myrrh, and Aloes,* and *Caſſia,* — מר
ואהלות קציעות כל בגדתיך] *Qu.* ought not the Verb Subſtantive rather
to be here ſupplied with the Prepoſition ב, thus — MYRRH, ALOES,
AND CASSIA are in ALL THY GARMENTS ? The Order of the
Words favours this Conjecture.

——— *out of the Ivory Palaces, whereby they have made thee glad.*
מ:

מִן הֵיכְלֵי שֵׁן מִנִּי שִׂמְּחוּךָ:] This Place ought I think to be rendered—brought OUT OF THE IVORY WARDROBES, IN ORDER TO PLEASE THEE. For no *Palace* was ever I believe built of *Ivory*; and here are more than one fuppofed to be mentioned. Whereas a *Wardrobe*, ornamented with Ivory, might not improperly be called by this Name; in the fame manner as we call a Repofitory for Things of great Value by the Name of *Cabinet*. In this Senfe I underftand what is faid of *the Ivory Houfe*, which Ahab made, 1 Kings XXII. 39. For בִית, *a Houfe*, is ufed for " a Place, or Cafe, wherein any Thing lieth, is contained, " or laid up," as Taylor well obferves. Ezekiel gives the Name of *Houfe* to CHESTS *of rich Apparel*. Ch. XXVII. 24. So does Euripedes,

——— εκ δ' ελαου κεδρινων δομων

Εσθητα, κοσμουντ ευπρεπως ητκηουτε.

And Homer makes ufe of a Word of the fame Sound and Signification to exprefs this Idea, (whence fome think that χηλοι are derived from

הֵיכְלֵי) Ηδ' αρ' εφ' υψηλης σανιδος βη, ενθαδε χηλοι

ΕσατΑν, εν δ' αρα τησι θυωδεα εματα κειτο. Odyf. *Lib.* XXI.

As to *dwelling Houfes*; the moft I think we can fuppofe in regard to them is, that they might have Ornaments of *Ivory*, as they fometimes have of *Gold*, *Silver*, or other precious Materials: thus Homer,

——— δωματα ηχηεντα

Χρυσω τ', ηλεκτρωτε, και αργυρω, ηδ' ελεφαντος.

V. 11. — *for he is thy Lord, and worfhip thou him.* כִּי הוּא אֲדֹנַיִךְ
וְהִשְׁתַּחֲוִי לוֹ:] Rather — with the old Verfion — AND REVERENCE THOU HIM.

V. 12. *And the Daughter of Tyre* fhall be there *with a Gift*, even *the rich among the People fhall intreat thy Favour.* וּבַת צֹר בְּמִנְחָה
פָּנַיִךְ יְחַלּוּ — עֲשִׁירֵי עָם:] Rather ——— AND THE DAUGHTER OF TYRE SHALL INTREAT THY FAVOUR WITH HER GIFT, EVEN THE RICH AMONG THE PEOPLE. I read here — יְחַל — וַעֲשִׁירֵי —. For the Verfe cannot be well conftrued, if this Lection be not admitted. For the Riches of the Tyrian Merchants, fee Ifa. XXIII. 8. Ezek. XXVII. throughout.

V. 13. *The King's Daughter is all glorious within*; — כְּבוּדָה בַת מֶלֶךְ
פְּנִימָה] Rather — THE KING's DAUGHTER is GLORIOUS in HER COUNTENANCE, or IN HER OUTWARD APPEARANCE; which Senfe would better fuit the next Hemiftic, as well as the whole Context: for *mental Accomplifhments* are not touched upon. See פְּנִים thus ufed, Pf. XI. 7.

R   P s A L M

PSALM XLVI.

V. 3. Though *the Waters thereof roar*, and *be troubled :* ——— יהמו
יחמרו מימיו] Rather, I think ——— LET THE WATERS THEREOF
ROAR; LET THEM BE TROUBLED.

PSALM XLVII.

V. 7. *For God* is *the King of all the Earth : sing ye Praises with*
Understanding. : אלהים זמרו משכיל — כי מלך כל הארץ] Rather —
FOR HE IS THE KING OF ALL THE EARTH : SING YE A
PSALM TO GOD. I render משכיל, *a Pfalm*, becaufe it is a common
Title to feveral of the Pfalms, and feems to denote one of a particular
Kind, which cannot now be afcertained. See XXXII, XLII, XLIV, &c.
and the concluding Note on the Titles.

V. 9. *The Princes of the People are gathered together,* even *the People*
of the God of Abraham : for the Shields of the Earth belong *unto God :*
he is greatly exalted. כי ——— עם אלהי אברהם — נדיבי עמים נאספו
: לאלהים מגני ארץ — מאד נעלה] Rather — THE PRINCES OF THE
PEOPLE ARE GATHERED BEFORE THE GOD OF ABRAHAM :
THE RULERS OF THE EARTH are THE LORD'S, who is GREATLY
EXALTED. עם is thus rendered, 1 Sam. II. 21. 2 Sam. VI. 7. 1 Kings
XV. 14. and מגן, Hof. IV. 18.

PSALM XLVIII.

V. 5. *They faw* it, and *fo they marvelled, they were troubled,* and
hafted away. : המה ראו כן — כן נבהלו נהפזו] Rather — THEY
SAW it was SO; THEY WERE TROUBLED, THEY WERE TERRI-
FIED, THEY HASTED AWAY. An Afyndeton, and a fine Climax.

V. 7. *Thou breakeft the Ships of Tarfhifh with an Eaft Wind.* ברוח
: קדים תשבר אניות תרשיש] *Tarfhifh* is frequently mentioned in Scripture; and various are the Places which are fuppofed to be meant by
it : but it is clear to me that it was a City in Spain. For Strabo fays
that *Tartaffus* in *Spain* was a Place of great Wealth, and that the
Phœnicians poffeffed it. The fame Author, Ariftotle, Pliny, and Polybius,

lybius obferve, that it produced Silver, Tin, Iron, and Lead; to which
Ariftotle adds, that the Phœnicians traded to Tartaffus for Silver. And
we read in Ezekiel, XXVII 12. *Tarfhifh was thy Merchant by reafon of
the Multitude of all kinds of Riches: with Silver, Iron, Tin, and Lead,
they traded in thy Fairs.* Polybius fays, that the Carthaginians were
not to fail beyond Ταρσηιον, and Stephanus, that Ταρσηιον was a City near
the Straits of Gibraltar.

V. 10. *According to thy Name, O God, fo is thy Praife unto the Ends
of the Earth :* — כשמך אלהים כן תהלתך — על קצוי ארץ] Rather
--- As thy Name is, so is thy Praise, unto the Ends of
the Earth.

V. 14. *For this God is our God for ever and ever: he will be our
Guide even unto Death.* כי זה אלהים אלהינו — עולם ועד הוא ינהגנו
(על מות)] Rather — For God Himself is our God; He will
be our Guide for ever and ever. זה has this Senfe, Judg. V. 5.
I pafs over the two laft Words, not only becaufe the Pfalm is complete
without them, but becaufe I am perfuaded they do not belong to it.
They are not acknowledged by any of the ancient Verfions, except
the Syriac: and there they may have been taken from *the Title* of the
next Pfalm, which it has in common with fome others; fee Pf. XLVI.

Psalm XLIX.

V. 5. — when *the Iniquity of my Heels fhall compafs me about?* עון
עקבי יסבני :] Rather — when the Iniquity of those that sup-
plant me compasseth me about? No Idea can be fixed to *the
Wickednefs of the Heels;* whereas עקבי is the regular Participle prefent
from עקב, *To fupplant, deceive,* or *trip up the Heels* of another.

V. 8. — *and it ceafeth for ever.* : וחדל לעולם] Thefe Words are
I think improperly connected with thofe that immediately precede, *viz.
For the Redemption of their Soul* (or *of his Soul,* according to the old
Verfions) *is precious.* Thofe ought I think to make Part of the foregoing Verfe, and the next Verfe begin with thefe, thus — But he
will cease for ever, though he would live to Eternity, and not see Corruption. The Verb חדל fignifies *to be
in a State of utter Ceffation; to be lifelefs,* or *dead.* Ifa. XXXVIII. 11.
Pf. XXXIX. 4.

V. 10. *For he feeth* that *wife Men die* —— כי יראה הכמים ימותו [Rather --- Though he see &c.

V. 11. *Their inward Thought* is that *their Houfes* shall continue *for ever.* קרבם בתימו לעולם [All the ancient Verfions, without Exception, read here קברם, instead of קרבם ; which yields a much better Senfe, (and ought doubtlefs to be admitted) *viz.* Their Sepulchre shall be their Houses for ever, their Dwelling to all Generations.

—— *they call* their *Lands after their own Names.* (12.) *Neverthelefs, Man being in Honour abideth not; he is like the Beafts that perifh.* קראו בשמותם עלי אדמות—ואדם ביקר בל ילין—נישמל כבהמות נדמו : These three Hemiftics ought I think to be connected into one Verfe, and thus rendered —— They call the Lands after their own Names : but Man abideth not in Honour ; as the Beasts perish, so doth he : literally, *as the Beafts perifh, he is made like.*

V. 13. *This their Way is their Folly :* —— זה דרכם כסל למו [Rather --- This their Proceeding is Folly in them.

V. 14. *Like Sheep they are laid in the Grave, Death shall feed on them :* —— כצאן לישאול שתו מות ירעם [This Hemiftic ought I think to be thus rendered --- They are cast under Ground like a Flock, whose Shepherd is Death ; *i.e.* like a Flock deftroyed by Difeafe, which are buried to prevent an Infection. The Idea of *Death being their Shepherd* cannot I think be thought a *Catachrefis,* but rather a fuitable Image in this Place.

—— *and the upright shall have Dominion over them in the Morning.* וירדו בם ישרים לבקר [The common Interpretation of this Verfe is very unfatisfactory. The principal Difficulty feems to me to lie in לבקר ; which I cannot but confider as a Miftake for לקבר, by the fame Tranfpofition as קרבם is put for קברם, Verfe 11. The Senfe I would therefore give this Hemiftic is this — They go down with them ; (*viz.* the Flock) they go straight to the Sepulchre. See ישרים ufed precifely in this Senfe, Prov. IX. 15. for the Introduction of *the righteous* here is out of Place. This conjectural Emendation feems to me to be ftrengthened by the correfponding Word, שאול, in the next Hemiftic.

—— *and their Beauty shall confume in the Grave, from their Dwelling.* וצירים לבלות שאול מזבל לו : [Rather — And the Grave,
THEIR

THEIR DWELLING, SHALL CONSUME THEIR BEAUTY. Thus the *Sepulchre* is faid V. 11. to be *their Houſes for ever, and their Dwelling to all Generations.* לבלות, the Infinitive, ſeems here uſed for the Future, as Pſ. LXX. 1. Ezek. XI. 7. &c.

V. 18. *Though whiles he lived he bleſſed his Soul; and* Men *will praiſe thee when thou doeſt well to thyſelf.* כי נפשו בחיי יברך—ויודך כי תיטיב לך :] Rather — THOUGH HE BLESS HIS SOUL IN HIS LIFE, AND COMMEND THEE WHEN THOU CHEEREST THYSELF; *i. e.* " though he gratify his Deſires in all the Enjoyments, which his Si- " tuation of Life affords him, and think thee right in indulging thy- " ſelf in like manner." This I apprehend is the true Senſe of this Paſ- ſage; for by *bleſſing* is frequently underſtood *giving freely and bounti- fully to* a Perſon; thus, *in bleſſing I will bleſs thee,* i. e. " when I be- "ſtow good Things, I will beſtow liberally on thee." Gen. XXII 17 So alſo Gen. XLIX. 25. Prov. XI. 25. And a *Bleſſing* is often uſed for *a Gift* or *Gratification,* Gen. XXVII. 12. Judg. I. 15. 2 Kings V. 15. and נפש ſignifies frequently *Luſt,* or *Appetite,* ſee Pſ. XXVII. 12. Eccl. VI. 7, 9. &c. So that by *bleſſing one's Soul* may very aptly be under- ſtood gratifying the Appetites and Deſires. בחיו, *in his Life,* ſignifies "in the Delights and Comforts of his preſent State," in the ſame manner as Eccl. XI. 9. *Rejoice, O young Man, in thy Youth,* ſignifies, "enjoy " freely thoſe Pleaſures and Gratifications, which that Seaſon of Life " offers thee;" ſo that the Senſe in both Places nearly coincides; for in the one it is ſaid of a Man that he gratifies his Deſires in the Com- forts and Delights of Life; in the other he is bidden (ironically) to enjoy freely all the Pleaſures that Youth admits of. But there is ſtill a nearer Correſpondence in the following Part in both Places, where the Words are almoſt the ſame; for in one we read ויטיבך לבך, *let thy Heart cheer thee,* in the other כי תיטיב לך, which I therefore render, *when thou cheereſt thyſelf;* and both evidently denote pleaſurable Indul- gence. Laſtly, this Interpretation moſt aptly ſuits with the Reaſoning of the Context. (V. 16.) "Be not thou concerned at the ſudden In- " creaſe of a Man's Wealth or Honour, (17.) for it will not follow " him into the Grave, (18.) though for the preſent he may gratify his " Deſires in the Enjoyments of this Life, and commend others for the " like Indulgence; (19.) yet after a while he ſhall leave all behind, " and go where his Forefathers are gone before him."

V. 19. *He ſhall go to the Generation of his Fathers; they ſhall never ſee Light.* תבוא עד דור אבותיו — עד נצח לא יראו אור :] Rather —

II2

HE SHALL GO TO THE HABITATION OF HIS FATHERS, who SHALL NEVER SEE LIGHT. דור signifies *to inhabit*, Pf. LXXXIV. 10. Dan. IV. 21, 25. Thus the Grave is ftiled *the Land of Darknefs*, Job. X. 21. Pf. LXXXVIII. 12.

V. 20. *Man that is in Honour, and underftandeth not,* — אדם ביקר ולא יבין] Rather — MAN being IN HONOUR, IF HE UNDERSTAND-ETH NOT, *i. e.* "if he be wicked and irreligious," which is the fcrip-tural Senfe of Folly and Want of Underftanding.

PSALM L.

V. 8. *I will not reprove thee for thy Sacrifices, or thy Burnt Offer-ings,* to have been *continually before me.* —— לא על זבחיך אוכיחך ועולתיך לנגדי תמיד :] Rather --- I WILL NOT REPROVE THEE ON ACCOUNT OF THY SACRIFICES; FOR THY BURNT OFFER-INGS are CONTINUALLY BEFORE ME.

V. 10. — and *the Cattle upon a thoufand Hills.* [בהמות בהררי אלף :] All the ancient Verfions feem to have read ואלפים, *viz.* THE CATTLE UPON MY HILLS, AND THE OXEN.

V. 13. *Will I eat the Flefh of Bulls, or drink the Blood of Goats?*] The Heathens thought that their Deities were nourifhed by the Smoke or Steam of their Sacrifices. See Lucian *de Sacrificiis;* and Arifto-phanes. But Euripedes fays,

Δειται γαρ ο Θεος, ειπερ εϛ' εντως Θεος,
Ουδενος· αειδαν ειδε δυϛηνοι λογοι.

V. 22. — *left I tear* you *in Pieces,* — פן אטרף] All the ancient Verfions, except the Chaldee, read יטרף — LEST HE TEAR.

V. 23. — *and to him that ordereth* his *Converfation* aright, *will I fhew the Salvation of God.* [ושם דרך אראנו בישע אלהים :] I take שם דרך to fignify the fame as בדרך *in the Way,* or *by thofe Means:* thus שם or שמה is ufed, Exod. XVI. 33. and XXX. 18. I would therefore render --- AND IN THAT WAY WILL I SHEW HIM THE SAL-VATION OF GOD.

PSALM

PSALM LI.

V. 4. *Against thee, thee only have I sinned:* — [לך לבדך חטאתי] Rather --- AGAINST THEE PERSONALLY HAVE I SINNED. See לבדך used in this Sense, Gen. XLIII. 32. Zech. XII. 12, 13. For David could not mean that he had sinned *only* against God *in the Matter of Uriah the Hittite:* but that *abstractedly* and *apart* from the Injury done to others, his Sin contained an *immediate* Offence against the Majesty of the supreme Governor of the World, and the Authority of his Laws; SO THAT (proceeds he) THOU ART JUST IN THY SENTENCE (meaning that which God had just pronounced against him by Nathan the Prophet, 2 Sam. XII. 11,12.) and PURE (or UNBLAMEABLE) IN THY JUDGMENT.

V. 5. *Behold I was shapen in Iniquity,* &c.] So Tully — *simul atque editi in lucem et suscepti sumus, in omni continuo pravitate versamur,* — *ut pæne cum lacte nutricis errorem suxisse videamur.* Tusc. Disp. *Lib.* III. *Cap.* i.

V. 6. — *and in the hidden* Part *thou shalt make me to know Wisdom.* [ובסתם הכמה הודיעני] As סתם certainly signifies THE HEART in this Place, ought it not to be so rendered in the Text, and the literal Version to be put in the Margin?

V. 12. — *and uphold me with thy free Spirit.* [ורוח נדיבה תסמכני] Rather --- AND LET A FREE SPIRIT UPHOLD ME.

V. 19. — *with burnt Offering, and whole burnt Offering:*] Though these two Words כליל and עולה signify the same Thing, it would I think be better to render them as in the old Version by OBLATION and BURNT OFFERING.

PSALM LII.

V. 1. — *the Goodness of God endureth continually.* [חסד אל כל היום] *Qu.* would not — THE GOODNESS OF GOD is EVERLASTING, be better?

V. 2. *Thy Tongue deviseth Mischief: like a sharp Razor, working deceitfully.* [הוות תחשב — לשונך כתער מלטש — עשה רמיה] Rather --- THOU DEVISEST MISCHIEFS; THY TONGUE, LIKE A SHARP RASOR, WORKETH DECEITFULLY.

V. 4.

V. 4. *Thou loveſt all devouring Words,* — אהבת כל דברי בלע [
Rather --- PERNICIOUS WORDS.

V. 9. — *and I will wait on thy Name;* — ואקוה שמך [קוה ought
I think to have here the Senſe of the Arabic Verb وفي, *To call upon.*

PSALM LIII.

V. 5. *There were they in great Fear, where no Fear was: for God
hath ſcattered the Bones of him that encamped* againſt *thee, thou haſt*
put them *to Shame, becauſe God hath deſpiſed them.* שם פחדו פחד לא
הירה פחד — כי אלהים פזר עצמות הנך — הבישתה כי אלהים מאסם: [
I read here with all the old Verſions, (except the Chaldee) הנף, inſtead
of הנך, and הובישו תהרה in lieu of הבישתה, and render thus ———
WHERE NO FEAR IS, THEY FEAR GREATLY; BECAUSE GOD
HATH BROKEN THE BONES OF THE IMPIOUS MAN: THEY ARE
GREATLY CONFOUNDED, BECAUSE GOD HATH REJECTED THEM:
OF, THEY WITHER AWAY TO NOUGHT, BECAUSE GOD HATH
CAST THEM OFF: making יבש the Root. תהרה is not ſtrictly perhaps an Hebrew Word, but Chaldee; though תהרו, *Confuſion,* is ma-
nifeſtly derived from it. The ף and ך are ſo like, that the Miſtake is
eaſily accounted for. By this Interpretation the Difficulty ariſing from
the Enallage of Perſons is ſurmounted.

PSALM LIV.

V. 1. — *and judge me by thy Strength.* ובגבורתך תדינני: [Rather
--- AND PLEAD THOU MY CAUSE WITH THY STRENGTH: as
Prov. XXXI. 9. or, with the Common Prayer Verſion, AND AVENGE
ME &c.

V. 7. ———— *and mine Eye hath ſeen his Deſire upon mine Enemies.*
ובאיבי ראתה עיני: [Rather — AND MINE EYE OVERLOOKETH (*i. e.*
DESPISETH) MINE ENEMIES: thus ראה ſignifies, Job. XL. 12. XLI. 34.

PSALM LV.

V. 6. — *O that I had Wings like a Dove!*] So Sophocles, *Æd. Col.*
Εἰτ', αἰλλαια ταχυρ-
ρωσες πελειας,
Αισθριας

Αἰθερίας νεφέλας
Κυρσαιμι.   And Euripedes,
Πιξαν πελειας ωκυτητ' εκ νοσενς.
—— *Quæ lachrymis noftris queftus*
Reddet Aëdon? cujus pennas
Utinam miferæ mihi fata darent!
Fugerem luctus ablata meos
Penna volucri, procul et cætus
Hominum trifles, cædemque feram:
Sola in vacuo nemore, et tenui
Ramo pendens, querulo poffem
Gutture mæftum fundere murmur.   Sen. in Agam.

V. 14. —— and *walked unto the Houfe of God in Company.* בבית
אלהים נהלך ברגש:] Our Tranflators have very properly borrowed
this Senfe of רגש from the Chaldee; for the ufual Signification in
Hebrew would be unfuitable.

V. 15. *Let Death feize upon them,* —— ישי מות עלימו] The Maffora
here directs us to feparate ישי from מות : but does not inform us of
the Signification, or how to fupply the Deficiency of, ישי. It feems to
me moft probable that the true Reading is —— ישים מות —— LET
DEATH BRING DESOLATION UPON THEM.

V. 18. *He hath delivered my Soul in Peace from the Battle* that was
againft me: —— פדה בשלום נפשי מקרב לי] Rather —— HE HATH
RESTORED MY SOUL TO PEACE FROM THE WAR AGAINST ME.
—— *for there were many with me:* כי ברבים היו עמדי] Rather,
I think --- FOR THEY were AT VARIANCE WITH ME. ברבים
or ברבים (for that Word is written either Way indifferently) fignifies
in Contentions, or *in Difputes.* This is the Senfe of the Syriac Verfion,
which feems more natural than to fuppofe that the Words refer to the
Affiftance given by Angels, as our old Verfion does. See Pf. LXXXIX. 50.

V. 19. *God fhall hear and afflict them, even he that abideth of old.*
ישמע אל ויענם וישב קדם] I think it cannot be doubted that וישב
קדם ought to be written ויש בקדם, *i. e.* EVEN HE THAT HATH
EXISTED FROM ETERNITY.

V. 21. *The* Words *of his Mouth were fmoother than Butter:* חלקו
מחמאת פיו] Rather —— HIS SPEECHES WERE SMOOTHER THAN
BUTTER : for פי is indifferently of either Number; and it fignifies A
S   SPEECH,

SPEECH, TALK, or SAYING, Exod. IV. 10. Eccl. X. 13. Pf. XLIX. 13. It is also frequently rendered WORD, or WORDS.

V. 22. *Caſt thy Burden upon the Lord,* — [השלך על יהוה יהבך] The Signification of יהב is *the Supply of what is needful,* as Taylor makes appear in various Inſtances; and the Verb שלך ſignifies *to throw* or *devolve* upon a Perſon; ſo Pſ. XXII. 10. *I was caſt upon thee,* i. e. *for Support.* This Place therefore may properly be rendered — CAST UPON THE LORD THE SUPPLY OF THY NECESSITIES, OR THE CHARGE OF THEE. Compare this Sentiment with Pſ. XXXVII. 5. 1 Pet. V. 7.

PSALM LVI.

V. 3. *What Time I am afraid* — [יום אירא] As this Hemiſtic wants a Word to complete it, and the preceding one has one ſupernumerary, *viz.* מרום, I would reſtore it to this Verſe, and render — WHAT TIME I MAY BE AFRAID OF THE HAUGHTY; for thus מרום is rendered, Iſa. XXIV. 4. whereas it ſignifies nowhere, *O moſt High.*

V. 4. *In God I will praiſe his Word* — [באלהים אהלל דברו] Rather, I think — THROUGH GOD (or, with his Aſſiſtance) I &c.

V. 12. *Thy Vows are upon me, O God:* — [עלי אלהים נדריך] The ך ſeems here to have got out of it's Place. The Syriac Verſion reads עליך אלהים נדרי, *I will pay my Vows unto thee*; or, more literally, MY VOWS are UNTO THEE, O LORD; which Reading makes the Senſe clearer, and better correſponds with the next Hemiſtic. Ανα- διχομαι Θεε α ευξαμην. Symmachus. Εν εμει ο Θεος αι ευχαι Ο.

V. 13. *For thou haſt delivered my Soul from Death :* wilt *not* thou deliver *my Feet from falling ?* [כי הצלת נפשי ממות—הלא רגלי מדחי] All the ancient Verſions in this Place, and Pſ. CXVI. 8. where the ſame Words occur, ſhew that הלא ought to be written ואת: the Senſe will then be --- FOR THOU HAST DELIVERED MY SOUL FROM DEATH, AND MY FEET FROM FALLING.

PSALM LVII.

V. 1. — *until theſe Calamities be overpaſt.* [עד יעבר הוות :] Rather --- UNTIL IT CAUSE CALAMITIES TO PASS AWAY. The Antecedent

Antecedent to the Pronoun is *the Shadow*, immediately preceding. The Verb is in *Pihel*, in which Conjugation it has a tranfitive Senfe as well as in *Hiphil*. See Gen. VIII. 1. XXXII. 23, 24. Our Verfion here labours under a double Solecifm, *viz.* of Number and Gender.

V. 2. — *unto God that performeth* all Things *for me.* : [לאל נמר עלי] All the ancient Verfions read here, and Pf. CXXXVIII. 8. גמל, *viz.* UNTO GOD WHO DEALETH BOUNTIFULLY WITH ME : which feems to be the true Lection in both Places ; for the Verb גמר never fignifies elfewhere *to perform* : only *to ceafe*, or *fail*.

V. 4. — and *I lie* even among *them that are fet on Fire*, even *the Sons of Men* ;—[אשכבה להטים בני אדם] Rather — I LIE DOWN among INCENDIARIES, EVEN THE SONS OF MEN.

PSALM LVIII.

V. 1. — *O ye Congregation,* — [אלם] Probably a Miftake for אלים, O YE MIGHTY.

V. 5. *Which will not hearken to the Voice of Charmers, charming never fo wifely.* : [אשר לא ישמע לקול מלחשים — חובר חברים מחכם] This Verfe does not feem to be rendered with fufficient Precifion. The Verfion following would approach nearer to the Text — WHICH WILL NOT HEARKEN TO THE VOICE OF THE INCHANTERS, though THE CHARMER OF CHARMS be SKILFUL ; or, though THE CHARMER be SKILFUL in CHARMS. It was an Opinion which prevailed very early and very univerfally, that Serpents might be charmed : See Bochart, *Hier.* B. III. Ch. VI. Thus Tzetzes (a Poet of the XIIth Century) fuppofes that Orpheus, well fkilled in this Art, could recal Eurydice, bitten by a Serpent, from Tartarus ———

——— ὑπὸ ὀφεως αυτὴν τῳ οντι δεδηγμενην,
Καὶ κινδυνευσιν θανειν, ταις ΕΠΩΔΑΙΣ, ΑΙΣ ΟΙΔΕ,
Καὶ ΑΓΧΙΝΟΙΑ,, ΜΟΥΣΗ, τε, καὶ ΠΟΛΥΜΑΘΕΙΑ,
Αυτὴν ἐζωπυρησεν *Chil.* II. Hift. 54.

And in Apollonius Rodius Medea is faid to have charmed the Serpent, Ἡδη ΕΝΟΠΗ, ΘΕΛΞΑΙ τερας. *Argon.* B. IV. V. 147.

And, to quote no other Authority than Virgil, *Æneid.* VII. V. 750.

Quin et Marrubia venit de gente Sacerdos,
Fronde fuper galeam et felici comptus oliva,

Archippi

Archippi regis miſſu, fortiſſimus Umbro ;
VIPEREO GENERI, ET GRAVITER SPIRANTIBUS HYDRIS
SPARGERE QUI SOMNOS CANTUQUE MANUQUE SOLEBAT,
MULCEBATQUE IRAS, *et morſus arte levabat.*

V. 7. *Let them melt away as Waters,* which *run continually :* יִמָּאֲסוּ
[כְּמוֹ מַיִם יִתְהַלְּכוּ לָמוֹ] Rather — LET THEM BE DISREGARDED AS
THE FLOWING WATER : for otherwiſe we ought to read יִמַּסּוּ or
יִמֵּסּוּ, if מסס *to diſſolve* were the Root.

——— when *he bendeth* his Bow to ſhoot *his Arrows, let them be as
cut in Pieces.* [יִדְרֹךְ חִצּוֹ כְּמוֹ יִתְמֹלָלוּ] I would either read בָּמוֹ with
the Chaldee, or give כְּמוֹ the Signification of *when,* with the reſt of the
ancient Verſions, thus --- when HE SHOOTETH HIS ARROWS
AGAINST THEM, LET THEM BE CUT IN PIECES ; or ironically,
LET HIM SHOOT HIS ARROWS WHEN THEY ARE CUT IN PIECES.
The Phraſe דָּרַךְ חִצּוֹ is not *elliptical,* for דָּרַךְ ſimply ſignifies to *ſhoot,*
1 Chron. V. 18. בָּמוֹ is the ſame as בָּהֶם, as לָמוֹ for לָהֶם, Iſa. XLIV.
15. XXX. 5. and ב ſignifies *againſt,* Gen. XVI. 12. Lev. XVII.10. כְּמוֹ
when, Gen. XIX. 15. Ezek. XVI. 57.

V. 8. *As a Snail* which *melteth, let* every one of them *paſs away :*
like *the untimely Birth of a Woman,* that *they may not ſee the Sun.*
[כְּמוֹ שַׁבְּלוּל תֶּמֶס — יַהֲלֹךְ נֵפֶל אֵשֶׁת — בַּל חָזוּ שָׁמֶשׁ :] Rather thus —
THOU WILT DISSOLVE them LIKE WAX : like THE UNTIMELY
FRUIT OF A WOMAN that PASSETH AWAY, THEY SHALL NOT
SEE THE SUN. The Word שַׁבְּלוּל occurs nowhere elſe. The Chaldee
gives it the Signification of *a Snail :* but the reſt of the Verſions, with
more Propriety, render it *Wax ;* from שבל, which in Syriac, Chaldee,
and Arabic, ſignifies *to flow,* which all know is a Property of Wax,
when in a State of Liquefaction.

V. 9. — *he ſhall take them as with a Whirlwind, both living,* and in
his *Wrath.* [כְּמוֹ חַי כְּמוֹ חָרוֹן יִשְׂעָרֶנּוּ :] Rather thus — THE LIVING
ONE IN WRATH WILL TAKE THEM AS WITH A WHIRLWIND.
I read here בְּמוֹ חָרוֹן, with the Syriac and Vulgate Verſions, inſtead of
כְּמוֹ הָרוּן, the preſent Lection, adopted by our Verſion and ſome of the
ancient Interpreters. See Pſ. XI. 2. כְּמוֹ implies IN A SHORT TIME,
or IN LIKE MANNER, as 1 Kings XXII. 4. and Pſ. LXXIII. 15. חַי
ſignifies THE LIVING ONE " He who is the Source of Life," as Gen.
XVI. 14. בְּאֵר לַחַי רֹאִי — *the Well* OF HIM THAT LIVETH, *ſeeing*
me :

me : and that this can be referred to none but God, the 13th Verfe fhews. לחי, 1 Sam. XXV. 6. may alfo admit of the fame Senfe : and in Pf. XVIII. 46. חי יהוה וברוך — may be rendered, as it is by the Arabic Verfions, حي هو الرب, THE LIVING ONE HE IS THE LORD &c. See alfo Pf. CXLIII. 2. where חי fimply is ufed for *every One living.*

PSALM LIX.

V. 2, 3, 4, 5. feem improperly divided in our Verfion. The Senfe I think would be clearer were they thus read —— (2.) DELIVER ME FROM THE WORKERS OF INIQUITY, AND SAVE ME FROM BLOODY MEN : FOR LO, THEY LIE IN WAIT FOR MY SOUL ; THE MIGHTY ARE GATHERED AGAINST ME : (3.) I HAVE NOT TRANSGRESSED, NEITHER HAVE I SINNED, O LORD : (4.) yet WITHOUT PROVOCATION THEY RUN AND PREPARE THEM- SELVES. (5.) STIR UP THYSELF TO MEET ME, AND BEHOLD ; EVEN THOU, O LORD GOD OF HOSTS, thou GOD OF ISRAEL, AWAKE &c.

V. 9. Becaufe of *his Strength will I wait upon thee : for God is my Defence.* עזו אליך אשמרה כי אלהים משגבי] All the ancient Ver- fions read עזי; which doubtlefs is the true Reading, and makes a better Senfe, thus --- O MY STRENGTH, UPON THEE WILL I WAIT ; FOR thou, O GOD, art MY DEFENCE. See Verfe 17. where we read עזי, as here propofed.

V. 10. *God fhall let me fee* my Defire &c.] See Pf. LIV. 7.

V. 12. For *the Sin of their Mouth,* and *the Words of their Lips,* — חטאת פימו דבר שפתימו] Perhaps — THE WORDS OF THEIR LIPS are THE SIN OF THEIR MOUTH ; or, if we read with the Syriac דברו, thus --- THEIR LIPS SPEAK THE SIN OF THEIR MOUTH.

—— *let them even be taken in their Pride : and for the curfing and lying* which *they fpeak.* וילכדו בגאונם —— ומאלה ומכחש יספרו] Ra- ther, I think --- LET THEM THEREFORE BE TAKEN IN THEIR PRIDE, SEEING THEY UTTER CURSING AND FALSEHOOD.

PSALM

Psalm LX.

V. 3. — *thou haſt made us to drink the Wine of Aſtoniſhment.* השקיתנו
[יין תרעלה :] Though the Syriac Verſion renders תרעלה, *full of Lees*, and عل, ſignifies *evaporated*, there is no Occaſion to depart from the uſual Senſe of the Word, *viz.* TREMBLING, or ASTONISHMENT. *The Wine of Aſtoniſhment* may be conſidered as equivalent to the *Cup of Fury*, or *of Trembling*, Iſa. LI. 17. Zech. XII. 2. For it is uſual to denote the Diſpenſations of Providence, good or bad, by ſome ſimilar Metaphor. See Pſ. XXXVI. 8. Job. XXI. 20. Iſa. XXX. 20. Jer. XXIII. 15. — XXV. 15. Matt. XX. 22, 23. John. XVIII. 11. Rev. XIV. 10.

V. 4. — *that it may be diſplayed becauſe of the Truth.* [להתנוסס מפני קשט :] Rather, I think --- THAT IT MAY BE DISPLAYED IN THE FRONT OF (or BEFORE) TRUTH: for otherwiſe the Allegory is loſt. קשט occurs only here and Prov. XXII. 21. In Chaldee and Samaritan it ſignifies both *Truth* and *Juſtice*, which Senſes will ſuit either Place.

V. 6. *God hath ſpoken in his Holineſs;* — [אלהים דבר בקדשו] Rather —— IN HIS SANCTUARY.

V. 8. — *Philiſtia, triumph thou becauſe of me.* [עלי פלשת התרועעי :] Rather — COME UP, O PHILISTIA, TRIUMPH THOU : for עלי is the 2d. Perſon fem. ſingular of the Imperative of the Verb עלה, in the ſame Manner as התרועעי, but of a different Voice.

Psalm LXI.

V. 5. — *thou haſt given* me *the Heritage of thoſe that fear thy Name.* [נתת ירשת יראי שמך :] ירשת ſeems here contracted for ירשות. I would therefore render — THOU HAST GIVEN INHERITANCES TO THOSE THAT FEAR THY NAME.

V. 7. —— *O prepare Mercy and Truth, which* may preſerve him. [חסד ואמת מן ינצרהו :] Or — LET MERCY AND TRUTH PRESERVE HIM : for מן is frequently uſed as a mere Expletive Particle, ſee Noldius, Art. 19.

Psalm LXII.

V. 9. — and *Men of high Degree* are *a Lie :* — [כזב בני איש] Rather
—— A

—— A Deceit, or deceitful; for the Hebrews delight in using the Abstract for the Concrete.

—————— *to be laid in the Balance, they are altogether* lighter *than Vanity.* [במאונים לעלות המה נהבל יחד :] Rather —— when laid in the Balance, they are altogether Vanity. The Gerund has here the Force of the Preter, and the Preposition כ is redundant: It is prefixed to a Nominative, Judg. X. 11, 12. Ezek. XVI. 20. &c.

V. 10. —— *if Riches increase, set not your Heart* upon them. היל כי [ינוב אל תשיתו לב :] Rather —— Set not the Heart on Riches, when they increase.

Psalm LXIII.

V. 5. *My Soul shall be satisfied as* with *Marrow and Fatness*; —— כמו [הלב ודשן השבע נפשי] It is not improbable that the true Lection is במו : in which Case I would render —— My Appetite shall be satisfied with Marrow and Fatness.

V. 9. *But those* that *seek my Soul to destroy* it, —— והמה לשואה יבקשו [נפשי] Rather —— But those that seek my Soul for Destruction &c.

V. 10. *They shall fall by the Sword:* —— יגירהו על ידי חרב [ ] Our Translators, not knowing what to make of יגירהו, gave it the best Sense that offered. As the Words are now read, they signify —— *he will make him run out upon the Hands of the Sword.* It is hence evident that יגירהו is corrupt; and it is also highly probable that יגורו is the true Reading; for all the ancient Versions seem to have read so; and this Word suits the Context; thus —— They shall abide in the Power of the Sword: *i. e.* be always subject to it.

Psalm LXIV.

V. 3. —————— and *bend* their Bows to shoot *their Arrows,* even *bitter Words.* [דרכו חצם דבר מר :] Rather —— They shoot bitter Words like their Arrows. See Note Ps. LVIII. 7.

V. 4. *That they may shoot* —————— [לירות] That they may hit, or strike.

V. 5.

V. 5. — *they fay, Who fhall fee them?* : אמרו מי יראה למו] The Syriac and Arabic read here לנו — *who fhall fee* us? This Reading feems better adapted to the Context; except we underftand by למו *them,* viz. *the Snares.*

V. 6. — *both the inward* Thought *of every one* of them, *and the Heart is deep.* : וקרב איש ולב עמק] Rather — BUT THE INWARD PART OF A MAN, AND THE HEART are DEEP: *i. e.* " notwithftanding " their diligent Search they cannot penetrate into another Man's " Thoughts, who may be contriving to render their Machinations " abortive."

V. 8. *So they fhall make their own Tongue to fall upon themfelves:* ויכשילהו עלימו לשונם] The Hebrew feems here faulty: for יכשילהו fignifies *he fhall make him fall,* which cannot be connected with the reft of the Sentence. Remove the ה, you have the proper Number, ויכשילו, as in the old Verfions, and get clear of that furreptitious Perfon. See the fame Error in the laft Pfalm, V. 10.

—— *all that fee them fhall flee away.* : יתנודדו כל ראה בם] Here again is another Solecifm: but this may perhaps be remedied by only reading יהנודד וכל — AND EVERY ONE THAT SEETH &c.

Psalm LXV.

V. 3. *Iniquities prevail againft me; as for our Tranfgreffions, thou fhalt purge them away.* : דברי עונת גברו — מני פשעינו אתה תכפרם] Rather --- THE PORTIONS OF INIQUITIES PREVAIL: but THOU WILT PURGE AWAY THE NUMBER OF OUR TRANSGRESSIONS. דברי, which is not tranflated in our Verfion in this Place, is rendered *a Portion,* Neh. XII. 47. Jer. LII. 34, &c. and I confider מני as a Noun *in regimine,* (as Ifa. LXV. 11. 1 Kings X. 17. &c.) from מנה *to number.* In refpect to the Affix Pronoun, fee Pf. X. Ver. 5. It is properly rendered, Pf. LXVII. 4.

V. 4. *Bleffed is* the Man whom *thou choofeft, and caufeft to approach unto thee, that he may dwell in thy Courts: we fhall be fatisfied* &c. אשרי הבחר ותקרב — ישכן חצריך — נשבעה וגו "] Rather — THOU CHOOSEST AND BRINGEST THE BLESSED ONE that HE MAY DWELL IN THY COURTS; HE WILL BE SATISFIED &c. אשרי is here confidered as the Participle prefent, which frequently admits the ' *paragogic,* and נשבעה, as the third Perfon of the Preter *Niphal* with ה alfo redundant, as Gen. L. 5. Ruth II. 2. Ezek. XXIII. 20. &c.

—— even

———— even *of thy holy Temple.* : קדש היכלך] I add here a Part of the next Word, *viz.* נורא, and render — even OF THY HOLY TEMPLE, which IS TO BE HAD IN REVERENCE. So נורא is rendered, Pf.LXXXIX. 7. CXI.9. All the ancient Verſions (except the Chaldee) read ſo: and the Hemiſtic wants here a Word, than which a properer could not be found.

V. 5. By *terrible Things in Righteouſneſs wilt thou anſwer us,* ———— נוראות בצדק תעננו] Our Verſion gives נוראות a Senſe oppoſite to the whole Scope of the Pſalm: for all the Inſtances ſubjoined are ſo many Proofs of the MERCY, not of the *Wrath* of the Almighty; and therefore fitter Objects to excite THANKFULNESS than *Terror.* For this Reaſon, having already divided the Word נוראות, and aſſigned the former Part a Place in the preceding Verſe, I here read אות, by a Repetition of the א; which ſeems to have been dropped, either caſually, or perhaps by the unſkilful Criticiſm of ſome Tranſcriber; who finding the two Words נורא אות written cloſe together, (as is uſual in Hebrew MSS; without a Point of Separation, as in Greek and Latin Inſcriptions) and being unable to make the proper Diſtinction, boldly cut the Knot, which he could not untie, and diſcarding the ſecond א as an Intruder, blended the two Words into one, ſo as to occaſion the preſent Difficulty. I render אות *a Sign,* or *Token,* as V.8. and connect it with the Reſt of the Sentence thus — THOU IN RIGHTEOUSNESS ANSWEREST with A SIGN, or, THOU IN KINDNESS SUPPLIEST US WITH A TOKEN — for ſo צדק ſignifies, Judg. V. 11. 1 Sam. XII. 7. &c. and ענה — Iſa. XLI. 17. XLIX. 8.

———— *and of them that are afar off* upon *the Sea.* : וים רחקים] וים may ſeem to be a Miſtake for וימים: but we ſhould not too haſtily draw Concluſions. The preſent Lection may well be juſtified if the Words be thus diſtinguiſhed, וים רהק ים, *viz.* AND OF THE SEA, THE moſt DISTANT SEA: the Words being in Appoſition: and by this Conſtruction they become nearly parallel to thoſe that precede, *viz. of all the Ends of the Earth.*

V. 8. *They alſo that dwell in the uttermoſt Parts are afraid at thy Tokens:* ———— וייראו ישבי קצות מאותתיך] Rather — REVERENCE THY SIGNS, as V. 4.

V. 9. ———— *thou greatly enricheſt it with the River of God,* which *is full of Water:* ———— תעשרנה פלג אלהים מלא מים] Rather — THOU, O GOD, ENRICHEST IT with THE RIVER which IS FULL OF WATER.

T V. 12.

V. 12. —*and the little Hills rejoice on every Side.* : ‏וגיל נבעות תהגרנה‎]
Rather, with the old Verſion — AND THE HILLS SHALL BE (or
ARE) COMPASSED WITH GLADNESS.

V. 13. *The Paſtures are clothed with Flocks :* — ‏לבשו כרים הצאן‎]
All the old Verſions ſeem to have read ‏כרי‎ *in regimine* — THE LAMBS
OF THE FLOCKS ARE CLOTHED.

PSALM LXVI.

V. 12. — *but thou broughteſt us out into a wealthy Place.* ‏ותוציאנו‎
‏לרויה :‎] All the ancient Verſions read here ‏לרוחה‎ — TO A PLACE
OF REFRESHMENT ; which is doubtleſs the true Reading : for ‏רויה‎
ſignifies only *moiſt*, or *well watered*.

PSALM LXVII.

V. 1. *God be merciful &c.*] See Pſ. XLV. 4.

PSALM LXVIII.

V. 4. — *by his Name Jah,* ‏ביה שמו‎] None of the ancient Verſions ſeem to have read the ‏ב‎ in their Texts : or, if they did, they
conſidered it as redundant ; which it frequently is before all Caſes.
However, theſe two Words cannot be joined to the ſecond Hemiſtic,
as they are in our Verſion : but ought to be rendered, and connected
with the latter, thus --- (HIS NAME IS JAH ;) AND REJOICE BE-
FORE HIM. *Jah* ſeems to be only a Contraction of ‏יהיה‎, *Jehovah*.

V. 8. *The Earth ſhook, the Heavens alſo dropped at the Preſence of
God :* even *Sinai itſelf* was moved *at the Preſence of God, the God of
Iſrael.* ‏ארץ רעשה אף שמים נטפו — מפני אלהים זה סיני — מפני‎
‏אלהים אלהי ישראל :‎] Rather —— THE EARTH SHOOK, THE
HEAVENS ALSO DROPPED, AT THE PRESENCE OF THE GOD,
WHO WAS AT SINAI ; AT THE PRESENCE OF GOD, THE GOD OF
ISRAEL.

V. 9. *Thou, O God, didſt ſend a plentiful Rain, whereby thou didſt
confirm thine Inheritance, when it was weary.* ‏גשם נדבות תניף אלהים‎
‏נחלתך — ונלאה אתה כוננתה :‎] Rather — THOU, O GOD, DIDST
SEND

SEND A GRACIOUS RAIN TO THINE INHERITANCE; AND, WHEN
IT WAS EXHAUSTED, THOU DIDST ESTABLISH IT.

V. 10. — *thou, O God, haſt prepared of thy Goodneſs for the poor.*
[תכין בטובתך לעני אלהים:] Rather— THOU, O GOD, ACCORDING
TO THY GOODNESS, DIDST PROVIDE FOR THE POOR.

V. 11. *The Lord gave the Word, great* was *the Company of thoſe
that publiſhed* it. [אדני יתן אמר — המבשרות צבא רב:] Rather, per-
haps, in one Hemiſtic --- THE LORD GAVE THE WORD OF GLAD
TIDINGS TO THE GREAT ARMY: or, in two, thus --- THE LORD
GAVE THE WORD; there were GLAD TIDINGS TO HIS NUMEROUS
HOST. This is the very Word our Lord uſes, Iſa. LXI. 1. where he
ſpeaks of his *Goſpel*; and which He quotes and applies to Himſelf,
Luke IV. 18. So alſo Ch. VII. 22. we read — *to the poor the* GOSPEL *is
preached*, which implies the ſame Idea as we have in the foregoing
Verſe. But notwithſtanding the ſecondary Alluſion, what is here ſaid
refers primarily to the total Diſcomfiture of Siſera and Jabin by
Deborah, Judg. IV.

V. 12. *Kings of Armies did flee apace:* — [מלכי צבאות ידדון ידדון]
I ſuſpect that the true Reading here is — ידדון נדוד, *flying did fly*.

V. 13. *Though ye have lien among the Pots, yet ſhall ye be as the
Wings of a Dove, covered with Silver, and her Feathers with yellow
Gold.* אם תשכבון בין שפתים—כנפי יונה נחפה בכסף—ואברותיה בירקרק
[חרוץ:] The Word שפתים never ſignifies *Pots*; and there ſeems to be
no Occaſion to add any Words to the Text, which appears ſufficiently
clear without: thus --- DID NOT YE LIE AMONG THE SHEEP-
FOLDS, O YE WINGS OF A DOVE, COVERED WITH SILVER,
AND WITH BURNISHED GOLD IN HER FEATHERS? See אם thus
uſed, Eſt. IV. 14. Jer. XXXI. 20. שפתים I render as in our Verſion,
Judg. V. 16. though it properly ſignifies *Rails* or *Bars*, which were
uſed for that Purpoſe: ſee Par. Proph. P. 78. and to ירקרק I give the
Senſe of *burniſhed*, becauſe in Chaldee it ſignifies *a Topaz*, a Stone
both *bright* and *yellow*: or, as the Word generally ſignifies *green*, it
may mean the greeniſh Caſt which Gold ſometimes has; thus Martial,
 Miratur Scythicas VIRENTIS AURI
 Jupiter flammas ——. B. XII. Epig. 15.
This Allegory appears to me to have a clear Reference to the Tribes
of Reuben, Part of Manaſſeh, Dan and Aſher, which did not aſſiſt

        Deborah

Deborah in the Battle againſt Siſera ; and which ſhe reproaches in her Song, Judg. V. 15, 16, 17. They are called *Doves*, as being the fitteſt Emblems of their Cowardice. The *Gold and Silver* to which the Wings are compared may allude to the *Riches*, which theſe Tribes ſeem to have acquired, by preferring a domeſtic, to a warlike, Life. Thus Iſſachar is called *an Aſs* ; Judah, *a Lion*, &c. to denote their reſpective Qualities, Gen. XLIX.

V. 14. *When the Almighty ſcattered Kings in it, it was* white *as Snow in Salmon.* : בֿרה תשלג בצלמון — בפרש שרי מלכים] Rather --- WHEN THE ALMIGHTY DISCOMFITED THE KINGS, ON HER ACCOUNT THOU DIDST BECOME AS THE SNOW OF SALMON. The Verbs פרס, פרע, פרץ, and פרש, are all ſo like in Form, Sound, and Senſe, that they are often confounded. I render מלכים *the Kings*, as Siſera and Jabin appear evidently to be meant. בֿרה I tranſlate *on her Account*, viz. Deborah's ; whoſe Reproaches made them *pale* with Indignation : ſo many Inſtances occur in Scripture, particularly in the poetical Books, of Relatives uſed in this Manner without Antecedents, when the Subject is ſo well known that it cannot be miſtaken, that it is needleſs to cite them. תשלג I make the ſecond Perſon, as the Tribes are ſtill addreſſed in the ſame Character.

V. 15. *The Hill of God* is as *the Hill of Baſhan, an high Hill* as *the Hill of Baſhan.* : הר גבננים הר בשן — הר אלהים הר בשן] Rather, I think, thus --- THE HILL OF BASHAN IS AN EMINENT HILL, THE HILL OF BASHAN IS A VERY HIGH HILL. I tranſlate הר אלהים, *an eminent Hill*, becauſe, according to the Hebrew Phraſeology, any Thing diſtinguiſhed in it's kind has the Addition of *God* after it, as Gen. XXIII. 6. XXX. 8. 1 Sam. XXVI. 12. &c. הר גבננים ſignifies a *Hill with many Tops*, as in Homer πολυδειρας. Our Tranſlators, as it ſhould ſeem by the old Verſion, thought that this Verſe referred to Mount Zion. But it ſeems to me more probable, that it is to be conſidered as an Apoſtrophe to the Victory, ſo often mentioned in Scripture, which the Iſraelites gained over Og the King of Baſhan, and Sihon King of the Amorites.

V. 16. *Why leap ye, ye high Hills ?* למה תרצדון הרים גבננים] Rather---WHY DO YE LOOK WITH JEALOUSY, YE HIGH HILLS ? So this Verb, which occurs nowhere elſe, ſignifies in Arabic. This ſeems addreſſed to other Hills, which are repreſented as jealous that God had made Baſhan the Inheritance of his People.

V. 17.

V. 17. *The Chariots of God* are *twenty thoufand*, even *thoufands of Angels:* — [רכב אלהים רבתים אלפי שנאן] Rather perhaps — THE LORD RODE with MYRIADS, with THOUSANDS OF THOUSANDS.

—— *the Lord* is *among them* as in *Sinai, in the holy* Place. אדני [בם סיני בקרש] Rather perhaps — THE LORD is AMONG THEM; it (*viz.* Bafhan) is A SINAI IN RESPECT TO HOLINESS. See ב thus ufed, Pf. XC. 10.

V. 18. — *yea, for the rebellious alfo, that the Lord might dwell among them.* [ואף סוררים לשכן יה אלהים:] Rather —— THAT THE LORD MIGHT HAVE THE HABITATION OF THE REBELLIOUS. Thus is לשכן rendered, Pf. CIV. 12. The Meaning of this Verfe feems to be — " That God had intirely defeated the Kings of " Canaan, or made them Tributaries, in order that his chofen might " poffefs their Country."

V. 19. *Bleffed* be *the Lord*, who *daily loadeth us* with Benefits, even *the God of our Salvation.* [ברוך אדני יום יום — יעמם לנו האל ישועתנו:] Rather ——— BLESSED be GOD DAILY, THE GOD OF OUR SALVATION, who BURDENETH HIMSELF WITH US. See the Word thus ufed, Zech. XII. 3.

V. 20. *He that is our God, is the God of Salvation, and unto God the Lord* belong *the Iffues from Death.* וליהוה — האל לנו אל למושעות [אדני למות תוצאות:] Rather — GOD is TO US A GOD OF SALVATION; AND UNTO THE LORD, THE GOD OF DEATH, belongs THE DETERMINATION, OR EFFICIENCY: for למות תוצאות. cannot be conftrued *the Iffues from Death.*

V. 23. *That thy Foot may be dipped in the Blood* of thine *Enemies*, and *the Tongue of thy Dogs in the fame.* למען תמחץ רגלך בדם — לשן [כלביך מאיבים מנהו:] This Verfe feems very corrupt; for מהץ can only fignify *to wound.* All the ancient Verfions read here מרחץ, as Pf. LVIII. 10. which is doubtlefs the true Reading, and there is the greateft Probability that מאיבים is another Miftake for מאדם: or perhaps מארמים (as Ex. XXV. 5.) agreeing with the laft Antecedent, though an uncommon Conftruction. Wherefore I would render this Verfe according to the Common Prayer Verfion — THAT THY FOOT MAY BE WASHED IN BLOOD; (or, THAT THOU MAYEST WASH THY FOOT IN BLOOD) and THE TONGUE OF THY DOGS MAY BE RED THROUGH THE SAME.

V. 26.

V. 26. — *even the Lord, from the Fountain of Ifrael.* אדני ממקור
ישראל:] I read — אדנים מקור — THE GOD, THE FOUNTAIN OF
ISRAEL. God is faid to be מקור היים, *the Fountain of Life*, Pf.
XXXVI. 9. and this I fuppofe to be the Senfe here intended.

V. 27. — *the Princes of Judah*, and *their Counfel*, — ישרי יהודה רגמתם]
רגמתם can only fignify *their Heap of Stones*. As all the old Verfions
(the Chaldee excepted) have here their *Princes* or *Generals*, I conclude
they read רומתם, THEIR EXCELLENCY: for Judah is called *the Lawgiver*, (Pf. LX. 7. CVIII. 8.) and was diftinguifhed above all the other
Tribes, not only by taking the Lead in War, by having the Metropolis
and Temple within his Diftrict, but principally by being the Anceftor
of the great Lawgiver of the whole World.

V. 28. *Thy God hath commanded thy Strength*: — עוך אלהיך צוה]
I would read אלהים with all the ancient Verfions, and render — COM-
MAND THY STRENGTH, O LORD; which would fuit better with the
next Hemiftic.

V. 30. *Rebuke the Company of Spearmen, the Multitude of the Bulls
with the Calves of the People*, till every one *fubmit himfelf with Pieces
of Silver: fcatter thou the People that delight in War.* — גער חית קנה
עדת אבירים בעגלי — עם ים מתרפס ברצי כסף — בזר עמים קרבות
יחפצו:] Thus ought I think the Hemiftics to be diftinguifhed; and
thus rendered — REBUKE THE BEAST OF THE REED, THE CONGRE-
GATION OF BULLS, WITH THE CALVES; THE PEOPLE OF THE
SEA, WHO HUMBLE THEMSELVES BEFORE FRAGMENTS OF SIL-
VER: SCATTER (I fay) THE PEOPLE WHO DELIGHT IN WAR.
By the *Beaft of the Reed* is clearly meant *the Hippopotamus*, which denotes *the Egyptians. The Company of Bulls and Calves* is a plain Allufion to their *Apis* and *Serapis*, or *Ifis* and *Ofiris*, which they worfhip-
ped; and to which the third Hemiftic refers, calling thefe Idols contemptuoufly *Fragments of Silver*, becaufe, I fuppofe, overlaid or plated
with that Metal. A third Characterriftic of this Nation is alfo mentioned: they are called *the People of the Sea.* Ifaiah defcribes their
Country *by the Tongue of the Egyptian Sea*, and by *the Seven Streams.*
XI. 15. And Ezekiel defcribes the Tyrians by the Appellation of *Princes
of the Sea* for the fame Reafon, becaufe they bordered upon the Sea,
and carried on a great Commerce. This Defcription is doubtlefs more
applicable to the latter than the former: but, when accompanied
with the other diftinguifhing Marks, could not fail of being eafily underftood.

derstood. Lastly, in the fourth Hemistic they are pointed out by a fourth Circumstance, viz. *a People* that *delight in War* ; where the Psalmist concludes, as he had begun, by requesting God to repress their Fury It may be objected to this Interpretation, that בעגלי is *in regimine :* but if it be considered how often such Words are used *specially*, the Objection will have little Weight. This Word cannot be construed with עמים without destroying the Hemistics, and with them the Sense of the Verse ; hence it is probable the מ was dropped by some unskilful Transcriber, who might officiously herein attempt to mend the Text. See the Particle ב used in the Sense here proposed, Nold. 4 & 9.

V. 31. — *Ethiopia shall soon stretch out her Hands unto God.* כוש תריץ ידיו לאלהים :] We ought I think to read the Text thus —— תפרש ידיה — see Pf. XLIV 20. for רוץ never signifies *to stretch*, but always *to run*.

V. 34. *Ascribe ye Strength unto God. his Excellency is over Israel, and his Strength is in the Clouds.* תנו עז לאלהים על ישראל — גאותו ועוז בשחקים :] Or thus — ASCRIBE YE STRENGTH UNTO GOD ON ACCOUNT OF ISRAEL ; WHOSE MAJESTY AND WHOSE STRENGTH IS IN THE HEAVENS.

V. 35. *O God thou art terrible out of thy holy Places :* — נורא אלהים ממקדשיך] Rather — O GOD thou art TO BE REVERENCED ON ACCOUNT OF THY HOLY PLACES. See Pf. LXV. 4.

PSALM LXIX.

V. 4. — *then I restored that which I took not away.* אשר לא גזלתי אז אשיב :] אז ought here to be rendered THEREFORE, as Jer. XXII. 15. Mich. III. 4.

V. 10. *When I wept and chastened my Soul with Fasting,* — ואבכה בצום נפשי] Rather — WHEN I WEPT WITH THE FASTING OF MY APPETITE.

V. 13. *But as for me, my Prayer is unto thee,* —————— ואני תפלתי לך] The Syriac reads———התפללתי———in *Hithpahel*, BUT I PRAY UNTO THEE.

V. 22 *Let their Table become a Snare before them : and that which should have been for their Welfare, let it become a Trap.*] The last Hemistic — ולשלומים למוקש — ought I think to be rendered — AND
THEIR

THEIR PEACE OFFERINGS A TRAP: the Verb being underſtood from the preceding Clauſe. This is the uſual Senſe of שלמים; which in the Text appears to have the ו redundant; and the Targum omits it : and *Table* being mentioned ſeems to determine for that Signification. For it was uſual after theſe Sorts of Sacrifices *to feaſt* upon ſome Parts of the Victims. Here we have an *Antiptoſis.* See Job. XXX. 31.

V. 26. — *and they talk to the Grief of thoſe whom thou haſt wounded.* ואל מכאוב חלליך יספרו :] Almoſt all the ancient Verſions read here יספו —AND THEY ADD TO THE GRIEF &c. which is a better Reading, and adopted by our old Verſion.

V. 27. *Add Iniquity to their Iniquity :* תנה עון על עונם] *Qu.* ought not עון to be tranſlated, THE PUNISHMENT OF INIQUITY, as in the Margin, and Lam. IV. 6. 1 Sam. XXVIII. 10. or תנה rendered —— SUFFER INIQUITY TO BE ADDED ?

V. 31. — *a Bullock that hath Horns and Hoofs.*] *i. e.* that is of full Age for Sacrifice, which was three at leaſt ; So Virgil, Ecl. III. V. 87.
Jam cornu petat, et pedibus qui ſpargat arenam.
And Juvenal, Sat. XII. V. 7.
Quippe ferox vitulus, templis maturus et aræ,
Spargenduſque mero, quem jam pudet ubera matris
Ducere, qui vexat naſcenti robora cornu.

V. 32. *The humble ſhall ſee* this, *and be glad : and your Heart ſhall live that ſeek God.* : ראו ענוים — יſֿבחו דרſֿי אלהים — ויחי לבבכם] Rather --- THE HUMBLE SHALL SEE this ; THEY THAT SEEK GOD SHALL REJOICE : AND YOUR HEART SHALL LIVE. Thus the old Verſion.

PSALM LXX.

V. 1. *Make haſte, O God, to deliver me ;* אלהים להצילני] There is clearly a Word wanting in this Hemiſtic. Now the Word of the Title, which immediately precedes, is very obſcure and ſeems redundant, *viz.* להזכיר; it might perhaps be a Miſtake for הזכר, REMEMBER : or the Word omitted may have been רצה, *be pleaſed*, as Pſ. XL. 13.

PSALM LXXI.

V. 15. — *for I know not the Numbers thereof.* : כי לא ידעתי ספרות] ספרות ſeems to be a Miſtake for ספרים, the Infinitive with the Affix, and

and כי ought to be rendered THOUGH (as Gen. VIII. 21. Exod. XIII. 17.) *viz.* I CANNOT NUMBER THEM, *i. e.* the feveral Inftances of them.

V. 16. *I will go in the Strength of the Lord God:* אבא בגברות אדני יהוה] As אבא (the Future of בוא) is often written אבא, fo I am perfuaded it ought to be here. For thefe Words, as we now read them, will not I doubt bear the Senfe which our Verfion gives them, *viz.* "I will abide ftedfaft, being upholden by the Power of God." See the old Verfion. And, though this Senfe were admitted, yet would it be unconnected with the Context. I would therefore read אבא, the Future of נבא, and render —— I WILL CELEBRATE THE MIGHTY ACTS OF THE LORD GOD: fo this Verb fignifies, 1 Chron. XXV. 1,3. (though improperly rendered *prophefy*) and גברות has this Senfe, Pf. CVI. 2. CXLV. 4. &c. Or, (retaining the prefent Reading) thus — I WILL GO ON (or, PROCEED) WITH THE MIGHTY ACTS OF THE LORD.

V. 18. *Now alfo when I am old and graybeaded,* — וגם עד זקנה ושיבה] This Hemiftic doubtlefs belongs to the preceding Verfe, and ought to be rendered --- EVEN UNTO OLD AGE AND GRAY HAIRS.

V. 19. *Thy Righteoufnefs alfo, O God, is very high, who haft done great Things.* וצדקתך אלהים עד מרום — אשר עשית גדלות:] Rather ---THY RIGHTEOUSNESS ALSO, O GOD, IS A WITNESS ON HIGH, THAT THOU HAST DONE GREAT THINGS. אשר is thus ufed, Lev. V. 5. 1 Sam. XVIII. 15. This feems to be an Allufion to the Cuftom of fetting up Witneffes in an elevated Place, when they delivered their Evidence in Courts of Juftice, that they might be feen and heard by all.

V. 23. *My Lips fhall greatly rejoice when I fing unto thee;* — תרננה שפתי כי אזמרה לך] Rather — MY LIPS SHALL SHOUT FOR JOY &c.

PSALM LXXII.

V. 3. *The Mountains fhall bring Peace to the People, and the little Hills, by Righteoufnefs.* ישאו הרים שלום לעם — וגבעות בצדקה:] Rather — AND THE HILLS RIGHTEOUSNESS: for ב in בצדקה is not acknowledged by moft of the ancient Verfions. The Miftake feems owing to בצדק occurring in the preceding Line.

U

V. 5.

V. 5. They shall fear thee as long as the Sun and Moon endure,] So Ovid, *Amor. Lib.* I. *Eleg.* 15.

Cum Sole et Luna semper Aratus erit.

V. 6. — as Showers that water the Earth. : כרביבים זרזיף ארץ] זרזיף is an ἅπαξ λεγ. and feems to be a Miftake for זרפים, the Participle prefent of זרף, which in Syriac fignifies *to water*, whence comes زنبאל, *Pluvia, Imber, Nimbus.* In Chaldee זרף has the Senfe of זרז, *Irrigatio.*

V. 7. In his Days shall the righteous flourish: — יפרח בימיו צדיק] Moft of the ancient Verfions read צדק, RIGHTEOUSNESS, which is preferable.

V. 16. There shall be an handful of Corn in the Earth — יהי פסת בר בארץ] I read here with the Syriac פשרת or פ׳ש, ABUNDANCE. For *an Handful* is contrary to the Idea intended to be conveyed.

—— *upon the Top of the Mountains —* בראש הרים] This ought doubtlefs to be Part of the fecond Hemiftic, thus — UPON THE TOP OF THE MOUNTAINS HIS FRUIT SHALL SHAKE LEBANON.

—— *and they of the City shall flourish —* ויציצו מעיר] Rather — AND HE WILL MAKE IT TO FLOURISH ABOUT THE CITY: for the latter ו in ויציצו feems to be the Affix Pronoun, which has פרי for it's Antecedent.

V. 17. — his Name shall be continued —— ינין שמו] The Verb נון occurs nowhere elfe : but, as נין fignifies *a Son*, Critics have fuppofed that this Root muft mean *to be as a Son*, to continue the Father's Name. But I think it can hardly be doubted that the true Reading is ילין, SHALL REMAIN.

—— *and Men shall be bleffed in him ;* ויתברכו בו] According to the LXX, Vulgate, Arabic, and Ethiopic Verfions, the Words here wanting are כל שבטי לארץ — ALL THE TRIBES OF THE EARTH.

V. 20. The Prayers of David &c.] See the Note Job XXXI. 40. If the Pfalms of David end here, how comes it to pafs that fo many of them occur afterwards? See CXXXI.—II.—III. &c. It is not worth while to inquire into this Matter, as thefe Places are evidently unau-thentic Interpolations: and we might with as much Propriety admit into the Body of the Text the Words that immediately follow thefe, *viz.* ספר שלישי *The third Book,* or תפלים, or הצי הספר *The Half of the Book,* or *of the Pfalms,* inferted in the Middle of Pf. LXXVIII, and other Maſſoretical Fancies.

PSALM

Psalm LXXIII.

V. 4. *For* there are *no Bands in their Death :* [כי אין הרצבות למותם]
That is, fays our old Verfion, *by Sicknefs,* which is Death's Meſſenger :
but this may perhaps be better underſtood of their " not being led
" bound to Death," like other Malefactors. The Word הרצב occurs
nowhere elfe, except Ifa. LVIII. 6.

—— *but their Strength is firm.* [ובריא עולם :] בריא cannot I think
convey the Idea of *Firmnefs.* The LXX, Symmachus, Arabic, and
Vulgate, feem to have read בריח, like *Bars.*

V. 5. *They* are *not in Trouble* as other *Men :* —— [בעמל אנוש אינימו]
THEY are IN NO HUMAN TROUBLE.

V. 7. —— *they have more than Heart could wiſh.* [עברו כשכיות לבב :]
Rather --- THEY EXCEED THE THOUGHTS OF THE HEART :
i. e. "they are wicked beyond Conception." The fame Sentiment,
probably borrowed from hence, occurs, Jer. V. 28. *viz. They are waxen
fat, they ſhine ; yea, they overpaſs the Deeds of the wicked.*

V. 8. —— *and ſpeak wickedly* concerning *Oppreſſion : they ſpeak loftily.*
[—וידברו ברע — עשק מרום ידברו :] Rather —— AND SPEAK OF
WICKEDNESS ; THEY TALK OF CONTENDING AGAINST THE
MOST HIGH ; or, THEY TALK INJURIOUSLY AGAINST THE
MOST HIGH. The Words which immediately follow eſtabliſh either
of thefe Senfes.

V. 10. *Therefore his People return hither :* —— [לכן ישוב עמו] According to our prefent Verfion *his* has here no Antecedent : but if the
Conſtruction of מרום, V. 8. be admitted, THE MOST HIGH will be
the Subject.

—— *and Waters of a full Cup* —— [ומי מלא] Rather —— AND
MUCH WATER IS WRUNG OUT TO THEM, *viz.* the wicked :
for the Words fignify literally *Waters of Fulnefs.*

V. 14. *For all the Day long have I been plagued, and chaſtened every
Morning.* [ואהי נגוע כל היום — ותוכחתי לבקרים :] Rather —— FOR
I HAVE BEEN CONTINUALLY PLAGUED, AND CHASTENED WITH
SCOURGES. So בקר fignifies, Lev. XIX. 20. ל is fometimes the Sign
of the Ablative Cafe. See Noldius.

V. 17.

V. 17. — then *understood I their End.*] So the Poet,
Abstulit hunc tandem Rufini pœna tumultum,
Absolvitque Deos ——. Claud. *Lib.* I. *Cap.* 21.

V. 19. *How are they* brought *into Desolation as in a Moment!* איך
ברגע [היו לשמה כרגע] Read with all the Versions, and render ——
How suddenly are they in Desolation!

V. 20. *As a Dream when* one *awaketh;* [כחלום מהקיץ אדני] Rather
— As a Dream on awaking, O Lord: for the Verb seems to be
in the Infinitive.

—— *so, O Lord, when thou awakest, thou shalt despise their Image.*
[בעיר צלמם תבזה] Rather — THOU WILT DISREGARD THEIR
FOOLISH VAIN SHEW.

V. 23. — *thou hast holden* me *by my right Hand.* [אחזת ביד ימיני]
These Words may be rendered --- THOU HAST TAKEN MY RIGHT
HAND BY THE HAND: or, THOU HAST TAKEN HOLD OF MY
RIGHT HAND.

PSALM LXXIV.

V. 2. —— *the Rod of thine Inheritance* which *thou hast redeemed;*
[נאלת שבט נחלתך] Rather — THE TRIBE &c. as in the Margin;
for Mount *Zion* in the next Hemistic determines that this Word is to
be taken in this Sense, and that the Tribe hereby meant is *Judah's.*

V. 3. *Lift up thy Feet unto the perpetual Desolations:* [הרימה פעמיך
למשאות נצח] Rather — UNTO THE TOTAL DESOLATIONS; as Ps.
XLIX. 19.

—— even *all that the Enemy hath done wickedly in the Sanctuary.*
[כל הרע אויב בקדש] Rather — SUPPRESS THE EVIL OF THE ENE-
MY IN THE SANCTUARY. כל is here considered as the Imperative
of כול, which has this Sense, Jer. VI. 11. XX. 9.

V. 5. *A Man was famous according as he had lifted up Axes upon the*
thick Trees. [יודע כמביא למעלה—בסבך עץ קרדמות] I read יודע מביא,
and render --- A MAN HAS BEEN SEEN BY THEE LIFTING UP
AXES AGAINST THE THICKEST PART OF THE TIMBER ON
HIGH. That is, I imagine, "against the Beams and Rafters of the
"Covering of the Temple."

V. 7.

V. 7. — *they have defiled* by casting down *the dwelling Place of thy Name to the Ground.* : לארץ הללו משכן שמך [Rather —— THEY HAVE BROKEN DOWN TO THE GROUND AS PROFANE THE DWELLING PLACE OF THY NAME. See חלל thus used, Pf. LXXXIX. 34.

V. 9. — *neither* is there *amongft us any that knoweth how long.* ולא : אתנו יודע עד מה [Rather — THAT KNOWETH WHEREFORE, *i. e.* " this Calamity is come upon us." See Noldius.

V. 11, 12. *Why withdraweft thou thy Hand, even thy right Hand?* *pluck* it *out of thy Bofom. For God is my King* &c. — למה תשיב ידך וימינך מקרב היקך — כלהו אלהים וגו [Thefe two Verfes ought I think to make but one, the Hemiftics to be thus divided, read, and rendered --- WHY DOST THOU RETURN BACK THINE HAND, EVEN THY RIGHT HAND FROM OUT OF THY BOSOM? DRAW IT FORTH QUITE, O GOD, MY KING OF OLD &c. כלה fig- nifies *to complete what was begun,* which in this Cafe feems to be *the drawing out of the Hand:* for God is reprefented as beginning to draw it out, and then returning it back again; for which Reafon the Pfal- mift prays him not to break off at the Attempt only, but to carry the Work quite through.

V. 18. *Remember this,* that *the Enemy hath reproached,* — זכר זות : איב הרף [Rather — REMEMBER that THE ENEMY DISPARAGETH THESE THINGS: *i. e.* thy Works, juft mentioned.

V. 19. *O deliver not the Soul of thy Turtle Dove unto the Multitude* of the wicked : — אל תתן לחית נפש תורך [Rather — UNTO WILD BEASTS : לחית being contractedly written for לחיות.

—— *forget not the Congregation* ——] חית here feems rather to fignify LIFE, anfwerable to נפש.

PSALM LXXV.

V. 1. *Unto thee, O. God, do we give Thanks,* unto thee *do we give Thanks :* — הודינו לך אלהים הודינו [Rather — WE GIVE THANKS UNTO THEE, O GOD, WE GIVE THANKS.

—— *for that thy Name* is near, *thy wonderous Works declare.* וקרוב : שמך ספרו נפלאותיך [Moft of the ancient Verfions read here וקראנו and ספרנו — AND WE CALL UPON THY NAME, and DECLARE THY WONDEROUS WORKS.

V. 8.

V. 8. —*and the Wine is red* :— [ויין חמר] Rather — IS TROUBLED, or THICK.

—— *but the Dregs thereof all the wicked of the Earth shall wring them out*, and *drink* them. [אך שמריה ימצו ישתו כל רשעי ארץ :] I read here וישתו ימין, and render — SURELY HE WILL WRING OUT THE DREGS THEREOF, AND ALL THE WICKED OF THE EARTH SHALL DRINK them.

V. 9. *But I will declare for ever* ;—[ואני אגיד לעלם] I read with the LXX, Ethiopic, and Arabic, אגיל, I WILL REJOICE : which suits better with the Context.

PSALM LXXVI.

V. 4. *Thou art more glorious* and *excellent than the Mountains of Prey*. [נאור אתה — אדיר מהררי טרף :] If this Verse were an Apostrophe to Zion, the Construction might be applicable to it : but it seems more natural to make it relate to God. In this Case I would render —THOU art become GLORIOUS, yea MIGHTY AT THE MOUNTAINS OF PREY. See מהר thus rendered, Exod. XXXIII. 6.

V. 6. — *both the Chariot and Horse are cast into a deep Sleep.* [נרדם ורכב וסוס :] Rather — BOTH THE RIDER AND HORSE &c. or if we read נרדו, we may render — BOTH THE CHARIOT AND HORSE ARE OVERCOME.

PSALM LXXVII.

V. 2. — *my Sore ran in the Night, and ceased not* : [ידי לילה נגרה ולא הפוג] It is not clear that יד can signify *a Sore*, nor yet *a Stroke*; for the only Place that may seem to countenance either of these Senses admits of another Sense. See Job XXIII. 2. The Syriac seems to have read נגעי or נגפי — ידו — HIS HAND STRIKES ME IN THE NIGHT, AND CEASETH NOT : or (by only reading ירו) HIS HAND EXHAUSTETH me. See Taylor.

V. 5. *I have considered the Days of old, the Years of ancient Times.* [השבתי ימים מקדם — שנות עולמים :] There is a Word wanting in the last Hemistic, and none is more proper than that which immediately follows, *viz.* אזכרה : it is accordingly made a Part of it in nearly all the ancient Versions, *viz.* thus —— I HAVE CALLED TO REMEMBRANCE THE YEARS OF ANCIENT TIMES.

V. 6.

V. 6. *I call to Remembrance my Song in the Night : I commune with mine own Heart: and my Spirit maketh diligent Search.* נגינתי בלילה [עם לבבי — אשיחה ויחפש רוחי: Inflead of נגינתי, I read הגיתי, as V. 12. with the LXX, Syriac, Arabic, and Vulgate, and render — I MEDITATE IN THE NIGHT IN MY HEART ; I COMPLAIN, AND MY SPIRIT INQUIRETH thus --- WILL THE LORD &c.

V. 10. — but I will remember *the Years of the right Hand of the most High.* [שנות ימין עליון: Rather, I think, with moſt of the old Verſions — for there are CHANGES IN THE RIGHT HAND OF THE MOST HIGH : *i. e.* "that fame Hand which lately afflicted me with "it's Stroke. (V. 2.) will ſoon *take hold of my own Hand :*" (as Pſ. LXXIII. 23. and LXXIV. 11.) ſo God is ſaid ανθρωποπαθως *to repent,* when He means to deſiſt from inflicting Puniſhments. Thus I think שנות ought alſo to be rendered, V. 5.

V. 18. *The Voice of thy Thunder was in the Heaven :* [קול רעמך בגלגל] גלגל ſignifies properly the HOLLOW ARCH, the *Cælorum convexa.*

PSALM LXXVIII.

V. 4. — *and his Strength, and his wonderful Words that he hath done.* [ועזוזו ונפלאתיו אשר עשה: Would not — AND HIS MIGHTY AND HIS WONDERFUL WORKS THAT HE HATH WROUGHT --- be better ?

V. 25. *Man did eat Angels' Food : he ſent them Meat to the full.* לחם [אבירים — צידה שלח להם לשבע: אבירים ſeems to ſignify OXEN in this Place, as Pſ. XXII. 12. L. 13. LXVIII. 30. Iſa. XXXIV. 7. Jer. L. 11. but this Word is uſed in no other Place to denote *Angels.* The correſponding Word צידה, which ſignifies any *Food procured by hunting,* countenances the firſt Senſe. I would therefore tranſlate --- EVERY ONE EAT THE FLESH OF OXEN : HE SENT THEM VENISON (or, VICTUALS) IN PLENTY. See לחם rendered *Fleſh,* Zeph. I. 17.

V. 31. — *the fatteſt of them* —— במשמניהם] Rather —— THE STRONGEST, with the old Verſion, or THE WEALTHIEST, as Pſ. XXII. 29.

V. 32. — *and believed not for his wonderous Works.* ולא האמינו [בנפלאתיו: Rather, with the old Verſion — AND BELIEVED NOT HIS WONDEROUS WORKS.

V. 41.

V. 41. — *and limited the Holy One of Ifrael.* [וקדוש ישראל התוו:] AND SET BOUNDS TO (i. e. *circumfcribed*) Him whom the Heavens cannot contain within the narrow Limits (as they fuppofed) of an Idol : or by this Phrafe may be meant *fetting Bounds to His Power*, which they did, when they fuppofed Him unable to bring them into the Land of Promife. Numb. XIV. 2, 3.

V. 49. — *by fending evil Angels* among them. [מישלחת מלאכי רעים:] מישלחת is here a Noun, put in Appofition, and governed of the Verb ישלח : it fignifies *the fending forth*. I would therefore render this Hemiftic thus --- THE MISSIONS OF EVIL MINISTERS : *viz.* not *Angels*; but THE FIERCE ANGER, WRATH, INDIGNATION, AND TROUBLE, which God employed as the Inftruments of his Vengeance. Thus is *the Fire* called *his Minifter.* Pf. CIV. 4.

V. 50. *He made a Way to his Anger;* — [יפלס נתיב לאפו] Rather --- HE LEVELLED A WAY --- i. e. "He made it plain and direct, "fo as not to mifs thofe whom it was intended to ftrike." See Taylor.

V. 63. *The Fire confumed their young Men;* [בחוריו אכלה אש] I read אכל האש —and render—THE FIRE CONSUMED THEIR CHOICEST YOUNG MEN; for fo בהור fignifies. ——— *and their Maidens were not given to Marriage.* [ובתולתיו לא הוללו:] Rather—AND THEIR MAIDENS WERE NOT CELEBRATED WITH A MARRIAGE SONG, had no *Epithalamium*; which correfponds to *the Lamentations* of the Widows in the next Verfe.

V. 69. *And he built his Sanctuary like high Palaces:* [ויבן כמו רמים מקדשו] I read במו with the Syriac — AND HE BUILT HIS SANCTUARY ON HIGH : for the Temple, wherein was the Sanctuary, was on Mount Zion, the higheft Part of Jerufalem. ——— *like the Earth which he hath eftablifhed for ever.* [כארץ יסדה לעולם:] Read again with the fame, and almoft all the other old Verfions, בארץ, — HE HATH ESTABLISHED IT IN THE EARTH FOR EVER.

V. 72. *So he fed them according to the Integrity of his Heart:* [וירעם כתם לבבו] I read here again with all the old Interpreters בתם --- AND HE FED THEM IN THE INTEGRITY &c. See alfo next Pfalm, Verfe 11.

PSALM LXXIX.

V. 2. — *unto the Beasts of the Earth.* לחיתו ארץ] A clear Mistake for לחיות.

V. 5. *How long, Lord, wilt thou be angry for ever? shall thy Jealousy burn like Fire?* [עד מה יהוה תאנף—לנצה תבער כמו אש קנאתך Rather --- HOW LONG, LORD, WILT THOU BE ANGRY? SHALL THY JEALOUSY BURN LIKE FIRE FOR EVER?

V. 8. *O remember not against us former Iniquities:* אל תזכר לנו עונת ראשנים] Rather, as in the Margin — THE INIQUITIES OF THEM THAT WERE BEFORE US, equivalent to *our Forefathers.*

PSALM LXXX.

V. 2. — *and come and save us.* ולכה לישעתה לנו:] Rather — AND COME TO OUR SALVATION; or, more literally, AND COME TO US FOR SALVATION.

V. 3. *Turn us again* — השיבנו] Rather — RESTORE US: so also V. 7, & 19.

V. 5. *Thou feedest them with the Bread of Tears:* — האכלתם לחם רמעה] Thus *Bread of Care, Bread of Affliction, Bread of Adversity,* are Scriptural Phrases.

—— *and givest them Tears to drink in great Measure.* ותשקמו בדמעות שליש:] Or — MAKEST THEM TO DRINK OF TEARS A THIRD PART: a definite Number used for an indefinite.

V. 6. — *and our Enemies laugh among themselves.* ואיבינו ילעגו למו:] All the old Versions, except the Chaldee, read לנו, viz. LAUGH AT US.

V. 9. *Thou preparedst Room before it;* שנית לפניה] Rather —— THOU DIDST REMOVE INCUMBRANCES FROM IT. See Taylor.

V. 10. *The Hills were covered with the Shadow of it, and the Boughs thereof were like the goodly Cedars.* [כסו הרים צלה — וענפיה ארזי אל I would render the latter Hemistic thus — AND THE GOODLY CEDARS WITH IT'S BOUGHS, the Verb understood from the preceding Hemistic:

X

tic: for a Vine may with more Propriety be faid to cover a Cedar with it's Boughs, than to be like that Tree.

V. 15. *And the Vineyard which thy Right Hand hath planted:* וכנה אשר נטעה ימינך] Lexicographers give כנה the Signification of *Vineyard*, merely becaufe they think the Senfe requires it in this Place. But, though this Senfe might be better adapted to the Continuance of this beautiful Allegory, yet I think we have not Authority to wreft the Word from it's ufual Signification, which is A FOUNDATION : I would therefore render --- AND THE FOUNDATION WHICH THY RIGHT HAND HATH SETTLED. The Pfalmift begins to proceed gradually from Figurative, to *Proper*, Terms. For feven Verfes a regular Series of Metaphors is preferved. Here is a Tranfition from a Vine to an Edifice. At V. 17. the Pfalmift advances one Step farther, and confiders the whole Congregation of Ifrael as one Individual. And at the 18th and 19th Verfes he ends in abfolutely Proper Terms.

—— *and the Branch that thou madeft fo ftrong for thyfelf.* ועל בן אמצתה לך:] *Qu.* may not בן be here rendered A BUILDING, as well as בת, בנה, or בנין, all which are derived from בנה, *ædificavit*? for בן, Gen. XLIX. 22. does not fignify there *a Branch*. See *Par. Proph.*

V. 16. — *they perifh at the Rebuke of thy Countenance.* מגערת פניך יאבדו:] The Antecedents to יאבדו are I apprehend *the Foundation* and *the Building* juft before mentioned.

PSALM LXXXI.

V. 5. — *where I heard a Language that I underftood not.* שפת לא ידעתי אשמע:] Our old Verfion obferves in the Margin that this is fpoken by God in the Perfon of the People, becaufe He was their Leader. But this Senfe feems very forced ; I would rather read, with moft of the old Verfions, ידע שמע viz. HE (*i. e.* Jofeph) HEARD A LANGUAGE that HE UNDERSTOOD NOT; or, with lefs Variation from the Text, read ידעת אשמיע—I MADE thee HEAR A LANGUAGE which THOU UNDERSTOODEST NOT. The two following Verfes would juftify this Change of Perfons.

V. 7. — *I anfwered thee in the fecret Place of Thunder.* אענך בסתר רעם] Rather — I ANSWERED THEE BY (HIDING, or) STOPPING

THE

THE THUNDER. בסתר is here I apprehend the Gerund; and this is a manifest Allusion to that Thunder which accompanied the Delivery of the Law of the two Tables, which we are told greatly alarmed the People. Exod. XX. 18, 19.

V. 8. *Hear, O my People, and I will testify unto thee : O Israel, if thou wilt hearken unto me.* :שמע עמי ואעידה בך—ישראל אם תשמע לי] The Syriac adds after, *Hear, O my People,* וארבור, *and I will speak :* but there is no Occasion for any Addition, if we render — HEAR, O MY PEOPLE, FOR I WILL BEAR WITNESS AGAINST THEE. O ISRAEL, IF THOU HADST HEARKENED UNTO ME;

V. 9. *There shall no strange God be in thee;* —לא יהיה בך אל זר] THERE WOULD HAVE BEEN NO &c. and so in the next Hemistic. The 11th Verse confirms this Sense.

V. 10. —*open thy Mouth wide, and I will fill it.* :הרחב פיך ואמלאהו] הרחב is here I imagine to be construed as the Preter Hiphil, as Isai. XXX. 33. Pf. IV. 1. &c. thus — WHO OPENED THY MOUTH AND FILLED IT. This seems clearly to refer to the miraculous Manner, in which the Israelites were fed with Manna in the Wilderness.

V. 15. —*but their Time should have endured for ever.* ויהי עתם :לעולם] *Qu.* might not we read —— ואהי אתם לעולם —— AND I WOULD HAVE BEEN WITH THEM FOR EVER ?

V. 16. *He should have fed them* — ויאכילהו] If we read ואכילהו— AND I SHOULD HAVE FED THEM --- the whole Context would be clearer.

PSALM LXXXII.

V. 1. —*he judgeth among the Gods.* :בקרב באלהים ישפט] The Word אלהים is not, like the incommunicable Name יהוה, *Jehovah,* (Pf. LXXXIII. 18.) confined to the Supreme Being, but is sometimes extended to MAGISTRATES, as in this Place and V. 6. and at other Times to *Angels,* as Pf. CIII. 20. The Reason seems to be, that by their Office they are God's Representatives, commissioned to execute his Commands. This Name is also given to *Idols,* Pf. XCVII. 7, 9. &c.

V. 5. —*all the Foundations of the Earth are out of Course.* ימוטו :כל מוכדי ארץ] Rather —— TOTTER, or ARE SHAKEN. When

Justice

Juſtice is perverted, and *Partiality ſhewn*, when *the poor, the afflicted, and the fatherleſs* are oppreſſed by the *Magiſtrates*, the *Foundations of the moral World* may very juſtly be ſaid to be *ſhaken*.

V. 6. *I have ſaid, Ye are Gods ; and all of you are Children of the moſt High.* : אני אמרתי אלהים אתם — ובני עליון כלכם] This Verſe ought I think to be connected with the next, and rendered —Though I HAVE CALLED YOU GODS, YEA, ALL OF YOU THE CHILD-REN OF THE MOST HIGH ;

V. 7. *But ye ſhall die like Men, and fall like one of the Princes.* : אכן כאדם תמותון — וכאחד השרים תפלו] Rather —— NEVER-THELESS YE SHALL DIE LIKE A COMMON MAN ; AND YE SHALL FALL, O PRINCES, LIKE A SINGLE INDIVIDUAL ; in Oppoſition to Magiſtrates, who repreſent the Body of the People.

PSALM LXXXIII.

V. 3. — *and conſulted againſt thy hidden ones.* : ויתיעצו על צפוניך] Rather --- AGAINST THOSE WHOM THOU ESTEEMEST ; or lite-rally, AGAINST THINE ESTEEMED, or TREASURED, ONES, (ſee the Verb צפן thus uſed, Job XXXIII. 12.) in the ſame Senſe as God's People are frequently ſtiled his סגלה, *His peculiar Treaſure* ; Pſ. CXXXV. 4. Exod. XIX. 5.

V. 11. *Make their Nobles like Oreb* ——— ישיתמו נדיבמו כערב] Read here — שיתם ונדיבמו — MAKE THEM AND THEIR NOBLES ----. That this is the true Lection, ſee the Chaldee and Syriac Verſions.

V. 13. *O my God, make them like a Wheel :* אלהי שיתמו כגלגל] In Iſaiah, where the ſame Compariſon occurs, גלגל is rendered *a rolling Thing* (which is doubtleſs the general Idea of the Word) and in the Margin, *Thiſtle Down :* (Ch. XVII. 13.) either of which Senſes ſeems preferable to that of *Wheel.*

V. 14. *As the Fire burneth the Wood, and as the Flame ſetteth the Mountains on Fire :*] So Homer, Iliad II. v. 455.

Ηυτε πυρ αιδηλον επιφλεγει αστετον υλην
Ουρεος εν κορυφις.   And Virgil, *Georg.* II. V. 305.
*Robora comprendit, frondeſque elapſus in altas,
Ingentem cælo ſonitum dedit ; inde ſecutus
Per ramos victor perque alta cacumina regnat,
Et totum involvit flammis nemus.* ———

Psalm LXXXIV.

V. 2. — *my Heart and my Flesh crieth out for the living God.* לבי
[ובשרי ירננו אל אל חי׃ Rather, with the old Version — REJOICE IN
THE LIVING GOD.

V. 3. *Yea, the Sparrow hath found an House, and the Swallow a
Nest for herself, where she may lay her young,* even *thine Altars* &c.
גם צפור מצאה בית — ודרור קן לה — אשר שתה אפרחיה — את מזבחותיך
[וגו״ As את feems rather redundant here, might not we read אתה or
אתן, and render — AS THE SPARROW FINDETH AN HOUSE, AND
THE SWALLOW A NEST, WHERE SHE MAY LAY HER YOUNG, fo
LET ME APPROACH (or LET ME BE PLACED at) THINE ALTARS
&c ? גם is ufed as a Particle of Comparifon, Jer. LI. 49.

V. 5. — *in whose Heart are the Ways of them.* [מסלות בלבבם׃
Rather, I think --- IN WHOSE HEART are PRAISES : for the
Verb סלל fignifies *to extol,* or *praise,* Pf. LXVIII. 4.

V. 6. Who *paffing through the Valley of Baca, make it a Well :*
the Rain alfo filleth the Pools. עברי בעמק הבכא — מעין ישיתוהו גם
[ברכות — יעטה מורה׃ Thus I think ought the Hemiftics to be
diftinguifhed, which will give this Senfe --- PASSING THROUGH
THE VALE OF WEEPING, THEY WILL MAKE IT A SOURCE EVEN
OF BLESSINGS : IT WILL PUT ON A NEW FACE ; or IT WILL
BE CLOTHED WITH A CHANGE. מורה is here confidered as a
Noun, from מור, which fignifies *to make a Change in the Circumftan-*
ces, or *to alter to the reverfe.* See Hof. IV. 7. Mic. II. 4. and I read,
with the ancient Verfions, הבכה.

V. 7. — *every one of them in Zion appeareth before God.* יראה אל
[אלהים בציון׃ Rather — THE GOD OF GODS WILL LOOK UPON
ZION ; i. e. *his Church.*

V. 10. *For a Day in thy Courts is better than a thoufand :*] So Tully,
Tufc. V. *O vitæ Philofophia dux, unus dies bene et ex præceptis tuis*
actus peccanti Immortalitati eft anteponendus.

Psalm LXXXV.

V. 13. — *and fhall fet us in the Way of his Steps.* [וישם לדרך פעמיו׃
Rather --- AND SHALL DIRECT HIS STEPS IN THE WAY : i. e.
Righteoufnefs

Righteousnefs shall direct God. A poetical Image, to intimate that He will act agreeably to Justice.

PSALM LXXXVI.

V. 8. —— *neither* are there any Works *like unto thy Works.* ואין
[כמעשיך:] Rather — AND there is NOTHING LIKE THY WORKS.

V. 11. — *unite my Heart to fear thy Name.* [יהד לבבי ליראה שמך:]
Or --- MY HEART WILL REJOICE IN FEARING THY NAME.
See the Verb חדה.

PSALM LXXXVII.

V. 1. *His Foundation is in the holy Mountains.* [יסודתו בהררי קדש:]
I read יסוד תו — A DESIRE (A MARK, or SIGN) SHALL BE SET
UP IN THE HOLY MOUNTAINS. Though the Temple upon
Mount Moriah might be confidered as *a Beacon,* to be feen by all Na-
tions, yet it does not feem to be *the Idea* intended to be here fpecified.
What this is will appear at V. 5.

V. 3. *Glorious Things are fpoken of thee* — [נכבדות מדבר בך] If
this Verfion be right, the Text ought to be מדברות, the Participle
Pyhal: but the Words may I think be divided better, thus — נכבד
ובך דבר ובתם, and rendered — A GLORIOUS AND PERFECT SUBJECT
IS IN THEE, O CITY OF GOD.

V. 4. *I will make mention of Rahab and Babylon to them that know
me; behold Philiftia, and Tyre, with Ethiopia; this Man was born there.*
[אזכיר רהב ובבל לידעי — הנה פלשת וצור עם כוש — זה ילד שם:]
Rather --- I WILL SPEAK TO THOSE THAT KNOW ME OF EGYPT
AND BABYLON; BEHOLD OF PHILISTIA, AND TYRE, WITH
ETHIOPIA, faying, SUCH A ONE WAS BORN THERE. The
fame as ο δεινα: זה is ufed contemptuoufly, viz. *as for* THIS MOSES,
*the Man that brought up us out of the Land of Egypt, we wot not
what is become of him.* Exod. XXXII. 1. The Meaning of this Verfe
I conceive to be no other than this; *viz.* "that in fpeaking to my
" Acquaintance concerning Egypt, Babylon, and all the other neigh-
" bouring Countries, I fhall make mention of the greateft Perfons
" born in them as mere ordinary Characters, from whofe Births their
" refpective

" refpective Countries will derive no great Credit, in Comparifon of
" that infinitely more eminent Native of Judea, who is the Subject of
" the following Verfe."

V. 5. *And of Zion it fhall be faid, This and that Man was born in
her: and the Highefl Himfelf fhall eftablifh her.* איש ואיש יאמר ולציון
יכוננה עליון והוא—ילד ברד:] Rather — BUT OF ZION IT SHALL
BE SAID, THE MOST EMINENT OF MEN WAS BORN IN HER; AND
HE, THE MOST HIGH, SHALL ESTABLISH HER. איש put in Oppofition to זה (as before explained) fignifies *a Man of Confequence*:
and, according to the oriental Phrafeology, by the Reduplication, muft
mean the Superlative or highefl Degree: or *the Man, even the
Man,* fignifies the MAN OF MEN, THE GREATEST OF ALL MEN.
According to this Interpretation every one will fee who this eminent
Perfonage was to be, from whofe Birth Zion (ufed by *a Synecdoche* for
Judea) was to acquire fo much Glory. The latter Hemiftic feems to
me to have reference, not to God the Father, but to his Son: it ap-
pearing to be exegetical of the preceding one, and to defcribe His Divine, as the other does His Human, Nature.

V. 6. *The Lord fhall count when he writeth up the People,* that *this
Man was born there.* זה ילד שם : עמים בכתוב יספר יהודה] Rather --- THE LORD WILL HAVE THIS RECORDED IN REGISTER-
ING THE PEOPLE, that HE WAS BORN THERE. ספר fignifies *a
Genealogy,* Gen. V. 1. Neh. VII. 5. כתב, *a Regifter.* Ezra. II. 62. Jer.
XVII. 13. זה is ufed to denote *this very Thing, this particular Circumftance,* Eccl. VI. 9. Efth. IV. 5. &c. This I think can poffibly relate to nothing elfe than the Pedigree of our Lord, which had been recorded among the Jews, and which the Evangelifts have given us with
the Hiftory of his Birth, &c. in the Gofpels.

V. 7. *As well the Singers as the Players on Inftruments* fhall be there:
all my Springs are in thee. כל מעיני בך — כחללים ושרים] Rather
---ALL THAT DWELL IN THEE will SING WITH THE DANCERS:
literally, will be *Singers,* the Part. prefent. חלל fignifies *to dance* in
feveral Places; Judg. XXI. 21, 23. &c. I read בחללים, with the Chaldee and the old Verfions; and confider מעיני as the Part. *Hiphil,* from
עין *to inhabit*; which is here *fpecial,* as in a Multitude of Places. Here
the Pfalmift returns to Sion, his firft Subject, from which he might
be thought to have digreffed, by talking of it as of a third Perfon;

and

and concludes with predicting the Joy which would accompany the Advent of the Defire of all Nations.

Psalm LXXXVIII.

V. 5. — *free among the dead* —— במתים חפשי] *Qu.* might not the true Lection be הפשתי (in *Pihel*) — I AM SOUGHT FOR — correfponding to נחשבתי, I AM COUNTED, in the preceding Verfe? However I fhall confider it as the Part. prefent, and render — THEY SEEK ME AMONG THE DEAD.

V. 6. — *in the Deeps.* :במצלות] All the ancient Verfions, the Chaldee excepted, read בצלמות, IN THE SHADOW OF DEATH; which feems a better Senfe.

V. 10. — *fhall the dead arife* —— אם רפאים יקומו] Rather — SHALL THE DECEASED —. See this and the following Verfes explained, Job XXVI. 5.

V. 18. *Lover and Friend haft thou put far from me,* and *mine Acquaintance into Darknefs.*] Thefe two laft Words — מידעי מחשך, in order to have the Senfe which our Verfion gives them, muft have a Verb, a Conjunction, and a Prepofition fupplied: they ought to be rendered --- KEEPING BACK MINE ACQUAINTANCE; viz. *from coming to fee me:* agreeably to V. 8. מחשך is the Participle *Pihel.* אהב ורע, at the Beginning of the Verfe, fhould be tranflated, FRIEND AND COMPANION, as Pf. XXXVIII. 11.

Psalm LXXXIX.

V. 2. *For I have faid* —— אמרתי] All the old Verfions, except the Chaldee, read אמרת, THOU HAST SAID: which is preferable.

V. 5. *And the Heavens fhall praife thy Wonders, O Lord: thy Faithfulnefs alfo in the Congregation of the Saints.* — ויודו שמים פלאך יהוה :אף אמונתך בקהל קדשים] The latter Hemiftic ought to be thus rendered --- THE SAINTS ALSO THY FAITHFULNESS IN THE CONGREGATION; the Verb יודו being either underftood or repeated from the preceding Member. For though it be a beautiful Image to fay that the *Heavens praife God,* by making Men admire their wonderful Structure and ftated Motions, it feems harfh to imagine them joining with Saints in Divine Worfhip.

V. 8.

V. 8. O Lord God of Hosts, who is a strong Lord like unto thee? or to thy Faithfulness round about thee?] The latter Clause is hardly intelligible as here rendered. ואמונתך סביבותיך ought to be translated— AND THY TRUTH IS ROUND ABOUT THEE.

V. 11. — as for the World, and the Fulness thereof, thou hast founded them. : תבל ומלאה אתה יסרתם] Rather — THE WORLD, AND ALL THAT IS THEREIN; THOU HAST FOUNDED THEM: the Words ARE THINE being underſtood from the preceding Clauſe, ſo Pſ. XCV. 5. *The Sea is his; for he made it:* the Property of them being founded in Creation.

V. 14. Juſtice and Judgment are the Habitation of thy Throne: צדק ומשפט מכון כסאך] Rather — are THE FOUNDATION, or THE ESTABLISHMENT, as in the Margin; ſo Prov. XXV. 5. and Iſa. XVI. 5.

V. 25. I will ſet his Hand alſo in the Sea, ושמתי בים ידו] Rather — OVER THE SEA; ſo likewiſe in the next Hemiſtic —— OVER THE RIVERS. That is, "I will give him Power over them." This doubtleſs has reference to God's Promiſe to the Patriarch Abraham, in regard to the Extent of the Land of Promiſe: hence *the Sea* here mentioned muſt mean *the Mediterranean,* as well as the *Red Sea,* and the *Rivers,* the *Euphrates* and *Nile.* See this Point particularly examined, *Par. Proph.* App. Nᵒ. I. P. 153. and the Reaſons why the Promiſe was never fully accompliſhed.

—— *and his right Hand in the Rivers.*] So the Scythians tell Alexander in Q. Curtius, *Si Dii habitum corporis tui aviditati animi parem eſſe voluiſſent, Orbis te non caperet; altera manu orientem, altera occidentem contingeres.* Lib. VII. Cap. 8.

V. 29. His Seed alſo will I make to endure for ever: ושמתי לעד זרעו] Rather — HIS SEED ALSO WILL I ESTABLISH FOR EVER: as Gen. XLV. 7. 2 Sam. XXIII. 5. &c.

V. 37. It ſhall be eſtabliſhed for ever as the Moon, and as a faithful Witneſs in Heaven. : כירח יכון עולם —ועד בשחק נאמן] There is here no *Ellipſis* of the comparative Particle, for ו, coming after ſuch a Particle, has that Force. See Noldius 60. §. 2.

V. 39. — thou haſt profaned his Crown, by caſting it to the Ground.] חללת ought to be rendered here — THOU HAST CAST DOWN AS PROFANE, as Ezek. XXVIII. 16.

V. 44. *Thou haſt made his Glory to ceaſe, and caſt his Throne* down to the Ground. : טהר [השברת מטהרו — וכסאו לארץ מגרתה] does not ſignify *Glory:* but the Words חשברת מטהרו, as they are now read, ought to be rendered --- THOU HAST MADE him CEASE FROM HIS SPLENDOR. But I have no doubt but that inſtead of מטהרו we ought to read מעטרו, and render — THOU HAST MADE HIS CROWN TO CEASE, &c. to which כסאו, *his Throne,* in the next Hemiſtic correſ-ponds. מ is here prefixed to the Accuſative, as שׂמת מעיר לגל — *Thou haſt made the City an Heap,* Iſa. XXV. 2.

V. 46. *How long, Lord, wilt thou hide thyſelf for ever? ſhall thy Wrath burn like Fire?* : [עד מה יהוה תסתר — לנצח תבער כמו אש המתך] Rather --- LORD, HOW LONG WILT THOU HIDE THYSELF? SHALL THY WRATH BURN LIKE FIRE FOR EVER? See Pſ. LXXIX. 5.

V. 48. — *ſhall he deliver his Soul from the Hand of the Grave?* : [ימלט נפשו מיד שאול] Rather, I think — FROM THE POWER.

V. 50. — *I do bear in my Boſom* the Reproach of *all the mighty People.* : [שאתי בחיקי כל רבים עמים] Rather — I BEAR (or lite-rally, MY BEARING) IN MY BOSOM ALL THE REPROACHES OF THE PEOPLE. The Syriac and Aquila ſeem to have read רבי *in re-gimine,* as the Conſtruction requires. See Pſ. LV. 18. For רב is the ſame as ריב : it is as frequently written one Way as the other.

PSALM XC.

V. 1. *Lord, thou haſt been our dwelling Place* — אדני מעון אתה היית [לנו] Rather — LORD, THOU HAST BEEN TO US A REFUGE: as Deut. XXXIII. 27.

V. 2. — *even from everlaſting to everlaſting thou art God.* ומעולם : [עד עולם אתה (אל)] Rather, I think —— EVEN FROM EVER-LASTING TO EVERLASTING THOU art, *or* doſt exiſt. So Habak-kuk, I. 12. Art *not thou from everlaſting, O Lord my God?* So alſo Pſ. XCIII. 2. &c.

V. 3. *Thou turneſt Man to Deſtruction and ſayeſt, Return, ye Child-ren of Men.* : [אל תשב אנוש עד דכא — ותאמר שובו בני אדם] DO NOT BRING MEN TO DESTRUCTION: BUT SAY, RETURN &c.

&c. I confider יַהֲל as belonging to this Verfe, and השב the fame as תשוב, which is as often written this Way as the other.

V. 4. — *and as a Watch in the Night.* ‏:‏ואשמורה בלילה] Rather, OR A WATCH OF THE NIGHT.

V. 5. — *they are* as *a Sleep: in the Morning* they are *like Grafs* which *groweth up.* ‏:‏כחציר יהלף — שנה יהיו בבקר ‏[‏ישנה‏]‏ Rather, I think --- THEY ARE as A SLEEP IN THE MORNING; LIKE THE GRASS which CHANGETH.

V. 10. *The Days of our Years* are *threefcore Years and ten :* ימי שנותינו בהם שבעים שנה ‏[‏ These Words I apprehend are to be conftrued as if we read ביְמֵי, inftead of בהם ; the Pronouns being frequently redundant in Hebrew. From what is here afferted, we may I think conclude that this Pfalm was not written by Mofes, notwithftanding the Title bears his Name. For he himfelf lived to the Age of 120; Aaron to 121; their Sifter Miriam to 130; and, to mention no other, Jofhua was 110 Years old when he died. And as thefe Ages are not mentioned as being extraordinary, it may be inferred that they were the common Period of human Life about Mofes's Time. It is therefore highly probable that this Pfalm could not be written more early than David's Reign, who attained only to the Age of 70 : about which Time God was pleafed to fix upon 70 or 80 Years for the common Duration of the Life of Man; after having reduced it twice before, *viz.* from near *one thoufand* to about *three Hundred* ; and from that Number to about *one Hundred and twenty*, as was before obferved. Solon (who lived in the Time of the Babylonifh Captivity) fays in Herodotus, ες έβδομηκοντα ετεα ουρον της ζωης ανθρωπω προτιθημι ; and dividing the Life of Man into ten Periods of feven Years each adds (according to Philo *de Mundi opificio* ;)

Τη δ' ενατη ετι μεν δυναται, μαλακωτερα δ' αυτη
Προς μεγαλην αρετην γλωσσα τε και σοφιη.
Τη δεκατη δ' ειτις τελεσας κατα μετρον ικοιτο,
Ουκ αν αωρος εων μοιραν εχει θανατου.

V. 11. *Who knoweth the Power of thine Anger ? even according to* thy *Fear*, fo is *thy Wrath.* ‏:‏וכיראתך עברתך — מי יודע עז אפך ‏]‏ I would read here ויראתך with the Syriac and Arabic Verfions, thus — WHO KNOWETH THE POWER OF THINE ANGER, AND THE TERRIBLENESS OF THY WRATH ?

V. 13.

V. 13. *Return, O Lord, how long?* שובה יהוה עד מתי] Rather --- WHEN will there be A RETURNING, O LORD ? or perhaps thus --- RETURN, O LORD, BEFORE MY DEATH. עד ſignifies before; ſee Noldius, Art. 7. and מות is ſometimes written without the ו as מתך *their Death,* and מתיו, Iſa. LIII. 9.

— *and let it repent thee concerning thy Servants.* והנחם על עבדיך] Rather --- AND CONSOLATION WITH THY SERVANTS ? or, AND A CHANGE OF PURPOSE IN RESPECT TO THY SERVANTS ? for נחם has both Senſes : and the Verb is to be underſtood from the preceding Clauſe.

V. 17. *And let the Beauty of the Lord our God be upon us :* ויהי נעם יהוה אלהינו עלינו [נעם ought to be tranſlated in this Place — THE GRACIOUSNESS, or THE SWEET FAVOUR, inſtead of *Beauty.*

—— *and eſtabliſh thou the Work of our Hands upon us ; yea, the Work of our Hands eſtabliſh thou it.* ומעשה ידינו כוננה עלינו — ומעשה ידינו כוננהו] As the Repetition of this latter Clauſe does not appear to be *emphatical,* and is not acknowledged by the Chaldee Paraphraſe, I am inclined to conſider it as a Miſtake of the Tranſcriber. At leaſt, if I retained it, I would read ידיו in the firſt Hemiſtic, and rejeĉt the laſt ו with the Syriac, and render — AND LET HIM ESTABLISH THE WORK OF HIS HANDS UPON US ; LET HIM ALSO ESTABLISH THE WORK OF OUR OWN HANDS.

PSALM XCI.

V. 2. *I will ſay of the Lord,* He is *my Refuge, and my Fortreſs ; my God, in him will I truſt.* אמר ליהוה מחסי — ומצודתי אלהי אבטח בו :] Rather, I think --- CALLING THE LORD MY REFUGE AND MY FORTRESS, MY GOD, IN WHOM I WILL TRUST. See Job XXXI. 24. Pſ. LXXXII. 6. and the ſame Uſe of the Particle ו, Pſ. XLV. 4.

V. 8. *Only with thine Eyes ſhalt thou behold,* —— רק בעיניך תביט] רק muſt either be conſtrued in an excluſive Senſe, as Gen. VI. 5. thus, THOU SHALT ONLY BEHOLD (i. e. *and nothing more*) or it may be conſidered as a Subſtantive ; thus --- WITH THINE EYES SHALT THOU BEHOLD THE VANITY, AND SEE THE REWARD, OF THE WICKED. See רק thus uſed, Gen. XXXVII. 24. Deut. XXXII. 47.

V. 9. *Becauſe thou haſt made the Lord* which is *my Refuge,* even *the moſt High, thy Habitation.* כי אתה יהוה מחסי — עליון שמת מעונך :]
Our

Our Tranſlators, in order to avoid *the Apoſtrophe*, run into *an Hyper-baton*. But, admitting that this Conſtruction were juſtifiable, yet could not the double *Enallage* of Perſons be avoided at V.14. I would there-fore give the Words their apparent genuine Senſe, *viz.* SURELY THOU, O LORD, art MY REFUGE; O MOST HIGH thou HAST FIXED THINE HABITATION; *viz.* in Sion. God's having fixed his Reſi-dence there affording a ſure Ground of Confidence that he would ſtill protect his King there, as David (or as Solomon, if he be Speaker) had experienced. The *Targum* makes this Pſalm *a Dialogue* between *God* and *Solomon:* and the Thought does not ſeem to be ill founded. For it is certain that the Cuſtom of repeating alternate Parts, or ſome-times the ſame Parts, by different Perſons, prevailed very early among the Iſraelites. We have an Inſtance of ſuch a Song, in which Moſes and his Company bore their Parts, and his Siſter Miriam and her At-tendants bore their's; and where all I think joined in the Chorus. See Exod. XV. 1, 20, 21. and 18, 19. Thus alſo Virgil, *Ecl.* III. 59, 60.

Incipe, Damœta; tu deinde ſequere, Menalca:
Alternis dicetis: amant alterna Camœnæ

PSALM XCII.

V. 7. — *and when all the workers of Iniquity do flouriſh: it is that they ſhall be deſtroyed for ever.* [ויציצו כל פעלי און‏—‏להשמדם עדי ער :] The Conſtruction is here very harſh and ungrammatical: but it may be remedied, I conceive, by referring the firſt Sentence of this Verſe to the preceding one, and reading thus, (V. 6.) A BRUTISH MAN DOTH NOT DISCERN, NOR DOTH ONE OF SLOW UNDERSTANDING PERCEIVE THIS (i. e. *the Profundity of God's Counſels*) IN THE FLOURISHING OF THE WICKED LIKE GRASS. (V. 7.) FOR ALL THE WORKERS OF INIQUITY DO FLOURISH UNTO (or IN ORDER TO) THEIR EVERLASTING DESTRUCTION: according to that Adage of Solomon, *The Proſperity of Fools ſhall deſtroy them.*

V. 11. *Mine Eye alſo ſhall ſee my Deſire on mine Enemies,* ותבט עיני בשורי] FOR MINE EYE SHALL LOOK DOWN ON MINE ENEMIES: and in the next Clauſe --- MINE EAR SHALL HEAR IT OF THE WICKED. אזני is ſingular as well as עיני, and therefore the Affix נדה refers to the Deſtruction, V. 9.

PSALM

Psalm XCIV.

V. 9. He that planted the Ear — הנטע אזן] Rather — He that
fixed the Ear ——.

V. 10. — *he that teacheth Man Knowledge,* shall not he know?
[המלמד אדם דעת:] I would rather connect this with the next Verse,
thus --- He that teacheth Man Knowledge is the Lord.;
who knoweth the Thoughts &c.

V. 20. — *which frameth Mischief by a Law.* [יצר עמל עלי חק:]
Rather perhaps — against the Law: as Pf. XXVII. 3.

Psalm XCVI.

V. 7. — *O ye Kindreds of the People* —— [משפחות עמים] O ye
Families of the People, as in the old Version.

V. 13. Before the Lord: for he cometh, —— [לפני יהוה כי בא]
לפני יהוה *(Before the Lord)* certainly belongs to the preceding Verse.

Psalm XCVII.

V. 11. Light is sown for the righteous —— [אור זרע לצדיק] We
ought I think to read here זרח is risen; for all the old Versions so
read the Text, and the Sense requires it. The Mistake is easily accounted for from the Similarity of Sound. Some, however, may think
that the Lection of the Text may be justified from the Authorities
which follow. Thus Virgil represents the Dawn,

   Et jam prima novo spargebat lumine terram. Æn. IV. 584.
So Pindar, *Isthm.* Od. VI. 15.

   Ει γαρ τις ανθρωπων δαπανα τε χαρεις
   Και πονω, πρασσει θεοδματεις αρετας,
   Συν τε οι δαιμων φυτευει
   Δοξαν επηρατον, εσχατιαις
   Ηδη προς ολβυ βαλλετ αγκυ-
   ραν θεοτιμος εων·

Whence it may be observed by the by that the blending of Metaphors
is not peculiar to the Hebrew Poetry.

Psalm

PSALM XCIX.

V. 3. *Let them praife thy great and terrible Name : for it is holy.*
יורו שמך גדול—ונורא קדוש הוא :] Rather—LET THEM PRAISE
THY NAME, WHICH IS GREAT, VENERABLE, AND HOLY. See
Pf. XLV. 4.

V. 4. *The King's Strength alfo loveth Judgment,* ——— ועז מלך משפט
אהב] Rather, I think —— FOR thou, O MIGHTY KING, who
LOVEST JUSTICE, DOST &c. I confider אהב as the Participle prefent ;
in order to avoid the Enallage in the next Hemiftic. Our Tranflators
feem to have underftood *the King's Strength* in the fame Senfe as
Homer ufes Βιη Ηρακληιη.

PSALM CI.

V. 2. *I will behave myfelf wifely in a perfect Way; O when wilt
thou come unto me ?* אשכילה בדרך תמים—מתי תבוא אלי] Without Interrogation —— WHEN THOU COMEST UNTO ME. So מתי is
ufed, Prov. XXIII. 35.

PSALM CII.

V. 7. *I watch, and am as a Sparrow alone upon the Houfe top.* שקדתי
ואהיה כצפור בודד על גג :] The Word צפור is a generic Name for
any Bird : that it cannot mean here *the Sparrow,* is I think evident
from the Circumftances ; for it is intimated that it is *a Bird of the
Night, a folitary,* and *a mournful* one ; none of which Characteriftics
are applicable to the Sparrow, which refts by Night, is gregarious, and
cheerful. I therefore think the Word muft here denote fome particular Species of the Owl. Thus Virgil, *Georg.* I. 402.
——— DE CULMINE SUMMO
Nequicquam feros exercet noctua cantus.
And ftill more to the Purpofe, *Æneid* IV. 462.
SOLAQUE CULMINIBUS, *ferali carmine bubo*
Sæpe queri, et longas in fletum ducere voces.

PSALM CIII.

V. 9. — *neither will he keep* his Anger *for ever.* ולא לעולם יטור :]
Rather--- NEITHER WILL HE BEAR A GRUDGE (or, RETAIN RE-
SENTMENT.)

SENTMENT) FOR EVER: for the Verb נטר has that Signification, and is fo rendered, Lev. XIX. 18. and ought to be, Jer. III. 12.

V. 20. — *hearkening unto the Voice of his Word.* [לשמע בקול דברו:] This Clauſe is omitted in all the old Verſions, except the Vulgate: and it appears redundant both as to the Senſe, as well as Verſe.

PSALM CIV.

V. 4. *Who maketh his Angels Spirits: his Miniſters a flaming Fire.* [עשה מלאכיו רוחות — משרתיו אש להט:] Rather — WHO MAKETH THE WINDS HIS MESSENGERS; AND THE FLAMING FIRE HIS MINISTERS.

V. 13. — *the Earth is ſatisfied with the Fruit of thy Works.* מפרי [מעשיך תשבע הארץ:] Rather — THE EARTH IS FILLED WITH FRUIT BY THY MEANS: for מעשיך is the Participle preter, which rejects the ה on account of the Affix. The מ prefixed is the Prepoſition.

V. 16. *The Trees of the Lord are full* of Sap: [ישבעו עצי יהוה] I prefer our old Verſion in this Place, *viz.* THE HIGH TREES ARE SATISFIED; *i. e.* are fufficiently watered, as the Context ſhews.

V. 25. So is *this great and wide Sea, wherein* are *Things creeping innumerable, both ſmall and great Beaſts.* — [זה הים גדול ורחב ידים] [שם רמש ואין מספר — חיות קטנות עם גדלות:] Rather — THE SAME IS THE SEA, GREAT AND WIDE IN EXTENT; WHEREIN are THINGS MOVING INNUMERABLE, BOTH SMALL AND GREAT CREATURES. For רהב ידים ſignifies literally *wide of Arms*; a Name very applicable to the Ocean, whoſe many Streights and narrow Gulphs are not improperly called *Arms.* רמש is not confined abſolutely to *Reptiles*, but is ſometimes uſed, as well as חיות, for *all the Brute Creation.* See Gen. IX. 3.

V. 26. — there is *that Leviathan* ——— [לויתן] As the *Leviathan* here doubtleſs means A WHALE, ought it not to be ſo rendered?

PSALM CV.

V. 20. — even *the Ruler of the People, and let him go free.* משל [עמים ויפתחהו:] By the Omiſſion of ו, the old Verſion in much clearer,

clearer, *viz.* THE RULER OF THE PEOPLE DELIVERED HIM: or might not we read, מישל עמימו יפתחהו, THE RULER OF THEIR PEOPLE LET HIM GO FREE?

V.28. — *and they rebelled not against his Word.* [ולא מרו את דבריו:] If the Negative be retained, what is here said must be understood of Moses and Aaron: but if this refer to the Egyptians, it must be omitted as in the LXX and Syriac Versions; except ולא could be construed NEVERTHELESS, or interrogatively, thus, AND DID THEY NOT REBEL AGAINST HIS COMMAND?

PSALM CVI.

V. 4. *Remember me, O Lord, with the Favour* that thou bearest unto *thy People.* [זכרני יהוה ברצון עמך] Rather — REMEMBER ME, O LORD, WITH THY FAVOUR: or thus — *with thy wonted Favour*; literally, *the Favour with thee*; for עמך in this Place signifies literally *with thee*, the Verb Substantive being understood, as in this Instance, אין עם יהוה אלהינו עולה: There is *no Unrighteousness* WITH *the Lord our God.* 2 Chron. XIX. 7.

V. 7. — *but provoked* him *at the Sea*, even *at the Red Sea.* וימרו על ים ביס סוף: [I read עלים the Participle present, with the LXX and Arabic, and render --- BUT REBELLED AS THEY MARCHED BY THE RED SEA: (Exod. XIII. 18. — XIV. 11,12.) for the present Lection of the Text is not only pleonastic, but also embarrassed by inconsistent Prepositions as well as Persons.

V. 15. *And he gave them their Request; but sent Leanness into their Soul.* [ויתן להם שאלתם—וישלה רזון בנפשם:] All the ancient Versions, except the Chaldee, read רוון, or רויה, instead of רזון, for they render the latter Hemistic thus—AND SENT ABUNDANCE TO THEIR SOULS, or APPETITES.

PSALM CVII.

V. 10. — being *bound in Affliction and Iron.* [אסירי עני וברזל:] By this *Hendyadis* the Sense is the same as if it were written — *bound in afflictive Iron.*

Z   V. 26.

V. 26. *They mount up to the Heaven, they go down again to the Depths; their Soul is melted because of Trouble.*] Thus Virgil, Æneid III. 564.

> Tollimur in cælum curvato gurgite, et idem
> Subducta ad manes imos descendimus unda.

And Ovid, *de Trist.* Eleg. II.

> Me miserum! quanti montes volvuntur aquarum?
> Jamjam tacturos sidera summa putes.
> Quantæ diducto subsidunt æquore valles?
> Jamjam tacturas Tartara nigra putes.
> Rector in incerto est, nec quid fugiatve, petatve,
> Invenit; ambiguis ars stupet ipsa malis.

V. 39. *Again they are minished* —— וימעטו] This Verse ought to be connected with the next, and ו ought to be rendered WHEN.

PSALM CVIII.

V. 1. —*I will sing and give Praise, even with my Glory.*] These Words, אף כבודי, ought I think to be joined to the next Word עורה, and rendered --- AND THOU MY GLORY AWAKE: for it appears by the Syriac, Vulgate, and Arabic, that they read עורה twice.

PSALM CIX.

V. 4. —*but I give myself unto Prayer.* :ואני תפלה] All the old Versions seem to have read ואתפלל, or ואתפללה, BUT I PRAY.

V. 10. *Let his Children be continually Vagabonds, and beg: let them seek their Bread also out of their desolate Places.* ——ונוע ינועו בניו ושאלו :ודרשו מהרבותיהם] The latter Hemistic ought I think to be thus rendered --- LET THEM BE SOUGHT FOR (or HURRIED) OUT OF THEIR DESOLATE PLACES: Or, if we give the Verb the Sense of درس, thus — LET THEM BE EXTERMINATED: דרס also in Chaldee signifies *to tread under Foot:* most of the old Versions render, *let them be expelled* &c. ודרשו is here considered as the Preter *Pyhal.*

V. 21. *But do thou for me, O God the Lord, for thy Name's Sake* —ואתה יהוה אדני—עשה אתי למען שמך —] Rather — BUT THOU, O LORD MY GOD, DEAL WITH ME ACCORDING TO THY NAME:

i. e.

i. e. according to thy moral Attributes of *Mercy* and *Goodnefs* : as Pf. VIII. 1. IX. 10. XXV. 11. &c. עשׂה is thus ufed, 2 Kings XXI. 6. 2 Chron. XXXIII. 6.

V. 28. *Let them curfe, but blefs thou :* — יקללו המה ואתה תברך] Doctor Sykes (in his Comment on the Epiftle to the Hebrews) takes occafion from this Verfe to conclude, that all the bitter Imprecations of this Pfalm from V. 6. are fpoken againft David by his Adverfaries : becaufe one Perfon only is the Subject ; and becaufe it cannot be fuppofed that an infpired Prophet could be fo devoid of Charity, as to utter fuch Curfes. I wifh I could acquiefce in this Interpretation : but it is fraught with infuperable Difficulties. For V. 20. may be thought to give a fatal Blow to this *Hypothefis :* for that Verfe feems to make the Compofer of the Pfalm the Speaker throughout. Befides, could that Objection be removed here, it would ftill remain triumphant in many other Pfalms, and Parts of the Old Teftament. The common Opinion is, that thefe Imprecations are *prophetic Denunciations* of God's Judgments upon impenitent Sinners. This in fome Cafes may be true : but furely it cannot be fo in all thofe Parts, where they are announced by the Imperative ; where the Author imprecates, not againft *God's* Enemies, not againft the Enemies of *the State,* but againft *his own* Enemies. The moft probable Account of this Matter in my humble Opinion is this, that God Almighty (though in a particular Senfe *the God of Abraham and his Offspring*) did not interpofe by his *Grace,* or act upon the Mind of his peculiar People, not even of their *Prophets,* in an extraordinary Manner, except when He vouchfafed to fuggeft fome future Event, or any other Circumftance that might be for the public Benefit of Mankind. In all other refpects (I apprehend) they were left to the full Exercife of their Freewill, without Control of the Divine Impulfe. Now God had abundantly provided, in that Code of moral and ceremonial Inftitutes which he had given his People for their Law, that the *poor, the fatherlefs, the Widow,* and *Stranger* fhould be particularly regarded ; whence they ought to have learnt *to be merciful as their Father in Heaven is merciful :* and it muft be confeffed that we fometimes find fuch Behaviour and Sentiments in the Jews with refpect to their Enemies as may be deemed truly Chriftian. See Pf. XXXV. 13, 14. &c. But, in that very Syftem of Laws, it was alfo for wife Reafons ordained that they fhould have no Intercourfe with the Seven Nations of the *Canaanites* ; but fhould abfolutely exterminate them ; whence they unwarrantably drew this Inference, that they *ought to love their Neighbours* ; *but* HATE THEIR ENEMIES, as our

Lord

Lord declares, Matt. V. 43. From these devoted Nations they extended the Precept to the rest of Mankind, that were not within the Pale of their Church; nay sometimes to their own *domestic* Enemies, those of their own Blood and Communion, with whom they were at Variance. Hence therefore the horrid Picture which is drawn of that Nation by the Greek and Roman Authors: from whom I forbear to bring any Instances, as they are well known; and so numerous, that they might fill a Volume.

How far it may be proper to continue the Reading of these Psalms in the daily Service of our Church, I leave to the Consideration of the Legislature to determine. A Christian of Erudition may consider those Imprecations only as the natural Sentiments of Jews, which the benign Religion he professes abhors and condemns: but what are the illiterate to do, who know not where to draw the Line between the Law and the Gospel? They hear both read, one after the other, and I fear too often think them both of equal Obligation; and even take Shelter under Scripture to cover their Curses. Though I am conscious I here tread upon slippery Ground, I will take Leave to hint, that, notwithstanding the high Antiquity that sanctifies as it were this Practice, it would in the Opinion of a Number of wise and good Men be more for the Credit of the Christian Church to omit a few of those Psalms, and to substitute some Parts of the Gospel in their stead. See *Les Sentimens des Theologiens de Hollande;* attributed to Le Clerc in his younger Days.

PSALM CX.

V. 1. — *Sit thou at my Right Hand.*] So Callimachus says of Apollo in his Hymn, V. 29.

—— δυνα⸗) γαρ, επει Δ‖ι δἰξιος ητται·

And Pindar in his Address to Vesta, intreating her to receive Aristagoras and his Friends, and admit them into her Temple at the Right Hand of her Sceptre, says,

Ευ μεν Αρι⸗αγοραν δὲξαι τεον ες Θαλαμον,
Ευ δ' εταιρ⸗ς αγλαω σκαπ‖ρω πελας.   *Nem.* Od. XI. 1.

V. 2. *The Lord shall send the Rod of thy Strength out of Zion:* מטה [מטה עזך ישלח יהוה מציון] is a Word exactly of the same Import as שבט: both signify primarily *a Shoot* or *Branch* of a Tree; whence they came to be used for *a Tribe,* (*issuing* out from a *Patriarch,* as a *Branch* from it's *Stock;*) for *any Rod,* or *Staff;* and hence they
have

have an appropriate Signification, viz. *that particular Staff* or SCEP-
TRE, used by a Sovereign Magistrate in Token of his Supreme Au-
thority. The Context in this Place clearly points out that this latter
Sense is that which ought to be received.

V. 3. *Thy People* shall be *willing in the Day of thy Power,* עמך
נדבת ביום חילך] Rather, I think — WITH THEE shall be FREE-
WILL OFFERINGS &c.

—— *in the Beauties of Holiness* —— בהדרי קדש] IN THE GLO-
RIOUS SANCTUARY, the Words signifying literally *in the Glories of
the Sanctuary.*

—— *from the Womb of the Morning: thou hast the Dew of thy
Youth.* מרחם משחר לך טל ילדתך :] I read here with most of the
old Versions ילדתיך; and, supposing that י before לך has dropped out,
render --- I HAVE BROUGHT THEE FORTH OUT OF THE WOMB
BEFORE THE MORNING BROUGHT ON THE DEW. The Prepo-
sition כ prefixed to שהר signifies BEFORE. See Noldius 4, 5. ילך is in
Hiphil (though defective for יולך, or rather יוליך) as 2 Kings VI. 19.
XXV. 20. &c. The Meaning of the Words thus interpreted is obvious. God is the Speaker, the Messiah is the Person addressed; and
the Sentence relates to the latter's Existence long before the Creation
of any Being. It is remarkable that none of the old Versions, except
the Chaldee, take any Notice of either טל or. לך

V. 5. *The Lord at thy right Hand shall strike* —— אדני על ימינך
מחץ —] Rather, I think, in two Sentences, thus — THE LORD is
AT THY RIGHT HAND; HE WILL STRIKE ---.

V. 6. — *he shall fill* the Places *with the dead Bodies: he shall wound
the Heads over many Countries.* מלא גויות — מחץ ראש על ארץ רבה :]
מלא and מחץ being both Participles, the Verse I think ought to be
thus rendered --- HE WILL JUDGE AMONG (*i.e.* RULE OVER) THE
NATIONS, after BEING SATISFIED WITH DEAD BODIES, and
HAVING WOUNDED MANY A CHIEF UPON THE EARTH: because
the Exercise of his Dominion is consequent upon his Conquest. The
Verb מלא is thus used, Eccl. I. 8. VI. 7. Isa. XXXIV. 6. and I here
read רבים, with all the ancient Versions.

V. 7. *He shall drink of the Brook in the Way:* מנחל בדרך ישתה]
As *Torrents* or *the overflowing of Rivers* frequently denote in the Scripture Language AFFLICTIONS (Ps. XVIII. 4. CXXIV. 4, 5. CXLIV. 7.
&c.)

&c.) and *the being oppreſſed by them* is alſo deſcribed by the Idea of DRINKING (Pſ. LX. 3. LXXV. 8. &c.) we may eaſily conclude what the Senſe of this Place muſt be, and ſee how this is applicable to the *Meſſiah*. The ſame Sentiment is here expreſſed as Iſa. LIII. 12.

PSALM CXI.

V. 10. *The Fear of the Lord is the Beginning of Wiſdom: a good Underſtanding have all they that do his Commandments.*] This latter Hemiſtic is thus read in the Hebrew, שכל טוב לכל עשיהם, *a good Underſtanding to all that do them*, as in the Margin. The Word *Commandments* ſeems borrowed from the 7th Verſe; but that is too far fetched: and the Pronoun *them* has here no proper Antecedent. It is therefore very probable, that there is an Error in the Pronoun, which ſhould be נה instead of הם. All the ancient Verſions, except the Chaldee, read ſo. In this Caſe we might render — A GOOD UNDERSTANDING HATH EVERY ONE WHO PRACTISETH IT, viz. *Wiſdom* juſt mentioned.

PSALM CXIV.

V. 1. *When Iſrael came out of Egypt, the Houſe of Jacob from a People of a ſtrange Language.* בצאת ישראל ממצרים — בית יעקב מעם לעז:] The Word לעז occurs only in this Place: but in Chaldee it ſignifies, *foreign, barbarous:* ܠܥܙ in Syriac is *barbarè locutus eſt*, and لوز, in Arabic, *peregrina verba habuit*. All the ancient Verſions render the Word BARBAROUS, and ſo I think it ought to be in our Verſion; for that Word is applicable to the Egyptians in reſpect to the Hebrews in every Senſe of it. The Etymology of *barbarous* is to be ſought for in the Eaſt. In Chaldee ברבר ſignifies *qui lingua ignota loquitur*, כֻרזֻברا, *extraneus*, and بربر, *quod multas voces edit*, derived from بر *extra*; whence بربري *Barbarus*, an Inhabitant of *Barbary*. The Word is uſed in this Senſe, 1 Cor. XIV. 11. *I ſhall be to him that ſpeaketh* A BARBARIAN, *and he that ſpeaketh ſhall be* A BARBARIAN *to me*. And Acts XXVIII. the ſame People who are called *barbarous*, V. 2. are ſtyled *Barbarians*, V. 4. So Ovid, *Am*.

BARBARUS *his ego ſum, quia non intelligar ulli*.

PSALM CXV.

V. 6. *They have Ears, but they hear not:*] To the ſame Effect the Satyriſt, ——— *Audis*,

Jupiter,

Jupiter, hæc, nec labra moves ? ———
— Ut video, nullum discrimen habendum
Effigies inter vestras, statuamque Bathilli. Juv. Sat. XIII. 113. & 118.

V. 8. *They that make them are like unto them :*] So again, *Sat.* VIII. 53.
——————— *Truncoque simillimus Hermæ* ;
Nullo quippe alio vincis discrimine, quam quod
Illi marmoreum caput est, tua vivit imago.

V. 16. *The Heavens, even the Heavens are the Lord's :*] השמים
שמים ליהוה] All the ancient Versions read השמי שמים — THE
HEAVEN OF HEAVENS ---.

PSALM CXVI.

V. 1. *I love the Lord, because he hath heard my Voice,* and *my Supplications.* : אהבתי כי ישמע יהוה — את קולי תחנוני] These two last
Words, את קולי תחנוני, as there is no Conjunction between them, ought
I think to be rendered the VOICE OF MY SUPPLICATIONS ; for את קולי
seems to be the Plural *in regimine.* Most of the ancient Versions give
this Construction accordingly to the Words.

PSALM CXVIII.

V. 5. *I called upon the Lord in Distress : the Lord answered me,* and
set me *in a large Place.*] The latter Hemistic — עני במרחב יה ——
ought I think to be thus rendered — THE LORD ANSWERED BY SET-
TING ME AT LARGE.

PSALM CXIX.

V. 9. *Wherewithal shall a young Man cleanse his Way ? by taking*
Heed thereto *according to thy Word.*] The latter Clause is thus read in
the printed Text, לשמר כדברך : but all the ancient Versions doubtless read בדברך, *viz.* BY TAKING HEED TO THY WORD. As this
Verb שמר is sometimes construed with the Preposition ב, this Reading
seems not only more agreeable to the Rules of Grammar, but gives a
better Sense.

V. 21. *Thou hast rebuked the proud* that are *cursed, which do err*
from thy Commandments. : נערת זדים — ארורים השגים ממצותיך]
Rather,

Rather, with the old Version ---- THOU HAST REBUKED THE PROUD: CURSED are THEY WHICH DO &c.

V. 38. *Stablish thy Word unto thy Servant, who is devoted to thy Fear.*] The two laſt Words, אשר ליראתך — ought I think to be here rendered — GUIDE him TO THY FEAR. For it is evident that אשר conſidered as a Relative in this Place perplexes the Sentence. See this Word thus uſed, Prov. XXIII. 19.

V. 48. *My Hands alſo will I lift up unto thy Commandments.*] This I apprehend is done in Token of Admiration and Reſpect: for ſo is Tully to be underſtood, where he ſays, (after having received a Favour which he had aſked of Cæſar) *ſuſtulimus manus, et ego et Balbus, tanta fuit opportunitas, ut illud neſcio quod, non fortuitum, ſed divinum videretur.* Famil. Epiſt. V.

V. 66. *Teach me good Judgment, and Knowledge:* — טוב טעם ודעת למדני] Rather, I think — TEACH ME GOODNESS, DISCRETION, AND KNOWLEDGE.

V. 96. *I have ſeen an End of all Perfection:* — לכל תכלה ראיתי קץ] תכלה occurs nowhere elſe in this Form: it ought I think to be rendered here — EVERY PURPOSE, or RESOLUTION. (See 1 Sam. XX. 7, 9.) that is, " to all that has been contrived and executed by human " Art or Power: BUT THY COMMANDMENT IS EXCEEDINGLY " EXTENSIVE —— is of eternal Obligation." This Verſe ſeems to comprehend the whole Scope and Deſign of the Book of Eccleſiaſtes; for the Preacher found, after many Reſearches, that all was Vanity, except the Fear of the Lord. Ch. XII. 13.

V. 109. *My Soul is continually in my Hand:* — נפשי בכפי תמיד] All the ancient Verſions read here בכפיך, IN THY HANDS; but there is no Occaſion to admit another Lection; ſee Job. XIII. 14.

V. 112. *I have inclined mine Heart to perform thy Statutes alway, even unto the end.*] The Conſtruction of the two laſt Words לעולם עקב is not only very harſh in our Verſion, but gives alſo but little or no Senſe. For what End can there be to an infinite Duration? I would rather conſider them as put in Appoſition, or ſupply the Pronoun and Verb Subſtantive, thus --- I HAVE INCLINED MINE HEART TO PERFORM THY STATUTES, which are AN EVERLASTING REWARD.

WARD. The fame Idea and nearly the fame Expreffion occurs, Pf. XIX. 11. viz. — *in keeping of them* (thy Judgments) there is *great Reward.* The Word there is עקב.

V. 118. — *for their Deceit is Falfhood.* : כי שקר תרמיתם] Rather, I think --- FOR THEIR DECEIT IS A DISAPPOINTMENT : *i. e.* their fraudulent Schemes have not met with the defired Succefs.

V. 123. *Mine Eyes fail for thy Salvation:* — : עיני כלו לישועתך] Rather --- MINE EYES LONG FOR (or, EARNESTLY EXPECT) THY SALVATION. See this Verb כלה thus ufed, Pf. LXXXIV. 2. and 2 Sam. XIII. 39.

V. 126. It is *Time for* thee, *Lord, to work :* — עת לעשות ליהוד] Rather --- It is TIME FOR THE LORD TO WORK.

V. 128. *Therefore I efteem all* thy *Precepts* concerning *all* Things to be *right* ; and *I hate* &c. — על כן כל פקודי כל ישרתי] The Text is here very obfcure, owing I believe to the Redundancy of one Letter, *viz.* the ל at the End of the fecond כל. All the ancient Verfions feem to have read only, על כן כל פקודיך ישרתי — FORASMUCH AS I ESTEEM ALL THY PRECEPTS, I HATE &c. which is much clearer, and was moft probably the original Lection. על כן ought alfo to be thus rendered in the preceding Verfe.

V. 130. *The Entrance of thy Words giveth Light :* פתח דבריך יאיר] Rather, I think --- THE UNFOLDING (or EXPLICATION) OF THY WORDS &c. thus the Word is ufed, Cant. VII. 12.

V. 138. *Thy Teftimonies* that *thou haft commanded are righteous, and very faithful.* : צוית צדק עדתיך — ואבונה מאד] The Words of the Text will not I believe bear the Conftruction of our Verfion : but ought I think to be thus rendered —THOU HAST GIVEN IN CHARGE THY RIGHTEOUS TESTIMONIES, AND TRUTH ABUNDANTLY : for צדק עדתיך fignify literally *the Righteoufnefs of thy Teftimonies*; and feveral of the old Verfions conftrue them accordingly. See Verfe 144. where the fame Words are thus rendered.

V. 160. *Thy Word* is *true* from *the Beginning :* — ראש דברך אמת] This feems to be a forced Conftruction : and the literal Verfion of the Hebrew in the Margin (viz. *The Beginning of thy Word is true*) cannot be admitted. But if the Word ראש be here rendered THE SUM

A a

(*i. e.*

(*i. e.* the whole) of thy Word is true, the Conſtruction will be eaſy, and the Senſe clear. See this Word thus uſed, Exod. XXX. 12. Numb. I. 2. &c.

Psalm CXXI.

V. 6. *The Sun ſhall not ſmite thee by Day, nor the Moon by Night.* [יומם השמש אל יככה — וירח בלילה:] The Meaning ſeems to be, that the COLD OF THE EVENING ſhould not hurt him, any more than THE HEAT OF THE SUN. Not that the Moon is really the Cauſe of the Cold: but it is ſufficient if it were at the Time a prevailing popular Idea. For the Holy Scriptures are not to be conſidered as unerring Guides in *natural*, although they are in *moral* and *Divine*, Matters.

Psalm CXXIV.

V. 1, & 2. *If* it had not been *the Lord, who was on our Side;* [לולי יהוה שהיה לנו] Surely our old Verſion is here preferable, *viz.* EXCEPT THE LORD HAD BEEN ON OUR SIDE. For לולי is not a mere hypothetical Particle, as לו is; but a *Negative* hypothetical one, as will appear wherever it occurs. And the Affix Particle ש does not ſeem here to be relative, but rather redundant; ſee Noldius.

V. 5. *Then the proud Waters had gone over our Soul.* [עזו עבר על נפשנו — המים הזידונים:] As עבר cannot be conſtrued with המים, it would be better to render the Verſe thus — THEN IT (viz. *the Torrent* juſt beforementioned) HAD GONE OVER OUR SOUL, even IT'S PROUD WATERS; or with IT'S PROUD WATERS.

Psalm CXXVI.

V. 1. *When the Lord turned again the Captivity of Zion, we were like them that dream.*] That is, "when Cyrus iſſued his Decree for "our Reſtoration, it appeared to us as a Dream; and we could ſcarcely "truſt our Senſes. So the Greeks, when they were aſſured that Flaminius had re-eſtabliſhed their Liberty: το δε πληθυμμι των ανθρωπων Διαπιςαμενον και δοκαν ωσανει και ἐνυπνιον ακουειν των λεγομενων Δια το παραδοξον τε συμβαινοντος, ως τις ἐ αλλης αρχης εἰσα πεπαυκειν τον κηρυκα· Polybius, excerpt. Legat. Cap. IX. Which Livy thus expreſſes, Lib. XXXIII. 23. *Audita voce præconis, majus gaudium fuit, quam quod univerſum homines caperent.*

caperent. Vix fatis credere fe quifque audiffe; alii alios intueri mirabundi veluti fomni vanam fpeciem, &c. Le Clerc.

V. 4. *Turn again our Captivity, O Lord, as &c.* שובה יהוה את [שביתנו וגו״ שובה] is not here the Imperative, but a Noun; and את is to be confidered as a Sign of the Genitive Cafe, thus —— THE TURNING OF OUR CAPTIVITY, O LORD, IS AS STREAMS IN THE SOUTH, *i. e.* as delightful. See Taylor's Conc. Befides the Grammatical Exigence of this Conftruction, the Context requires this Senfe. For the Pfalmift muft otherwife be fuppofed to be entreating God to do what he acknowledges had already been done.

PSALM CXXVII.

V 2. — for *fo he giveth his beloved Sleep.* [כן יתן לידידו שנא :] The old Verfion is more appofite, and lefs equivocal, *viz.* BUT HE GIVETH REST TO HIS BELOVED.

PSALM CXXVIII.

V. 2. *For thou fhalt eat the Labour of thine Hands: happy* fhalt *thou* be &c. [יגיע כפיך כי תאכל — אשריך וגו״] Rather, I think — WHEN THOU EATEST THE LABOUR OF THINE HANDS, HAPPY fhalt THOU be &c. For the Particle כי does not feem to be caufal in this Place.

V. 4. *Behold, that thus fhall the Man be bleffed &c.* הנה כי כן יברך [גבר וגו״] Rather — BEHOLD, SURELY THUS &c.

V. 5. *The Lord fhall blefs thee out of Zion, and thou fhalt fee &c.* [יברכך יהוה מציון וראה וגו״] As the laft Verb and the Verb in the next Verfe are in the Imperative, it would I think be more accurate to render thus --- MAY THE LORD BLESS THEE OUT OF ZION, AND MAYEST THOU &c.

PSALM CXXXII.

V. 17. — *I have ordained a Lamp for mine anointed.* ערכתי נר [למשיחי :] That is, *a Succeffor,* as is evident from 1 Kings XI. 36. and 2 Sam. XXI. 17. The Metaphor is taken from the Light being conti-

nually

nually kept in by fresh Supplies successively. Theocritus uses the same Expression, *Idyl.* XXVII. — νεον Φαες ο|εαι γας.

PSALM CXXXIII.

V. 3. *As the Dew of Hermon*, and as the Dew *that descended upon the Mountains of Zion:* — על הררי ציון — כטל הרמון שירד] Critics have been much embarrassed in accounting how the Dew of Hermon could fall upon the Mountains of Zion, in Jerusalem, at the Distance of upwards of sixty Miles. Our Translators indeed overcome that Difficulty by the Addition of a few Words: but by such Expedients most Difficulties may easily be mastered. The Sense of this Place seems however very obvious, and the Construction is easy, thus — As THE DEW OF HERMON THAT DESCENDETH UPON THE DRY HILLS: for so is ציון used, Isa. XXV. 5. and XXXII. 2. The Psalmist having mentioned the Satisfaction which the Community feels on contemplating the Affection and Harmony subsisting between Brothers living under the same Roof, (for that I apprehend is the Meaning of the Words יחד גם, V. 1.) makes use of two Comparisons to illustrate his Idea; the one is the precious Oil used in consecrating the High Priest, which diffused it's odoriferous Effluvia far and wide; and the other, the Dew falling upon and invigorating the parched Ground; and then adds in the Conclusion --- THERE (in that House) HATH THE LORD FOR EVERMORE COMMANDED A BLESSING, even LIFE. For it is well known that one of the Sanctions of the Mosaic Dispensation was Long Life: and it is particularly promised to those who observed the fifth Commandment of the Decalogue, or *the first with Promise,* Eph. VI. 2. But as to LIFE ETERNAL, it made no part of that Temporary Institution.

PSALM CXXXV.

V. 3. *Praise ye the Lord, for the Lord* is good: *sing Praises unto him, for* it is *pleasant.*   : הללו יה כי טוב יהוה — זמרו לשמו כי נעים] The latter Hemistic does not quadrate in our Version with the preceding one, though it does so in the Text. If it be rendered thus, SING PRAISES UNTO HIM, FOR he is FAVOURABLE; both the Clauses will correspond exactly. That נעים has the Sense here proposed is clear from Ps. XC. 17.

V. 19. *Sihon, King of the Amorites,* — [לסיחון מלך האמרי] Rather, NAMELY SIHON, &c. for the ל has here that Force, as 1 Chron. V. 26. 2. — XXV. 10.

PSALM CXXXVII.

V. 3. — *and they that wasted us* required of us *Mirth*, — ותוללינו שמחה] I cannot find from what Verb our Translators derive the Word תוללינו, so as to give it the Sense of *wasting*. It must I think be deduced, either from תלל, and then it may signify — THEY THAT LAID HEAPS UPON US; (which Sense is countenanced by the Arabic Verb تل, *prostravit, conjecit in collum &c.*) or from ילל, *ejulavit*, in which Case we might render it *Lamentation*, thus — AND instead of OUR LAMENTATIONS they required MIRTH. But all the ancient Versions read ויולכינו, *they that brought us, viz.* into Captivity: if this Reading were admitted, it would be proper to render שובינו, (in the preceding Clause) *they that kept us Captives.*

V. 5 *If I forget thee, O Jerusalem, let my right Hand forget* her Cunning. [אם אשכחך ירושלם תשכח ימיני:] There is nothing in the Text expressive of *Cunning* or *Skill*; neither is any Word wanting to complete the Sense: thus --- IF I FORGET THEE, O JERUSALEM, LET MY RIGHT HAND BE FORGOTTEN, q. d. *let it ever be rejected as useless:* an Imprecation similar to those which immediately follow.

V. 6. — *if I prefer not Jerusalem above my chief Joy.* אם לא אעלה [את ירושלם — על ראש שמחתי:] *Qu.* ought not this Hemistic to be thus rendered --- IF I DO NOT ESTEEM JERUSALEM, LET ME REJOICE IN BITTERNESS? *i.e.* " may an oppressive Captivity be my " Doom and only Comfort." Each of the Words will I believe be found to admit of this Sense, and that without Violence; and the Antithesis of the preceding Verse, as well as of the former Part of this Verse, will hereby be exactly preserved.

V. 7. — *Rase it, rase it, even to the Foundation thereof.* ערו ערו עד [היסור בה:] The Translation would be more exact, were it to run literally thus --- RASE, RASE, TO THE VERY FOUNDATION OF IT. For it does not seem improbable that the original Lection might have been היסורנה: the ה however appears to be demonstrative.

PSALM

PSALM CXXXVIII.

V. 2. — *for thou hast magnified thy Word above all thy Name.* כי
[הגדלת על כל שמך אמרתך:] Neither the LXX, Syriac, Arabic,
Ethiopic, or Vulgate Versions, acknowledge this last Word, אמרתך.
It moreover greatly perplexes the Sense; and ought therefore I think
to be rejected as a Gloss. In this Case the Sentence would run thus—
FOR THOU HAST MAGNIFIED THY NAME ABOVE EVERY THING.

V. 5. — *Yea, they shall sing in the Ways of the Lord:* —— וישירו
בדרכי יהוה,] Our Translators and most of the ancient Interpreters
derive ישירו from שור *cecinit*, because of the Word *Praise*, I imagine,
in the preceding Verse. But the Verb ישר, *rectum, planum fuit*, was
certainly as obvious, and is infinitely better adapted to the Text. It is
used in *Hiphil*, (Prov. IV.25.) and, besides it's transitive Sense of *direct-
ing*, signifies also TO PROCEED FORWARD; which is doubtless the true
Meaning of it in this Place.

V. 6. *Though the Lord be high, yet hath he respect unto the lowly:
but the proud he knoweth afar off.*] This latter Clause, *viz.* וגבוה
מימרחק יידע, ought I think to be rendered — BUT THE PROUD HE
REGARDETH WITH AVERSION; which is clearly the Meaning of
the Phrase, *he beholdeth afar off*: the literal Version might better
suit the Margin.

V. 8. *The Lord will perfect* that which *concerneth me:* —— יהוה יגמר
בעדי] There can be no Doubt that all the ancient Versions read here
יגמל instead of יגמר: which makes a better Sense; thus—THE LORD
WILL DEAL BOUNTIFULLY WITH ME. See Pf. LVII. 2.

PSALM CXXXIX.

V. 5. *Thou hast beset me behind and before,* [אחור וקדם צרתני] All
the ancient Interpreters read יצרתני, THOU HAST FORMED ME &c.
which does not suit the Context so well as the other Verb.

V. 6. — *I cannot attain unto it.* : [לא אוכל לה] Here seems to
have been a Transposition of Letters, *viz.* אוכל for אבול; for יכל signifies only *To be able*, whereas the Signification of כול is that which
is here wanted, viz. TO COMPREHEND.

V. 7.

V. 7. *Whither shall I go from thy Spirit? &c.*] In a similar Manner does Xenophon expres the same Sentiment, *viz.* τον γαρ θεων πολεμον εκ οιδα ετ απο ποιε αν ταχες φευγων τις αποφυγοι, ετ εις ποιαν αν σκοτος αποδραιη, εδ οπως αν εις εχυρον χωριον απεςαιη. Παντη γαρ παντα τοις θεοις υποχα, και πανταχη παντων ισον οι θεοι κρατεσι. *Anab. Lib.* II. P. 158. Hut.

V. 14. *I will praise thee, for I am fearfully* and *wonderfully made:* אודך על כי נוראות נפליתי] All the ancient Versions read here נפלית, which seems to be the true Sense of this Place, *viz.* I WILL PRAISE THEE, FOR THOU HAST WONDERFULLY DONE TERRIBLE THINGS.

V. 16. *Thine Eyes did see my Substance yet being imperfect; and in thy Book all my Members were written,* which *in Continuance were fashioned, when* as yet there was *none of them.* גלמי ראו עיניך — ועל ספרך כלם — יכתבו ימים יצרו — ולא אחד בהם:] Each Hemistic in this Verse contains a distinct Sentence, which I think ought to be thus translated --- THINE EYES SAW MINE IMPERFECT PARTS, AND THEY were ALL IN THY BOOK; MY MEMBERS WERE REGISTERED FOR A WHILE, WHEN there was NOT ONE OF THEM. I read יצרו (instead of יצרו) which is the slightest Alteration possible, as Job XVII. 7. and this Lection seems to remove every Difficulty from the Construction of the Pronouns. גלם is not found elsewhere in SS. in this Sense: but גולם, in Chaldee, is an *Embryo,* a rude and unformed Mass of Matter; جلم also signifies *a Body mangled and torn in Pieces;* and ימים is used to express *a Season,* or a long undetermined Space of Time, Gen. XL. 4.

V. 17. *How precious also are thy Thoughts unto me, O God;* ולי מה יקרו רעיך אל] Rather — CONCERNING ME.

V. 18. *If I should count, them they are more in Number than the Sand: when I wake, I am still with thee.* אספרם מחול ירבון — הקיצתי ועדי עמך:] I cannot see the Connection between these two Clauses as they stand in our Version: but if we give to the Verb קוץ the same Signification in *Hiphil* which it has in *Kal,* as Isa. VII. 6. that Objection will be removed: thus --- If I COUNT THEM, THEY ARE MORE IN NUMBER THAN THE SAND: I GROW WEARY; (or, AM VEXED;) AND AM STILL WITH THEE: that is, " I find it an impracticable At-
" tempt; for in the End I am where I began, and lost in the Con-
" templation of thy glorious Perfections."

V. 20.

V. 20. — and *thine Enemies take* thy Name *in vain*. : [נשוא לשוא עריך]
Rather ---- and THINE ENEMIES STIR (or, LIFT UP THEM-
SELVES) IN VAIN. See Exod. XXXV. 26.

PSALM CXL.

V. 1. *Deliver me, O Lord, from the evil Man : preserve me from the
violent Man.* : [חלצני יהוה מאדם רע — מאיש חמסים תנצרני] Though
the Hebrew abounds in Anomalies, yet is there none in this Place,
provided אדם and איש be here conftrued in the plural Number. Both
thefe Words are ufed indifferently for one fingle Man, or any Number
of Men : the firft has no plural ; and the fecond is ufed only three
Times in Scripture in that Number.

V. 7. *O God the Lord, the Strength of my Salvation* : יהוה אדני
[עז ישועתי] Rather — O LORD, THE MIGHTY GOD OF MY SAL-
VATION.

V. 8, 9. —*further not his wicked Device, left they exalt themfelves.
As for the Head of thofe that compafs me about, let the Mifchief of their
own Lips cover them.* זממו אל תפק — ירומו ראש מסבי — עמל שפתימו
: [יכסומו] Thefe two Verfes ought I think to be divided and rendered
differently from what they are in our Verfion ; by which Means the
Hemiftics will be regular, the Senfe clearer, and the Anomaly removed :
thus —— FURTHER NOT HIS WICKED DEVICE. V. 9. As for thofe
who LIFT UP THE HEAD ROUND ABOUT ME, LET THE MIS-
CHIEF OF THEIR OWN LIPS COVER THEM ; or fimply --- THEY
LIFT UP THE HEAD &c. This Phrafe רום ראש is the fame I apprehend as נשא ראש, *to lift up the Head*, for we find רום קרן, *to lift up
the Horn*, ufed in the fame Senfe in refpect to Perfons who boaft, or
make Oftentation, of their Power. See Gen. XL. 13. 2 Kings XXV.
27. and Pf. LXXV. 4, & 5. מסבי is ufed adverbially, 1 Kings VI. 29.
2 Kings XXIII. 5. as well as here.

PSALM XLI.

V. 4. —*and let me not eat of their Dainties.* : [ובל אלהם במנעמיהם]
Or — PLEASANT MEATS ; by which feem to be underftood their
IDOL OFFERINGS.

V. 5. *Let the righteous fmite me*, it fhall be *a Kindnefs ; and let him
reprove me*, it fhall be *excellent Oil*, which *fhall not break my Head* :
יהלמני

יהלמני צדיק חסד ויוכיחני — שמן ראש אל יני ראשי] There are here I believe but two Hemiftics, which may be thus divided and rendered — LET THE RIGHTEOUS rather SMITE ME with KINDNESS, AND REPROVE ME; --- THE PRECIOUS OIL WILL NOT BREAK MY HEAD. *i. e.* "the kind Correction will do me no Prejudice;" which by a *Litotes* fignifies much Good. The Expreffion שמן ראש, *precious Oil*, is countenanced by one fimilar, Exod. XXX. 23. *viz.* שמים ראש, *principal* or *precious Spices*. Or if this be a Prayer of David, when he fled to Achifh, this Verfe may be thus rendered —— THOUGH THE RIGHTEOUS KINDNESS (fhewn in fparing Saul's Life twice) BRUISE ME AND REPROVE ME, LET NOT THE ANOINTED HEAD BREAK MY HEAD: *i. e.* "Though I fuffer for my confcientious Tendernefs, "and find by Experience that I have mifplaced it, yet let not my royal "Enemy quite deftroy me." See David's own Words, 1 Sam. XXVI. 23, 24. where he fpeaks of his Behaviour, as both *righteous* and *kind*, as Saul alfo did, Ch. XXIV. 17. and Strefs alfo is laid upon Saul's being the Lord's anointed.

—— *for yet my Prayer alfo* fhall be *in their Calamities.* כי עוד והפלתי ברעותיהם:] Rather, I think — FOR HITHERTO MY PRAYER ONLY hath been AGAINST THEIR WICKEDNESSES. The ו has this exclufive Force, as may be feen by confidering it's proper Force, Gen. XXIII. 15. 1 Sam. XIII. 22. 2 Sam. XV. 16.

V. 6. *When their Judges are overthrown in ftony Places, they fhall hear my Words, for they are fweet.* נשמטו בידי סלע שפטיהם — ושמעו אמרי כי נעמו:] We have here the Words בידי סלע, which fignify literally *in the Hands of the Rock*: but as ידים, when applied to the Sea, Pf. CIV. 25. is ufed for it's *Gulphs* and *Windings*; fo here it may denote the *Receffes, Holes*, or *Sides of the Rock*, where Saul and his Officers were *let go free* by David; for this evidently is the true Senfe of שמט in this Place. I would therefore render the Verfe thus —— THEIR RULERS WERE LET GO IN THE SIDES OF THE ROCK, AND HEARD MY WORDS, which WERE KIND.

V. 7. *Our Bones are fcattered at the Grave's Mouth, as when one cutteth and cleaveth* Wood *upon the Earth.* — כמו פלח ובקע בארץ נפזרו עצמינו לפי שאול:] Rather — OUR BONES ARE SCATTERED AT THE MOUTH OF THE GRAVE, AS SHREDS OR CHIPS UPON THE GROUND. Thefe Words, I fuppofe, are defigned to exprefs in a beautiful poetical Image "the continual Danger, to which David and

B b

"his

" his Men were continually expofed." פלח and בקע are not here Verbs, but Subftantives, and fynonymous: the firft is often ufed in the Senfe here propofed; and the latter occurs once, Gen. XXIV. 22. and figni-fies *a Part*, or *Portion*; which, together with the general Signification of the Verb from which it is derived, and the Exigence of the Place, may be deemed fufficient to eftablifh the foregoing Verfion.

V. 8. *But mine Eyes* are *unto thee*, *O God the Lord:* כי אליך יהוה אדני עיני] The old Verfion feems preferable, *viz.* BUT MINE EYES look UNTO THEE, O LORD GOD.

PSALM CXLII.

V. 4. *I looked on* my *right Hand, and beheld*, &c. הביט ימין וראה וגו] הביט muft be either the 3 perf. of the Preter, the Imperative, or Infi-nitive; none of which are here fuitable, except the Imperative. I fhould therefore adopt the Marginal Verfion, *viz.* LOOK ON THE RIGHT HAND AND BEHOLD; FOR there is NONE THAT KNOWETH ME: REFUGE FAILETH; NO ONE CARETH FOR MY LIFE.

PSALM CXLIII.

V. 1. — *give Ear to my Supplications: in thy Faithfulnefs anfwer me,* and *in thy Righteoufnefs.* האזינה אל תחנוני באמנתך — עני בצדקתך :] Rather, with moft of the ancient Verfions, thus —— GIVE EAR TO MY SUPPLICATIONS IN THY FAITHFULNESS; ANSWER ME IN THY RIGHTEOUSNESS. For though the Hemiftics are by this Divifion not fo uniform, yet it is not very uncommon for the latter to be fhorter than thofe which have preceded. See Pf. XVII. 7. &c.

V. 6. — *my Soul* thirfteth *after thee, as a thirfty Land.* נפשי כארץ עיפה לך :] As there is no Verb in this Sentence, it feems more na-tural to conftrue עיפה with נפש than with ארץ; which may be done indifferently, as they are both of the feminine Gender. But, if in that cafe an Epithet be thought wanting, I would fupply *dry* or *parched* in another Charaƈter.

V. 8. *Caufe me to hear thy loving Kindnefs in the Morning.* השמיעני בבקר חסדך] Would not בבקר be more properly rendered EARLY, as Pf. XLVI. 5. and XC. 14. fo as to be confidered as equivalent to מהר, *fpeedily*, in the preceding Verfe?

V. 9.

V. 9. — *I flee unto thee to hide me.* אליך כסתי :] The Text expreffes only --- HIDE ME NEAR THEE : and this is fufficient. See the Prepofition thus ufed, Gen. XXIV. 11. Exod. XXIX. 12. &c. Or thus --- I HAVE HIDDEN myfelf WITH THEE, *i. e.* taken Shelter. כסתי is ufed as the 1ft Perf. pret. Ezek. XXXI. 15. Vander Hoogt's Edition reads here כסיתי.

V. 10. — *thy Spirit is good; lead me into the Land of Uprightnefs.* רוחך טובה תנחני בארץ מישור :] Rather, with the old Verfion — LET THY LOVING (or GOOD) SPIRIT LEAD ME &c.

PSALM CXLIV.

V. 2. *My Goodnefs, and my Fortrefs,* &c. חסדי ומצודתי ונו׳] Thefe two Words do not well agree together. The whole Scope of this Place has evidently a reference to War. I therefore fufpect that, inftead of חסדי, we ought to read חסתי, MY REFUGE, or TRUST, as Ifa. XXX. 3. The Syriac feems to have fo read the Text. And in all the parallel Places Terms of the fame Import are ufed : thus — *The Lord is my Rock, and my Fortrefs, and my Deliverer. The God of my Rock, in whom I will truft : he is my Shield, and the Horn of my Salvation, my high Tower and* MY REFUGE. 2 Sam. XXII. 2, 3. And — *The Lord is my Rock, and my Fortrefs, and my Deliverer : my God, my Strength, in whom I will truft, my Buckler, and the Horn of my Salvation, and my high Tower.* Pf. XVIII. 2. &c.

V. 7. *Send thine Hand from above;* שלח ידיך ממרום] Rather — STRETCH FORTH &c. as Exod. XXIV. 11. 1 Sam. XXVI. 9. &c.

— *rid me, and deliver me out of great Waters ;* פצני והצילני ממים רבים] This Hemiftic does not feem at firft Sight to correfpond with the next, viz. *from the Hand of ftrange Children :* but if inftead of the proper, we take the figurative, Senfe ; that is, underftand *by many Waters* GREAT AFFLICTIONS, the Harmony will be reftored. See Pf. CX. 7.

V. 12. *That our Sons may be as Plants grown up in their Youth :* אשר בנינו כנטעים מגדלים בנעוריהם] Rather — THAT OUR SONS IN THEIR YOUTH may be AS THRIVING (or VIGOROUS) PLANTS.

—— that *our Daughters may be as Corner-Stones, polifhed after the Similitude of a Palace.* בנותינו כזוית מחטבות תבנית היכל :] Rather, I think --- that OUR DAUGHTERS may be AS THE POLISHED CORNER STONES in the STRUCTURE OF A PALACE.

V. 13.

V. 13. — *our Sheep may bring forth Thousands, and ten Thousands in our Streets.* : צאוננו מאליפות מרבבות בחוצתינו [בחוצתינו ought here furely to be tranflated IN OUR FIELDS, as Job V. 10. Prov. VIII. 26.

V. 14. — that there be *no Breaking in, nor going out :* אין פרץ ואין יוצאת] The Signification of יוצאת, as it is here rendered, feems to be too indeterminate. The Verb is ufed for *putting away ftrange Wives;* Ezra X. 3, 19. whence it might be inferred that it may have reference here to *Divorces.* But, as פרץ and יוצאת appear to be put in Oppofition to each other, I rather think that the firft of thefe Words means either A PLAGUE or PESTILENCE, *breaking in* to depopulate a Country; (fee Exod. XIX. 22. Pf. CVI. 29. which is called *a Breach,* 2 Sam. VI. 8. 1 Chron. XIII. 11. Pf. CVI. 23.) or THE BREAKING IN *as an Enemy,* (as Judg. XXI. 15. 2 Sam. V. 20. Pf. CXLIV. 14.) or, *as a Robber,* (as Pf. XVII. 4.) confequently that the latter fignifies THE REPELLING, or DRIVING OUT, and ought to be fo rendered here. The Intention of the Pfalmift may perhaps have been, that there might be no *Irruption* of Aliens into their Commonwealth; nor *Emigration* of his own People into foreign Countries; or carrying into Captivity; for יוצאת fignifies *Women going into Captivity out of their own Land,* Ezek. XII. 4. And thefe Senfes fuit very well with what follows, viz. *no complaining,* (rather, CRYING OUT,) *no bewailing in our Streets.*

PSALM CXLV.

V. 1. *I will extol thee, my God, O King,* — ארוממך אלהי המלך] Rather, I think --- I WILL EXTOL THEE, MY GOD, THE KING, (or, who art THE KING) for the Articular ה does not feem to be here the Vocative, but rather denotes Excellency.

V. 5. *I will fpeak of the glorious Honour of thy Majefty, and of thy wonderous Works.* : ודברי נפלאתיך אשיחה [הדר כבוד הודך] All the old Verfions (except the Chaldee) read ישיחו, THEY (*viz.* the Generation) WILL SPEAK &c. and fo likewife יספרנה (contracted for יספרונה) THEY WILL DECLARE, inftead of אספרנה, *I will declare,* in the next Verfe. By thefe Lections the prefent Embarraffment of the Text, owing to the *Enallage* of Perfons, is removed.

V. 12. *To make known to the Sons of Men his mighty Acts, and the glorious Majefty of his Kingdom.* להודיע לבני האדם גבורתיו — וכבוד הדר

הדר מלכותו׃] The Pronouns in the two foregoing Verſes, and in that which immediately follows, are all of the *ſecond* Perſon ; and ought doubtleſs to be ſo in this Verſe. Whether the Text had originally the Affix ו or ך, may poſſibly never be determined. This, however, is certain, that all the ancient Verſions, without Exception, have here — THY mighty Acts, and THY Kingdom ; and I think we might admit their Reading without Scruple.

Psalm CXLVI.

V. 8. *The Lord openeth* the Eyes of *the blind :* יהוה פקח עורים] There is no Neceſſity for ſupplying the Word *Eyes* in the Verſion ; for the Verb פקח ſignifies TO GIVE LIGHT, or TO CAUSE ONE TO SEE, Exod. IV. 11. XXIII. 8.

Psalm CXLVII.

V. 1. — *for it is pleaſant*, and *Praiſe is comely.* כי נעים נאוה תהלה׃] There ſeems to be but one Member in this Hemiſtic, which may be thus rendered — FOR A BECOMING PRAISE IS PLEASANT.

V. 14. *He maketh Peace* in *thy Borders :* השם גבולך שלום] Rather — HE MAKETH THY COUNTRY PEACEABLE ; for שלום is the *Abſtract* for the *Concrete*, as in a thouſand other Inſtances.

V. 16. *He giveth Snow like Wool :* — הנתן שלג כצמר] Rather, I think — HE SENDETH FORTH &c. Thus Virgil, *Georg.* I. 397.
  Tenuia nec lanæ per cælum vellera ferri.
And Martial, *Lib.* IV. Epig. III. V. 1.
 —— *Denſum tacitarum vellus aquarum.*
Herodotus ſays, that the Scythians called the Flakes of Snow πτερα, *Feathers* — ᵅᵘ εια τε ειναι ετι πϱοσωτερω ᵘτε οραν, ᵘτε διεξιεναι ᵘπο πτερων κεχυμενων· πτερων γαρ την γην και τον αερα ειναι πλεον. *Lib.* IV. *Cap.* vii.

V. 18. — *he cauſeth his Wind to blow*, and *the Waters flow.* ישב רוחו יזלו מים׃] The Syriac reads — רוח ויזלו — *viz.* HE CAUSETH THE WIND TO BLOW, AND THE WATERS FLOW : or, THE WIND BLOWETH, AND THE WATERS FLOW, as Iſa. XL. 7.

V. 20. — *and* as for his *Judgments, they have not known them.* ומשפטים בל ידעום׃] Rather —— NOR HAVE JUDGMENTS IN-
STRUCTED

STRUCTED THEM. So ירד in *Hiphil* fignifies; and in this Form and Senfe we may find it, Judg. VIII. 16. Ezek. XLIV. 23. &c. This is exactly the Senfe of what Mofes fays, Deut. IV. 8.

PSALM CXLVIII.

V. 7. — *ye Dragons and all Deeps.*   תנינים וכל תהמות :] Rather --- YE GREAT SERPENTS, AND ALL DEEP CAVERNS : *viz.* where they dwell. I tranflate תהמות, *Caverns*, becaufe it fignifies *the deep Parts of the Earth.* Pf. LXXI. 20.

V. 14. *He alfo exalteth the Horn of his People, the Praife of all his Saints*, &c. " וירם קרן לעמו — תהלה לכל חסידיו וגו] It is not eafy to diftinguifh whether our Tranflators meant to put תהלה, *the Praife*, in Appofition to *He* (*viz.* God) or *to Horn*; though I think the latter. The former would be preferable; and I am perfuaded is the true Senfe. Thus it would be better and more clearly expreffed — HE ALSO EXALTETH THE HORN OF HIS PEOPLE; he is A PRAISE AMONG ALL HIS SAINTS, AMONG THE CHILDREN OF ISRAEL.

PSALM CXLIX.

V. 4. — *he will beautify the meek with Salvation.*   יפאר ענוים בישועה :] Rather, I think — HE WILL ADORN &c.

V. 5. *Let the Saints be joyful in Glory;* יעלזו חסידים בכבוד] Rather I think in the Future —— THE SAINTS WILL TRIUMPH GLORIOUSLY.

—— *let them fing aloud upon their Beds.*   ירננו על משכבותם :] We read of *Songs in the Night*, Job XXXV. 10. and Pf. XLII. 8. but thefe it is prefumed were uttered in an erect, not in a recumbent or horizontal, Attitude. For befides that the Singer could not exert his Voice with fo much Advantage, there is a manifeft Impropriety of Behaviour in a Perfon *finging aloud in Bed*, whether he be alone or in Company. I would therefore underftand this Place and Pf. IV. 4. (where exactly the fame Phrafe occurs) agreeably to the Genius of the Arabic Language, which delights in calling *the Heart* A BED; and this it muft be confeffed is no improper Metaphor, the Affections being there quietly

quietly compofed as in a Bed, till they are roufed by fome unexpected
Accident: thus the Poet Motanabbius, *Carm.* XVI. 8.

يرى حده غامضاة القلوب ۞

i. e. *Gladius ejus infpicit* CUBILIA CORDIS. And, *Carm.* XLVI. 25.

مقبل حب ؏عبة فرح به
ومقبل غبظ عدوة مقروح ۞

i. e. CUBILE AMORIS *amici fui lætatur, fed* CUBILE ODII *in adverfa-
rium vulneratum eft.* The Scholiaft Wahedienfis explains مقبل by القلب;
and though neither of thefe Words, or غبض, be found in Golius or
Caftle in the Senfe of *Bed,* yet I doubt not of their having that Signification in the *Camus* or other Lexicons; for both the Verbs غبض and
تاب fignify *to fleep,* and قلب *to roll, to turn about.* I would therefore
render this Place thus --- THEY WILL SING ALOUD FROM THE
HEART; which Senfe it is evident is well connected with the Context, which contains an Exhortation to prepare for an offenfive War,
to which nothing can be more oppofite than the Notion of *rolling on a
Bed:* but, on the contrary, if this be underftood to have reference to
a martial Song before the Engagement, the Climax will be kept up,
and the Harmony preferved. See the Prepofition על ufed in this Senfe,
Noldius, II.

V. 6. Let *the high* Praifes *of God be in their Mouth:* רוממות אל
בגרונם] Rather — GOD will be EXALTATIONS (or, HIGHLY EX-
ALTED) IN THEIR MOUTHS, AND A TWO EDGED SWORD &c.

V. 9. — *this Honour have all his Saints. Praife ye the Lord.* הדר
הוא לכל חסידיו — הללו יה:] Thefe Words are an Epiphonema, as
in the laft Verfe of the preceding Pfalm, and fhould be thus tranflated
--- HE IS AN HONOUR AMONG ALL HIS SAINTS. PRAISE YE
THE LORD.

PSALM CL.

V. 1. — *Praife God in his Sanctuary: praife him in the Firmament
of his Power.* : הללו אל בקדשו — הללוהו ברקיע עזו] Rather — PRAISE
GOD ON ACCOUNT OF HIS HOLINESS: PRAISE HIM ON AC-
COUNT OF THE EXTENT OF HIS POWER, (or, HIS EXTENSIVE
POWER.) That the Prepofition ב has this Force here, is evident from
the Ufe made of it in the next Verfe; and that רקיע is not confined to
the Firmament (or fpacious Extenfion between the Earth and the
Clouds) but fignifies alfo any Extenfion, may be inferred from the general Senfe of the Verb רקע, *To fpread forth, To ftretch out.*

I CANNOT

I CANNOT conclude my Remarks on the Book of Pſalms without making a few general Obſervations on the Authors, and the Titles of them ; and this I thought might beſt be done by bringing the whole into one View.

This Collection of Divine Hymns has always been held in the higheſt Degree of Veneration, both by Jews and Chriſtians ; and it muſt be confeſſed that their Excellence is obvious, either in the Light of Compoſitions, or in reſpect to the Subject Matter of them. But this very Circumſtance has proved prejudicial to them ; for as they have been more frequently tranſcribed, they abound more in Faults, than any other of the ſacred Books ; a Circumſtance unavoidable without the Divine Interpoſition, which we cannot ſuppoſe would have interfered further than in providing that they ſhould be tranſmitted down to Poſterity ſufficiently intire.

By the Word *Pſalms*, the Jews ſeem ſometimes to have underſtood the whole of the *Hagiographa*, or moral Books, when put in Contradiſtinction to the *Pentateuch*, and the *Prophets* ; which laſt Diviſion comprehended alſo the *Prior Prophets*, (as they called them) or the Hiſtorical Books. See Luke XXIV 44. This Collection has been divided into different Parts, and in different Modes, according as their Fancy, or perhaps ſome more ſolid Reaſon, now unknown to us, ſuggeſted. It is certain however, that in their preſent State neither the Order of Time, the Unity of the Subject, nor the Diſtinction according to the Authors ſeem to have been much regarded ; that ſome of the Pſalms are a literal Tranſcript one from the other ; and that two of them have been made from what was originally but one, and this perhaps with no other View than that of making a round Number of the Sum total.

Some of the Fathers held that all theſe Pſalms were compoſed by David. But though this Opinion was abetted by Chryſoſtom, Theodoret, Ambroſius, Auguſtin, and ſome other reſpectable Names, yet it is ſo weak that it will not bear the Teſt of Examination ; no more than the Inference which ſome of them made on another Occaſion, *viz.* that our Lord's Miniſtry had continued *only one Year*, becauſe they thus underſtood *the acceptable Year*, propheſied of by Iſaiah, LXI. 2. When theſe Men, more remarkable for their Piety than their critical Skill, were preſſed by their Opponents with the Titles which ſome of the Pſalms bore, and the Matter they contained, which proved the contrary, they gave evaſive Replies to the firſt Point, and aſſerted that David could predict all the Circumſtances relative to the Captivity and other

Periods,

Periods, in as ample a Manner as if he had been an Eye Witnefs to the Tranfactions there mentioned; an Abfurdity equal to that of the Romanifts, who reprefent the **Almighty** as conftantly engaged in working Miracles without Neceffity.

WHEN thefe Titles were firft added is a Point which cannot now be determined: That they were not added by the Authors of the refpective Pfalms, is I think probable; becaufe few or no Compofitions had any Titles anciently, (this being a later Refinement) and many of them have none to this Day. Who they were that made this Addition is alfo very uncertain. It is generally fuppofed to have been the Work of Ezra, Nehemiah, or fome of the latter Prophets. Others have imagined that " they might have been prefixed by Tranfcribers " upon their own Conjectures, and perhaps upon fome uncertain Tra-" ditions. And if fo, they can have little more Authority, than if " modern Commentators were to affix their Opinions or Conjectures, " as the Occafions of writing any of thefe Pfalms." See Fenwick on the Titles of the Pfalms; P. 4. Thefe Additions feem however to be prior to the Exiftence of the Verfion of the LXX, as they appear there.

THAT feveral of thefe Pfalms could not have been compofed by the Authors whofe Names they bear, appears evident from internal Marks. The following Inftances may fufficiently prove this Point. The XIVth is faid to be David's, though the laft Verfe proves that the Author lived during the Captivity. Calmet entertains the fame Idea of the XXVIIIth, from what is faid V. 2d. The LXXXIXth has the Title of Ethan, the Ezrahite, a cotemporary with David, (1 Kings IV. 31.) and yet from the laft 15 Verfes it feems to have been written during the laft mentioned Epocha. The XCth is attributed to Mofes: but, from the common Period of human Life there mentioned, muft have been written feveral Centuries after his Time. And among the feveral Pfalms which are diftinguifhed by the Name of Afaph, the Mafter of David's Band of Mufic, the following are thought by the moft judicious Critics to be of the fame Æra, *viz.* the LXXIVth, LXXVth, LXXVIth, LXXXth, as are the LXXXIVth, and CIId, the Songs of *Degrees* (as they are called) from the CXXth to CXXVIth, fo likewife thofe that are anonymous from the CXLVIth to the End.

BESIDES the Hiftorical Titles, there are other Words prefixed to many of the Pfalms, which feem to denote their Quality; as MAS-CHIL, *inftructive*, XXXIId; MICHTAM, *golden*, XVIth; NEGINOTH, *merry*, LIVth; SHIGGAION, *plaintive*, VIIth; &c. or to have reference to Seafons, as SHOSHANNIM, to *Feftivity*, wherever it occurs;

or to particular Tunes, as THE HIND OF THE MORNING, THE SILENT DOVE (as the Words are rendered in our Version) &c. or to musical Instruments, as HIGGAION, &c.   But in what Class, SHEMINITH, SHIGGAION, MAHALATH, MUTHLABEN, ALMOTH, &c. are to be reduced I know not ; neither does it seem material to inquire, particularly as they are no Part of the Psalms, but only an Appendage.

WHATEVER may be the Meaning of the Word SELAH, it is also certain that it is no Part of the Composition, wherever it occurs, though inserted within it ; and even at Pf. XLIX. 13. where it is found in the Midst of a Sentence ; see also Pf. CXL. 8, 9. We have it in this Book seventy one Times, and thrice in Habakkuk.   The LXX render it Διαψαλμα ; which, according to Suidas, is *An Alteration of the Tune*. Meibomius (the most fanciful Critic, that perhaps ever wrote on the sacred Books) says that the three Letters, of which the Word is composed, stand for three distinct Words, viz. סוב למעלרה השר, *Redi sursum, cantor*. HIGGAION is another unconnected Word, the Meaning of which can by no Means be ascertained.

LASTLY, Pf. XXIVth, LXXVth, LXXXIst, and XCIst, seem to have been composed with a View that they might be sung in different Parts, and with Choruses ; in singing which they seem to have admitted Women. See 1 Chron. XXV. 5, 6. 2 Chron. XXXV. 25. Neh. VII. 67.   In respect to the Music, and the Musical Instruments which the Jews used in their Temple Service, see Calmet's Dissertations.

CRITICAL REMARKS

ON THE

BOOK OF PROVERBS.

CHAPTER I.

VERSE I. *The Proverbs of Solomon* —— משלי שלמה] The six first Verses contain a Prefatory Introduction to the Book: The first is properly to be confidered as *the Title*, with the Author's Name and Quality. The Word *Proverbs* here means fententious Maxims and Obfervations. The three next Verfes fpecify the Subject treated of under three general Heads: the 5th and 6th befpeak Attention to them, by making it a Mark of Wifdom and good Underftanding.

V. 2. *To know Wifdom and Inftruction* —— [לדעת חכמה ומוסר The ל with the Infinitive fupplies the Place of the Gerund in *do*, when ufed by the Latins with the Prepofition *de* preceding it, in this Verfe and the two following: as Exod. V. 14. *Wherefore have ye not fulfilled your Tafk in making Brick*, ללבן, properly, CONCERNING THE MAKING OF BRICK. 1 Sam. XII. 17. *Your Wickednefs is great, which ye have done, in afking You a King*, לשאול, CONCERNING THE ASKING &c. So Eccl. II. 11. &c. In all thefe Cafes the Reference is to the preceding Noun, as *the Sayings of Solomon concerning the knowing of &c.* in thefe Verfes.

The Author in thefe three Verfes judicioufly diftributes his Matter under three general Heads, correfponding to each Verfe refpectively. For his Maxims or Sentences are either 1°. declarative of the Nature and Excellence of Wifdom &c. or 2°. contain Exhortations to the Practice of what is right; or 3°. fupply Rules for the Conduct of the

fimple

fimple and unexperienced. It may be of Ufe to afcertain the Force of
the Terms. By הכמה is certainly meant *Religion*, properly fo called,
or *Piety towards God*, which is Wifdom κατ' ἐξοχήν. Compare Ch. IX.
10. XV. 33. with Pf. XC. 12. Job XXVIII. 28. מוסר, from it's De-
rivation, appears to be *Moral Difcipline*, reftraining Men from what is
wrong, and leading them to what is right : fo that the firft Hemiftic
may be rendered --- CONCERNING THE KNOWLEDGE OF WISDOM
AND VIRTUE. From the Prepofition בין is derived הבין, which fignifies *to difcern* between oppofites, as Truth and Falfhood, Good and
Evil, and therefore להבין אמרי בינה is, CONCERNING THE DIS-
CERNMENT OF THE WORDS OF UNDERSTANDING, i. e. *of found
Doctrine*.

V. 3. *To receive the Inftruction of Wifdom, Juftice, and Judgment,
and Equity.* לקחת מוסר השכל — צדק ומשפט ומשרים: The Verb
לקח, whofe Infinitive is קהת, fignifies not fimply *to receive*; but *to
receive, fo as to obey* or *improve*. See Ch. XXIV. 32. Job XXII. 22.
Jer. VII. 28. &c. צדק fignifies *Juftice*, which confifts in giving to all,
both God and Man, their ftrict due ; משפט feems to denote properly
the Prefcriptions of the written Law, human and divine ; and משרים
what is ftrait or *even, according to the Rule of Right Reafon* and *Equity* :
fo that this Verfe may be rendered --- CONCERNING THE IM-
PROVEMENT OF MORAL DISCIPLINE IN THE WISE PRACTICE
OF JUSTICE, LAW, AND EQUITY.

V. 4. *To give Subtilty to the fimple, to the young Man Knowledge and
Difcretion.* לתת לפתאים ערמה — לנער דעת ומזמה: פתאים
ftands for *weak filly Perfons*, who are eafily impofed upon ; ערמה is
the oppofite Quality taken in a good Senfe, which may be properly
called *Prudence*, as Ch. VIII. 5, 12. for *Subtilty* is generally ufed in a
bad Senfe for *Craft* and *Cunning*. What giddy Youth generally wants
is a *Knowledge* of Things, founded upon *Obfervation* and *Thought* ;
and thus much is implied in the Words דעת and מזמה, taken as an
Hendyadis ; the latter of which comes from זמם, *to confider*, or *think
with a fixed Attention*. This Verfe may then be rendered —— CON-
CERNING THE FURNISHING OF THE SIMPLE WITH PRUDENCE,
AND OF THE YOUNG MAN WITH CONSIDERATE KNOWLEDGE :
i. e. laying down for them fuch Rules and Precepts as may fupply the
Place of thofe ufeful Qualities, in which they are refpectively moft
deficient.

V. 5.

V. 5. *A wife* Man *will hear, and will increase Learning : and a Man of Understanding shall attain unto wife Counsels.* — ישמע הכם ויוסף לקח ונבין תחבלות יקנה:] Or, THE WISE WILL HEAR AND INCREASE WHAT IS RECEIVED, (or, IMPROVE IN LEARNING) AND A MAN OF UNDERSTANDING WILL AVAIL HIMSELF OF WISE COUNSELS.

V. 6. *To understand a Proverb and the Interpretation ;* — להבין משל ומליצה] Rather — BY CONSIDERING A PROVERB AND IT'S FI-GURATIVE SENSE.

V. 17. *Surely in vain the Net is spread in the Sight of any Bird.* כי חנם מזורה הרשת — בעיני כל בעל כנף:] The Hemistics ought I think to be thus distinguished --- SURELY THAT NET IS SPREAD IN VAIN, which is IN THE SIGHT OF ANY BIRD.

V. 32. *For the turning away of the simple shall slay them :* כי משובת פתים תהרגם] Rather — THE BACKSLIDING — as in all other Places.

CHAP. II.

V. 2. *So that thou incline thine Ear unto Wisdom,* and *apply thine Heart to Understanding :* להקשיב לחכמה אזנך — הטה לבך לתבונה:] Instead of the Copulative " and" the Conjunction אם is to be supplied from the last Verse, and prefixed to the Beginning, thus — IF WHILST THINE EAR HEARKENETH UNTO WISDOM, THOU INCLINE THINE HEART TO UNDERSTANDING :

V. 7. *He layeth up sound Wisdom for the righteous : he is a Buckler to them that walk uprightly.* וצפן לישרים תושיה — מגן להלכי תם:] Rather --- AND HE LAYETH UP SOLID HAPPINESS (or TRUTH) FOR THE RIGHTEOUS : HE GIVETH it TO THEM &c.

V. 9. — *and Equity ; yea, every good Path.* ומישרים כל מעגל טוב:] This Hemistic ought not to make more than one Sentence, thus --- AND THE RECTITUDE OF EVERY GOOD PATH. Most of the old Versions read ומישרי.

V. 12. *To deliver thee from the Way of the evil* Man ; להצילך מדרך רע] Rather — DELIVERING THEE FROM THE EVIL WAY, OR THE WAY OF THE WICKED : So also V. 16.

— *from the Man that speaketh froward Things.* מאיש מדבר תהפכות:] Rather — FROM EVERY ONE &c. because all the Verbs which follow are in the Plural.

CHAP.

V. 4. *So shalt thou find Favour, and good Understanding in the Sight of God and Man.* : ‏ומצא הן ושכל טוב — בעיני אלהים ואדם‎] Rather --- SO SHALT THOU FIND FAVOUR AND GOOD SUCCESS &c. The Verb ‏שכל‎ has this Sense, Deut. XXIX. 9. Josh. I. 7, 8. 1 Kings II. 3. &c.

V. 8. *It shall be Health to thy Navel,* — ‏רפאות תהי לשרך‎] The LXX, Syriac, and Arabic Versions seem to have read ‏לבשרך‎, TO THY FLESH; for ‏בשר‎ is sometimes thus used: see Ch. IV. 22. We have a like Antithesis, where *Flesh* is opposed to *Bones.* Pf. XXXVIII. 3. &c.

V. 18. *She is a Tree of Life to them that lay hold upon her; and happy is every one that retaineth her.* — ‏עץ חיים היא — למחזיקים בה‎ — ‏ותמכיה מאשר‎ :] The Construction our Version gives to the last Hemistic is unjustifiable, as it joins a singular to a plural, besides the Enallage of Numbers it creates between the two Sentences in the Verse: I would therefore render it --- AND SHE GUIDES (or, DIRECTS) THEM THAT RETAIN HER; the ‏ה‎ formative of the feminine having by some Accident dropped out of the Text.

V. 24. *When thou liest down thou shalt not be afraid: yea, thou shalt lie down, and thy Sleep shall be sweet.* ‏אם תשכב לא תפחד — ושכבת‎ ‏וערבה שנתך‎ :] It is not probable that Solomon would use the same Word in both the Hemistics. If we look into the old Versions, we shall find that they all, except the Chaldee, read in the first Hemistic ‏השכך‎ : whose Lection I would therefore adopt, and render — WHEN THOU ART SUNK DOWN, THOU SHALT NOT BE AFRAID; NAY, THOU SHALT LIE DOWN &c.

V. 32. — *but his Secret is with the righteous.* : ‏ואת ישרים סודו‎] Rather --- BUT HIS COUNSEL IS WITH THE RIGHTEOUS. As Pf. LV. 14. LXXXIII. 3.

V. 35. — *but Shame shall be the Promotion of Fools.* ‏וכסילים מרים‎ ‏קלון‎ :] Rather, with the Margin — SHAME EXALTETH FOOLS; or, still better, EXPOSETH TO PUBLIC VIEW: except this be said ironically.

CHAP. IV.

V. 3. *For I was my Father's Son, tender and only* beloved *in the Sight of my Mother.* : כי בן הייתי לאבי רך — ויחיד לפני אמי] Rather --- FOR I WAS A SON TENDER TO MY FATHER, AND A DARLING IN THE SIGHT OF MY MOTHER. By this Construction one Hemistic reflects Light upon the other. יחיד signifies both *an only one* and *a Darling* : the Reason of which is obvious.

V. 18. *But the Path of the just is as the shining Light, that shineth more and more unto the perfect Day.* וארח צדיקים כאור נגה — הולך : ואור עד נכון היום] Rather — AS A SHINING LIGHT, THAT GOETH FORTH AND SHINETH LIKE THE PERFECT DAY, or *the Day in it's Meridian Brightness.* See עד thus used, Nah. I. 10. 1 Chron. IV. 27.

V. 22. *— and Health to all their Flesh.* : ולכל בשרו מרפא] Rather --- AND THEY (viz. *my Words* or *Sayings*) BEAR TIDINGS OF HEALTH TO ALL : *i. e.* are replete with wholesome and salutary Counsels.

V. 23. *Keep thy Heart with all Diligence; for out of it are the Issues of Life.* : מכל משמר נצר לבך — כי ממנו תוצאות חיים] Rather — THE GOINGS FORTH (or perhaps, THE PROGRESS) OF LIFE : *i. e.* (as it is added in the old Version) " as the Heart is pure or corrupt, so " is the whole Course of a Man's Life."

CHAP. V.

V. 3. *For the Lips of a strange Woman —* כי — שפתי זרה] Ought not זרה here, and in the other Places where it occurs in this Book, to be rendered A DEBAUCHED or LEWD WOMAN ; for the Import of the Word is — ONE WHO IS ALIENATED in her Affections, *viz.* from her Husband, or from her God ?

V. 6. *Lest thou shouldest ponder the Path of Life, her Ways are moveable,* that *thou canst not know* them. ארח חיים פן תפלס — נע מעגלתיה : לא תדע] The first Hemistic does not well connect with the latter, or the Context, in our Version ; and that because our Translators assign a wrong Person to the Verb : for תפלס is equally *the 2d. Per. masc.* or

the

the 3d. fem. of the Future, as every *Tyro* knows. This Overfight is the more remarkable, as they had doubtlefs the old Verfion before them, which renders the Word properly, thus —— SHE WEIGHETH NOT THE WAY OF LIFE: HER PATHS ARE MOVEABLE; THOU CANST NOT KNOW them.

V. 8. *Remove thy Way far from her,* —— [הרחק מעליה דרכך] This Ex-prefsion is harfh, either in the Proper, or the Figurative, Senfe. I would therefore either render with the old Verfion —— KEEP THY WAY FAR FROM HER; or, KEEP FROM HER in THY WAY.

V. 9. *Left thou give thine Honour unto others,* —— [פן תתן לאחרים הודך] אחרים does not feem to be a Noun in this Place, but the Participle pre-fent; which I would render *(Left thou give up &c.)* TO THE IDLE, as Deut. VII. 10. XXIII. 21. &c. AND THY YEARS TO THE UNRE-LENTING; meaning the jealous Hufband. See Chap. VI. 33, 34, 35. which may be confidered as a Kind of Paraphrafe upon this Verfe.

V. 14. *I was almoft in all Evil, in the midft of the Congregation and Affembly.* [כמעט הייתי בכל רע — בתוך קהל ועדה:] As the Words *Congregation* and *Affembly* are generally ufed in a good Senfe for *re-ligious Meetings,* and the Meaning here feems directly oppofite; I would render the latter Hemiftic thus — IN THE MIDST OF COMPANY AND THE MULTITUDE. See the firft Word fo rendered, Gen. XXXV. 11. and the latter, Pf. LXVIII. 30.

V. 15. *Drink Waters out of thine own Cistern; and running Waters out of thine own Well.* [שתה מים מבורך — ונוזלים מתוך בארך:] The latter Hemiftic ought to be rendered —— AND STREAMS (or, STREAMING DRAUGHTS) FROM THE BOTTOM OF THINE OWN WELL. מתוך has this Senfe by Conftruction, Zech. V. 4. where it is faid *that the Curfe fhall remain in the midft* (*i. e.* fhall penetrate INTO EVERY, THE MOST DISTANT, PART) *of the Houfe.* What is meant by this Allegory is explained at Ver. 18, 19, 20. There we find the Key to unlock this Proverb; which is hereby reftrained to *the Marriage Bed, and connubial Benevolence.* It does not feem therefore to be a general Maxim (according to the old Verfion) relative to So-briety and Charity.

V. 16. *Let thy Fountains be difperfed abroad,* — [יפצו מעינתיך חוצה] I would here render מעינתיך THY SPRINGS, to diftinguifh it from מקורך

מְקוֹרֶךָ (at V. 18.) which is alfo tranflated *Fountain*; not merely on Account of the Sound, but becaufe a different Sentiment is thereby conveyed: the firft being *the Effects*, the latter *the Caufe*. For Solomon himfelf interprets the בְּקוֹר, or *Fountain*, by THE WIFE; and by Parity of Reafon we may conclude, that *the Springs*, or RIVULETS, here mentioned muft mean THE CHILDREN, produced from that Union. And if there ftill could remain any Doubt, the next Verfe muft I think intirely remove it: which fays, *Let them be only thine own, and not Strangers with thee*; and feems capable of no other Interpretation, than that of an Exhortation TO KEEP THE BED OF WEDLOCK UNDEFILED.

V. 19. Let her be as *the loving Hind, and pleafant Roe* : — אילת אהבים וְיַעֲלַת הֵן] Rather — THE BELOVED HIND, AND FAVOURITE ROE. The Comparifon is here very appofite; for it is well known, that all the Males of the Deer Kind are remarkably fond of their Females at the Time in which the εισρος operates; and, though at other Seafons timid Animals, they will then, at the Hazard of their Lives, encounter any Danger, rather than forfake their beloved Partners.

— *and be thou ravifhed always with her Love*. באהבתה תשגה תמיד:] The Verb שנה in all other Places, befides this and the next Verfe, fignifies *to err*, or *go aftray*: fee V. 23. but the Senfe in Arabic of شغا is *Lætitiam attulit, anxius fuit, illum exhilaravit.*

V. 22. — *and he fhall be holden with the Cords of his Sins*. ובחבלי חטאתו יתמך :] In the Margin — *his Sin*; which is right according to the prefent Lection: but the correfponding Word and all the old Verfions point out חטאותו.

CHAP. VI.

V. 1. *My Son, if thou be Surety for thy Friend*, — בני אם ערבת לרעך] This Maxim againft being Surety for a Friend (which Solomon inculcates in different Places) feems to favour more of œconomical Prudence than of Benevolence. It borders upon a Saying of Thales, mentioned by Diogenes Laertius — εγγυα, παρα δε ατη. He means I fuppofe hereby to recommend the greateft Circumfpection before we become bound for any one, and not to forbid this Act of Friendfhip abfolutely in all Cafes whatever. See the Note Job. XVII. 3.

V. 5. *Deliver thyfelf as a Roe from the Hand* of the Hunter, הנצל כצבי מיד] Our Tranflators feem to have thought that the Word ציד had

D d

had dropped out of the Text: but I think it is more probable that there is only the ע wanting; and that the Word was originally מציר --- DELIVER THYSELF AS A ROE FROM THE HUNTER: for by this Reading the Hemiflics correfpond better in Length; and it feems to have been the Reading of all the old Verfions, except the Vulgate.

V. 8. *Provideth her Meat in the Summer* — תכין בקיץ לחמה, Modern Naturalifts feem to queftion this Fact: but it may be thought fufficient for the Purpofe, if it were in Solomon's Time but a popular Notion. See the Note on Pf. CXXI. 6. and Ray, on the Creation, &c. (Part I. P. 135.) His Words are — " Another Infect noted for her " Prudence, in making Provifion for the Winter, propofed by Solo" mon to the Sluggard for his Imitation, is the Ant, which (as all Na" turalifts agree) hoards up Grains of Corn againft the Winter for her " Suftenance: and is reported by fome to bite off the *Germen* of " them, left they fhould fprout by the Moifture of the Earth; which " I look upon as a mere Fiction: neither fhould I be forward to credit " the former Relation, were it not for the Authority of Scripture; " becaufe I could never obferve any fuch ftoring of Grain by our " Country Ants." The Author referred to by Ray is Pliny, B. X. Ch. 72. See alfo B. XI. Ch. 30. Ælian in feveral Places confirms the Account of the Induftry of the Ant. B. II. Ch. 25. B. VI. Ch. 43. &c. So likewife the Poets,

> *Hic nos frugilegas afpeximus agmine longo*
> *Grande onus exiguo formicas ore gerentes,*
> *Rugofoque fuum fervantes cortice callem.* Ovid. Met. B. VIII. 624.

So Horace in the firft Satyr — V. 32.

> *Parvula, nam exemplo eft, magni formica laboris;*
> *Ore trahit quodcunque poteft, atque addit acervo*
> *Quem ftruit, haud ignara ac non incauta futuri.*

And Virgil, —— *populatque ingentem farris acervum*
(Curculio, atque) inopi metuens formica feneêtæ. Georg. B. 1. V. 184.

> *Ac veluti ingentem formicæ farris acervum*
> *Cum populant, hyemis memores, tectoque reponunt:*
> *It nigrum campis agmen, prædamque per herbas*
> *Convectant calle angufto; pars grandia trudunt*
> *Obnixæ frumenta humeris: pars agmina cogunt,*
> *Caftigantque moras; opere omnis femita fervet.* Æneid. IV. V. 402.

V. 10. Yet *a little Sleep, a little Slumber,* מעט שנות מעט תנומות]
By the Plurals being ufed here feems to be implied *Sleep and Slumber
often repeated* at different Intervals. The Apoftrophe from the Pre-
ceptor to the Sluggard is beautiful.

V. 11. *So fhall thy Poverty come* —— ובא — ראשך] The Senfe
feems to require that the ו in this Place fhould be confidered as an adverfative Conjunction; or an illative one, as in the old Verfion.

V. 12. *A naughty Perfon, a wicked Man, walketh with a froward
Mouth.* אדם בליעל איש און — הלך עקשות פה :] Rather — A
BASE (or WORTHLESS) FELLOW IS A WICKED MAN, WALKING
&c. This Conftruction feems more agreeable to the Genius of the oriental Languages; which have feldom two Subjects put in Appofition;
and to the Nature of Hemiftics, each of which almoft univerfally contains a Propofition.

V. 26. *For by Means of a whorifh Woman* a Man is brought *to a
Piece of Bread :* — כי בעד אשה — זונה עד ככר לחם] Rather —
FOR BY MEANS OF A WOMAN, THE FORNICATOR is brought
TO A PIECE OF BREAD. For זונה may as well be here confidered
as the Participle prefent, as a Noun.

—— *and the Adulterefs will hunt for the precious Life.* ואשת איש
נפש יקרה תצוד :] Rather, by Way of *αυξησις* — YEA, THE ADUL-
TERESS WILL HUNT FOR THE PRECIOUS LIFE.

V. 30. Men *do not defpife a Thief, if he fteal to fatisfy his Soul,
when he is hungry.* לא יבוזו לגנב כי יגנוב — למלא נפשו כי ירעב :]
Rather, I think --- IS NOT A THIEF TAKEN WHEN HE STEAL-
ETH; THOUGH HE LONG TO SATISFY HIS APPETITE? This
Conftruction preferves the Hemiftics diftinct from each other, and
conveys a clearer Senfe than the other. Inftead of יבוזו, which has no
Antecedent, and is befides a Verb foreign to the Purpofe, I read יבוז
with all the old Verfions; and give רעב the Senfe of *longing* (to avoid
Tautology in the next Words) for *to hunger and thirft after* Righteouf-
nefs &c. is *to long earneftly* for that particular Thing.

V. 32. — *he that doeth it, deftroyeth his own Soul.* משחית נפשו]
הוא יעשנה :] Rather --- HE that EMBRACETH HER, or HATH
COMMERCE WITH HER. See Ezek. XXIII. 3, 8, 21.

V. 34. *For Jealoufy is the Rage of a Man:* — כי קנאה חמת גבר] Rather --- FOR THE RAGE OF A MAN (or rather, OF THE HUS-BAND) IS MOVED BY JEALOUSY.

CHAP. VII.

V. 2. — *and my Law as the Apple of thine Eye.* : ותורתי כאישון עיניך] Rather --- AND let MY LAW be AS THE PUPIL OF THINE EYES.

V. 3. *Bind them upon thy Fingers,* — קשרם על אצבעתיך] Solomon could not mean that this Precept fhould be underftood literally, any more than the next, *write them upon the Table of thine Heart;* and yet it was upon fuch Texts as thefe (fee Exod. XIII. 16. Deut. VI. 5. XI. 18.) that the Pharifees founded their Practice of binding *Philacteries* upon their Foreheads. And hence perhaps alfo the popular Phrafe among us *of having a Thing at the Finger's End,* when we are perfectly acquainted with it.

V. 11. *She is loud and ftubborn,* — המיה היא וסררת] Rather — SHE CANNOT REST QUIET, BUT BACKSLIDETH. The Verb המה fignifies *to be difquieted, hurried,* or *violently agitated:* and the primary Senfe of סרר is *to go backward* or *backflide.* This Senfe is in perfect Harmony with the next Hemiftic, — *her Feet abide not in her Houfe.* Befides that *the being loud and ftubborn* are Qualities which do not correfpond with *the meretricious Arts of captivating.*

V. 14. *I have Peace Offerings with me;* — זבחי שלמים עלי] That is, "I have an Entertainment, or Feaft, at my Houfe:" for in thefe Sorts of Sacrifices the Perfon that offered referved a Part of the Victim for convivial Purpofes. See the Note Pf. LXIX. 22. and Ch. XVII. 1.

V. 15. — *diligently to feek thy Face, and I have found thee.* לשהר : פניך ואמצאך] Rather — TO SEEK THEE, or THY COMPANY: for פני has frequently thefe Senfes.

V. 16. — *with carved* Works, *with fine Linen of Egypt.* חטבות אטון מצרים] Rather (I think with all the ancient Verfions) — with TAPESTRY OF THE TEXTURE OF EGYPT. For חטב in Chaldee fignifies, *effigiavit, figuravit, figuris aliquid exornavit,* &c : and in refpect to אטון, as it occurs in no other Place, and no Affiftance is to be derived in the Explanation of it from the Eaftern Languages,

we

we can follow no better Guide than the old Verſions; except we give it the Senſe of ⲁⲛ̅ⲗ, which in Coptic ſignifies, *Incenſum, Aroma*; (and this may not be thought improper, as it relates to ſome coſtly Egyptian Manufacture;) in this Caſe, the Hemiſtic ought to be rendered --- with PERFUMED TAPESTRY, or COVERLETS FROM EGYPT. The next Verſe may be thought to countenance this Senſe. Note, that as the Word מרבדים in the preceding Hemiſtic (which is another *ἀπαξ λεγομενον*) is rendered *Tapeſtry*, I would give it the Senſe of *Blankets* with the old Verſions, and from the Arabic سبخ, which ſignifies, *diverſicolores lanæ partes*, or سبخ, *Manipulus lanæ, Panniculus*.

V. 18. *Come, let us take our fill of Love unto the Morning; let us ſolace ourſelves with Loves.* לכה נרוה דדים — עד הבקר נתעלסה באהבים:] Thus I think the Hemiſtics ought to be rendered —— COME, LET US TAKE OUR FILL OF LOVE; LET US SOLACE OURSELVES WITH ARDENT LOVE UNTIL THE MORNING. I give אהבים the Force of the Superlative, becauſe the Hebrews having properly no ſuch Degree of Compariſon, expreſs it by an additional Particle, or by a Repetition of the ſame Word, or by a Plural.

V. 21. *With her much fair Speech ſhe cauſed him to yield; —* הטתו ברב לקח] Rather — BY THE MULTITUDE OF HER ALLUREMENTS SHE PERVERTED HIM, BY THE FLATTERY OF HER LIPS SHE SEDUCED HIM. *Allurements* is a Word not only more expreſſive, as it extends to Signs, Acts and Geſtures, but is more immediately connected with the Verb לקח, *to catch*. So in Engliſh the Words *Lure*, or *Allure*, (ſomething ſet up to entice Birds, or other Things, to it) are derived from a Verb of the ſame Senſe as the Hebrew.

CHAP. VIII.

V. 2. *She ſtandeth in the Top of high Places, by the Way in the Places of the Paths.* בראש מרמים עלי דרך — בית נתיבת נצבה:] This Verſe would I think be more juſtly tranſlated thus — SHE IS ON THE TOP OF EMINENCES NEAR THE ROAD; SHE STANDETH IN THE HIGHWAYS. I ſupply the Verb Subſtantive in the firſt Hemiſtic, as ſome Verb is there wanted; or connect this with the preceding Verſe, thus --- DOTH NOT UNDERSTANDING PUT FORTH HER VOICE FROM THE TOP OF EMINENCES &c?

V. 3.

V. 3 *She crieth at the Gates* —— תרנה — [ליד שערים] Rather — BY THE SIDE OF THE GATES, as in several other Places : which corresponds to לפי and כבוא, AT THE ENTRANCE, and AT THE THRESHOLD, immediately after.

V. 5. *O ye simple, understand Wisdom ; and ye fools, be ye of an understanding Heart.* : [הבינו פתאים ערמה — וכסילים הבינו לב] Rather --- O YE SIMPLE, DISCERN PRUDENCE ; AND, YE FOOLS, UNDERSTAND JUDGMENT. For ערמה seems to have this Sense here, and is so rendered at V. 12. See Ch. I. 4. And לב is used figuratively for *Judgment* or *Discretion* ; see Ch. VI. 32. XIV. 33. &c.

V. 6. — *and the Opening of my Lips* shall be *right Things.* ומפתח : [שפתי מישרים] Rather—WITH RIGHT THINGS, or WITH EQUITY. For the מ prefixed to ישרים is here a Preposition ; which is wanted to complete the Sense : or, by construing ומפתח as the Participle *Benoni,* thus --- AND OPEN MY LIPS WITH EQUITY.

V. 10. *Receive my Instruction, and not Silver* ; — [קחו מוסרי ואל כסף] Rather --- RECEIVE MY INSTRUCTION WITHOUT MONEY : thus is ואל rendered, Job. XII. 25. and ought to be Jer. XVII. 11.

V. 13. *The Fear of the Lord* is *to hate evil :* — [יראת יהוה שנאת רע] Wisdom, which is here personified, speaks in the preceding Verse in the first Person, so likewise in this Verse, and throughout the Remainder of the Chapter. The religious Precept before us (though most worthy to be inculcated) must therefore appear to be here unseasonable ; whence I conclude that Solomon did not put these Words in her Mouth : but made her say יראתי, and שנאתי, *viz.* I FEAR THE LORD ; I HATE THE EVIL OF PRIDE AND ARROGANCY ; BOTH THE WICKED PATH, AND THE PERVERTED MOUTH, DO I HATE.

V. 16. *By me Princes rule, and Nobles,* even *all the Judges of the Earth.* : [בי שרים ישרו — ונדיבים כל שפטי ארץ] The latter Hemistic ought I think to be thus rendered—AND THE NOBLES are ALL GOVERNOURS OF THE EARTH. The Verb שפט is used for *governing.* 2 Chron. I. 10. Gen. XIX. 9. &c.

V. 19. — *and my Revenue than choice Silver.* : [ותבואתי מכסף נבחר] Rather — MY PRODUCE ; which answers better to MY FRUIT in the preceding Hemistic.

V. 21.

V. 21. *That I may caufe thofe that love me to inherit Subftance ; and I will fill their Treafures.*] The latter Hemiftic — : ואצרתיהם אמלא, might be rendered — WHOSE TREASURES I WILL SURELY FILL.

V. 22. *The Lord poffeffed me in the Beginning of his Way ;* — יהוה קנני ראשית דרכו] Rather — THE LORD POSSESSED ME when HE FIRST WENT FORTH : *viz.* when He exerted Himfelf in the Work of Creation.

V. 26. *While as yet he had not made the Earth, nor the Fields :* עד לא עשה ארץ וחוצות] The ufual Signification of חוץ is *a Street*, as in the Margin ; but that of *Fields* is not much better : in either Cafe we may conclude this could never have been Solomon's Idea. The Chaldee, Syriac, and Vulgate have here *the Rivers :* but that does not yet feem to come up to the Thing intended. I would therefore give this Word the Senfe of حوض *Pifcina, Conceptaculum aquæ majus ;* and underftand by it THE GRAND COLLECTION OF WATERS, which were mixed with the Firmament at the Creation of the World, to which Mofes gives no particular Name. This Interpretation agrees with the whole Context.

—— *nor the higheft Part of the Duft of the World.* וראש עפרות : תבל] What Idea can be affixed to thefe Words, I cannot conceive. In the old Verfion there is no Note ; which feems to be a tacit Acknowledgment of the Tranflators' Ignorance of the Meaning. I would therefore with Submiffion propofe this Verfion — NOR THE FIRST PART OF THE WORLDS OF THE UNIVERSE. Now עפר frequently fignifies this *Earth* that we Inhabit, the fame as ארץ. Solomon does not ufe this latter Expreffion, probably becaufe it goes immediately before. He ufes the Plural, I imagine, becaufe he wanted to give an Idea of other *Earths* or *Worlds* befides, *viz.* the whole Planetary Syftem. And the Hebrew has no other Word to exprefs thofe fpacious Regions, in which they all move, than תבל.

CHAP. IX.

V. 9. *Give* Inftruction *to a wife* Man, *and he will yet be wifer :* — תן להכם ויחכם עוד] Rather — DIRECT THE WISE &c. The Verb נתן has that Senfe, Ifa. LXI. 8.

V. 12. *If thou be wife, thou fhalt be wife for thyfelf : but if thou fcorneft, thou alone fhalt bear it.* : אם חכמת חכמת לך—ולצת לבדך תשא]
The

The LXX, Syriac, and Arabic, Verſions add after *thyſelf* — AND TO THY FRIENDS : probably becauſe *others beſides the wiſe* Man receive Benefit from his Wiſdom. But the Senſe of the Maxim ſeems to be this — " If thou art truly religious, thou thyſelf ſhalt fare the better " for it : but if thou art a Scorner, thou ſhalt alſo ſuffer in thine own " Perſon :" לבדך, *ſeparately*, and *diſtinctly*, from any Evil it may oc-caſion to others. This is the true Senſe of לבדך, ſee Pſ. LI. 4. It is remarkable that the three Verſions abovementioned ſubjoin here the following Hemiſtics : which I ſhall not attempt to reſtore to their original Hebrew ; (as that might be deemed too preſumptuous an Attempt ;) but content myſelf with tranſlating their Verſions, which are to the following Effect,

HE that *TRUSTETH IN FALSEHOOD FEEDETH THE WINDS : HE ALSO PURSUETH THE BIRDS OF THE AIR*

HE FORSAKETH THE WAY OF HIS OWN VINEYARD ; AND FOR-GETTETH THE PATHS TO HIS FIELD :

THAT HE MAY WANDER THROUGH DESOLATE AND PARCHED PLACES, WHERE there is *NO WATER TO QUENCH THE THIRST, AND HE GATHERETH WITH HIS HANDS UNPROFITABLENESS.*

As theſe Hemiſtics were doubtleſs in their Copies, (which in this re-ſpect ſeem to have been better than thoſe which have come down to us,) and they have beſides all the internal Marks of Genuineneſs, I would reſtore them in our Verſion, but diſtinguiſh them by Brackets, and another Character.

V. 13. — *ſhe is* ſimple, פתיות] This Word occurs only in this Place : but we may notwithſtanding conclude that it is the feminine Plural of פתי, which is rendered SIMPLICITY, Ch. I. 22. The Ab-ſtract is here, as it often is, put for the Concrete, and the Plural uſed for the Superlative, in the ſame manner as חכמות, *the moſt excellent Wiſdom*, Pſ. XLIX. 3. Ch. I. 20. IX. 1. &c. The Word therefore ſignifies SHE IS SIMPLICITY ITSELF IN THE HIGHEST DEGREE, yet ſhe ſitteth &c. or ſhe alſo ſitteth &c. *i. e.* as well as Wiſdom. See הומיה explained, Ch. VII. 11.

V. 16. — *and as for him that wanteth Underſtanding, ſhe ſaith to him.* וחסר לב ואמרה לו :] Neither the preſent Lection of the He-brew ſeems genuine, nor is our Verſion exact. I would therefore read לבו אמרה — and render, AND TO HIM THAT IS BEREAVED OF HIS UNDERSTANDING, SHE SAITH &c. or omit the ו as in V. 4.

V. 17.

V. 17. —*and Bread* eaten *in secret is pleasant.* :נעם סתרים ולחם]
Rather --- AND THE BREAD OF CONCEALMENT (or, THE BREAD
WITHHOLDEN) IS PLEASANT; *i. e.* " the Bread procured by clan-
" destine and indirect Means;" answerable to THE STOLEN WATERS
of the preceding Hemistic. The Meaning of this *Adage,* couched under two similar Phrases, is but too obvious, considering from whose
Mouth it issues.

V. 18. *But he knoweth not that the dead* are *there;* — ולא ידע כי
שם רפאים] See the Word רפאים explained, Job. XXVI. 5.

CHAP. X.

V. 1. *The Proverbs of Solomon.* משלי שלמה] These detached Words
are I imagine a Massoretical Gloss, such as we have seen, Job XXXI.
40. and Pf. LXXII. 20. They were probably placed in the Margin
originally by the latter Jews, to denote some particular Division of this
Book. Our old Versions properly consider them as a Title, and distinguish them by capital Letters. This, however, is certain, that no
old Version, except the *Targum,* acknowledges them.

V. 3. —*but he casteth away the Substance of the wicked.* והות רשעים
יהדף:] Rather — BUT HE DRIVETH OFF THE MISCHIEF OF THE
WICKED, *i. e.* " from the righteous," just mentioned; or, HE
THRUSTETH AWAY (viz. from himself) THE DEPRAVITY OF THE
WICKED. The Sense our Version gives הות seems very apposite: but
there is no Authority for it.

V. 4. *He becometh poor that dealeth* with *a slack Hand:* ראש עשה
כף רמיה] Rather —— THE DECEITFUL (or, THE SLOTHFUL)
HAND MAKETH POOR; as in the old Version, and as the Antithesis
in the next Clause points out.

V. 6. —*but Violence covereth the Mouth of the wicked.* ופי רשעים
יכסה חמס:] Rather —— BUT THE MOUTH OF THE WICKED
CLOKETH (or, EXTENUATETH) VIOLENCE; as V. 12. Ch. XXVIII.
13. or, PASSETH it BY, and *buries it in Oblivion,* as Ch. XVII. 9.
The 11th Verse countenances this Construction.

V. 8. — *but a prating fool shall fall.* :לבט ואויל שפתים ילבט] לבט
occurs only here and Hof. IV. 14. but the Arabic Verb لبط, *in terram
conjecit,* confirms this Sense.

E e

V. 9. — *but he that perverteth his Ways shall be known.* ומעקש : דרכיו יודע] Rather — SHALL BE DETECTED; as Pf. LXXVII. 19.

V. 10. *He that winketh with his Eye causeth Sorrow :* — קרץ עין יתן עצבת] Rather, I think — HE THAT WINKETH WITH HIS EYE SHALL BE PUT TO SORROW. This Proverb is explained by Ch. VI. 13, 14, 15. where the same Expreſſion occurs, and it is added that he meditates Miſchief, though he ſeems to conſent by the Motion of his Eyes, and other ſignificative Geſtures. I conſtrue יתן as the Participle *Hophal;* (as Lev. XI. 38. Numb. XXVI. 54, &c.) becauſe the Paralleliſm of the next Verſe ſeems to require it. The Copulative Particle which follows ought to be rendered, AND.

V. 14. — *but the Mouth of the fooliſh is near Deſtruction.* ופי אויל מחתה קרבה:] Rather — BUT THE MOUTH OF THE FOOLISH PRODUCETH DESTRUCTION : for קרב is here a Verb in *Pihel,* and is thus rendered, Iſai. XLI. 21. See alſo Pf. LXV. 4. But as פי is of the Maſculine Gender, I would remove the ה from קרבה to the Beginning of the next Word ; where, though it already begins with that Letter, there is no Objection againſt receiving it : for the ה articular is prefixed to all Sorts of Words, except Proper Names, Pronouns of the firſt and ſecond Perſon, and undeclinables.

V. 15. *The rich Man's Wealth is his ſtrong City : the Deſtruction of the poor is their Poverty.* [הון עשיר קרית עזו — מחתת דלים רישם:] I read here with the LXX, Syriac, and Arabic Verſions — עז ומחתת — and render --- THE RICH MAN'S WEALTH IS A STRONG CITY : BUT THE DREAD OF THE POOR IS THEIR POVERTY.

V. 17. *He is in the Way of Life that keepeth Inſtruction : but he that refuſeth Reproof erreth.* [ארח לחיים שומר מוסר — ועוב תוכחת מתעה:] Rather --- THE WAY OF LIFE KEEPETH INSTRUCTION : BUT THAT WHICH REJECTETH Reproof, CAUSETH TO ERR.

V. 18. *He that hideth Hatred* with *lying Lips, and he that uttereth a Slander, is a Fool.* [מכסה שנאה שפתי שקר — ומוציא דבה הוא כסיל:] Rather, in two Hemiſtics, with all the ancient Verſions —— LYING LIPS are THE TRIBUTE OF HATRED &c. thus is מכסה rendered, Numb. XXXI. 28, 38. The Meaning ſeems to be, that a Perſon hated is often falſely aſperſed in his Reputation.

V. 20.

V. 20. — *the Heart of the wicked is little worth.* : כמעט רשעים לב] כמעט signifies literally — AS A LITTLE, or THE LEAST, THING.

V. 21. *The Lips of the righteous feed many* : —שפתי צדיק ירעו רבים] Rather, I think --- THE LIPS OF THE RIGHTEOUS DO GOOD TO MANY ; for the Verb רעה has that Senſe both in Chaldee and Syriac.

V. 22. *The Bleſſing of the Lord, it maketh rich :* היא יהוה ברכת תעשיר] Rather — is THAT WHICH MAKETH RICH. So alſo V. 24.

V. 25. — *but the righteous is an everlaſting Foundation.* יסוד וצדיק עולם] Rather — BUT TO THE RIGHTEOUS is &c. Or, if we read יסד, with the LXX and Arabic, thus — BUT THE RIGHTEOUS IS ESTABLISHED FOR EVER.

V. 32. *The Lips of the righteous know what is acceptable : but the Mouth of the wicked* ſpeaketh *Frowardneſs.* רצון ידעון צדיק שפתי — ופי הֹהפכות רשעים] It is not improbable that the ſecond י has dropped from ידעון, for the Senſe requires that it ſhould be in *Hiphil.* In that Caſe the Verſe would run thus --- THE LIPS OF THE RIGHT-EOUS DECLARE WHAT IS ACCEPTABLE ; BUT THE MOUTH OF THE WICKED, FROWARDNESS. All the old Verſions ſeem to read ידיעון.

CHAP. XI.

V. 13. *A Talebearer revealeth Secrets :* — סוד מגלה רכיל הולך] Rather --- A TALEBEARER WALKETH ABOUT REVEALING A SECRET.

V. 15. *He that is Surety for a Stranger ſhall ſmart* for it : *and he that hateth Suretiſhip is ſure.*] This latter Clauſe, *viz.* תוקעים ושונא בוטח ought doubtleſs to be rendered — BUT HE THAT HATETH &c. on account of the Oppoſition.

V. 19. *As Righteouſneſs* tendeth *to Life :* ſo *he that purſueth evil* purſueth it *to his own Death.* : למותו רעה ומרדף — לחיים צדקה כן] A Verb is manifeſtly wanted in this Verſe, as it appears by the Words ſupplied in our Verſion. But if we read כנר inſtead of כן, a Particle of Compariſon unneceſſary in this Place, the whole will be clear, and may be thus rendered — RIGHTEOUSNESS DIRECTETH TO LIFE : BUT THE PURSUIT OF EVIL, TO DEATH. The Vulgate read ſo.

Or thus, according to the prefent Reading, As RIGHTEOUSNESS UNTO LIFE, SO WICKEDNESS PURSUETH UNTO DEATH. See ברדף, the Participle *Pihel*, thus ufed, Deut. XXVIII. 22, 45. &c.

V. 20. —— *but fuch as are upright in their Way, are his Delight.* ורצונו תמימי דרך׃] Inftead of fupplying as many Words as thofe that are already in the Text, I would render fimply thus — BUT THEY THAT ARE OF AN UPRIGHT WAY, HIS DELIGHT; the Verb being underftood from the preceding Hemiftic, viz. *They that are of a froward Heart* are *an Abomination to the Lord.*

V. 21. Though *Hand* join *in Hand, the wicked fhall not be unpunifhed :* — יד ליד לא ינקרה רע] I fufpect that יד ליד is a Miftake for יליד, THE POSTERITY. If this Lection were admitted, the two Hemiftics would correfpond exactly thus — THE POSTERITY OF THE WICKED SHALL NOT BE UNPUNISHED : BUT THE SEED OF THE RIGHTEOUS SHALL BE DELIVERED.

V. 25. *The liberal Soul fhall be made fat :* — נפש ברכה תרשן] Rather — THE LIBERAL MAN &c. for *Soul* is ufed by a Synecdoche for *Man,* as Numb. IX. 10. XXXI. 19. &c. or — The Man of a LIBERAL SOUL — with the Margin.

V. 31. *Behold, the righteous fhall be recompenfed in the Earth : much more the wicked and the Sinner.* הן צדיק בארץ ישלם — אף כי רשע וחוטא׃] The united Particles אף כי ought doubtlefs to be rendered here, YEA ALSO, as Gen. III. 1. Neh. IX. 18. &c. For the Affertion that God punifhes more the wicked, than He rewards the good, is not confonant with our Idea of the Supreme Being, nor founded in Fact, either under the Theocracy, or in the more general Adminiftration of Providence.

CHAP. XII.

V. 7. *The wicked are overthrown* —— הפוך רשעים] As הפוך muft be either the Imperative or Infinitive, neither of which are fuitable in this Place; it is very probable that the two laft Letters have been tranfpofed ; for הפכו in the 2d Conj. fignifies — *they overthrow themfelves ;* which is the Senfe here wanted, and this Lection the ancient Verfions for the moft part acknowledge.

V. 12. — *but the Root of the righteous yieldeth* Fruit. וְשֹׁרֶשׁ צַדִּיקִים
יִתֵּן] Rather — BUT THE ROOT OF THE RIGHTEOUS SHOOTETH
FORTH, as Ezek. XXXI. 14. XXXVI. 8.

V. 13. *The wicked is snared*] See Ch. XXIX. 6.

V. 18. — *but the Tongue of the wise is Health.* וּלְשׁוֹן הֲכָמִים מַרְפֵּא :]
Rather — A MEDICINE, as Ch. IV. 22.

V. 23. *A prudent Man concealeth Knowledge:* — אָדָם עָרוּם כֹּסֶה
דָּעַת] " Prudence requires that Knowledge should be displayed only
" on proper Occasions; whereas the fool proclaimeth his inconsiderate
" Thoughts, without regard to the Circumstances of Time, Place, or
" Persons."

V. 24. — *but the slothful shall be under Tribute.* וְרְמִיָּה תִּהְיֶה לָמַס :)
It is remarkable that the Verb רָמָה, and it's Derivatives signify only
to deceive, *Deceit*, and *deceitful*: but in this Book, they are used three
Times besides in the Sense of *Slackness*, or *Idleness*. See Ch. X. 4.
V. 27. and XIX. 15.

V. 26. *The righteous is more excellent than his Neighbour: but the
Way of the wicked seduceth them.* יָתֵר מֵרֵעֵהוּ צַדִּיק — וְדֶרֶךְ רְשָׁעִים
תַּתְעֵם :] There seems to be no great Connection between these Hemistics in our Version; which is owing to the not giving יָתֵר it's proper Signification. It may be derived from תּוּר; or from נָתַר. in the
first Case, the Hemistic ought to be thus rendered — THE RIGHTEOUS
ENDEAVOURETH TO FIND OUT HIS FRIEND: *i. e.* " in order to
" be useful to him:" and in the latter Case, thus — THE RIGHTEOUS
MOVETH WITH ACTIVITY ON ACCOUNT OF HIS FRIEND; *i. e.*
for the same benevolent Purpose; " But the wicked, unmoved by the
" Feelings of Humanity, and insensible to social Affection, continually
" proceeds in the devious Path which tends to the Gratification of his
" inordinate Appetite." According to the first Construction here proposed, מֵרֵעֵהוּ is a Substantive with only the Affix: but, according to
the latter, it has besides the Preposition prefixed; which is thus used,
Exod. VI. 9. Deut. VII. 7. &c. Or יָתֵר may be considered in a figurative Sense for STRETCHING BEYOND; the Metaphor being taken
from a Race, to which Life is often compared; in which the Righteous, pursuing his Way strait forward with Vigour and Diligence, ad-
vanceth beyond others: but the Way, or Manners of the Wicked,
pointing out Objects inconsistent with the main End which they ought

to

to have in View, caufes them to deviate from the ftrait Road, by which Means they come fhort, and lofe the Prize. St. Paul (Phil. III. 14.) ufes the fame Metaphor, and a Word very fimilar to יתר; τις δε εμ-προσθεν ΕΠΕΚΤΕΙΝΟΜΕΝΟΣ, κατα σκοπον διωκω; STRETCHING AFTER *thofe that are before, I pufh forward to the Mark.* Again, fpeaking of his own Courfe of preaching the Gofpel, (2 Cor. X. 14.) he fays, Ου γαρ ως μη εφικνεμενοι εις υμας, ΥΠΕΡΕΚΤΕΙΝΟΜΕΝ εαυτες, αχρι γαρ και υμων εφθασαμεν εν τω ευαγγελιω τε Χριςν. *We did not* STRETCH OUR-SELVES FORWARD BEYOND our Line, *as not regularly coming to you ; but we have been the firft who have reached fo far as you &c.* In the latter Claufe, תתעם, CAUSETH THEM TO WANDER, correfponds with another Expreffion ufed by the fame Apoftle in a like Senfe, 1 Cor. IX. 26. Εγω τοινυν ουτω τρεχω, ως ουκ αδηλως; where by αδηλως he evidently means, *running at random,* without minding whether he was in the ftrait Path to the Goal. The Apoftle is thought to have borrowed thefe Terms from the Grecian Games : but might he not have fetched them from the facred Writings belonging to his own Country, in which he feems to have been particularly converfant ?

V. 28. *In the Way of Righteoufnefs is Life ; and in the Path-way* thereof there is *no Death.* : בארח צדקה היים — ודרך נתיבה אל כות] This Verfe ought doubtlefs to be thus tranflated — IN THE HIGHWAY OF RIGHTEOUSNESS is LIFE : BUT IT'S BYE-PATH LEADETH TO DEATH. ארח is always ufed in a good Senfe : but נתיב fometimes in a bad one. See Ch. I. 15. VII. 25. Hof. II. 6. By this Conftruction the Verfe is cleared of all Difficulties, the Antithefis is preferved, and there is neither a Redundancy or Deficiency in the Words.

CHAP. XIII.

V. 1. *A wife Son heareth his Father's Inftruction* : — בן חכם מוסר — אב] Rather perhaps — A WISE SON IS INSTRUCTED by his FA-THER : for מוסר may be confidered here as the Participle *Pahul.*

V. 2. *A Man fhall eat good by the Fruit of his Mouth : but the Soul of the Tranfgreffors* fhall eat *Violence.* מפרי פי איש יאכל טוב — ונפש בגדים חמס :] Rather — EVERY GOOD MAN WILL EAT OF THE FRUIT OF THE WORD : BUT VIOLENCE COMFORTETH THE TRANSGRESSORS. Our Tranflators feem here to have miftaken the Senfe of the Text ; and that which they fubftitute is involved in Ob-fcurity.

THE BOOK OF PROVERBS.

fcurity. I join איש and טוב together in the Conſtruction, as the Syntax ſeems to require: and as the Phraſe EATING THE WORD OF
GOD, for *ſtudying* and *digeſting* it, is ſcriptural, (ſee Jer. XV. 16. Ezek.
III. 3.) I give פי the Signification *of the Word*, as our Verſion does,
Numb. III. 16, 51. IV. 45. XXII. 18. XXXVI. 5. &c. which being
left indefinite, and being often uſed for the Divine Commandments,
may be ſo taken here, as well as דבר and מצוה, V. 13. And as a
Verb is wanted in the latter Hemiſtic, I conſider נפש in that Light,
and give it the Senſe it has, Exod. XXIII. 12. XXXI. 17. and 2 Sam.
XVI. 14. or it may be conſidered as a Noun, but with the Idea of
Luſt, or *Appetite*, (as Exod. XV. 9. Eccl. VI. 7.) thus — BUT THE
LUST OF THE TRANSGRESSORS is for VIOLENCE, or VIOLENCE
is THE LUST &c. In either Caſe the Senſe is the ſame, and the Antitheſis preſerved in every correſponding Member.

V. 3. *He that keepeth his Mouth, keepeth his Life:* — נצר פיו שמר
נפשו] Rather — HE THAT WATCHETH OVER HIS MOUTH &c.
for this is one of the Senſes of נצר, whence נצר, *a Watchman*, is derived: beſides as the Verbs in the Hebrew are different, ſo ought
they to be in the Verſion.

V. 4. *The Soul of the Sluggard deſireth, and hath nothing:* מתאוה
ואין נפשו עצל] Rather — THE SLUGGARD DESIRETH, BUT hath
NOT HIS WILL; or *the Thing he deſireth:* ſo נפש frequently ſignifies.
—— *but the Soul of the diligent ſhall be made fat.* ונפש חרצים
חרצן:] Rather — BUT THE DESIRE OF THE DILIGENT SHALL
BE SATISFIED. See דשן in the Note on Pſ. XX. 3.

V. 5. *A righteous Man hateth lying: but a wicked Man is lothſome,
and cometh to Shame.* דבר שקר ישנא צדיק — ורשע יבאיש ויהפיר:]
Rather --- THE RIGHTEOUS HATETH A FALSEHOOD: BUT THE
WICKED IS AN ABOMINATION, AND COMETH TO SHAME: thus
is the Verb באיש rendered, 1 Sam. XIII. 4. 2 Sam. XVI. 21. But all
the old Verſions ſeem to have read here הוביש; for they agree in rendering it — HE IS CONFOUNDED; which ſeems to be the true Lection.

V. 6. *Righteouſneſs keepeth* him that is *upright in the Way:* צדקה
נצר תם דרך] Rather — RIGHTEOUSNESS KEEPETH THE RIGHT
WAY.
—— *but Wickedneſs overthroweth the Sinner.* ורשעה תסלף חטאת:]
Rather --- BUT WICKEDNESS MAKETH THE WRONG WAY SLIP-
PERY:

PERY : *i. e.* "finds continual Dangers and Difappointments attending "a criminal Courfe of Life." See כלף in Taylor's Conc. and as the Verb הטא fignifies *to mifs the Mark,* or *to turn from the ftrait Way,* I make הטאת have reference *to the Way,* mentioned immediately before ; which I here fupply for the fake of Perfpicuity.

V. 8. *The Ranfom of a Man's Life* are *his Riches : but the poor heareth not Rebuke.* כפר נפש איש עשרו — ורש לא שמע גערה :] Rather --- DOTH NOT THE POOR HEAR REBUKE ? "That is, (I ima-"gine) the rich by his Wealth can always extricate himfelf out of "Difficulties ; while the poor Man, who has nothing to offer by Way "of Atonement for his Faults, meets with Rebukes." The old Verfion is to the fame Effect as that we now ufe ; and the marginal Note is, "For his Poverty, he is not able to efcape the Threatnings, which "his cruel Oppreffors ufe againft him." Which Explanation, abftractedly confidered, appears to be good : but, compared with the Verfion of the Text, is diametrically oppofite to it. The Interrogation however relieves from the Embarraffinent.

V. 10. *Only by Pride cometh Contention :* רק בזרון יתן מצה:] Rather --- A VAIN Man BY PRIDE CAUSETH CONTENTION. See רק (contracted for ריק) thus ufed, Gen. XXXVII. 24. Deut. XXXII. 47.

V. 11. *Wealth* gotten *by Vanity fhall be diminifhed :* הון מהבל ימעט] *Qu.* ought not this Hemiftic to be rendered — WEALTH IS DIMINISHED BY VANITY ?

—— *but he that gathereth by Labour fhall increafe.* וקבץ עד יד ירבה:] יד is never ufed to exprefs the *Labour of the Hand* ; though it may appear naturally to admit of that Senfe. All the ancient Verfions, as far as we can collect from their difcordant Readings, feem to have had רי, inftead of יר, in their refpective Texts : and it muft be confeffed that nothing is more probable than fuch a Metathefis. Admitting this Lection, the Senfe is clear, *viz.* BUT HE THAT GATHERETH UNTO COMPETENCY SHALL HAVE PLENTY. This Maxim, thus reftrained, inculcates an excellent Leffon. It exhorts to Induftry, and checks Avarice, by drawing between them the precife Line of Separation.

V. 12. *Hope deferred maketh the Heart fick,* but when *the Defire cometh,* it is *a Tree of Life.* תוהלת ממשכה מהלה לב — ועץ חיים האות באה:] Rather — EXPECTATION PROLONGED CAUSETH AN

ANXIETY

ANXIETY OF HEART: BUT THE DESIRE APPROACHING IS A
TREE OF LIFE. I conſtrue באר, as the Participle, rather than as the
Preter; becauſe it ſeems to improve the Senſe; for it is well known,
that we generally derive more Satisfaction from Expectation than
from actual Fruition; unleſs when by repeated Diſappointments the
Hope ſeems to be removed farther off from Day to Day; which is
juſtly ſaid to *ſicken the Heart*.

V. 13. *Whoſo deſpiſeth the Word ſhall be deſtroyed:* בז לרבר יהבל
לו] Our Verſion paſſes over the Pronoun לו; and alſo does not ſeem
to give the true Senſe of this Hemiſtic; which I think ought to
be thus tranſlated --- WHOEVER DESPISETH A DECREE (or, THE
LAW) SHALL BE HOLDEN (or, BOUND) TO IT: *i. e.* " if he treat
" the Laws with Scorn, they ſhall be executed againſt him; or he
" ſhall be bound over, or made to give a Pledge for the Obſervance of
" them." רבר, though a Word of a moſt extenſive Signification, is here
reſtrained by the parallel Word, *Commandment*, in the next Hemiſtic,
to a ſynonymous Senſe: it is tranſlated by this ſame Word in a Multitude of Places; but, for Variety, I render it *Decree* or *Law*, as
2 Chron. XXX. 5. And in reſpect to the Verb יהבל, it's primary Senſe
is *to bind*; and it is thus rendered, Ezek. XVIII. 16.

₀ There is here doubtleſs a Verſe wanting in our preſent Hebrew
Texts; for all the ancient Verſions, except the Chaldee (which in theſe
Caſes is no Authority, as the Jews have certainly reduced it to the
Standard of their Texts) read to this Effect, *viz.*

"*TO THE FRAUDULENT MAN NO GOOD WILL COME: BUT THE*
"*WORK OF THE WISE PROSPERETH, AND HIS WAY SUCCEEDETH.*"

V. 14. *The Law of the wiſe is a Fountain of Life, to depart from
the Snares of Death.* הורת חכם מקור חיים — לסור ממקשי מורת:
I conſider תורת, not as *in regimine*, but as the Plural, with the Ellipſis
of the formative ן, which is not uncommon; and read לסור ממקשי
thus — לסורים ניקשי. The Verſion, according to this Conſtruction and
Reading, will be this --- THE LAWS are TO THE WISE A FOUN-
TAIN OF LIFE; TO THE REBELLIOUS they are THE SNARES OF
DEATH. By this Interpretation the Antitheſis is reſtored to every correſponding Word in the Verſe; and hence another Argument beſides
might be drawn by an Induction of every Verſe, not only in this Chapter, but of the far greater Part of this Book, to prove that it is the
moſt probable Senſe.

F f

V. 15. *Good Underſtanding giveth Favour : but the Way of Tranſ-greſſors is hard.* : שכל טוב יתן חן — ודרך בגדים איתן] Rather — A GOOD CONDUCT CONCILIATETH (or, PROCURETH) FAVOUR : BUT THE WAY OF THE WICKED IS RUGGED. So שכל ſignifies, 1 Sam. XVIII. 14, 15. &c.

V. 19. *The Deſire accompliſhed is ſweet to the Soul :* תאוה נהיה תערב לנפש] All the ancient Verſions read here נוה, *viz.* THE DESIRE OF WHAT IS HONEST, or COMELY &c.

V. 23. *Much Food is in the Tillage of the poor : but there is* that is *deſtroyed for Want of Judgment.* רב אכל ניר ראשים — ויש נספה בלא משפט] The moſt obvious Conſtruction of this Verſe is —— There is MUCH FOOD IN THE TILLAGE OF RULERS (or, CHIEF MEN) BUT IT HAPPENETH that it is DESTROYED &c. It is a Fact founded in Experience, that where there is great Abundance, there is generally great Waſte. The Word ראיש indeed (probably a Miſtake for ריש) in ſome few Places ſignifies *a poor Man :* but he cannot be deemed poor who has a Superfluity : beſides that the latter Hemiſtic has no Coherence according to that Senſe.

V. 25. *The righteous eateth to the ſatisfying of his Soul :* —— צדיק אכל לשבע נפשו] Rather — APPETITE.

CHAP. XIV.

V. 1. *Every wiſe Woman buildeth her Houſe :* — חכמות נשים בנתה ביתה] Theſe four Words are very anomalous ; and that owing ſolely to the Inſertion of the ו in חכמות ; which makes it the Nominative Plural, inſtead of Singular. Moſt of the ancient Verſions read חכמת ; and ſo indeed muſt we, if we pay any Regard to the Syntax.

V. 3. *In the Mouth of the fooliſh is a Rod of Pride :* — בפי אויל חטר גאוה] Rather — PRIDE IN THE MOUTH OF FOOLS IS A ROD, viz. *for their Chaſtiſement* &c.

V. 7. *Go from the Preſence of a fooliſh Man, when thou perceiveſt* not *in him the Lips of Knowledge.* לך מנגד לאיש כסיל — ובל ידעת שפתי דעת] The LXX, Syriac, and Arabic Verſions, read the Text thus — ילך, and add כל at the Beginning of the Verſe ; and in the latter Hemiſtic — וכלי דעת. According to this Lection the Senſe

is

is --- EVERY THING SUCCEEDETH ADVERSELY TO THE FOOLISH MAN : BUT THE INSTRUMENTS OF KNOWLEDGE are THE KNOWING LIPS. The Verb ילך *to go*, is ufed figuratively in this Senfe, Lev. XXVI. 41. Deut. XXIX. 19. &c. and כלי, which primarily fignifies *Veſſels*, is alfo ufed for *Inſtruments*, Numb. IV. 32. XXXV. 16. &c. See the laſt Chap. Ver. 14.

V. 8. — *but the Folly of fools is Deceit :* — ואולת כסילים מרמה] Rather --- FOLLY DECEIVETH (or, MISLEADETH) FOOLS. This anſwers to the former Hemiſtic by Way of Antitheſis. מרמה is here conſtrued as the Part. preſ. *Pihel*, which has a tranſitive Senfe.

V. 9. *Fools make a Mock at Sin : but among the righteous* there is *Favour.* : אולים יליץ אשם — ובין ישרים רצון] The Syntax will not bear the Senfe which our Verſion gives the firſt Hemiſtic : neither does it correſpond by that Conſtruction with the latter Clauſe. I would therefore render it thus --- GUILT EXPOSETH FOOLS TO SCORN ; as it is faid Ch. III. 35. *Shame exalteth fools.*

V. 14. *The Backſlider in Heart ſhall be filled with his own Ways : and a good Man* ſhall be fatisfied *from himſelf.* — מדרכיו ישבע סוג לב : ומעליו איש טוב] Rather — THE BACKSLIDING HEART IS SATISFIED WITH IT'S OWN WAYS : BUT THE GOOD MAN, WITH HIMSELF : *i. e.* the wicked is pleafed with the vicious Courſe in which he is engaged, while the good Man has the Approbation of a good Conſcience.

V. 19. *The evil bow before the good ; and the wicked at the Gates of the righteous.* : שחו רעים לפני טובים — ורשעים על שערי צדיק] Our Tranſlators feem to have miſtaken the Senfe in this Place ; for they underſtood *bowing* to be a Token of Reverence, or a Mark of Reſpect ; as appears by the old Verſion ; which adds in the Margin, by Way of Illuſtration, *viz.* " If this come not daily to paſs, we muſt " confider, that it is becauſe of our Sins, which let God's Workings." The Miſtake lies in this, that they derive שחו from שחה, whereas it comes from שחח. I would therefore tranſlate thus — THE EVIL ARE BROUGHT LOW BEFORE THE GOOD ; &c. The latter Hemiſtic is here not adverſative, but exegetical of the former ; and by *Gates* we are to underſtand, according to the Scripture Phraſe, *the Courts of Judicature*, which were uſually over the Gates of the Jewiſh Cities ; fo that the Meaning feems clearly and fimply to be this, " That the

F f 2   " wicked

" wicked are brought low, when they are arraigned before the Tribu-
" nal of the Judge."

V. 22. — *but Mercy and Truth* ſhall be *to them that deviſe good :*
ט‎וב חרשי ואמרת ו‎הסד‎]   Rather, as in the preceding Hemiſtic ——
BUT MERCY AND TRUTH DEVISE GOOD.

*** Here again another Verſe ſeems wanting ; for the LXX, Syriac,
and Vulgate add,

" *THEY THAT DO EVIL KNOW NEITHER MERCY NOR TRUTH : BUT*
" *MERCY AND TRUTH* are *WITH THEM THAT DO GOOD.*"

V. 23. *In all Labour there is Profit : but the Talk of the Lips* tendeth *only to Penury.* למחסור אך שפתים ודבר — מותר יהיה עצב בכל]
Qu. ought not the two laſt Words to be thus read, מחסור אכל, and
the laſt Hemiſtic rendered — BUT THE TALK OF THE LIPS FEEDETH
ON PENURY ? thus Ephraim is ſaid *to feed on Wind,* Hoſ. XII. 1.

V. 24. *The Crown of the wiſe is their Riches :* — עשרם הכמים עטרת]
Rather — RICHES CROWN THE WISE : or, literally, are THE CROWN
&c. *i. e.* " their Reward."

—— but *the Fooliſhneſs of fools* is *Folly.*   אולת כסילים אולת]
I read here מאולת, having omitted the מ in the preceding Word, עשרם,
and render --- but FROM THE FOLLY OF FOOLS cometh FOLLY :
i. e. " while the prudent Man by his Induſtry and Circumſpection ac-
" quires Wealth, the inconſiderate Knave reaps only the Reproach
" of his iniquitous and fooliſh Proceedings."

V. 25. — *but a deceitful* Witneſs *ſpeaketh Lies.*   מרמה כזבים ויפח]
Rather --- BUT A DECEIVER SPEAKETH LIES : מרמח being the
Part. Pih. as V. 8.

V. 26. *In the Fear of the Lord* is *ſtrong Confidence : and his Child-*
ren ſhall have a Place of Refuge. ולבניו — עז מבטח יהוה ביראת
מחסה יהיה]   Rather — HE THAT TRUSTETH IN THE FEAR OF
THE LORD IS STRONG, AND HIS CHILDREN &c.

V. 29. He that is *ſlow to Wrath* is *of great Underſtanding :* ארך
תבונה רב אפים]   Rather — ABOUNDETH IN UNDERSTANDING,
as Ch. XXVIII. 20. XXIX. 22.

—— but *he that is haſty of Spirit exalteth Folly.* רום רוח וקצר
אולת]   Rather — BUT THE HASTY SPIRIT EXALTETH FOLLY
(or EXPOSETH it) TO PUBLIC VIEW ; as Ch. III. 35.

V. 32.

V. 32. *The wicked is driven away in his Wickedness* : — ברעתו ידחה
רשע] Rather — IS RUINED, or DESTROYED BY &c. as Pf. XXXVI.
12. and CXL. 4.

V. 33. — *but* that which is *in the Midst of fools is made known.*
ובקרב כסילים תודע :] Rather, according to the LXX, Syriac, and
Arabic --- BUT IT IS NOT KNOWN IN THE INWARD THOUGHTS
OF FOOLS : or, interrogatively, IS IT KNOWN &c. The Antecedent
to the Pronoun is *Understanding*, mentioned in the preceding Hemiftic :
and קרב is here rendered, as Pf. XLIX. 11.

V. 35. — *but his Wrath is* againft *him that caufeth Shame.* ועברתו
תהיה מביש :] Rather — BUT HIS WRATH IS that which CAUSETH
SHAME. מביש cannot agree with עברתו on account of the Difference
of Genders : but feems to be equivalent to the neuter.

CHAP. XV.

V. 4. *A wholefome Tongue is a Tree of Life* : — מרפא לשון עץ חיים]
Rather — A SOUND (or, AN HEALING) TONGUE &c. *i. e.* a Tongue
that giveth found Advice, or pacifieth great Offences.

—— *but Perverfenefs therein is a Breach in the Spirit.* וסלף בה
שבר ברוח :] Or — BUT PERVERSENESS THEREIN AFFLICTETH
THE SPIRIT.

V. 7. *The Lips of the wife difperfe Knowledge : but the Heart of the
foolifh doeth not fo.* ולב כסילים לא כן :] —— BUT THE HEART
OF THE FOOLISH DOTH NOT ESTABLISH it. כן is here confidered as the Preter of כון. Perhaps the original Reading might have
been לא כל (inftead of כן) DOTH NOT TAKE, or RECEIVE it.

V. 11. *Hell and Deftruction are before him* :] See this Verfe explained, Job. XXVI. 5.

V. 18. *A wrathful Man ftirreth up Strife* : — איש חמה יגרה מדון]
מדון ought here to be rendered CONTENTION, as ריב is alfo rendered
Strife in the next Claufe.

V. 20. *A wife Son maketh a glad Father : but &c.* בן חכם ישמח
אב — וגו"] Rather — A WISE SON REJOICETH HIS FATHER :
but &c. I here fupply the adverfative Particle, which feems to have
dropped out of the Text, as the copulative has, Verfe 10th and 30th.
This Conftruction makes the two Hemiftics correfpond more exactly.

V. 24.

V. 24. *The Way of Life is above to the wise, that he may depart from Hell beneath.* :מטרה מְשְׁאוֹל סוּר לְמַעַן — לְמִשְׂכִּיל לְמַעֲלָה חַיִּים אֹרַח] Rather ---- THE WAY OF LIFE ABOVE IS FOR THE WISE ; THEREFORE HE WILL AVOID THE REGIONS OF THE DEAD BE- NEATH. לְמַעַן seems to have the Sense here proposed, Neh. VI. 13. Pſ. LI. 6. Jer. XLIV. 8. Hoſ. VIII. 4. or thus — THE WAY OF LIFE IS UPWARD TO THE WISE ; IN ORDER THAT HE MAY DEPART FROM THE GRAVE, which is DOWNWARD.

V. 26. *The Thoughts of the wicked are an Abomination to the Lord : but* the Words *of the pure are pleasant Words.* :נֹעַם אִמְרֵי וּטְהֹרִים—] Rather --- BUT THE PURE SPEAK WHAT IS ACCEPTABLE to him.

V. 27. *He that is greedy of Gain troubleth his own House ;* בֵּיתוֹ עֹכֵר בָּצַע בּוֹצֵעַ] Rather —— THROWETH HIS HOUSE (viz. *his Family*) INTO CONFUSION.

V. 30. *The Light of the Eyes rejoiceth the Heart : and a good Report maketh the Bones fat.* :עֶצֶם תְּדַשֶּׁן טוֹבָה שְׁמוּעָה—לֵב יְשַׂמַּח עֵינַיִם מְאוֹר] Rather --- THE HEART REJOICETH THROUGH THE LIGHT OF THE EYES ; AND A GOOD REPORT MAKETH THE BODY FAT. The Eye, of all the Senſes, is that which gives the moſt laſting Plea- ſure ; and we find by Experience that Cheerfulneſs, from whatever Cauſe it may proceed, contributes to Corpulence.

V. 31. *The Ear that heareth the Reproof of Life abideth among the wiſe.* :תָּלִין חֲכָמִים בְּקֶרֶב — חַיִּים תּוֹכַחַת שֹׁמַעַת אֹזֶן] Rather, I think --- THE EAR THAT HEARETH REPROOFS hath LIFE, and ABI- DETH AMONG THE WISE.

V. 32. *He that refuſeth Inſtruction deſpiſeth his own Soul : but he that heareth Reproof getteth Underſtanding.*] The latter Hemiſtic — :לֵב קוֹנֶה תּוֹכַחַת וְשׁוֹמֵעַ — I would render literally, that it may anſwer more exactly to the preceding one, thus — BUT HE THAT HEARETH REPROOF GAINETH A HEART : *i. e.* " ſecures his own from the " Attack of bad Impreſſions, whilſt the fool makes Shipwreck of his " Soul."

CHAP. XVI.

V. 1. *The Preparations of the Heart in Man, and the Anſwer of the Tongue is from the Lord.* :לָשׁוֹן מַעֲנֵה וּמֵיְהוָה — לֵב מַעַרְכֵי לְאָדָם]
The

The Oppofition between God and Man and the other Members of thefe two Hemiftics feems to fhew, that they ought (as moft of thefe Proverbs are, particularly V.9.) to be conftrued feparately, thus —To MAN belong THE INCLINATIONS OF THE HEART: BUT BY THE LORD IS THE TONGUE ASSISTED. That is (as I apprehend) "Man " contrives: but the Succefs of his Defigns depends upon God:" the fame Sentiment as at V. 9. but differently exprefled. For *the affifting of the Tongue*, in order to execute any Purpofe, feems clearly to imply this Idea. I conftrue מענה as the Participle *Pahul:* and give it the Senfe it has, Pf. XXII. 21. LXV. 5. &c.

V. 4. — *yea, even the wicked for the Day of Evil.* וגם רשע ליום : רעה] According to our Verfion the Verb פעל, *made*, is underftood from the preceding Hemiftic: but moft of the ancient Verfions read here ונצר, IS RESERVED, inftead of וגם.

V. 5. *Every one that is proud in Heart is an Abomination to the Lord:* though *Hand* join *in Hand*, he *fhall not be unpunifhed.* תועבת יהוה : כל גבה לב — יד ליד לא ינקה] This Verfe I read, diftinguifh, and render thus —תועבת יהוה כל גבה — לב ידל יד לא ינקה, EVERY PROUD Man IS AN ABOMINATION TO THE LORD: THE HEART THAT IS LIFTED UP with POWER SHALL NOT BE DEEMED INNOCENT. By this Conftruction the Parallelifm is reftored; the Hemiftics are rendered more regular; and the Senfe made clearer.

V. 10. *A divine Sentence* is *in the Lips of the King:* — קסם על שפתי מלך] Rather—DIVINATION &c. This Word is in all other Places, where it occurs, taken in a bad Senfe, *viz.* for an Intercourfe with familiar or evil Spirits, or the Practice of magical Arts, in order to difcover future Events: but here it feems to mean that Portion of *the Divine Spirit*, which God imparted under the Theocracy to fuch as he appointed *his Vicegerents.* That this is the Senfe will I think be evident on confulting the following Texts, Numb. XI. 17. Deut. XXXIV. 9. Judg. III. 10. VI. 34. XI. 29. XIII. 23, 25. 1 Sam. X. 9. XVI. 13, 14. 1 Kings III. 12.

V. 11. *A juft Weight and Balance* are *the Lord's:* — פלס ומאזני משפט ליהוה] Rather—THE WEIGHT AND THE BALANCE are THE ORDINANCE OF THE LORD; *i. e.* of His Appointment. So is משפט rendered, Exod. XV. 25. Lev. XXIV. 22. 2 Chron. XXXV. 13.
Neh.

Neh. VIII. 18. &c. There seems to be no Occasion to add any Epithet; for if they be not true according to the Standard, they are not then *Weights* or *Balances*; and still less can they be called the Lord's Appointment. They are therefore here used *κατ᾽ ἐξοχὴν*, as when Solomon says, that whoso *findeth a Wife, findeth a good* Thing, Ch. XVIII. 22.

V. 13. — *and they love him that speaketh right.* : ודבר ישרים יאהב [
Rather --- AND THE WORDS OF THE UPRIGHT ARE BELOVED, or LOVED by them.

V. 17. At the End of this Verse the Maſſora adds הצי, to denote that we are arrived precisely at the Middle of this Book. Instead of these Sorts of Remarks (and these are by no means the moſt frivolous that appear in this Book) it is much to be wished, that the Compilers of it had spent their Time in collating the several Copies of their Texts, in order to correct the Miſtakes, which have crept into them.

V. 21. — *and the Sweetneſs of the Lips increaseth Learning.* ומתק
: שפתים יסיף לקה [Here the old Verſion has this Note, "The ſweet "Words of Conſolation, which come forth of a godly Heart." But how Learning can hereby be increaſed, I cannot conceive. I would therefore give מתק the Senſe of مَتَك, *viz.* FAITHFULNESS, underſtanding by the *Faithfulneſs of the Lips* the declaring without Reſerve and with Sincerity of ſuch uſeful Obſervations as are ſtored up in the Memory. Or *by Sweetneſs of Lips* may be meant *Eloquence*; as in Homer, Il. I. 249.

Του γαρ απο γλωσσης μελιτος γλυκιων ρεεν αυδη.

V. 24. *Pleaſant Words* are as *an Honey-Comb, ſweet to the Soul, and Health to the Bones.* : צוף דבש אמרי נעם — מתוק לנפש ומרפא לעצם [
The latter Hemiſtic ought I think to be thus rendered — SWEETNESS TO THE SOUL, (or TASTE,) AND A MEDICINE TO THE BODY: for מתוק, as an Adjective, cannot agree with אמרי : and עצם in the Singular muſt here ſignify *Body*.

V. 26. *He that laboureth, laboureth for himſelf: for his Mouth craveth it of him.* : נפש עמל עמלה לו — כי אכף עליו פיהו [Our Verſions appear to me to have totally miſtaken the Senſe of this Verſe, which notwithſtanding is very obvious, *viz.* THE SOUL OF THE AFFLICTED LABOURETH WITHIN HIM, WHEN HIS MOUTH (or, UTTERANCE) PRESSETH HARD UPON HIM: *i. e.* "when he "ſtrives

"ſtrives to give Vent to his Sorrow, but cannot." Thus Ovid, *Triſt.*
Lib. V. El. I. v. 59. *& alibi.*

> *Strangulat incluſus dolor, atque æſtuat intus,*
> *Cogitur et vires multiplicare ſuas.*

V. 27. *An ungodly Man diggeth up Evil: —* איש בליעל כרה רעה]
Rather, I think — PREPARETH EVIL : thus כרה is uſed, 2 Chron.
XVI. 14.

V. 28. *— and a Whiſperer ſeparateth chief Friends.* ונרגן מפריד
אלוף] אלוף ought here I think to be rendered CHIEFS, or GOVER-
NOURS ; ſo alſo Ch. XVII. 9. It ſeems to be uſed as a Noun of Multitude.

V. 29. *A violent Man enticeth his Neighbour :* איש חמס יפתה רעהו]
Rather — A FALSE MAN &c. as Exod. XXIII. 1.

V. 32. *— and he that ruleth his Spirit than he that taketh a City :*
ומשל ברוחו מלכד עיר :] Thus Horace to the ſame Effect, *Lib.* I.
Ode ii. *Latius regnes avidum domando*
> *Spiritum, quam ſi Lybiam remotis*
> *Gadibus jungas, et uterque Pœnus*
> *Serviat uni.*

And Claudian *de 4to. Conſ. Honor.* V. 257.
> *Tu licet extremos late dominere per Indos,*
> *Te Medus, te mollis Arabs, te Seres adorent :*
> *Si metuis, ſi prava cupis, ſi duceris ira ;*
> *Servitii patiere jugum ; tolerabis iniquas*
> *Interius leges : tunc omnia jure tenebis,*
> *Cum poteris rex eſſe tui.*

V. 33. *The Lot is caſt into the Lap :* בחיק יוטל את הגורל]
The את prefixed to the Nominative is juſtified by other ſimilar Inſtances, Gen. XVII. 5. Exod. X. 8. &c. What our Tranſlators underſtood by *Lap* in this Place, I do not know but am clear, that בחיק
ought to be rendered INTO THE MIDST, (as 1 Kings XXII. 35.) viz. *of
the Urn,* or *Veſſel,* into which the different Billets were caſt. In Homer
we find they were put in an Helmet, *Iliad.* II. V. 175, & 181.

> —— ει δε κληρον εσημηναντο εκαςος,
> Εκ δ' εϐαλον κυνεη Αγαμεμνονος Ατρειδαο·
> —— παλλεν δε Γερηνιος ιππετα Νεςωρ·
> Εκ δ' εθορε κληρος κυνης, ον αρ ηθελον αυτοι.

G g

—— but

— *but the whole difpofing thereof is of the Lord.* ; וּמֵיהוה כל מִשְׁפָּטוֹ]
Rather — BUT THE SOLE (or WHOLE) DISPOSAL &c. Among the
Jews their moſt important Concerns were determined by Lot. The
whole Country of Canaan was thus divided among the Tribes, and
again ſubdivided among the Heads of Families : and I have endea-
voured to ſhew that the Hand of an overruling Providence was eaſily
perceivable in the wiſe Allotment of the reſpective Portions. (See Par.
Proph.) The laſt Inſtance of deciding by Lot recorded in Holy Writ,
is that Acts I. 26. for the Purpoſe of filling up the Apoſtleſhip of the
Traitor Judas.

CHAP. XVII.

V. 1. — *than a Houſe full of Sacrifices with Strife.* מבית מלא
: זבחי ריב] As זבחי is *in regimine*, and ſignifies the *Sacrifices of Strife,*
it would be more accurate to render theſe two Words — CONTENTIOUS
SACRIFICES, or the *riotous Feaſts after Sacrifices*, which are here very
properly oppoſed to *a dry Morſel with Quietneſs*. See Ch. VII. 14.

V. 3. *The fining Pot is for Silver, and the Furnace for Gold : but
the Lord trieth the Hearts.* : ובחן לבות יהוה — מצרף לכסף וכור לזהב]
Rather thus --- THE FINING POT TRIETH SILVER, AND THE
FURNACE GOLD : BUT GOD, THE HEARTS.

V. 8. — *whitherſoever it turneth, it proſpereth.* אל כל אשר יפנה
: ישכיל] The Antecedent here is השחד, which generally ſignifies *a
Bribe*, as V. 23. As it cannot have that Senſe here, it muſt mean either
a Reward, as in the old Verſion ; or *a Gift*, as in the laſt ; either of
which, wherever they are beſtowed, generally ſucceed in gaining Favour to the liberal Donor.

V. 16. *Wherefore is there a Price in the Hand of a fool to get Wiſdom, ſeeing he hath no Heart to it ?* למה זה מחיר ביד כסיל — לקנות
: חכמה ולב אין] The Diviſion of the Hemiſtics ſeems to require
that we ſhould render thus --- WHEREFORE is THIS, that there
ſhould be A PRICE IN THE HAND OF A FOOL, SINCE HE HATH
NO HEART TO ACQUIRE WISDOM?

V. 19. — *and he that exalteth his Gate ſeeketh Deſtruction.* מגביה
: פתחו מבקש שבר] This may be underſtood literally, for *raiſing the
Gates* about a Man's Houſe for Oſtentation : or figuratively, for a
haughty

haughty Carriage in general, as in the old Verſion ; or we may conſider this Expreſſion as parallel to Mic. VII. 5. and *by Gate* mean *the
Door of the Lips*; i. e. *proud diſdainful Language.*

V. 20. —*and he that hath a perverſe Tongue*——— ונהפך בלשונו]
Rather perhaps --- AND HE THAT HATH A DOUBLE TONGUE ;
or (as the Words ſignify literally) HE THAT IS VARIABLE IN HIS
TONGUE, *i. e.* " the Man who uſes Duplicity in his Speech."

V. 21. *He that begetteth a fool* doeth it *to his Sorrow :* ילד כסיל
לתונה לו] Rather— HE THAT BEGETTETH A FOOL HATH
SORROW : for לתונה is here uſed as the Nominative, not the Dative
Caſe. See Ch. XIV. 23.

V. 22. *A merry Heart doeth good* like *a Medicine :* — לב שמח יטב
נהה] Or— A MERRY HEART MAKETH A MEDICINE GOOD, or
EFFECTUAL. Or --- IS A MEDICINE that DOETH GOOD. The
old Verſions however ſeem to have read גוה, *viz.* DOETH GOOD TO
THE BODY.

V. 24. — *but the Eyes of a fool* are *in the Ends of the Earth.* ועיני
כסיל בקצה ארץ] " That is, (ſays the old Verſion) wander to and
" fro, and ſeek not after Wiſdom." But may not the contrary be the
Senſe ? In the preceding Hemiſtic, the Man of Underſtanding is ſaid
to have Wiſdom always preſent with him : but the fool upon every
Emergency, which requires more than ordinary Circumſpection, is reduced to caſt about, and wander for Counſel to direct him in his
Proceedings.

V. 26. *Alſo to puniſh the juſt* is *not good,* nor *to ſtrike Princes for
Equity.* גם ענוש לצדיק לא טוב — להכות נדיבים על ישר] Rather
thus --- SURELY it is NOT GOOD TO PUNISH THE JUST : it is
CONTRARY TO RIGHT TO STRIKE PRINCES. See both theſe
Particles thus uſed in Noldius.

V. 27. — *and a Man of Underſtanding is of an excellent Spirit.* וקר
רוח איש תבונה] The Maſſora reads ויקר — of A PRECIOUS *Spirit ;*
which Lection is followed by the Vulgate only. The other Verſions
read with our Text, *viz.* of A COOL *Spirit ;* which ſeems preferable.

V. 28. *Even a fool, when he holdeth his Peace, is counted wiſe :* and
he that ſhutteth his Lips is eſteemed *a Man of Underſtanding.*

אויל מחריש חכם — יחשב אטם שפתיו נבון:] Thus the Hemiſtics ſeem to require to be divided; the Conſtruction of which is this——EVEN A FOOL, WHEN HE HOLDETH HIS PEACE, IS WISE: HE THAT SHUTTETH HIS LIPS IS COUNTED A MAN OF UNDER-STANDING.

CHAP. XVIII.

V. 1. *Through Deſire a Man, having ſeparated himſelf, ſeeketh* and *intermeddleth with all Wiſdom :* לתאוה יבקש נפרד — בכל תושיה יתגלע:] Rather —THE CONTEMPLATIVE MAN SEEKETH THAT which is DESIRABLE, and INTERMEDDLETH WITH ALL WISDOM.

V. 4. *The Words of a Man's Mouth* are as *deep Waters*, and *the Well-ſpring of Wiſdom* as *a flowing Brook*. מים עמקים דברי פי איש — נחל נבע מקור הכמה:] Our Verſions conſider theſe Hemiſtics as *expla-natory* of each other : for the Note upon *deep* is, "which can never "be drawn empty, but bring ever Profit." But the two Propoſitions appear to me *adverſative*. A *Man's Words* are very properly compared to *deep Waters*, which are unfathomable, as the other are inſcrutable in reſpect to his Thoughts. That this is the Meaning, will I think be evident from Ch. XX. V. 4. where it is ſaid, that *Counſel in the Heart of Man* is as *deep Water, but a Man of Underſtanding will* (ra-ther *may*) *draw it out* ; for God is the ſole Καθιαγνωστης. The firſt Hemiſtics in both Places I conſider as parallel ; for *the Words of the Mouth* and *Counſel* differ only as *Cauſes* and *Effects*, which the beſt Writers uſe frequently one for the other ; ſee V. 6. On the other Hand, *the Source of Wiſdom* is ſaid to be *a flowing Brook*, which is ge-nerally *clear* as well as *ſhallow*, a fit Emblem of the ingenuous Mind, which knows no Diſguiſe or Diſſimulation, and whoſe Deſigns are eaſily diſcovered ; becauſe, as Good is always it's Object, it affects not Concealment. In Confirmation of what is here advanced, I would obſerve, that when *Deepneſs* is predicated of *Heart*, *Thoughts*, &c. it always means in Scripture *Unſcrutableneſs, deep Schemes,* or the like. If therefore any Particle is ſupplied to connect the Hemiſtics, it ought to be BUT, to denote the Oppoſition.

V. 8. *The Words of a Talebearer* are as *Wounds* ; —— דברי נרגן כמתלהמים] This Combination of Letters, כמתלהמים, occurs only in another Place, *viz.* Ch. XXVI. 22 where the ſame Verſe is re-peated. Our Tranſlators ſuppoſe that להם is here uſed by a Metatheſis

for

for הלם *to wound*; and that the Participle has the Force of the Subftantive: but this feems very harfh. The Arabic Verb ـﻞ, *infpiravit, infudit, infinuavit, effecit occulto modo*, feems to fuggeft this Senfe, *viz.* THE WORDS OF A TALEBEARER ARE LIKE SUBTIL POISONS, THAT INSINUATE THEMSELVES, and produce their Effects infenfibly; for THEY PENETRATE INTO THE INWARD PARTS OF THE BELLY, where they lie rankling and gnawing the Vitals. I cannot however but fufpect that thefe Letters, befides the Particle of Similitude, contain a Prepofition, a Subftantive, and a Verb; and that they ought to be thus feparated and read —— כמתלי הים: *The Words of the Talebearer* DESTROY AS Shafts FROM THE QUIVER. הים is the Participle prefent *Kal*, from הים; and the Word *Shaft* or *Arrow* is added merely for the Sake of Perfpicuity. All the old Verfions here difagree, and feem to have tranflated merely by Guefs.

V. 11. *The rich Man's Wealth is his ftrong City, and as an high Wall in his own Conceit.* הון שעיר קרית עזו — וכחומה נשגבה במשכתו: The Word conftantly ufed for *Conceit* or *Imagination* is משכית, and not משכת; befides that none of the ancient Verfions acknowledge that Reading. But the Chaldee and Syriac feem to have read במישכנהו, or במסכתו; which Word is well adapted to this Place. The latter Hemiftic ought therefore I think to be thus rendered —— AND it is AN HIGH WALL ABOUT HIS HABITATION.

V. 15. *The Heart of the prudent getteth Knowledge; and the Ear of the wife feeketh Knowledge.* לב נבון יקנה דעת — ואזן חכמים תבקש דעת: דעת in the latter Hemiftic being as properly taken for the Infinitive as for a Subftantive, it would be beft for the fake of Variety to render it thus --- AND THE EAR OF THE WISE SEEKETH TO KNOW.

V. 17. *He that is first in his own Caufe feemeth juft: but his Neighbour cometh and fearcheth him.* צדיק הראישון בריבו — ובא רעהו וחקרו: Rather --- HE IS ACQUITTED who is FIRST IN HIS OWN CAUSE: BUT HIS NEIGHBOUR COMETH AND FINDETH HIM OUT. צדיק is here the Preter, *Hiphil*; and ufed as a *forenfic* Term, Ifa. V. 23. L. 8. and חקר is here rendered as Job. IX. 10.

V. 19. *A Brother offended is harder to be won than a ftrong City:* אח נפשע מקירת עז Rather —— A BROTHER IS MORE APT TO REBEL THAN A STRONG CITY: *i. e.* Diffentions among Brothers,
from

from Motives of Intereſt or other Cauſes, more frequently ariſe, than Mutinies in Garriſons. ——— *tanta eſt diſcordia fratrum*; as the Poet obſerved, Ovid. *Met. Lib.* I. v. 60.

V. 20. *A Man's Belly ſhall be ſatisfied with the Fruit of his Mouth:* and *with the Increaſe of his Lips ſhall he be filled.*——מפרי פי איש תשבע : בטנו תבואת שפתיו ישבע] If we read with the LXX and Arabic, ישבע, the Hemiſtics may thus be divided and rendered ——— A MAN SHALL BE SATISFIED WITH THE FRUIT OF HIS MOUTH; and HIS BELLY FILLED WITH THE PRODUCE OF HIS LIPS. This Lection makes the Conſtruction more eaſy, and more agreeable to the other two Places, where theſe very Words occur, *viz.* Ch. XII. 14. and XIII. 2.

V. 22. Whoſo *findeth a Wife findeth a good* Thing, ——— מצא אשה מצא טוב] All the old Interpreters (except the Chaldee) have here *a good Wife:* but we are not haſtily to conclude, that they read טובה in their reſpective Texts. The Addition, I am perſuaded, is ſolely their own; who, ſenſible that the Propoſition did not hold true univerſally in a *moral* View, thus reſtrained it. Numerous are the Inſtances in Scripture which countenance this Expreſſion; thus, *Lo, Children* are *an Heritage of the Lord,* and *the Fruit of the Womb* is his *Reward.* Pſ. CXXVII. 3. So *Weights and Balances* are ſaid to be *the Ordinance* appointed by *God.* Ch. XVI. 11. But to return to the Text; if it can be doubted what *Sort of Wife* is meant here, this ſufficiently appears by the next Hemiſtic ——— *and obtaineth Favour of the Lord;* beſides that the former Hemiſtic would have one Word redundant as to Quantity, if טובה be added.

₀ Here the LXX, Vulgate, Arabic, and in Part the Syriac add —

" *HE THAT DRIVETH AWAY A (GOOD) WIFE DRIVETH AWAY A* " *GOOD THING: AND HE THAT RETAINETH AN ADULTEROUS WOMAN* " *IS FOOLISH AND WICKED.*"

V. 24. *A Man* that hath *Friends muſt ſhew himſelf friendly:* איש רעים להתרועע] The Want of Connection in this Hemiſtic does not proceed from the Omiſſion of any Word in the Text: but rather, I apprehend, from a wrong Lection. It is apparent that the Chaldee and Syriac Verſions read יש, inſtead of איש; which better correſponds with the next Member. According to this Reading the Senſe will be ———THERE ARE COMPANIONS who SHEW THEMSELVES SOCIABLE. See the ſame Conſtruction of the Infinitive for the Future, Ch. XIX. 8. ——— *and*

—— *and there is a Friend &c.* "וישׁ אהב גו] Rather —— BUT
THERE IS A FRIEND that *ſticketh cloſer than a Brother.*

CHAP. XIX.

V. 1. *Better is the poor that walketh in his Integrity, than* he that is
perverſe in his Lips, and is a fool. טוב רשׁ הולך בתמו — מעקשׁ שׂפתיו
:והוא כסיל] The Phraſe *he that is perverſe and is a fool* conveys
but one and the ſame Idea: the Terms are convertible; and neither
of them in the leaſt approaches to the Oppoſition we want to *the poor*
of the preceding Hemiſtic. But is this Fault in the Text, or in the
Verſion? A very little Attention will ſhew where the Miſtake lies.
Now the four principal Greek Interpreters, beſides the others collected
together by Origen, are here unfortunately deficient; the Arabic is
ſo likewiſe: but of the three remaining, the Syriac and Vulgate
plainly ſhew that there is a Metatheſis of the two laſt Letters in עקשׁ;
they having read עשׂק, the primary Senſe of which is *to be loaded with
a heavy Body.* שׂפרת ſignifies, according to our Verſion, *a Burden,*
Gen. XLIX. 14. But I lay no Streſs upon that Interpretation. I give
it the Senſe of the Arabic Verb غش *lucrum fecit,* whence comes شن,
Lucrum, augmentum. And it is remarkable that from the ſame Root
comes شه, *a Lip,* which has led the Tranſlators into the Miſtake.
Theſe Words therefore thus explained naturally admit of this Senſe ——
BETTER IS THE POOR MAN THAT WALKETH IN HIS INTE-
GRITY, THAN HE THAT IS LOADED WITH RICHES, AND IS A
FOOL.

V. 2. *Alſo, that the Soul be without Knowledge, it is not good.* גם
בלא דעת נפשׁ לא טוב] Rather — SURELY it is NOT GOOD to be
WITHOUT KNOWING ONESELF: for thus נפשׁ is often uſed; and
thus the Syriac alſo renders: according to which Interpretation the Senſe
is equivalent to the ſage Maxim of the Philoſophers, γνῶθι σεαυτόν.

—— *and he that haſteth with his Feet ſinneth.* ואץ ברגלים חוטא]
There ſeems to be here in our Verſion as little Connection between
theſe two Hemiſtics as in thoſe of the laſt Verſe. For what has *the
Knowledge of oneſelf* to do with *haſting with the Feet?* And not to
criticiſe upon the Quaintneſs of the Phraſe, where lies the *Sin in
haſting away?* This apparent Inconſiſtency will be removed, if we give
רגלים a Senſe, which it frequently has, *viz.* that of *Spies,* and render --- BUT HE THAT HASTILY GOETH WITH SPIES, SINNETH.

"*To know oneself* (which is the Work of Time) is declared in the pre-
"ceding Hemistic *to be good:* but to consort with Spies (who, con-
"scious they are concerned in a dangerous Sort of Knowledge, are
"hasty in their Motions) is a Sin." Or thus, HE THAT IS HASTY IN
HIS GOINGS (or, PROCEEDINGS) ERRETH ; i. e. *is liable to err.*

V. 7. — *he pursueth* them with *Words,* yet *they are wanting to him.*
מרדף אמרים לא המה:] In our Version there are more Words here
supplied than there are translated. The precise Sense of the Text seems
however sufficiently obvious, *viz.* HE PURSUETH them WHO SAY,
BE NOT THOU NOISY. I reject the Massoretical Lection ; and
construe המה as the Imperative of the Verb, which has the Sense here
given to it.

V. 8. *He that getteth Wisdom loveth his own Soul: he that keepeth*
Understanding shall find good. קנה לב אהב נפשו — שמר תבונה למצא
טוב:] Rather—HE THAT GETTETH UNDERSTANDING LOVETH
HIS OWN SOUL: HE GIVETH HEED TO DISCRETION, SO AS
TO FIND BENEFIT from it. For the ל with the Infinitive makes the
Gerund. Of this there are frequent Instances.

V. 10. *Delight is not seemly for a fool: —* לא נאוה כסיל תענוג] Rather — DELICACIES (i. e. *such Things as he is not a proper Judge of*)
ARE &c.

V. 11. *The Discretion of a Man deferreth his Anger* ; — שכל אדם
האריך אפו] Rather — THE DISCREET MAN &c. for שכל is here
the Participle.

V. 12. *The King's Wrath is as the Roaring of a Lion* ; — נהם ככפיר
זעף מלך] Rather —— THE KING'S WRATH ROARETH AS A
LION.

V. 13. — *and the Contentions of a Wife* are *a continual Dropping.*
ודלף טרד מדיני אשה:] The old Version explains *continual Drop-*
ping by " Rain that droppeth and rotteth a House." But I think this
must mean THE DROPPING OF THE EVES OF A HOUSE, or any
continued gentle falling of Water, than which nothing is more apt to
be tiresome and distracting. See Ch. XXVII. 15.

V. 18. — *and let not thy Soul spare for his Crying.* ואל המיתו
אל תשא נפשך:] Rather, as in the Margin — AND INCLINE NOT
THY SOUL TO HIS DESTRUCTION ; i. e. *by conniving too long at his*
Faults, which may prove his Destruction.   V. 19.

V. 19. *A Man of great Wrath shall suffer Punishment ; for if thou deliver* him, *yet thou must do it again.* גדל חמה נשא ענש — כי אם תציל ועוד תוסף] The latter Hemiftic ought I think to be thus rendered --- FOR, NOTWITHSTANDING THOU MAYEST HAVE INTERPOSED, THOU MUST DO IT AGAIN.

V. 21. There are *many Devices in a Man's Heart ; neverthelefs the Counfel of the Lord, that fhall ftand.* רבות מחשבות בלב איש — ועצת יהוה היא תקום] The Senfe I think would be clearer, if the Verfe were thus rendered --- MANY are THE DEVICES IN A MAN's HEART : BUT IT IS THE COUNSEL OF THE LORD THAT SHALL STAND.

V. 22. *The Defire of a Man* is *his Kindnefs :* — תאות אדם חסדו] Rather --- THE DESIRE OF A MAN is that IT MAY BE WELL WITH HIM. חסר is here the Infinitive for the Nominative.

——— *and a poor Man is better than a liar.* וטוב רש מאיש כזב :] In our Verfion there is neither Contraft nor Parallelifm between the Terms of this Hemiftic, nor between one Hemiftic and the other. Moft of the old Interpreters add the Word *rich* to *liar :* but there is certainly no more Ground for this Addition, than there was for reading A *good* WIFE, at V. 22. of the laft Chapter. But, admitting there were Ground, yet would there ftill be wanting an oppofite Term to *liar ;* and the two Propofitions would moreover labour under the fame Incoherence. I would therefore thus tranflate this Paffage — EVEN THE POOR MAN IS HAPPY NOT TO BE DECEIVED BY A GREAT MAN. This Senfe feems to reftore a general Harmony between all the difjointed Members of this Verfe. For the firft Part is an univerfal Propofition, expreffive of this Idea, that *all Men aim at Happinefs.* Here the Author defcends to a particular Inftance, and fixes upon that Clafs of Men, who from their Wants are fuppofed to be the greateft Strangers to that Bleffing ; and the very Inftance adduced is *negative :* " even " thefe (fays he) are comparatively happy, if they be not ill ufed and " impofed upon by the Rich." In the Conftruction I confider טוב as the Preter ; and give it the Senfe of *happy,* as 1 Sam. XXV. 8, 36. Efth. I. 10. VIII. 17. and make the Prepofition מ in מאיש anfwer a double Purpofe, *viz.* of giving a negative Force to the Infinitive כזב, and of reducing the Subftantive to the Ablative Cafe.

V. 23. *The Fear of the Lord* tendeth *to Life ; and he that hath it fhall abide fatisfied ; he fhall not be vifited with Evil.* יראת יהוה לחיים ושבע — ילין בל יפקד רע :] Rather — THE FEAR OF THE LORD

H h

tendeth TO LIFE AND PLENTY: IT SHALL ABIDE, AND SHALL NOT BE VISITED WITH EVIL.

V. 24. A slothful Man hideth his Hand in his Bosom, טמן עצל ידו בצלחת] Rather --- WHEN HE RECLINETH ON HIS SIDE: for that is the precise Idea of صلى, *viz. prostratus in latus dormivit.* The Chaldee, Vulgate, Aquila, and Symmachus render בצלחת, UNDER HIS ARM-PITS; which seems also to be a good Sense, if the Word would bear it; as either Representation paints Idleness in the most striking Colours.

V. 26. He that wasteth his Father, and chaseth away his Mother, is a Son that causeth Shame, and bringeth Reproach. משדד אב יבריח אם — בן כביש ומחפיר:] In this Verse (as in almost every other throughout the Part that contains what are strictly called *the Proverbs*) are two distinct Propositions; and, though our Version supplies four Words, there is no Need of the least Addition: for the Text may be thus rendered literally --- HE THAT ROBBETH A FATHER WILL DRIVE AWAY A MOTHER: THE SON THAT CAUSETH SHAME IS ALSO CONFOUNDED; for this Verb הפר is always used passively in *Hiphil.* The Sense, according to this Interpretation, is sufficiently obvious, *viz.* "That the Son who injures either of his Parents will "not hesitate at behaving disrespectfully toward the other: but because "he does not honour them, according to the fifth Commandment, "instead of a Blessing, he shall have a Curse."

V. 27. Cease, my Son, to hear the Instruction that causeth to err from the Words of Knowledge. חדל בני לשמע — מוסר לשגות מאמרי דעת:] Rather --- ABSTAIN, MY SON, FROM NEWS; BE THOU IN-STUCTED AGAINST ERRING (or, THE ERRORS) FROM THE WORDS OF KNOWLEDGE. Here is both *a Caution* and an *Exhorta-tion:* and *News,* or *idle Rumours,* are justly opposed to *the Words of true Knowledge.* שמע is rendered *News,* Ch. XXV. 25. מוסר is here the Imperative *Pyhal,* and שגות may be considered either as the Infinitive, or as a Noun. See Instances of the Prepositions thus used in Noldius.

CHAP. XX.

V. 6. Most Men will proclaim every one his own Goodness: רב אדם יקרא איש חסדו] Not one of the old Versions acknowledges this last ו;

which

which feems to have been borrowed from the next Word, beginning with that Letter; in the Room of which another has probably been added fince for the Connection. And as the Hemiftic would be clearer without, I pafs it over, and render thus —— A GREAT MAN WILL BE CALLED A BENEFICENT MAN: *i. e.* " A Man in an " eminent Station, if he live fuitably to his Rank, will not want Pa" negyrifts: but where is the truly fincere and righteous Man to be " found?" רב is ufed for *a great Man*, Eft. I. 8. whence comes the Title of *Rabbi*, which the Jews have fince fo much affected.

V. 8. *A King that fitteth in the Throne of Judgment fcattereth away all Evil with his Eyes.* [מלך יושב על כסא דין — מזרה בעיניו כל רע :] Rather --- A KING SITTETH ON THE THRONE OF JUDGMENT; HE SCATTERETH &c. For there are clearly two different Members in this Period.

V. 12. *The hearing Ear, and the feeing Eye, the Lord hath even made both of them.* [אזן שמעת ועין ראה — יהוה עשה גם שניהם :] Rather --- THE EAR HEARETH, AND THE EYE SEETH; BUT THE LORD HATH MADE THEM BOTH. So the LXX and Arabic Verfions.

V. 16. *Take his Garment that is Surety for a Stranger:* — לקח בגדו [כי ערב זר] Rather — TAKE HIS GARMENT, WHEN A STRANGER IS SURETY. Solomon repeatedly advifes to beware of being Surety for any Body: but here he intimates that it is not fafe to admit the Suretyfhip of a Stranger, without taking a fufficient Pawn, or Pledge, as an additional Security.

—— *and take a Pledge of him for a ftrange Woman.* ובעד נכרים [הבלהו :] Our Verfion adopts the Lection of the Maffora, and of Ch. XXVII. 13. *viz.* נכריה : but the prefent Text may be thus rendered --- AND TAKE A PLEDGE OF HIM WHERE STRANGERS ARE WITNESSES: literally, *in the Teftimony of Strangers.*

V. 18. *Every Purpofe is eftablifhed by Counfel:* [מהשבות בעצה הכון] Rather --- ESTABLISH PURPOSES BY COUNSEL. הכון is the Future fingular *Kal*: but as the Verb in the next Claufe is the Imperative, that Mood feems here preferable.

V. 19. *He that goeth about as a Talebearer revealeth Secrets:* גולה [סוד הולך רכיל] Rather — HE THAT REVEALETH SECRETS IS A WANDERING TALEBEARER.

V. 25. It is *a Snare to the Man* who *devoureth* that which is *holy* ; מוקש אדם ילע קדש] Rather — THE MAN IS INSNARED WHO DE- VOURETH AN HOLY THING. For יוקש is the Part. *Pahul.*

—— *and after Vows to make Inquiry.* ואחר נדרים לבקר :] Rather --- WHEN INQUIRY COMETH TO BE MADE AFTER VOWS. The ל with the Infinitive is here conſtrued as the Gerund.

V. 27. —*ſearching all the inward Parts of the Belly.* חפש כל הדרי בטן :] Rather — OF THE BODY ; as Job. XIX. 17. Mic. VI. 7.

CHAP. XXI.

V. 1. The King's Heart is in the Hand of the Lord, as the *Rivers of Water : he turneth it whitherſoever he will.*—פלגי מים לב מלך ביד יהוה על כל אשר יחפץ יטנו :] Rather —— THE KING'S HEART is A STREAM OF WATER IN THE HAND OF THE LORD; &c. פלג ſignifies any Part, be it ever ſo ſmall, that is divided from the Body to which it was before united. Hence appears the Aptneſs of the Com- pariſon. "God as eaſily influences the Minds of Kings, as a ſmall "Quantity of Water, upon a Table, may be directed by the Finger "into this or that Stream, as the Fancy ſuggeſts."

V. 4. An high Look, and a proud Heart, and *the plowing of the wicked,* is *Sin.* רום עינים ורחב לב — נר רשעים חטאת :] Rather HE THAT HATH AN HIGH LOOK HATH ALSO A PROUD HEART; and THE LIGHT OF THE WICKED IS SINFUL. חטאת ſeems to be here in *ſtatu conſtructo pro abſoluto,* and to be uſed by a Metonymy of the Effect for the Cauſe. The Senſe of the Verſe ſeems clearly to be this — "*The Eye* is the Index which points out the different Mo- "tions of *the Heart.* If therefore a Man harbours *Pride in his Breaſt,* "it will certainly betray itſelf *by his Eye* and his outward Carriage : "and *the Light,* or the Principle, *of a bad Heart,* muſt unavoidably "lead aſtray." In the ſame Senſe our Lord calls *the Eye the Light of the Body,* and cautions us *to take Heed that the Light within us be not Darkneſs.* Luke XI. 34, 35.

V. 5. The Thoughts of the diligent tend *only to Plenteouſneſs : but of every one* that is *haſty,* only *to Want.* כהשבות חרוץ אך למותר — וכל אץ אך למחסור :] Rather — THE THOUGHTS OF THE DILIGENT ARE CERTAINLY TOWARD PLENTY : BUT THE INCONSIDERATE

LAYS

LAYS HOLD ONLY OF WANT. I confider כל as the Preter of כול: it occurs in the fame Form and Signification, Ifa. XL. 12. and אץ (which as an Adjective, applicable to a Perfon, is found only, Ch. XXIX. 20.) I render *inconfiderate*; which Signification is clearly deducible from אוץ, *to haften, urge*, or *prefs forward*.

V. 6. *The getting of Treafures by a lying Tongue, is a Vanity tofled to and fro of them that feek Death.* פעל אצרות בלשון שקר — הבל נדף מבקשי מות:] There can be little Doubt that the prefent Reading of מבקשי is faulty. I would therefore read with the LXX, Arabic, and Syriac במוקשי, or contractedly במקשי, and render —HE DEALETH FALSELY THAT GETTETH TREASURES BY SLANDERING: THE VAIN MAN IS DRIVEN INTO THE SNARES OF DEATH: or, at leaft, read with Theodotion and Symmachus מבקש, in this Senfe —— THE ACQUISITION OF TREASURES BY ACCUSING (or, INFORMING) IS A DECEIT; even A VANITY DRIVEN ABOUT, SEEKING DEATH. See לישן ufed as a Verb, in the firft Senfe, Pf. CI. 5. and in the latter, Ch. XXX. 10.

V. 7. *The Robbery of the wicked fhall deftroy them*; שד רשעים יגורם] יגורם in this Place ought to be rendered — SHALL TERRIFY THEM. —— *becaufe they refufe to do Judgment.* כי מאנו לעשות משפט:] Rather — THAT WHICH IS RIGHT.

V. 8. *The Way of a Man is froward and ftrange:* הפכפך דרך איש וזר] All the ancient Verfions read here איש זר; which makes a much better Senfe, *viz.* THE WAY OF A STRANGER IS FROWARD. By this Reading we have a proper Term oppofed to *the pure* in the next Claufe; for *a ftrange Man* or *Woman*, in the Scripture Phrafe, are fuch *idolatrous Heathens*, as were Aliens from the Commonwealth of Ifrael, or *Perfons of depraved Morals*.

V. 9. — *than with a brawling Woman in a wide Houfe.* מאשת מדינים ובית חבר:] Rather — THAN WITH A BRAWLING WOMAN, AND IN A WIDE HOUSE, or WHERE there is A WIDE HOUSE, as Job XXIII. 3. &c.

V. 12. *The righteous Man wifely confidereth the Houfe of the wicked: but God overthroweth the wicked for their Wickednefs.* משכיל צדיק לבית רשע — מסלף רשעים לרע:] I read here with the LXX, Syriac, and Arabic, לבת; and render — THE RIGHTEOUS WISELY CON-

SIDERETH

SIDERETH THE HEART OF THE WICKED, PERVERTING THE
WICKED TO EVIL.

V. 15. It is *Joy to the juſt to do Judgment : but Deſtruction* ſhall be
to the workers of Iniquity.   שמחה לצדיק עשות משפט — ומחתה לפעלי
און :] Rather --- It is JOY TO THE RIGHTEOUS TO DO WHAT IS
RIGHT : BUT A TERROR TO THE WORKERS &c.

V. 16. *The Man that wandereth out of the Way of Underſtanding,*
ſhall remain in the Congregation of the dead. — ארם תועה מדרך השכל
בקהל רפאים ינוח :] · Or thus — A MAN MAY WANDER OUT OF
THE WAY OF UNDERSTANDING ; but HE SHALL &c.

V. 18. *The wicked* ſhall be *a Ranſom for the righteous,* — כפר לצדיק
רשע] Rather — THE WICKED IS CUT OFF INSTEAD OF THE
RIGHTEOUS : *i. e.* " the Miſchief he intended ſhould fall upon the
" righteou's falls upon his own Head." That this is the Senſe of the
Prepoſition ל, is I think evident from תחת, which correſponds to it
in the next Clauſe. And as כפר is uſed for *diſannulling* or *cancelling*
a Covenant, it may doubtleſs be uſed in general for *deſtroying.* See
Iſa. XXVIII. 18.

V. 20. There is *a Treaſure to be deſired, and Oil in the Dwelling of*
the wiſe ; — אוצר נחמד ושמן בנוה חכם] · If we omit the ו in ושמן
the Senſe will I think be clearer thus — OIL IN THE DWELLING OF
THE WISE IS A DESIREABLE TREASURE.

V. 24. *Proud and haughty Scorner is his Name, who dealeth in proud*
Wrath. זד יהיר לץ שמו — עושה בעברת זדון :] Rather — THE
PROUD, WHOSE NAME IS HAUGHTY SCORNER, MAY PREPARE
FOR THE RAGE OF PRIDE : *i. e.* which is reſerved for it. The
common Interpretation of this Verſe approaches to Tautology, and
contains no Sentiment : whereas that which is here propoſed may be
conſidered as a Diſſuaſive from Pride, from the Conſideration of the
Effects conſequent from it. The Verb עשה is thus uſed, 2 Chron.
XXXII. 29. Ezek. XLV. 22. and the Particle ב, Gen. XXIX. 18.
Deut. XIX. 21.

V. 26. *He coveteth greedily all the Day long :* — כל היום התאוה
תאוה] A Subject ſeems wanting here. The LXX and Arabic read
רשע, THE WICKED ; which anſwers to צדיק, THE RIGHTEOUS, in
the next Hemiſtic.

V. 27.

V. 27. *The Sacrifice of the wicked* is *an Abomination: how much more* when *he bringeth it with a wicked Mind?* — זבח רשעים תועבה : אף כי בזמה יביאנו]   The latter Hemiſtic ought I think to be rendered --- BECAUSE HE BRINGETH IT WITH A MISCHIEVOUS DEVICE.   See theſe united Particles thus rendered, Noldius, 6.

V. 28. — *but the Man that heareth ſpeaketh conſtantly.*   ואיש שומע : לנצח ידבר]   Rather — BUT THE OBEDIENT MAN SPEAKETH WITH STEADINESS, or AUTHORITY: *i. e.* ſo as not to be confounded.   Seé Taylor.

V. 29. — *but as for the upright, he directeth his Way.*   וישר הוא יבין : דרכו]   הוא is here a mere Expletive, without which the Hemiſtic would be too ſhort.   I would therefore render ſimply thus — BUT THE UPRIGHT DIRECTETH HIS WAY; except we adopt the Reading of the LXX and Arabic, יבין, he UNDERSTANDETH, or PONDERETH. Aquila and Symmachus read as we now do.

CHAP. XXII.

V. 2. *The rich and poor meet together:* — עשיר ורש נפגשו]   That is, ſays the old Verſion, " live together, and have Need the one of the " other:" which ſeems to be the true Senſe; for the Verb פגש ſo ſignifies, Iſa. LXIV. 5. and Jer. XV. 11.

V. 4. *By Humility,* and *the Fear of the Lord,* — עקב ענוה יראת יהוה] Rather --- THE REWARD OF THE HUMBLE IS THE FEAR OF THE LORD.

——— are *Riches, and Honour, and Life.* : עשר וכבוד וחיים] I read עשרו כבוד — and render — HIS RICHES are HONOUR AND LIFE.

V. 6. *Train up a Child in the Way he ſhould go*; חנך לנער על פי : דרכו] על פי ought here to be rendered AGREEABLY TO, *viz. the Way* &c.   See Taylor.

V. 8. *He that ſoweth Iniquity ſhall reap Vanity.* — זרע עולה יקצור : און]   Rather — AFFLICTION, as Job V 6. or EVIL, as Ch. XII. 21.

V. 11. *He that loveth Pureneſs of Heart,* for *the Grace of his Lips the King* ſhall be *his Friend.* : אהב טהר לב — חן שפתיו רעהו מלך] This Apothegm is doubtleſs much embarraſſed.   The firſt Part appears to be only a Subject without a Predicate : and the only Object of the King's Attention seems to be the graceful Conversation mentioned in the latter Part. For the Knowledge of another's Sincerity belongs not to Kings ; but is the sole Property of Him, who is emphatically called καρδιαγνωςης. Hence one would naturally be led to conclude, that the first Hemistic was defective as well in the Sense, as in the Metre, and that the Word GOD had dropped from the Text. We shall accordingly find it in the LXX, Chaldee, Syriac, and Arabic Versions : and surely on such Authorities we may presume to restore it, and render ---- GOD LOVETH THE PURE IN HEART, and he that hath GRACE IN HIS LIPS, THE KING MAKETH HIM HIS FRIEND. טהר is used as an Adjective, Job XVI. 9. and רעהו may be considered as the Participle with the Affix, signifying *does associate with him.*

V. 12. *The Eyes of the Lord preserve Knowledge*, [עיני יהוה נצרו דעת Rather --- OBSERVE (or, ARE ATTENTIVE TO) KNOWLEDGE, as Ch. XXIV. 12. &c.

—— *and he overthroweth the Words of the Transgressor.* ויסלף דברי : בגד] Either — AND HE CONFOUNDETH THE WORDS &c. or — HE OVERTHROWETH THE MATTERS &c. as in the Margin.

V. 16. *He that oppresseth the poor to increase his* Riches, *and he that giveth to the rich* shall *surely* come *to want.* עשק דל להרבות לו — נתן] לעשיר אך למחסור :] All the ancient Versions, the Vulgate excepted, read the first Hemistic thus—" He that oppresseth the poor increaseth " *Evil* upon himself :" but I do not think they read their Text differently from what we do our's ; which I would render thus —— HE THAT OPPRESSETH THE POOR TO INCREASE HIS OWN, IS AS HE THAT GIVETH TO THE RICH CLEARLY TO his own DETRIMENT. That is, they both act *equally* contrary to the Rules of Wisdom and Understanding, the great Objects of this Book ; and though they have Recourse to different Means, yet their Ends will be the same.

V. 18. *For it is a pleasant Thing, if thou keep them within thee ;* כי נעים כי תשמרם בבטנך [נעים has here no Antecedent to agree with : for *a pleasant Thing,* according to the Genius of the Hebrew, would have been expressed by the Substantive נועם, which has often the Force of a Neuter. As all the old Versions, except the Vulgate, read נעמו, which the Syntax requires, I adopt their Lection, and render — FOR THEY ARE PLEASANT, WHEN THOU KEEPEST THEM

WITHIN

WITHIN THY BREAST. The Antecedents are *the Words* and *Know-ledge* mentioned immediately before.

—— *they shall withal be fitted in thy Lips.* [יכנו יחדו על שפתיך :]
Rather --- THEY SHALL WITHAL BE READY UPON THY LIPS.

V. 19. —— *I have made known to thee this Day, even to thee.* הודעתיך
[היום אף אתה :] There seems to be something defective after the
Verb *made known* in our Version, as well as in the Text. But the LXX,
Aquila, Symmachus, and the Arabic read, instead of היום, חיים;
which not only completes the Sentence, but makes a better Sense.
The Words also אף אתה, as rendered in our Version, are not only
Tautology, but are incapable of that Meaning. I would therefore
supply *them* (viz. *the Instructions of Wisdom*, mentioned just before)
if we retain the Reading of our modern Text: or rather, adopting
the Lection of the Greek Copies, render the latter Hemistic thus —— I
HAVE MADE LIFE KNOWN TO THEE; THEREFORE DRAW NEAR.
Life in this Place seems to imply *the Path of Life*; and the Imperative, אתה is an Exhortation to proceed in it.

V. 20. *Have not I written to thee excellent Things —?* הלא כתבתי
[לך שלשים] Our Version without the least Authority gives to שלשים
the Signification of *excellent Things*: but in the old Version the Word
is with more Justice rendered THREE TIMES, with this Note in the
Margin, " That is, sundry Times." Le Clerc supposes that this refers
to the *three thousand Proverbs* mentioned, 1 Kings IV. 32. But I think
it is most probable, that this alludes to these *three Books*, which were
composed by Solomon and bear his Name; or, that it is only a general
determinate Number for an undetermined, and might be rendered
OFTENTIMES, as Job. XXXIII. 29. All the ancient Versions read
three Times.

V. 21. *That I might make thee know the Certainty of the Words of
Truth; that thou mightest answer the Words of Truth to them that send
unto thee.* [להודיעך קשט אמרי אמת. — להשיב אמרים אמת לשלחך]
The latter Hemistic ought doubtless to be rendered ——THAT THE
WORDS MIGHT BRING BACK THE TRUTH TO THEM THAT
SEND THEE. This is an Instance of the Figure Antimetabole, which
plays with the Words, and is not uncommon in the best Poets. The
Sense of the Verse is plainly this — " that I might acquaint thee with
" Truth, that thou mightest report it to them that apply to thee."

V. 24. *Make no Friendship with an angry Man: and with a furious Man thou fhalt not go.* אל תתרע את בעל אף ‒‒ ואת איש חמות לא תבוא:] The latter Hemiftic ought to be rendered ‒ AND GO NOT WITH A FURIOUS MAN: for both the Sentences are expreffed by the fame Tenfe.

V. 29. ‒ *he fhall not ftand before mean* Men. (בל יתיצב לפני השכים:) As the Noun ושך never denotes *a mean, low,* or *obfcure* Condition; I would render לפני חשכים IN OBSCURITY, as Ifa. LVIII. 10. LIX. 9. or DARKNESS, as Pf. LXXXVIII. 6.

CHAP. XXIII.

V. 2. *And put a Knife to thy Throat,* ‒ ושמת שכין בלעך] This is a bold Eaftern Phrafe, expreffive of the abfolute Neceffity *of reftraining the Appetites;* and intimating that there is as much Danger in indulging them, as there is in running againft a Knife applied to the Throat.

V. 4. *Labour not to be rich: ceafe from thine own Wifdom.* אל תיגע להעשיר ‒ מבינתך חדל:] The laft Hemiftic feems incapable of any other Senfe than that which is here given to it; but as this Senfe is directly contrary to the whole Purport of this Book, as well as to Reafon, we may conclude, that there is fome Fault in the Text. Now, no Omiffion is more common than that of the copulative ו between the Hemiftics: and we fhall find that every one of the ancient Verfions have it. I would therefore reftore it, and render ‒ LABOUR NOT TO BE RICH, NEITHER CEASE FROM THINE OWN WISDOM: *i. e.* " if thou be earneftly bent upon acquiring Wealth, thou muft neceffarily " be inattentive to the Purfuit of Wifdom, in which thou art engaged."

V. 5. *Wilt thou fet thine Eyes upon that which is not?* התעוף עיניך בו ואיננו] This is an Idiom which cannot bear to be rendered literally, it fignifying ‒ *Wilt thou let thine Eyes fly upon it, and it is not?* The Meaning however is clear, which I think ought to be thus expreffed ‒‒‒ WILT THOU SET THINE EYES UPON A TRANSIENT THING?

‒‒‒‒ *for* Riches *certainly make themfelves Wings;* ‒ כי עשה יעשה לו כנפים] Perhaps the original Reading was עשר (inftead of עשה) ‒‒‒ RICHES MAKE THEMSELVES WINGS: for at prefent there is neither *Riches,* nor *any other Subject* to the Verb, except it be a negative one, borrowed from the foregoing Hemiftic.

V. 7. *For as he thinketh in his Heart, so is he:* כי כמו שער בנפשו
כן הוא] Rather — FOR as he is VILE IN HIS SOUL, &c. i. e. *his*
Actions correspond to his Inclinations. שער occurs nowhere as a Verb
but is used as an Adjective in this Sense, Jer. XXIX. 17.

V. 8. *The Morsel* which *thou haft eaten shalt thou vomit up, and lose*
thy sweet Words. פתך אכלת תקיאנה, — ושחת דבריך הנעימים]
The Note in the old Version upon this Place is — "He will not cease
"till he hath done thee some Harm, and his flattering Words shall
"come to no Use." This Interpretation may be just, as far as it relates to the first Hemistic : but surely the Sense there given to the latter
cannot hold : it ought I think to be thus rendered —— AND THOU
SHALT PUT AN END TO THY PLEASANT DISCOURSES, or WORDS
OF COMMENDATION : that is, "the Treatment thou wilt receive
"from him, is so bad, that it will oblige thee to desist from convivial
"Mirth by the Nausea excited from the Badness of his Repast;" or,
"instead of the Compliments thou usest to bestow upon him, thou
"wilt be disgusted by reflecting upon his sordid and illiberal Usage."

V. 13. —— *for if thou beatest him* &c. — כי תכנו] Rather — WHEN
THOU BEATEST &c.

V. 14. *Thou shalt beat him* —— אתה — תכנו] The Imperative
would perhaps be preferable in this Place.

V. 15. — *my Heart shall rejoice, even mine.* ישמח לבי גם אני :]
This particular Idiom would perhaps be better translated thus — MY
HEART, EVEN I MYSELF, WILL REJOICE. It is an Hendyadis,
expressive of exceeding great Joy.

V. 17. —— *but be thou in the Fear of the Lord all the Day long.*
כי אם ביראת יהוה כל היום :] There is no Occasion to supply any
Word to complete the Sense ; for ביראת is governed by יקנא in
the preceding Clause, which ought to be rendered, AFFECT NOT ; for
this Verb is used in a good, as well as bad, Sense. See Taylor. The
proper Translation of the whole Verse seems therefore to be this ——
LET NOT THINE HEART AFFECT SINNERS : BUT ALWAYS THE
FEAR OF THE LORD.

V. 18. *For surely there is an End;* — כי אם יש אחרית] In the
Margin we have the Word REWARD ; which is doubtless the Force

of

of אחרית in this Place: thus Jer. XXIX. 11. we meet with the same two Words, *viz.* אחרית ותקורה, *the End and Expectation,* which are an Hendyadis for *the expected Reward.* אחרית has also the same Sense, Pf. XXXVII. 37. and is rendered a REWARD, Ch. XXIV. 14. & 20.

V. 20. — *amongst riotous Eaters of Flesh.* בזללי בשר למו׃] Rather --- AMONGST THEM THAT RIOTOUSLY EAT FLESH WITH EACH OTHER: for this I apprehend is the Meaning of למו in this Place; which our Version passes over, except in the Margin, where we read — *of their Flesh;* which cannot possibly be the Sense.

V. 21. —— *and Drowsiness shall clothe a Man with Rags.* וקרעים תלביש נומה׃] Rather —— AND DROWSINESS SHALL PUT ON RAGS; for thus this Verb in the same Voice is rendered, Exod. XXVIII. 41. XXIX. 5. XL. 13. or, SHALL CLOTHE ITSELF WITH; as Jer. IV. 30. for *Hiphil* in this Verb includes the Signification of *Hithpahel,* which is never used.

V. 22. *Hearken unto thy Father that begat thee, and despise not thy Mother, when she is old.* שמע לאביך זה ילדך — ואל תבוז כי זקנה אמך׃] Were we to read ינקבה, instead of זקנה, the Antithesis would be more direct, thus — AND DESPISE NOT THY MOTHER, BECAUSE SHE GAVE THEE SUCK.

V. 25. *Thy Father and thy Mother shall be glad, and she that bare thee shall rejoice.* ישמח אביך ואמך ותגל יולדתך׃] Rather, I think --- THY FATHER AND THY PEOPLE (or, COUNTRY) WILL BE GLAD &c.

V. 26. *My Son, give me thine Heart,* — תנה בני לבך לי] Rather --- MY SON, APPLY THINE HEART TO ME.

V. 27. *For a Whore is a deep Ditch; and a strange Woman is a narrow Pit.* כי שוחה עמוקה זונה — ובאר צרה נכריה׃] I would render the latter Hemistic thus — AND A PROSTITUTE IS A WELL OF DISTRESS, or A FOUNTAIN OF TRIBULATION.

V. 28. *She also lieth in wait as for a Prey;* — אף היא כחתף הארב] Rather, with the Margin, AS A ROBBER. For the Verb חתף, in the only Place where it occurs besides, signifies *to take away;* *viz.* Job. IX. 12.

V. 29.

V. 29. — *who hath Babbling?* — לְמִי שִׂיחַ] Rather — WHO HATH COMPLAINT? as Job. VII. 13. XXIII. 2. &c.

—— *who hath Wounds without Cauſe?* — לְמִי פְּצָעִים חִנָּם] Rather, I think — WITHOUT COST, or RECOMPENSE; *having no Proſpect of Advantage*, as 1 Chron. XXI. 24. Jer. XXII. 13.

V. 31. — *when it giveth his Colour in the Cup,* — כִּי יִתֵּן בַּכִּיס עֵינוֹ] Rather --- WHEN IT SHEWETH IT'S COLOUR IN THE CUP: thus is נתן uſed, Deut. XIII. 1, 17.

—— when *it moveth itſelf aright.* יִתְהַלֵּךְ בְּמֵישָׁרִים:] In the old Verſion — or *goeth down pleaſantly.* Neither of which ſeems ſtrictly exact: but the Truth lies between both; thus — that IT MAY GO DOWN ARIGHT; viz. *the Throat.*

V. 33. *Thine Eyes ſhall behold ſtrange Women,* — עֵינֶיךָ יִרְאוּ זָרוֹת] Rather --- THINE EYES then SHALL GAZE UPON STRANGE WO-MEN; for ſo ראה is uſed, Eccleſ. IX. 9. or — BEHOLD WITH PLEA-SURE — as Gen. XVI. 13. Pſ. LIV. 7. &c. The Particle is here added to preſerve the Connection.

V. 35. — *when ſhall I awake? I will ſeek it yet again.* מָתַי אָקִיץ אוֹסִיף אֲבַקְשֶׁנּוּ עוֹד:] Rather, without Interrogation — WHEN I SHALL AWAKE I WILL REPEAT it; AND WILL SEEK IT AGAIN: as Pſ. CI. 2.

CHAP. XXIV.

V. 5. *A wiſe Man is ſtrong; yea, a Man of Knowledge increaſeth Strength.* גֶּבֶר חָכָם בָּעוֹז — וְאִישׁ דַּעַת מְאַמֶּץ כֹּחַ:] Rather — THE WISE IS MIGHTY IN POWER, AND THE MAN OF UNDERSTAND-ING PREVAILETH IN STRENGTH. The two Verbs גבר and אמץ are ſynonymous. But I ſhould ſtill prefer the Senſe given by all the old Verſions, except the Vulgate, thus — THE WISE IS MORE EXCELLENT THAN THE POWERFUL, AND THE MAN OF UNDERSTANDING THAN THE MIGHTY IN STRENGTH. גבר is conſtrued with ב in this Senſe, 1 Chron. V. 2. XI. 21.

V. 10. If *thou faint in the Day of Adverſity,* — הִתְרַפִּיתָ בְּיוֹם צָרָה] Rather — DOST THOU FAINT &c? for the ה is here *interrogative* as well as *formative.*

V. 16.

V. 16. *For a just Man falleth seven times, and riseth up* again; כי
שבע יפול צדיק וקם] Rather — Though the just fall seven
Times, yet will he rise up again.

V. 21. — and *meddle not with them that are given to change.* עם
שונים אל תתערב :] Rather — and be not Surety for unsteady
Men. Thus this Verb is rendered, 2 Kings XVIII. 23. Isa. XXXVI. 8.
And the Prepofition is so used, 1 Sam. XIV. 45. Dan. XI. 39.

V. 22. — *and who knoweth the Ruin of them both?* ופיד שניהם
מי יודע :] The Note on this Place in the old Version is — "mean-
"ing, either of the wicked and seditious, as V. 19. & 21. or of them
"that fear not God, nor obey the King." But neither of these References seems to the Purpose. Whereas if the Interpretation of התערב
in the last Verse be admitted, the two Persons exposed to Ruin are *the*
Surety, and *the unsteady Person,* for whom the other is bound.

V. 23. *These* Things *also* belong *to the wise.* גם אלה לחכמים]
The old Version distinguishes these Words by other Characters, as it
does all the other supposed Interpolations. That this is the Addition
of some later Hand seems sufficiently clear from internal Marks: probably the same that added the first Verse, or more properly the Title,
to the next Chapter.

V. 26. Every Man *shall kiss his Lips that giveth a right Answer.*
שפתים ישק משיב דברים נכחים :] The obvious Construction of this
Sentence is --- he may kiss the Lips who giveth a right
Answer : the Sense of which seems plainly to be this in general —
"the Person who speaks properly, suitably to the Occasion, whatever
"it be, shall have particular Marks of Attention paid to him ; or, in
"a more confined Sense, he may be admitted to kiss the Lips of his
"Superiors, who consult him, whenever a pleasing Answer is given."

V. 28. — *and deceive* not *with thy Lips.* והפתית בשפתיך :] Rather surely --- nor deceive with thy Lips : for ו is negative,
when a negative Particle has preceded, which is the Case here. This
is so general a Rule, that I am surprized it escaped our Translators in
this Place, as they have observed it elsewhere.

Chap. XXV.

V. 1. —— *which the Men of Hezekiah, King of Judah, copied out.*
אשר העתיקו אנשי הזקיה מלך יהודה :] Rather, I think —— collected

LECTED TOGETHER. The Verb עתק fignifies primarily *to remove from one Place to another*: and the Notion of *collecting fcattered Pieces into one whole* feems as confiftent with that Idea, as that of *tranf- cribing*. The old Verfion, I find, explains the Word as I do. This is the only Place where it occurs in either of thefe Senfes.

V. 2. It is *the Glory of God to conceal a Thing : but the Honour of Kings is to fearch out a Matter.* כבד אלהים הסתר דבר—וכבד מלכים הקר דבר] Thefe Hemiftics are not I apprehend adverfative, but ex- egetical. For though *God* reveal not always to us the Caufes of His Difpenfations, or the final Caufes of the Works of Nature ; yet the *Con- cealment* here meant feems more applicable to *Magiftrates*, whofe Glory it is to keep State Matters impenetrably fecret, till they are ripe for Execution. An unremitted Inveftigation of the leaft Difpofition to form Cabals, either at home or abroad, in order to quafh them in their Birth, is another Characteriftic of a wife Prince. And thefe two may be con- fidered as cardinal Points in every well regulated Adminiftration. I would therefore render the firft Hemiftic thus — It is THE GLORY OF MAGISTRATES TO CONCEAL A THING, AND &c. See what was faid on the Word אלהים, Pf. LXXXII. 1, 6.

V. 3. *The Heavens for Height, and the Earth for Depth ;* שמים לרום וארץ לעמק] Here is no Propofition according to our Verfion. Some Verb appears to be wanting : but that is not the Cafe ; for there are two Verbs in this Sentence. לרום and לעמק are both Infinitives, and thefe Infinitives have here the Force of Preters or Prefent Tenfes. (See Inftances in Noldius, P. 415.) This Place ought therefore to be rendered --- THE HEAVENS ARE HIGH, AND THE EARTH DEEP. It is fo in the Chaldee and Syriac Verfions.

V. 5. *Take away the wicked* from *before the King ;* הגו רשע לפני מלך] Rather --- REMOVE THE WICKED FROM THE KING. לפני has that Force as well as מלפני ; fee Noldius. 2.

V. 6. *Put not forth thyfelf in the Prefence of the King,* אל תתהדר לפני מלך] Rather — BOAST NOT THYSELF ——.

V. 7. *For better* it is *that it be faid unto thee, Come up hither ;* &c. כי טוב אמר לך עלה הנה וגו"] This Verfe is almoft parallel to what our Saviour faid, Luke XIV. 8, 9, 10. *Sit down in the loweft Room, that when he that bade thee cometh, he may fay unto thee, Friend, go up higher,* &c.

—— *whom*

———— *whom thine Eyes have seen.* : אשר ראו עיניך] This Hemiſtic ſeems to be not only ſuperfluous both as to the Senſe and Metre, but alſo imperfect and out of Place. According to the LXX and Arabic the Word דבר is wanting. In my Opinion it ought to begin the 9th Verſe, and be rendered thus --- SPEAK WHAT THINE EYES HAVE SEEN; *and diſcover not a Secret to another.*

V. 8. *Go not forth haſtily to ſtrive, left* thou know not *what to do in the End thereof, when thy Neighbour hath put thee to Shame.* אל תצא : בהכלים אתך רעך — פן מה תעשה באחריתה — לרב מהר] Ra-ther --- GO NOT HASTILY TO STRIVE, LEST THOU DO ANY THING IN THE END THEREOF, WHEREBY THY NEIGHBOUR MAY PUT THEE TO SHAME.

V. 9. *Debate thy Cauſe with thy Neighbour* himſelf; *and diſcover not thy Secret to another.* : וסוד אחר אל תגל — ריבך ריב את רעך] There is neither Affinity nor Oppoſition between theſe Precepts. The Fault lies evidently in the Union of Parts of diſtinct Verſes : for the firſt Hemiſtic ſeems to belong to thoſe three other which immediately precede, with which it ought to be connected by ſupplying the Part. *But.*

V. 11. *A Word fitly ſpoken* is like *Apples of Gold in Pictures of Silver.* : דבר דבר על אפניו — הפוחי זהב במשכיות כסף] The mar-ginal Explanation of *fitly ſpoken* is, viz. *upon it's Wheels*; a bold Fi-gure truly! But as it favours too much of a Catachreſis; and does not anſwer the Purpoſe of the Compariſon; (for the only Idea that *a Word upon it's Wheels* ſeems to convey is a Word ſpoken *rapidly*, not *fitly*) I ſhould chuſe to give אפן the Chaldee Senſe: now אפנתי ſignifies, *occurſus, obviam itio, è contra,* and accordingly the Phraſe על אפניו would hence mean literally, *in it's Meeting, in it's Defence,* or, by a more liberal Conſtruction, *in Reply,* or *in Repartee*; and a good *Repartee,* it is al-lowed, is the ſtrongeſt Indication that can be given of true *Wit.* The Words תפוחי זהב may either be underſtood of *golden Balls* for Orna-ment, or of *Citrons* or *Oranges,* which have alſo that Name in He-brew, as well as in Latin. משכיות properly ſignifies *the Thoughts of the Mind,* or *the Imagination*; with reſpect to outward Objects, it is uſed for any *Works curiouſly wrought* or *figured*; and in this Place may there-fore be underſtood of any *Veſſel, Baſket,* or the like. Hence this Verſe may not improperly be thus rendered — A WORD SPOKEN IN REPLY is like ORANGES (or, GOLDEN APPLES) IN SILVER VESSELS. The Reply or Repartee is doubtleſs to be conſtrued κατ᾽ ἐξοχήν, as *the*
Weights

Weights or *Wife*, Ch. XVI. 11. XVIII. 22. See the Prepofition thus ufed, V. 20. The following Interpretation of this Verfe has been communicated to me by a Friend, *viz.* " As Apples of Gold in Silver " Vessels, fo is an excellent Saying expreffed in Terms " suited to it. דבר according to the Hebrew Idiom implies *Ex-* " *cellence*; and the paraphraftic Senfe given to על אפניו, which literally " fignifies, *on it's Wheels*, is agreeable to the Verfion of the LXX, " which renders this Paffage, ειπεν λογον επι αρμεζωσιν αυτω. The Meta- " phor may be taken from Carriages, which when mounted on their " Wheels are in the moft convenient State for Ufe. Perhaps the com- " mon Expreffion of a Simile or Proverbial Sentence *running upon all* " *four* may be derived from the fame Origin, as alfo the *Rotundity* of " *a Phrafe*."

V. 12. — fo is *a wife Reprover upon an obedient Ear.* מוכיח חכם : על אזן שמעת] Rather — unto an attentive Ear.

V. 13. *As the Cold of Snow* —— כצנת שלג] This Word צנת occurs nowhere elfe : the Signification of *Cold* is given to it from the Chaldee and Vulgate. The Syriac read צנח, *the falling*; and fo did the LXX, for they have here εξοδος χιονες.

V. 14. *Whofo boafteth himfelf of a falfe Gift, is like Clouds and Wind without Rain.* נשיאים ורוח וגשם אין — איש מתהלל במתת שקר] Rather --- The Man who boasteth of a Bribe &c. " He " hereby acknowledges, that he is not influenced by the Principles of " Rectitude; and though he may be thought by the World a virtuous " Man from his outward Deportment, yet he is not fo, but is like thofe " Clouds which threaten Rain, and produce nothing." The old Ver- fion is — *The Man that boafteth of a falfe Liberality.*

V. 22. *For thou fhalt heap Coals of Fire upon his Head,* — כי גחלים אתה חתה על ראשו] *Qu.* might not this difficult Place admit of this Senfe --- For thou wilt take away the Sparks left upon his Head ? Or thus --- For thou wilt remove the Coals of Fire from his Head ? For the Verb חתה never fignifies *to heap*, but always *to take away*; and גחל is ufed figuratively for *a Spark*, and that Spark for *an Offspring*: fo here *by Sparks*, or *burning Coals*, may ftill more naturally be underftood *the different De-* *grees of Wrath.* The Prepofition is ufed in the Senfe laft propofed, Pf. LXXXI. 5. By this Interpretation it is not meant to infinuate, that

the

the Head is the Seat of the Affections: but that it would be made anfwerable for the wrong Directions of them; agreeably to a well known Scriptural Phrafe, Jof. II. 19. *his Blood fhall be upon his Head.* 1 Sam. XXV. 39. *The Lord hath returned the Wickednefs of Nabal upon his Head* &c. So here the violent Indignation, which is not improperly compared to burning Coals, which refts on an Enemy's Head, and would therefore expofe him to Punifhment, is reprefented as quite extinguifhed in him by the good Offices and kind Behaviour of the Perfon, who before was the Object of his Wrath and Revenge. The common Expofition of this Place feems to me to be exceedingly harfh, *viz.* that *heaping Coals of Fire upon an Enemy's Head* means *to melt him into Love and Affection*; or, that this Phrafe fignifies, that by doing him good, he becomes thereby expofed to the moft fevere of all Punifhments, if he do not relent, and fhew a proper Senfe of Gratitude.

V. 23. *The north Wind driveth away Rain:* ─── [רוח צפון תחולל גשם]
Rather ─── THE NORTH WIND PRODUCETH RAIN: which it is not improbable it did in Judea, as in fome other Countries. Ο μεν βορεας (fays *Theophraftus*) και μαλλον οι Ετησιαι τοις προς μεσεμβριαν και ανατολην οικουσι υετιοι. *Lib. de Ventis.*

─── *fo* doth *an angry Countenance a backbiting Tongue.* ופנים [נזעמים לשון סתר:] According to our Verfion the Verb that is to be fupplied here is *driveth away:* but חולל has no fuch Signification. We muft therefore repeat, or underftand, the Verb *produceth;* which is at leaft equally applicable to this Place as the other Verb, thus ─── fo doth A BACKBITING TONGUE AN ANGRY COUNTENANCE. For injurious Reflections are more frequent behind the Back than in the Prefence of an angry Perfon.

V. 26. *A righteous Man falling down before the wicked* is as *a troubled Fountain, and a corrupt Spring.* [מעין נרפש ומקור משחת ─── צדיק כט לפני רשע:] That is ─── "A righteous Man forcibly thrown out of "Authority, by the prevailing Power of the ungodly, makes the State "of which he is a Member like a troubled Fountain &c."

V. 27. It is *not good to eat much Honey:* ─── [אכל דבש הרבות לא טוב] Though this Advice be true in the literal Senfe, yet it is clearly requifite to underftand it in the figurative, on account of it's Connection with the next Hemiftic, and becaufe it was thus to be confidered at V. 16. The Meaning therefore feems to be in both Places, "that we "ought to reftrain our Appetites in refpect to the Enjoyments of all "temporal Bleffings."

─── *fo*

—— *fo* for Men *to fearch their own Glory*, is not *Glory*. והקר
והקר כבד —— The Text ought I think to be thus read —— [כברם כבוד:
מכבוד —— and rendered —— NOR TO SEARCH AFTER GLORY BY GLO-
RYING ; *i.e.* "we ought not to proclaim our own Praifes, but leave
"that to others," as we are directed, Ch. XXVII. 2. The ו is here
negative, on account of the preceding negative. See Ch. XXIV. 28.
And מכבוד is here the Gerund with the Particle prefixed. See Noldius, P. 471.

V. 28. *He that* hath *no Rule over his own Spirit* —— איש אשר אין
מעצר לרוחו [Rather—THE MAN WHO REFRAINETH NOT HIS OWN
SPIRIT ; for מעצר here does not feem to be a Subftantive, but the
Participle prefent *Pibel*.

CHAP. XXVI.

V. 2. *As the Bird by wandering, as the Swallow by flying, fo the
Curfe caufelefs fhall not come.* כצפור לנוד כדרור לעוף —— כן קללת
חנם לא תבא :[Rather —— As THE BIRD WANDERETH, AS THE
SWALLOW FLIETH, SO THE CURSE WITHOUT CAUSE SHALL
NOT COME. See the Note Ch. XXV. 3. In the old Verfion the Word,
efcape, is added after *flying :* which makes the Verfe rather more intelligible than in the prefent Verfion. The Meaning feems to be "that
"Evils, natural or moral, owe not their Being to Chance, like the ac-
"cidental Flight of Birds in this or that Direction; but are all directed
"by the Will of a fuperintending wife Providence."

V. 4. *Anfwer not a fool according to his Folly,*—[אל תען כסיל כאולתו
As the preceptive Part of this Verfe and the next are contradictory,
fome have thought that one of the two muft be a Glofs: but the
Suppofition is furely groundlefs. Nothing is more confiftent than fuch
Precepts on different Occafions, as is plainly the Cafe here. The marginal Explanation in the old Verfion is here fhort, but proper. In refpect to the firft, it fays, "Confent not unto his Doings ;" and, as to
the latter — "Reprove him as the Matter requireth."

V. 6. *He that fendeth a Meffage by the Hand of a fool, cutteth off
the Feet,* and *drinketh Damage.* מקצה רגלים חמס שתה — שלה
דברים ביד כסיל :[The Meaning may be, that he that fends a
Meffage by a fool, will as furely fuffer Damage by not having it duly
performed, as if he cut off the Meffenger's Feet. See Ch. XIII. 2.

Or

Or perhaps the Verse may be rendered thus, according to the Syriac — HE THAT SENDETH A MESSAGE BY A FOOL DRINKETH WITH TORTURE FROM THE EXTREMITY OF HIS FEET. That is, " He that employs a fool to transact any Business of Consequence acts " as ridiculously as he that distorts his Body by bringing Neck and Feet " together, in order to drink at a Brook." See צצה thus used *in regimine*, Ch. XVII. 24. and חיים, considered as the Participle present, signifying *being in Torture*, or *suffering Violence*.

V. 7. *The Legs of the lame are not equal; —* דליו שקים מפסח [Rather --- THE LEGS OF THE LAME FAIL, or ARE EXHAUSTED: which is the common Signification of דלל; and corresponds better with the next Hemistic. דליו is irregular, and incapable of being reduced to any known Form : it is generally supposed to be 3. m. pl. Imp. *Pihel*, for דלהו : but is here considered as 3. m. pl. Preter *Kal*, for דלו, or rather for דללו. Symmachus seems to have so read the Word ; for thus he renders the Place — ἐξελίπον κνημαι απο χωλυ, και παραβολη εν στοματι ———.

V. 8. *As he that bindeth a Stone in a Sling ; so is he that giveth Honour to a Fool.* כצרור אבן במרגמה — כן נותן לכסיל כבוד : [The marginal Lection is — *As he that putteth a* precious *Stone in a Heap of Stones*. Both the Senses are good, abstractedly considered, but the Hebrew does not seem to justify either. For the Verbs צרר or צור never signify *to put*, or *place*, but always *to bind*; and מרגמה, which occurs only in this Place as a Noun, should seem to mean a Heap of Stones, from the Verb רגם, *to stone :* however the Chaldee and Arabic will here assist us, for מרגמא signifies *a Sling*, as does رجم : on which account the textual Lection is preferable. The Application of the Comparison to the moral Sentiment is obvious, *viz.* they are both (the Stone and the Honour) thrown away.

V. 9. As *a Thorn goeth up into the Hand of a drunkard, so is a Parable in the Mouth of Fools.* חוח עלה ביד שכור — ומשל בפי כסילים : [Rather --- AS A THORN ENTERETH INTO THE HAND OF A DRUNKARD, so doth A PARABLE &c. That is, they each expose themselves to Ridicule.

V. 10. *The great* God *that formed all* Things, *both rewardeth the fool, and rewardeth transgressors.* רב מחולל כל ושכר כסיל — ושכר עבריה : [None of the ancient Versions seem to have had the same Text

Text before them, as that which we now have in this Place. The Chaldee and Syriac read it thus — רב מהולל בשר כסיל ושבר עבר ים : — *The Flesh of a fool suffereth much : and a drunkard crosseth the Sea.* The Arabic has only one Word like our Text, *viz.* כל, which the others omit, viz. *All the Beauty of the wicked is hated in many Things, because their Aspect is grievous to them.* The LXX is as unintelligible, *viz.* Πολλα χειμαζεται πασα σαρξ αφρονων, συντριβεται γαρ εκστασις αυτων· Symmachus, Theodotion, and the Vulgate omit רב מהולל ; and render, as if they had read — כל שבר כסיל ישבר עברות : for their Versions, though differently worded, are all to this Effect — *Every one that restraineth the Madman restraineth Wrath.* Notwithstanding this unparalleled Diversity in the old Interpreters, the present Text is not only defensible, but affords us a better Sense than any they have given us. I would render it thus — EVERY ONE SUFFERETH MUCH, WHO EITHER HIRETH A FOOL, OR HIRETH TRANSGRESSORS. This Sense seems more pertinent to the Place, and more connected with the Context, than it would, if the Verse be so construed as to refer to God, as in our Version.

V. 12. —there is *more Hope of a fool than of him.* תקוה לכסיל ממנו :] Rather --- THOU MAYEST HOPE MORE OF A FOOL THAN OF HIM, תקוה being the 2. P. Fut. *Kal.*

V. 16. *The sluggard is wiser in his own Conceit, than seven Men that can render a Reason.* חכם עצל בעיניו — משבעה משיבי טעם :] As Self-Conceit does not properly enter into the Character of the Sluggard, what is here said must I think be understood with reference to the two preceding Verses : where it is said " that he continually turneth " upon his Bed as a Door upon it's Hinges, and chooseth to abide in a " reclining Posture upon his Arm, which he can hardly be prevailed " upon through Hunger to draw off from that Posture, in order to " feed himself — Then follows — Even though seven (or any Number " of) wise Men were to endeavour to argue with him on the Immora- " lity of these Proceedings, he will not suffer their Counsel to have " any Effect ;" so prevalent are inveterate Habits. Or the Meaning may be, that he adheres to his own Opinion more obstinately than seven Men of Judgment, because he will not give himself the Trouble to examine it.

V. 18. *As a mad Man who casteth Firebrands, Arrows, and Death.* כמתלהלה הירה זקים הצים ובות :] *Arrows and Death* are here put by an Hendyadis

Hendyadis for DEADLY ARROWS, in the fame Manner as Pſ. CVII.10. *being bound in Affliction and Iron:* the Hebrews, having few Adjectives, frequently ſupply their Place by uſing Subſtantives expreſſive of Qualities in the Abſtract. Note, this and the next Verſe properly make but one.

V. 23. *Burning Lips and a wicked Heart* — שפתים דלקים ולב רע] Rather —— WARM LIPS &c. or " Lips full of Expreſſions of the " warmeſt Friendſhip."

—— like a *Potſherd covered with Silver Droſs.* כסף סינים מצפה: על חרש] Literally, *like the Silver of Droſs laid on a Potſherd,* or *broken Veſſel.* So the warm Lips, though they may at firſt deceive by a falſe Appearance, will ſoon diſcover the Wickedneſs of the Heart, as what ſeemed to be Silver, on Examination, turns out to be only Droſs.

V. 25. *When he ſpeaketh fair* —— כי יחנן קולו] Rather — WHEN HIS VOICE IS GRACIOUS.

—— *for* there are *ſeven Abominations in his Heart.* כי שבע תועבות בלבו] Rather — FOR HE IS FULL OF ABOMINATIONS IN HIS HEART.

V. 26. *Whoſe Hatred is covered by Deceit* — תכסה שנאה במשאון] Rather --- HE THAT COVERETH HATRED WITH TRANQUILLITY; for that ſeems to be the Senſe of במשאון in this Place, from the Verb שאן, *to be tranquil.* תכסה is here conſidered as if written הכסה; for all the oriental and all the Greek Verſions ſeem to have ſo read.

V. 28. *A lying Tongue hateth* thoſe that are *afflicted by it* ; לשון שקר ישנא דכיו] All the ancient Verſions render this Place thus —— A LYING TONGUE HATETH TRUTH: whence I conjecture that, inſtead of דכיו, they read דכיות, PURE THINGS ; for ſo the Word ſignifies both in Chaldee and Syriac.

CHAP. XXVII.

V. 6. — *but the Kiſſes of an Enemy are deceitful.* ונעתרות נשיקות שונא:] As there is no Authority for rendering נעתרות *deceitful,* I would either adopt the marginal Lection EARNEST, or FREQUENT, or, give it the Senſe, which Taylor does from Schultens, *viz.* FETID, VIRULENT, POISONOUS.

V. 8.

V. 8. *As a Bird wandereth from her Neſt* ; *ſo* is *a Man that wandereth from his Place.* : כצפור נודדת מן נקה — כן איש נודד ממקומו]
Place ſeems here too general an Expreſſion : the Word I think ought
to be rendered FROM HIS HOME, or HOUSE, as 1 Sam. II. 20. and
2 Chron. XXV. 10. or perhaps FROM HIS POST or STATION.

V. 9. — *ſo* doth *the Sweetneſs of a Man's Friend by hearty Counſel.*
: ומתק רעהו מעצת נפש] Rather — SO THE COUNSEL OF THE
SOUL DELIGHTETH (or, IS SWEET TO) IT'S FRIEND : or as
נפש is of the common Gender, and not unfrequently uſed for a *Man*,
this Hemiſtic may be rendered, SO THE COUNSEL OF A MAN DE-
LIGHTETH HIS FRIEND.

V. 10. *Thine own Friend, and thy Father's Friend forſake not* ;
neither go into thy Brother's Houſe in the Day of thy Calamity : רעך
ורעה אביך אל תעזב — ובית אחיך אל תבוא ביום אידך] The Note
in the old Verſion upon *the Day of thy Calamity* is, " truſt not in any
" human Help." But I imagine the Meaning to be, " have Recourſe ra-
" ther in Times of Adverſity to a ſincere Friend of thy Father's, or of
" thine own, than to a Brother :" for it follows, *better* is *a Neighbour*
that is *near than a Brother far off* ; *i.e.* " even a good Neighbour that
" is ready at hand to aſſiſt, is preferable to a Brother, who keeps at a
" Diſtance, regardleſs of thy Trouble." See the Note Ch. XVIII. 19,
24. and XIX. 7.

V. 12. *A prudent* Man *foreſeeth the Evil,* — ערום ראה רעה] The
three connexive Particles, which the Tranſcriber has omitted in this
Verſe, are found Ch. XXII. 3.

V. 14. *He that bleſſeth his Friend with a loud Voice, riſing early in
the Morning, it ſhall be counted a Curſe to him.* מברך רעהו בקול גדול
: בבקר — השכים קללה תחשב לו] Rather — HE THAT SALUTETH
HIS FRIEND WITH A LOUD VOICE, RISING EARLY, IT SHALL
BE REPUTED TO HIM A LIGHT THING. See ברך and קלל, which
have theſe Senſes, *i.e.* " He who is over ſedulous and officious in his
" Attention upon his Friend creates a Suſpicion that he is hereby more
" influenced by private Views, than by his Friend's Welfare."

V. 16. *Whoſoever hideth her, hideth the Wind, and the Ointment of
his right Hand, which bewrayeth itſelf.* צפניה צפן רוח — ושמן ימינו
: יקרא] If we here read ריח for רוח, we may render — WHOSOEVER
HIDETH HER, HIDETH A SMELL, WHICH THE OINTMENT about

IIIS

HIS RIGHT HAND PROCLAIMETH. Or without reference to the contentious Woman, by reading צפן ירד (according to the MS. Interpretation of an ingenious Friend) thus—THE LORD LAYETH UP THE NORTH WIND, AND CALLETH FORTH THE PLENTEOUS SOUTH WIND: *i.e.* "He ruleth over fecond Caufes, and directeth them to "their due Effects."

V. 17. *Iron ſharpeneth Iron; ſo a Man ſharpeneth the Countenance of his Friend.* : ברזל בברזל יחד—ואיש יחד פני רעהו] Rather — As IRON IS SHARPENED BY IRON, SO A MAN IS SHARPENED BY THE COUNTENANCE OF HIS FRIEND: *i.e.* receives Alacrity and Spirits.

V. 19. *As in Water Face* anſwereth *to Face, ſo the Heart of a Man to a Man.* : כמים הפנים לפנים—כן לב האדם לאדם] Rather, I think --- AS THE FACE IS TO THE FACE IN WATER, SO IS THE HEART OF A MAN TO A MAN: That is (I apprehend) "the Actions of a Man ſhew as much his Heart, as the Reflection of "Water ſhews his Countenance."

V. 21. As *the fining Pot for Silver, and the Furnace for Gold; ſo is a Man to his Praiſe.* : מצרף לכסף וכור לזהב—ואיש לפי מהללו] Rather, I think---AS THE FINING POT TO SILVER, AND THE FURNACE TO GOLD, SO IS A MAN WITH RESPECT TO THE SPEECH OF HIM THAT PRAISETH HIM. That is (I imagine) "a Man's real "Character proves whether the Encomiaſt be a Flatterer or not."

V. 22. *Though thou ſhouldeſt bray a fool in a Mortar, among Wheat with a Peſtil, &c.* — אם תכתוש את האויל—במכתש בתוך הריפות בעלי ["ונו] Here we have no leſs than four Words that may be conſidered as απαξ λεγ. The Signification of the Verb כתש and it's Derivative מכתש may be aſcertained from the Chaldee and Syriac; the Verb ſignifies *to bruiſe* or *beat,* כתיש is *a Veſſel,* or *Fat, in which the Grapes are gently bruiſed before they are put in the Preſs.* הריפות is derived from רוף, which alſo ſignifies *to bruiſe,* and בעלי (which is rendered *with a Peſtil,* without any Sort of Authority that I can find) I conſider as an Error for בעלו or בעליו, compoſed of ב, עלי and the Affix. The Senſe therefore of this Place ſeems to be this—THOU MAYEST BRUISE A FOOL IN A FAT BY MEANS OF STAMPINGS UPON HIM &c. This ſeems to be the ſame Sentiment as that of Horace, *viz.*

Naturam expellas furca licet, uſque recurret.

V. 23.

V. 23. *Be thou diligent to know the State of thy Flock :* ידע הדע פני
צאנך] Our Version seems here to go too wide from the Text, which
is literally, *Knowing know thou the Faces of thy Sheep ;* and seems to
signify—"Be thou particularly acquainted with every one of thy Sheep."
It is remarkable that some Shepherds will know every Sheep in very
large Flocks merely by *their Faces.*

V. 24. *For Riches* are *not for ever : and doth the Crown* endure *to*
every Generation ? : כי לא לעולם הסן — ואם נזר לדור לדור (ו)דור] Rather
FOR RICHES are NOT FOR EVER ; NEITHER SURELY ARE THEY
APPROPRIATED FROM GENERATION TO GENERATION. It is
doubtless better to consider נזר as a Verb in this Place, which is wanted,
than to construe it *a Crown,* which is quite foreign to the Subject.

C H A P. XXVIII.

V. 2. *For the Transgression of a Land many* are *the Princes thereof :*
בפשע ארץ רבים שריה] Thus God says in Isaiah—— *I will give*
Children to be their Princes, and Babes shall rule over them, Ch. III. 4, 12.
—— *but by a Man of Understanding* and *Knowledge the State* thereof
shall be prolonged. : ובאדם מבין ידע כן יאריך] Rather perhaps —
SHALL OBTAIN RELIEF : for the Verb ארך has that Sense in Arabic,
and ארכה et ארוכה signify both *Health* and *a Cure.*

V. 3. *A poor Man that oppresseth the poor* —— גבר רש ועשק דלים]
Rather --- A MAN IN POWER THAT IS NEEDY AND OPPRESS-
ETH THE POOR.

V. 4. *They that forsake the Law praise the wicked :* — עזבי תורה
יהללו רשע] That is, they countenance them in their Iniquity, in
the same Manner as *they that keep the Law* are said *to contend with*
them, i. e. *reprove them.*

V. 12. — *but when the wicked rise, a Man is hidden.* ובקום רשעים
יחפש אדם :] Rather (as at Verse 28.) —MEN HIDE THEMSELVES,
viz. for Fear.

V. 21. *To have respect of Persons is not good ; for for a Piece of*
Bread that *Man will transgress.* הכר פנים לא טוב — ועל פרת לחם
יפשע גבר :] The latter Hemistic ought I think to be rendered interrogatively --- AND FOR A PIECE OF BREAD SHOULD A MAN
TRANSGRESS ?

L l

C H A P.

CHAP. XXIX.

V. 4. *The King by Judgment ſtabliſheth the Land. but he that re-ceiveth Gifts overthroweth it.* מלך במשפט יעמיד ארץ — ואיש תרומות יהרסנה:] The Word תרומית is doubtleſs a Miſtake for הרכית, *Fraud* or *Deceit:* for the firſt ſignifies only *Oblations*, or Gifts offered with a religious View; but is never uſed in a bad Senſe for *Bribes.* The Chaldee, Syriac, LXX, and Arabic, read תרמית; for which Rea-ſon I would render with them — BUT THE FRAUDULENT MAN &c.

V. 6. *In the Tranſgreſſion of an evil Man there is a Snare.* — בפשע איש רע מוקש] Rather — THE WICKED MAN IS ENSNARED BY TRANSGRESSION: thus theſe Words are rendered, Ch. XII. 13. See Ch. XXII. 25.

V. 7. — but *the wicked regardeth not to know* it. רשע לא יבין דעת:] Rather --- but THE WICKED REGARDETH NOT KNOWLEDGE.

V. 8. *Scornful Men bring a City into a Snare:* — אנשי לצון יפיחו קריה] Rather — INFLAME A CITY; *i. e.* occaſion Tumults and Diſcords; or SET A CITY ON FIRE, by blowing the Fire of the Divine Wrath upon it. The next Hemiſtic countenances either of theſe Senſes.

V. 9. *If a wiſe Man contendeth with a fooliſh Man, whether he rage or laugh, there is no Reſt.* איש הכם נשפט את איש אויל — ורגז ושחק ואין נחת:] Rather — A WISE MAN CONTENDETH WITH A FOOL; AND WHETHER HE RAGE OR LAUGH, HE IS NOT DISMAYED: that is, "the wiſe will continue to reprove the fool, whether he be " angry or laugh at his Admonitions." נחת is here conſidered as the *Niphal* of חתת.

V. 13. *The poor and the deceitful Man meet together : the Lord lighteneth both their Eyes.* רש ואיש תככים נפשו — מאיר עיני שניהם יהוה:] Rather — THE POOR AND OPPRESSED MAN &c. For, that theſe Words are not in Oppoſition, but are to be conſidered rather as ſynonymous, the latter Hemiſtic ſhews. The Word תככים oc-curs only in this Place: as it has no Root in Hebrew, the Senſe given to it here is borrowed from the Chaldee and Syriac.

V. 18. *Where there is no Viſion, the People periſh :* — באין חזון יפרע עם] Rather — WHERE there is NO INSTRUCTION, THE PEOPLE

ARE

STRIPPED. See הון joined to תורה, in the fame Manner as here, Ezek. VII. 26 : and the ufual Signification of the Verb הור in Job is *To underftand, to have learned* &c. Ch. XV. 17. XXVII. 12. &c.

V. 21. *He that delicately bringeth up his Servant from a Child, fhall have him become his Son at the length.* מפנק מנער עבדו — ואהריתו יהיה מנון :] Rather — SHALL HAVE HIM WEAK AT LAST ; for fo مَفْنُون fignifies, this Word occurring nowhere elfe in Hebrew ; it does not feem to have any Affinity with נין *a Son;* neither do any of the ancient Verfions give it that Senfe.

V. 25. —— *but whofo putteth his Truft in the Lord fhall be fafe.* ובוטח ביהוה ישגב :] Rather — SHALL BE EXALTED.

CHAP. XXX.

V. 1. *The Words of Agur the Son of Jakeh, even the Prophecy:* דברי אגור בן יקה המשא] Rather — THE WORDS OF AGUR, THE SON OF JAKEH, THE CHARGE (or, LESSON) which HE SPAKE &c. fo alfo in the next Ch. V. 1. — THE LESSON WHICH KING LEMUEL'S MOTHER TAUGHT HIM. משא is ufed frequently by the Prophets to fignify *what they were charged with,* and thence called *a Burden.* — *the Man fpake unto Ithiel, even unto Ithiel* — נאם הגבר לאיתיאל לאיתיאל] This Repetition of the Word *Ithiel* is doubtlefs an Error of the Tranfcriber ; for the two Words are not even joined by the connexive Particle, neither do any of the old Verfions (except the Chaldee) acknowledge more than one of them.

V. 2. *Surely I am more brutifh than any Man :* — כי בער אנכי מאיש] Rather — THAN ANY ONE, as איש frequently fignifies ; and becaufe אדם follows, which is rendered *Man* immediately after.

V. 3. — *nor have the Knowledge of the holy.* ודערת קדשים ארע :] Rather --- (with the old Verfion) NOR HAVE ATTAINED TO THE KNOWLEDGE OF HOLY THINGS : for *holy Things* correfponds better with *Wifdom* in the preceding Hemiftic ; and *holy Men* would have been expreffed by קדושים.

V. 4. — *who hath bound the Waters in a Garment ?* מי צרר מים בשמלה] So Job talking of the Sea fays — *when I made the Cloud*

the

the GARMENT *thereof, and thick Darkneſs* A SWADDLING BAND *for it.* Ch. XXXVIII. 9. See alſo Iſa. XL. 12.

—— *what is his Name, and what is his Son's Name, if thou canſt tell?* [מה שמו ומה שם בנו כי תדע׃] Some of the Fathers thought that Agur here referred to God *the Father* and *his only begotten Son*; and interpreted alſo the latter Clauſe of V. 19. of *the Incarnation* of the ſame Divine Perſon: but this Senſe ſeems inconſiſtent with what he ſays in his *Exordium*, V. 2, 3: beſides that it would imply a Degree of Communication of Divine Truths beyond what Providence choſe to reveal in ſo early a Period by any of his Prophets. I ſhould therefore underſtand the Phraſe, *what is his Son's Name*, to ſignify only in general, "What are his Connections, or the Name of his "Family?" For before the Introduction of Sirnames, it was uſual among moſt Nations, and among the Jews particularly, to diſtinguiſh the Son by the Father's Name. Or if the Son happened to be of greater Eminence than the Father, the Addition of the Son's Name was made Part of the Father's Deſcription; as *Ham, the Father of Canaan*, Gen. IX. 18. *Kiſh, Saul's Father*, 1 Sam. IX. 3. *Obed, the Father of Jeſſe, the Father of David*, Ruth. IV. 17. &c.

V. 9. — *and take the Name of my God* in vain. [ותפשתי שם אלהי׃] There is nothing wanting in the Text to complete the Senſe; for the Verb תפש ſometimes ſignifies *to lay hold with Violence*, right or wrong. I would therefore render --- LEST I VIOLATE (or, PROFANE) THE NAME OF MY GOD; *i. e.* ſwear audaciouſly and preſumptuouſly. See Taylor.

V. 13. There is *a Generation, O how lofty are their Eyes!* דור מה [רמו עיניו] Rather ſurely — There is A GENERATION WHOSE EYES ARE LOFTY: for מה is here a Relative undeclined; but the ſubſequent Affix gives it the Force of the Genitive.

V. 15. *The Horſeleech hath two Daughters,* crying, *Give, give.* [לעלוקה שתי בנות הב הב] Or — THE HORSELEECH HATH TWO DAUGHTERS, *viz.* GIVE, GIVE: or each of whom is called *Hab*, that is, *Give*. By this Image the Inſatiableneſs of Avarice is ſtrongly painted.

V. 19. — *the Way of a Serpent upon a Rock,* — [דרך נחש עלי צור] A Serpent ſeems here ſpecified rather than any other Animal; becauſe he would be more likely to diſcover himſelf by the Marks left behind him

him upon the Duſt: but upon a Rock he leaves no more Traces of his Track, than the Eagle in the Air, or the Ship in the Sea.

—— *and the Way of a Man with a Maid.* ‏ורדך גבר בעלמה׃‏] Agur's Meaning ſeems to be, not that the Tokens of Virginity were fallacious, as ſome have thought; but, as the next Verſe ſhews, that a Man could no more diſcover by his Wife when ſhe had been unfaithful to the Marriage Bed, than he could diſcern the Path of the Eagle through the Air, &c.

V. 20. — *ſhe eateth and wipeth her Mouth* —— ‏אכלה ומהתה פיה‏] A modeſt Way of expreſſing her unlawful Commerce.

V. 22. — *and a fool when he is filled with Meat.* ‏ונבל כי ישבע‏ ‏לחם׃‏] That is, a Man of no Principles, in affluent Circumſtances and pampered, is to be conſidered as a Peſt to Society.

V. 24. — *but they* are *exceeding wiſe.* ‏והמה חכמים מחכמים׃‏] Rather --- BUT THEY ARE WISER THAN THE WISE.

V. 25. *The Ants are a People not ſtrong*; — ‏הנמלים עם לא עז‏] So Phocylides in his *Carm. admonit.*
—— ΦΥΛΟΝ δ᾽ΟΛΙΓΟΝ τελεθει πολυμεχθον
And Ælian calls them likewiſe a *People,* ΔΗΜΟΣ. *Lib.* VI. *Cap.* 43. So Joel, Ch. I. V. 6. calls the Locuſts, *a Nation.*

V. 26. *The Conies* are but *a feeble Folk, yet they make their Houſes in the Rocks.* ‏שפנים עם לא עצום‏ — ‏וישימו בסלע ביתם׃‏] Rather — THE MOUNTAIN-MICE, though A PEOPLE NOT STOUT ----: for this is not true of *Rabbits,* who burrow in the Ground only: but the other Animal is found in the Crevices and Interſtices of Rocks. See Bochart's *Hieroz.* and Shaw's Travels.

V. 27. — *yet go they forth all of them by Bands.* ‏ויצא חצץ כלו׃‏] ‏חצץ‏ ought I think to be rendered TO PLUNDER, or TO DESTROY.

V. 28. *The Spider taketh hold with her Hands* — ‏שממית בידים תתפש‏] This Animal is not *the Spider,* but *the Stellio,* (according to moſt of the old Verſions) which is a Species of the *Lizard,* whoſe fore Paws, ſays Bochart, are not unlike a Man's Hand, which it uſes very dexterouſly; and, on account of it's Smalneſs, might as well be in Palaces as the Spider.

V. 29.

V. 29. *There be three* Things *which go well, yea, four* are *comely in going.* : שלשה המה מיטיבי צעד — וארבעה מטבי לכת] This is the fifth Time that Agur uses this Mode of Expression in the Compass of a few Verses: it is not inelegant in itself, but may perhaps be thought to recur too often. The Phrases מיטיבי צעד and מטבי לכת are equivalent, and mean *moving* or *advancing in a stately and majestic Manner.*

V. 31. *A Greyhound;* זרזיר מתנים] In the Margin — *A Horse:* but neither of these Animals seem here to be meant. All the ancient Interpreters, both Eastern and Greek, agree in the same Signification, *viz.* that of A COCK. But what the Description, *girt in the Loins,* implies, it is difficult to account for. Our Translators fixed upon *a Greyhound* and *a Horse,* from *their Speed:* but that Idea is foreign to the Purpose. The Syriac seems to have read זר זור instead of זרזיר; זר signifying *a Crown* or *Crest,* gave the Name I imagine to that Bird. If this Reading be admitted, the Words may be rendered — THE COCK, PROUDER THAN A WHALE: which Creature, conscious of it's great Strength, must necessarily look with Disdain on inferior Animals.

V. 32. — lay *thine Hand upon thy Mouth.* : יד לפה] Rather — let THE HAND be UPON THE MOUTH; for there is no Pronoun in the Text. In Judges we have the same Phrase more fully expressed, *viz.* חרש שים ידך על פיך, Ch. XVIII. 19.

CHAP. XXXI.

V. 2. *What, my Son? and what, the Son of my Womb? and what, the Son of my Vows?* : מה ברי ומה בר בטני — ומה, בר נדרי] Our Version is here almost unintelligible for Want of supplying a Verb in one of these elliptical Expressions. It would doubtless be better to render the Verse in some such Manner — WHAT shall I say, MY SON? OR WHAT, O SON OF MY WOMB? OR WHAT, O SON OF MY VOWS?

V. 4. — it is *not for Kings to drink Wine, nor for Princes strong Drink.* : אל למלכים שתו יין — ולרוזנים או שכר] Our Version intirely omits the Word או, or אי, as written in the Massora; which appears to be defective for אוה, in the same Manner as שתו, for שתות. This Place ought therefore to be rendered — it is NOT FOR

KINGS

KINGS TO DRINK WINE; NOR FOR PRINCES TO COVET STRONG
DRINK.

V. 21. —— *for all her Houſhold are clothed with Scarlet.*] שׁנים
would be more properly rendered DOUBLE GARMENTS, as theſe are
a better Security againſt the Cold than *Scarlet.*

V. 28. — *her Huſband alſo, and he praiſeth her.*   ;בעלה ויהללה]
Our Tranſlators by adding here the Word *alſo* ſeem to have thought
that there was ſomething wanting in the Text : and doubtleſs there is,
for the Hemiſtic is too ſhort by one Word, and the Order of the two
remaining Words plainly ſhew it.   They ſeem to have judged that it
was וקם that was defective : but, beſides that it is not ſuitable to the
Dignity of the Huſband *to ariſe,* in token of Subjection, to *the Wiſe,*
the Arabic Verſion has preſerved the Word ſought for : for we read
there —— رجلها ايضا ومدحها —— *her Huſband praiſeth her and*
applaudeth her : whence it is probable, that the Text was read thus
—— ויודה בעלה ויהללה.

V. 29. *Many Daughters have done virtuouſly, but thou excelleſt them*
all.]   This muſt neceſſarily be ſuppoſed to be ſaid by the Huſband, as
the Words immediately preceding intimate.   The Word *ſaying,* ſo frequently omitted in the Text, ought therefore to precede this Verſe.

V. 30. — but *a Woman that feareth the Lord, ſhe ſhall be praiſed.*]
The Picture which is drawn in this Chapter of a good Houſewife is
perhaps the moſt finiſhed of all Antiquity.   It is drawn at full Length,
and equally pleaſing in every Point of View.   The Character which
Iſchomachus gives of his Wife in Xenophon's Oeconomics is alſo very
engaging, and very ſimilar in moſt reſpects to this Child of Fancy,
which Solomon's Mother produced, in order to engage him in the
Search of ſuch a one to bleſs himſelf with.   But by neglecting this
pious Advice, his Wives and Concubines made him drink deep of the
Cup of Bitterneſs, ſhook his Throne, and from the moſt exalted Pitch
of Wiſdom reduced him to the Condition *of the Beaſts that periſh.*

CRITICAL REMARKS

ON THE

BOOK OF ECCLESIASTES.

CHAPTER I.

VERSE 9. — *and* there is *no new Thing under the Sun.* כל ואין
הרש תהרת השמש [: This Expression of the Preacher is not to be
understood in any other Sense than as a general Inference from what
he had said, *viz.* that there is nothing among the *Phænomena* of Nature, which happens now otherwise than it has done for some Generations before : and in the moral World, Men being subject to the same
Passions and Affections now as heretofore, it is no wonder the same
Causes should operate in the Production of like Effects.

V. 11. There is *no Remembrance of former* Things ; —— זכרון אין
[לראשנים That is, "Many past Events are totally buried in Obli-
" vion, and the Circumstances of other Facts are at a distant Period
" quite forgotten."

V. 13. *And I gave my Heart to seek* — לרדוש לבי את ונתחי [ונתחי
here and at V. 17. ought to be rendered —AND I APPLIED MY HEART.

V. 18. *For in much Wisdom is much Grief ; and he that increaseth
Knowledge, increaseth Sorrow.* רב חכמה ברב כי — דעת ויוסיף
[יוסיף מכאוב : What Solomon declares here may seem at first Sight
contradictory to his Assertion, Prov. III. 17, 18. that the *Ways of
Wisdom are Ways of Pleasantness,* &c. But it is evident that there he
means a *practical Wisdom,* or Religious Life ; and here *the Improvements of Science,* in which at least he appears to have excelled all his
cotemporaries.

Cotemporaries. Now, though every speculative Man must have experienced much Pleasure on the Discovery of Truth, yet he must confess that the Investigation of it is replete with Trouble and Anxiety, and that after long and painful Researches he frequently finds he has been pursuing a vain Phantom.

Chap. II.

V. 2. *I said of Laughter, It is mad; and of Mirth, What doeth it?*] לשחוק אמרתי מהולל — ולשמחה מה זה עשה: Or thus, with most of the old Versions — I said to Laughter, O thou fool! and to Mirth, Why doest thou that?

V. 3. *I sought in mine Heart to give myself unto Wine* — תרתי בלבי למשוך ביין את בשרי [Rather perhaps —— I purposed in mine Heart to gratify mine Appetite with Wine.

V. 8. — *I gat me Men-Singers and Women-Singers, and the Delights of the Sons of Men, as musical Instruments, and that of all Sorts.* עשיתי לי שרים ושרות—ותענגות בני האדם—שדה ושדות: [The Text seems corrupt in the two last Words before us; for what can a Singular and a Plural of the same Signification, thus joined together, mean; as, in the Margin of our Version, *musical Instrument and Instruments?* It is evident to me from the Agreement in all the ancient Versions, both Eastern and Greek, that they read ומשקים ומשקות, or contractedly ושקים ושקות — And Men and Women Cupbearers.

V. 12. — *for what can the Man do that cometh after the King? even that which hath already been done.* — כי מה האדם שיבא אחרי המלך את אשר כבר עשוהו: [The Syriac and Vulgate read here עשהו: according to them this Place may be rendered — But what is Man, that he should go against that King, even Him who long since made him? That is, "Why should Man take Pleasure in "Madness and Folly against the positive Commands of his Creator?" See אחרי thus used, Noldius, 5.

V. 16. — *seeing that which now is in the Days to come shall all be forgotten* · — בשכבר הימים הבאים הכל נשכח] Rather — Seeing that now the Days will come, when all shall be forgotten.

M m

—— and

—— *and how dieth the wife* Man ? *as the fool.* זאיך ימות החכם
עם הכסיל:] Rather, I think, without Interrogation, thus — AND
THE WISE DIETH IN THE SAME MANNER AS THE FOOL. So this
Particle is ufed, Ruth. III. 18. and ϖως likewife, Joh. XI. 36.

V. 18. *Yea, I hated all my Labour, which I had taken under the
Sun : becaufe I fhould leave it unto the Man that fhall be after me.*]
This is fo felfifh and narrow a Principle, that we cannot fuppofe Solo-
mon ever entertained it himfelf. I am perfuaded that he is here enu-
merating the different Purfuits of different Men after Happinefs. The
Ufe of the firft Perfon is common in moft Languages ; and is juftly
deemed the moft elegant and delicate Way of conveying Reproof. The
Line of Diftinction, which he feems to draw, is, I apprehend, at the
Epiphonema, which recurs fo frequently, viz. *This is alfo Vanity.*

V. 25. *For who can eat, or who elfe can haften* hereunto, *more than I ?*
כי מי יאכל ומי יחוש חוץ ממני:] The Tranflation of the old Verfion
is, *For who could eat, and who could hafte to outward Things, more
than I ?* But I much doubt whether the Words can bear either of
thefe Senfes ; and neither of them feems to be much to the Purpofe.
The LXX, Syriac, and Arabic read ממנו ; but what Verb they had
inftead of יחוש I know not : they however render it *drink,* viz *For
who can eat and drink without him,* i. e. *God,* juft before mentioned.
It is not improbable that יחצר was the Lection ; for Symmachus and
the Vulgate favour it. I would therefore adopt it, and render — FOR
WHO CAN EAT, OR WHO CAN DISTRIBUTE ABROAD, WITHOUT
HIM ? that is, " who is there that can fay he has not only enough to
" fupply his own Wants, but alfo to relieve the Wants of others,
" without being indebted to Providence for it ?" By admitting this
Senfe, we need not fupply a Subject, as our Verfions do, at the Beginning of the next Verfe.

C H A P.   III.

V. 11. — *alfo he hath fet the World in their Heart, fo that no one
can find out the Work that God maketh* — גם את העלם נתן בלבם
מבלי אשר לא ימצא האדם — את המעשה אשר עשה האלהים] Rather --- BUT HE HATH SET THEIR YOKE ON THEIR HEART, SO
THAT &c. that is (I apprehend) " God has fo circumfcribed the Fa-
" culties of Man, that he cannot thoroughly comprehend the Nature
                                                              " of

"of final Caufes:" the *Heart* as often denoting *the Faculties of the Mind* as *the Affections*. The Phrafe—*to fet a Yoke on the Heart*—occurs I believe nowhere elfe in Scripture; neither do we meet in any other Place with the Expreffion of *fetting the World in the Heart*: befides that this Place is the only one where עלם fignifies *the World*, according to the Hebrew Writers; in all other Places it means *Time* or *Eternity*. In our Verfion indeed it is thus rendered, Ifaiah LXIV. 4. *Yoke* in this Verfe feems to imply the fame as *Weight*, caufing an *Obftacle*; thus— *the Yoke of my Tranfgreffions*; Lam. I. 14.

V. 12. — *but for* a Man *to rejoice, and to do good in his Life.* כי אם לשמוח ולעשורת טוב בחיו] Rather— BUT FOR A MAN TO REJOICE, AND TO PROCURE HAPPINESS IN HIS LIFE. The next Verfe, relating to fenfual Gratifications, feems to confirm this Senfe.

V. 19. — *as the one dieth, fo dieth the other* — כמות זה כן מות זה] Thefe Infinitives are ufed for Preters: fee Prov. XXV. 3. &c. The Antecedents are *Man* and *Beafts*, which Solomon fays *have all one Breath, fo that a Man hath no Preeminence above a Beaft.* Here he doubtlefs perfonates thofe minute Philofophers, who, like the Sadducees, denied a Refurrection, and took Pleafure in degrading human Nature.

V. 21. *All go unto one Place, all are of the Duft, and all turn to Duft again.*] So the Poets,

Παντα κονις, και παντα γελως, και παντα το μηδεν *Epig. incerti.*
Σιας οναρ ανθρωποι. Pindar.
Pulvis et umbra fumus ——. Hor.
———— *Sed omnes una manet Nox,*
Et calcanda femel via Leti. Ibid. *Lib.* I. *Od.* 28.
Nobis cum femel accidit brevis Lux,
Nox eft perpetua una dormienda. Catul.

CHAP. IV.

V. 1. — *and behold the Tears of fuch as were oppreffed, and they had no Comforter; and on the Side of their Oppreffors there was Power, but they had no Comforter.* — והנה דמעת העשקים —ואין להם מנחם— ומיד עשקיהם כח—ואין להם מנחם] Rather— AND BEHOLD THE TEARS OF THE OPPRESSED, FOR THEY HAD NO COMFORTER, NOR STRENGTH AGAINST THE HAND (or, POWER) OF THEIR OP-
PRESSORS,

PRESSORS, FOR THEY HAD NO COMFORTER. This is an Epizeuxis, not unlike the following Inftance, Virg. Buc. Ecl. VIII. 89.

    Talis amor Daphnim, qualis, cum feffa juvencum
    Per nemora atque altos quærendo bucula lucos ——
    Talis amor teneat, nec fit mihi cura mederi.

V. 3. *Yea, better is* he *than both they, which hath not yet been* —— וטוב משניהם את אשר ערן לא היה] Rather — BUT BETTER is HE THAN BOTH THEY WHO DOTH NOT EXIST : or thus——WITH WHOM PLEASURE HATH NOT BEEN &c. For ערן is nowhere ufed for *yet :* but it fignifies *Delight* or *Pleafure* ; i. e. who has neither experienced Pleafure nor Pain. The Character which Solomon introduces here feems to be that of the *querulous,* who habitually complains of every Thing, and delights in ufing this Paradox, that *Nonentity is preferable to Exiftence.*

V. 5, 6. *The fool foldeth his Hands together, and eateth his own Flefh. Better is an Handful with Quietnefs, than both the Hands full with Travail and Vexation of Spirit.* הכסיל חבק את ידיו — ואכל [את בשרו : טוב מלא כף נחת — ממלא חפנים עמל ורעות רוח: Ra- ther --- THE INACTIVE FOLDETH HIS HANDS TOGETHER, AND CONSUMETH HIS OWN FLESH, faying, BETTER is AN HANDFUL &c. כסיל is fometimes ufed for *dull, unactive, Heavinefs.* See Taylor. Solomon draws here the Portrait of *Envy* and *Lazinefs.* Then follows *Covetoufnefs.* Thus Homer reprefents Bellerophon *confuming his own Soul;* Iliad. z. 202.   Ον θυμον κατεδων, πατον ανθρωπων αλεεινων·
So Horace, *Epift.* I. ii. 57.
    Invidus alterius macrefcit rebus opimis.

V. 8. *There is one* alone, *and there is not a fecond* ; יש אחד ואין שני] Rather --- THERE IS ONE WITHOUT A SECOND, or ANOTHER.
—— *neither* faith he, *For whom do I labour, and bereave my Soul of good ?* ולמי אני עמל — ומחסר את נפשי מטובה :] Our Tranf- lators underftood this as fpoken by the covetous Man : but may it not with as much Propriety be fuppofed to be a Reflection, by way of Epiphonema, made by the Author of this Book on what he had obferved, as the Words that immediately follow ? thus —— BUT FOR WHOM WOULD I thus LABOUR, AND BEREAVE MY SOUL OF GOOD ?

V. 9. *Two* are *better than one ; becaufe they have a good Reward for their Labour.* טובים השנים מן האחד — אשר יש להם שכר טוב בעמלם :]
                                             Rather

Rather --- Two are BETTER THAN ONE; BECAUSE THEY HAVE A GREATER Advantage in their Labour: for this Sense is more confistent with Truth, as well as the Context: and it is well known that the Hebrews are unacquainted with the comparative Degree, which the *Exigentia loci* alone can determine.

V. 14. *For out of Prifon he cometh to reign; whereas alfo he that is born in his Kingdom becometh poor.* — כי מבית הסורים יצא למלך — כי [גם במלכותו נולד רש] As סור and שור are often confounded, I read here הסורים, and render — THOUGH HE COME TO REIGN FROM THE HOUSE OF PRINCES, YET HE WILL CERTAINLY BECOME POOR IN HIS KINGDOM. See the Verb ילד thus ufed, Pf. II. 7. Or thus, according to the Reading of the Text —— FOR HE (the Child mentioned in the preceding Verfe) COMETH TO REIGN FROM THE HOUSE OF THE REVOLTERS, &c. *i. e.* is by a Revolution fet upon the Throne.

V. 15. *I confidered all the living which walk under the Sun, with the fecond Child that fhall fland up in his Stead.* — ראיתי את כל החיים [המהלכים תחת השמש — עם הילד השני — אשר יעמד תחתיו] Here we feem to have an *Hyfteron Proteron*, and a wrong Senfe given to השני. The natural Order and Meaning of the Verfe is, as I conceive, this --- I CONSIDERED THAT ALL THE LIVING UNDER THE SUN WALKED WITH (or, ATTACHED THEMSELVES TO) THE NEXT CHILD, WHO WOULD SUCCEED IN HIS STEAD. The Phrafe *to walk with another* in Scripture denotes *to be obedient to his Will*: thus Enoch is faid to have *walked with God.* Gen. V. 22, 24. So Noah, Gen. VI. 9. That שני is not always ufed for *fecond* appears from V. 8. where it fignifies *another*: that Word is perhaps ufed here in Preference to another Word, to denote that the Heir apparent is *fecond* in Dignity to the reigning Prince; and indeed the Words which immediately follow countenance this Conjecture: but furely it can have no Reference to *the fecond Child,* in Prejudice to his elder Brother; who among the Hebrews, as well as in all other civilifed Countries, was intitled to the Rights of Primogeniture.

V. 16. There is *no End of all the People,* even *of all that have been before them*; *they alfo that come after fhall not rejoice in him.* אין קץ [לכל העם — לכל אשר היה לפניהם — גם האחרונים לא ישמחו בו] I read with the Syriac and Vulgate לפניו, and render — There is NO END OF ALL THE PEOPLE, OF ALL THAT ARE IN HIS PRESENCE:

BUT

BUT THEY THAT COME AFTER WILL NOT REJOICE IN HIM; *i. e.* "The Number of those who from Vanity or Interest pay their "Devotions to the presumptive Heir of the Crown is innumerable: "but it will probably happen, that he, who has been for a Time sur-"rounded with a Troop of flatterers, when he comes to sway the "Sceptre, may make it a *Rod of Iron*, to their Sorrow, and that "of their Posterity." This Prediction was verified in Rehoboam, So-lomon's Son and Successor.

CHAP. V.

V. 1. *Keep thy Foot when thou goest to the House of God,* שמר רגליך [כאשר תלך אל בית האלהים] Rather --- ATTEND TO THY GO-INGS; or KEEP A GUARD ON THY FEET, WHEN &c. *i. e.* "to "thy Affections, or the Dispositions of thy Mind." רגל has this Sense, Job. XXXI. 5. Prov. VI. 8. Isa. LII. 7.

— *than to give the Sacrifice of fools :* — מתת הכסילים זבה] Rather --- THAN TO OFFER with FOOLS A SACRIFICE; for the Order and Form of the Words prevents their being considered as *in regimine*.

V. 3. *For a Dream cometh through the Multitude of Business; and a fool's Voice* is known *by Multitude of Words.* — כי בא החלום ברב ענין וקול כסיל ברב דברים:] Rather --- FOR AS A DREAM COMETH THROUGH A MULTITUDE OF BUSINESS, SO THE VOICE OF A FOOL THROUGH A MULTITUDE OF WORDS. Meaning, that he who talks a great deal will necessarily talk foolishly.

V 4. — *for* he hath *no Pleasure in fools :* כי אין חפץ בכסילים] There ought to be here no Italics; as חפץ is a Verb.

V. 6. *Suffer not thy Mouth to cause thy Flesh to sin;* — אל תתן את פיך להטיא את בשרך] Rather, I think — SUFFER NOT THY MOUTH TO SIN AGAINST THY BODY, *viz.* by rash Vows of Self-Denial, Abstinence, or Mortification, as the preceding Verse seems to shew.

—— *neither say thou before the Angel,* — ואל תאמר לפני המלאך] Rather, I think — NEITHER SAY THOU BEFORE HIM WHO PROVI-DETH FOR THEE. This Periphrasis is explained by the Word *God* in the next Clause, which is exegetical.

V. 7. *For in the Multitude of Dreams and many Words* there are *also* divers *Vanities :* — כי ברב חלמות והבלים ודברים הרבה] Rather — FOR

--- FOR as IN THE MULTITUDE OF DREAMS there are SURELY VANITIES, SO IN MANY WORDS. See Noldius.

V. 8. — *for he that is higher than the highest regardeth; and there be higher than they.* : כי גבה מעל גבה שמר ונבהים עליהם] Rather --- FOR he that is HIGH OBSERVETH him THAT IS HIGHER; AND THERE are HIGHER THAN THEY. That is, it is not to be wondered that a Country should be plundered, when the several Officers are countenanced by their Superiors, and these by the supreme Authority itself. This Sense seems more agreeable to the Context, than to interpret it, with our Version, of the Divine Providence.

V. 10. *He that loveth Silver* &c. ——— אהב כסף וגו׳] Rather — HE THAT LOVETH MONEY.

V. 17. *All his Days also he eateth in Darkness:* — גם כל ימיו בהשך יאכל] Rather —— HE CONSUMETH ALSO ALL HIS DAYS IN DARKNESS.

—— *and he hath much Sorrow and Wrath with his Sickness.* וכעס הרבה וחליו וקצף] Rather — AND ANGER, SICKNESS, AND WRATH MULTIPLY : for הרבה does not seem to be an Adverb here, but the Preter *Hiphil*, as Deut. I. 10. Hos. VIII. 14. which agrees with each of the singular Nouns separately ; and the ו final in וחליו is plainly a Mistake, occasioned by the next Word beginning with the same Letter ; for not one of the ancient Versions acknowledge it.

V. 19. *Every Man also to whom God hath given Riches and Wealth, and hath given him Power to eat thereof, and to take his Portion, and to rejoice in his Labour ; this is the Gift of God.*] Our Version in this Place is scarcely intelligible, the Words not being reducible to a Proposition. How much better is this expressed in the old Version — AND TO EVERY MAN TO WHOM GOD &c ? The same Mode of Expression occurs Ch. VI. 2. and ought to be rendered — To WHOMSOEVER GOD &c.

V. 20. *For he shall not much remember the Days of his Life:* כי לא הרבה יזכר את ימי חיו] Rather in the present Tense —— FOR HE DOTH NOT &c.

—— *because God answereth him in the Joy of his Heart.* כי האלהים מענה בשמחת לבו] Rather --- BECAUSE GOD MINISTRETH GROUND

GROUND FOR THE JOY OF HIS HEART ; *viz.* by the Gifts be-
stowed on him : for this Verb when construed with the Preposition ב
has that Sense.

CHAP. VI.

V. 3. *If a Man beget an hundred Children,* — אם יוליד איש מאה]
Rather --- THOUGH HE BEGET AN HUNDRED MALES ; *i. e.* Sons,
and Grandsons. That this is the Construction of this Place is evident ;
for איש of the preceding Verse is certainly the Nominative, which
would therefore be unnecessarily repeated here ; neither would it in
that Case be placed after the Verb ; and this shews that it is governed
by it in an oblique Case, as it cannot be used *absolutely,* on which account our Version adds the Word *Children.* But איש is here more
proper than בנים ; because it restrains the Offspring to the Issue Male :
and it is well known that in Hebrew this Word is used with any
Number, how great soever.

——— *so that the Days of his Years be many* ; ורב שיהיו ימי שניו]
The Construction here according to the present Reading and Translation is very harsh and ungrammatical, and the Sense a mere Tautology ;
for where is the Difference between *a Man's living many Years,* and
the Days of his Years being many ? But if instead of שיהיו we read שיהו,
which Word is used 1 Sam. XIV. 34. and translated HIS SHEEP,
which may be here taken for SUBSTANCE in general, we shall not
only avoid the Tautology, and remedy the Defects of Construction,
but find a Sense much more suited to the Context ; thus — THOUGH
HE BEGET AN HUNDRED MALES, AND LIVE MANY YEARS, AND
HIS SUBSTANCE BE GREAT all THE DAYS OF HIS LIFE, BUT HIS
SOUL BE NOT FILLED WITH GOOD, AND ALSO HE HAVE NO
BURIAL, &c. Three Species of Good are enumerated, *a numerous
Progeny, long Life,* and *great Possessions, during the whole Course of
that Life* ; in Opposition to these are placed *Want of Contentment* in
this Life, and *Want of Burial* after Death ; which Solomon says are
such Abatements of Happiness, that an Abortion is preferable to Life
in such Circumstances.

V. 5. *Moreover he hath not seen the Sun, nor known* any Thing : —
גם שמש לא ראה ולא ידע] Rather — MOREOVER HE HATH NOT
SEEN NOR KNOWN THE SUN : *i. e.* the Embryo, which can neither
see nor feel it's Influence.

V. 8.

--- For as in the Multitude of Dreams there are surely Vanities, so in many Words. See Noldius.

V. 8. — *for* he that is *higher than the highest regardeth; and* there be *higher than they.* : עליהם ונבהים שמר נבה מעל גבה כי] Rather ---for he that is high observeth him that is higher; and there are higher than they. That is, it is not to be wondered that a Country should be plundered, when the several Officers are countenanced by their Superiors, and these by the supreme Authority itself. This Sense seems more agreeable to the Context, than to interpret it, with our Version, of the Divine Providence.

V. 10. *He that loveth Silver* &c. —— וגו" כסף אהב] Rather— he that loveth Money.

V. 17. *All his Days also he eateth in Darkness :* — בהשך ימיו כל גם יאכל] Rather —— He consumeth also all his Days in Darkness.

—— *and* he hath *much Sorrow and Wrath* with *his Sickness.* וכעם : וקצף וחליו הרבה] Rather — and Anger, Sickness, and Wrath multiply : for הרבה does not seem to be an Adverb here, but the Preter *Hiphil*, as Deut. I. 10. Hof. VIII. 14. which agrees with each of the singular Nouns separately ; and the ו final in וחליו is plainly a Mistake, occasioned by the next Word beginning with the same Letter ; for not one of the ancient Versions acknowledge it.

V. 19. *Every Man also to whom God hath given Riches and Wealth, and hath given him Power to eat thereof, and to take his Portion, and to rejoice in his Labour ; this is the Gift of God.*] Our Version in this Place is scarcely intelligible, the Words not being reducible to a Proposition. How much better is this expressed in the old Version — And to every Man to whom God &c ? The same Mode of Expression occurs Ch. VI. 2. and ought to be rendered — To whomsoever God &c.

V. 20. *For he shall not much remember the Days of his Life :* לא כי חיו ימי את יוכר הרבה] Rather in the present Tense —— For he doth not &c.

—— *because God answereth* him in the *Joy of his Heart.* האלהים כי : לבו בשמחת מענה] Rather --- because God ministreth Ground

GROUND FOR THE JOY OF HIS HEART; *viz.* by the Gifts be-
stowed on him : for this Verb when construed with the Preposition ב
has that Sense.

CHAP. VI.

V. 3. *If a Man beget an hundred Children,* — אם יליד איש מאה]
Rather --- THOUGH HE BEGET AN HUNDRED MALES; *i.e.* Sons,
and Grandsons. That this is the Construction of this Place is evident ;
for איש of the preceding Verse is certainly the Nominative, which
would therefore be unnecessarily repeated here ; neither would it in
that Case be placed after the Verb ; and this shews that it is governed
by it in an oblique Case, as it cannot be used *absolutely,* on which account our Version adds the Word *Children.* But איש is here more
proper than בנים ; because it restrains the Offspring to the Issue Male :
and it is well known that in Hebrew this Word is used with any
Number, how great soever.

———— *so that the Days of his Years be many* ; ורב שיהיו ימי שניו]
The Construction here according to the present Reading and Translation is very harsh and ungrammatical, and the Sense a mere Tautology ;
for where is the Difference between *a Man's living many Years,* and
the Days of his Years being many ? But if instead of שיהיו we read שיהו,
which Word is used 1 Sam. XIV. 34. and translated HIS SHEEP,
which may be here taken for SUBSTANCE in general, we shall not
only avoid the Tautology, and remedy the Defects of Construction,
but find a Sense much more suited to the Context ; thus — THOUGH
HE BEGET AN HUNDRED MALES, AND LIVE MANY YEARS, AND
HIS SUBSTANCE BE GREAT all THE DAYS OF HIS LIFE, BUT HIS
SOUL BE NOT FILLED WITH GOOD, AND ALSO HE HAVE NO
BURIAL, &c. Three Species of Good are enumerated, *a numerous
Progeny, long Life,* and *great Possessions, during the whole Course of
that Life* ; in Opposition to these are placed *Want of Contentment* in
this Life, and *Want of Burial* after Death ; which Solomon says are
such Abatements of Happiness, that an Abortion is preferable to Life
in such Circumstances.

V. 5. *Moreover he hath not seen the Sun, nor known* any Thing :—
גם שמש לא ראה ולא ידע] Rather — MOREOVER HE HATH NOT
SEEN NOR KNOWN THE SUN : *i.e.* the Embryo, which can neither
see nor feel it's Influence.

V. 8.

V. 8. For what hath the wife more than the fool? what hath the poor, that knoweth to walk before the living? כי מה יותר לחכם מן [הכסיל — מה לעני יודע להלך נגד החיים:] The latter Part of this Verſe ſeems to be an Anſwer to the Queſtion propoſed in the former Part, and ought I think to be thus rendered —— THAT WHICH THE POOR HATH, WHO KNOWETH &c. *i. e.* in Point of Morals the wife has no Advantage over the poor who knows and practiſes his Duty.

V. 9. Better is the Sight of the Eyes, than the Wandering of the Deſire: —טוב מראה עינים מהלך נפש [] Rather — BETTER IS THE SIGHT OF THE EYES THAN THE PURSUIT OF THE APPETITE, as Verſe 7. *The Sight of the Eyes* is here uſed by a Metonymy for every Object of Sight, or whatever may be ſeen.

V. 12. For who knoweth what is good for Man in this Life, all the Days of his vain Life which he ſpendeth as a Shadow? כי מי יודע [מה טוב לאדם בחיים מספר ימי חיי הבלו ויעשם כצל] Rather — BUT WHO KNOWETH WHAT IS BETTER IN LIFE FOR A MAN, THAN TO NUMBER THE DAYS OF HIS LIFE &c? that is, to take an Account of them, ſo as to turn them to Profit.

CHAP. VII.

V. 8. Better is the End of a Thing than the Beginning thereof: and the patient &c. טוב אחרית דבר מראשיתו טוב וגו׳ [] The two laſt Words ought to be thus read, מראשית וטוב; and the Verſe thus rendered --- BETTER IS THE END OF A THING THAN THE BEGINNING: AND THE PATIENT &c.

V. 10. Say not thou, What is the Cauſe that the former Days were better than theſe? אל תאמר מה היה שהימים הראשנים היו טובים מאלה [] Rather --- SAY NOT, WHY DOTH IT HAPPEN THAT &c.

V. 11. Wiſdom is good with an Inheritance: and by it there is Profit to them that ſee the Sun. טובה חכמה עם נחלה ויתר לראי השמש: [] Rather, with the Margin --- WISDOM IS AS GOOD AS AN INHERITANCE; NAY BETTER TO THEM &c.

V. 12. For Wiſdom is a Defence, and Money is a Defence: — כי בצל צל [ההכמה בצל הכסף] occurs Numb. XIV. 9. in this Senſe, but

N n

without

without the Prepofition; but the ב is not unfrequently prefixed to the Nominative, as well as other Cafes: fee Exod. XXXII. 22. 1 Kings XIII. 34. Or בצל may fignify the fame as بَضَعٌ, A WEAPON.

—— *but the Excellency of Knowledge is, that Wisdom giveth Life to them that have it.* ויתרון דעת החכמה תחיה בעליה:] Rather — BUT THE EXCELLENT KNOWLEDGE OF WISDOM GIVETH LIFE TO THEM THAT HAVE IT.

V. 13. *Confider the Work of God: for who can make that ſtraight which he hath made crooked?* ראה את מעשה האלהים — כי מי יוכל לתקן את אשר עותו:] Rather — CONSIDER THE WORK OF GOD, WHETHER ANY ONE CAN MAKE STRAIGHT THAT WHICH HE HATH MADE CROOKED. See thefe feveral Particles thus ufed in Noldius's Concordance.

V. 14. *In the Day of Profperity be joyful, but in the Day of Adverfity confider: God alfo hath fet the one over againſt the other, to the End that Man ſhould find nothing after him.* ביום טובה היה בטוב וביום רעה ראה גם את זה לעמת זה עשה האלהים על דברת שלא ימצא האדם אחריו מאומה:] Our Tranflators explain the latter Claufe thus — "That Man ſhould be able to controul nothing in his " (God's) Works." See the Margin of the old Verfion. But that does not feem to be the Meaning, neither will the Words bear that Senfe. I would render them, with all the ancient Verfions, thus — TO THE END THAT MAN MIGHT FIND NO BLAME AGAINST HIM. That is, God hath ordered that Good and Evil ſhould be fo intermixed, that no Man is without his Share of either, and therefore cannot arraign his Providence. מאומה may here fignify *any Thing:* but as מום *Blame* is twice written מאום, it may be alfo confidered as having the paragogic ה: it occurs exactly in this Form and Senfe, 1 Sam. XXIX. 3. and אחריו is here ufed as Lev. XXVI. 33. viz. והריקתי אחריכם חרב —— *and I will unſheath the Sword* AGAINST YOU. See alfo 1 Sam. XIV. 37. &c.

V. 15. *All Things have I feen in the Days of my Vanity:* את הכל ראיתי בימי הבלי] Rather — ALL THIS HAVE I SEEN &c. as Gen. XXIV. 50. מיהוה יצא הדבר — THIS THING *cometh from the Lord.* See alfo Ch. VIII. 9.

—— *there is a juſt* Man *that periſheth in his Righteoufnefs, and there is a wicked* Man *that prolongeth his Life in his Wickednefs.* יש צדיק אבד בצדקו — ויש רשע מאריך ברעתו:] Rather, I think — THERE IS

IS A JUST Man THAT IS DISAPPOINTED IN HIS RIGHTEOUS-
NESS; AND A WICKED Man THAT CONTINUETH LONG IN HIS
WICKEDNESS. אבד has the Senſe of *loſing* or *miſſing the Way of Life
or Happineſs*, Job. VI. 18. Pſ. II. 12. See Taylor. ארך, ſimply, ſignifies to continue long, Ch. VIII. 12.

V. 16. — *why ſhouldeſt thou deſtroy thyſelf?* למה תשומם :] Rather — BE DESOLATE; or *left alone*, as in the Margin, and in the old
Verſion: for a Man *overrighteous* or *overwiſe* (*i. e.* one who carries
his Religion as far as Superſtition, or whoſe Prudence degenerates into
Pyrrhoniſm) bids fair to be forſaken by all his Companions.

V. 18. — *for he that feareth God ſhall come forth of them all.* כי
ירא אלהים יצא את כלם :] Rather — SHALL PROCEED IN (or, AC-
CORDING TO) ALL THESE, viz. *Precepts*. See Noldius, Art. 10 & 19.

V. 25. —— *and to know the Wickedneſs of Folly, even of Fooliſhneſs*
and Madneſs. ולדעת רשע כסל והסכלות הוללות :] The old Verſion is here more agreeable to the Text, *viz*. AND TO KNOW THE
WICKEDNESS OF FOLLY, AND THE FOOLISHNESS OF MADNESS.

V. 26. — *whoſe Heart is Snares and Nets, and her Hands as Bands:*
אשר היא מצורים וחרמים לבה אסורים ידיה] Rather, I think —
WHO HERSELF IS SNARES, WHOSE HEART IS NETS, and WHOSE
HANDS are BANDS: for the Pronoun היא ſeems here to be emphatical.

V. 27. *Behold, this have I found, (ſaith the Preacher) counting* one
by one, to find out the Account. ראה זה מצאתי אמרה קהלת אחת
לאחת למצא השבון :] Rather, I think thus — BEHOLD THIS HAVE
I FOUND, SAITH THE PREACHER, OF ONE WITH THE OTHER,
IN THE END OF THE ACCOUNT. מצא is here conſidered as a Subſtantive derived from יצא, and ſignifying literally the *going forth*. The
ל has the Force of the Prepoſition *in*; or it denotes that the Verb Subſtantive היות is underſtood. *Qu*. ought not we to read אמר הקהלת?

V. 29. *Lo, this only have I found, that God hath made Man upright:*
but they have ſought out many Inventions. לבד ראה זה מצאתי אשר
עשה האלהים את האדם ישר וגו'] Rather, I think, thus — THIS
ONLY BY EXAMINING HAVE I FOUND, THAT GOD HATH MADE
MEN UPRIGHT &c. For ראה is not here I apprehend an Interjection,
or the Imperative; if it were, it would claim the firſt Place in the

Sentence,

Sentence, like הנה; but it is the Participle prefent of the Verb ראה, which has this Senfe, Lev. XIII. 10. &c. and אדם fignifies not only the firſt Man ſo called, or any other particular Man; but alſo the whole Aggregate of Mankind.

CHAP. VIII.

V. 1. —*a Man's Wiſdom maketh his Face to ſhine,* חכמת אדם תאיר פניו] Rather — ENLIGHTENETH HIS FACE, or MAKETH IT GLO-RIOUS; as the Word is rendered in other Places.

—— *and the Boldneſs of his Face ſhall be changed.* [ועז פניו ישנא : Rather --- BUT HE THAT HATH AN IMPUDENT COUNTENANCE SHALL BE HATED: thus עז פנים is rendered, Prov. VII. 13. Here the Prepoſition ב is ſupplied before פניו; the literal Conſtruction being —*He that is impudent in his Face.* In regard to ישנא, it is the regular Future *Niphal* from שנא, as Prov. XIV. 17. which is there rendered in our Verſion HATED: ſo that it is amazing our Tranſlators would prefer to torture this Word by deriving it from שנה; and this too, for the ſake of adopting a worſe Senſe.

V. 2. *I counſel thee to keep the King's Commandment:* אני פי מלך שמר] I think it is more probable that אני is a Miſtake for אנא or אנה, than that a Word ſhould have dropped from the Text; wherefore I would render — KEEP, I PRAY THEE, &c. None of the old Verſions, the Vulgate excepted, ſeem to have had this Word in their Texts.

V. 3. *Be not haſty to go out of his Sight: ſtand not in an evil Thing:* אל תבהל מפניו תלך אל תעמד בדבר רע] Rather — RUSH NOT HASTILY FROM HIS PRESENCE: (viz. *as impatient*) GO THY WAY, STAND NOT IN AN EVIL THING.

V. 6. *Becauſe to every Purpoſe there is Time and Judgment; there-fore the Miſery of Man is great upon him.* — כי לכל חפץ יש עת ומשפט כי רעת האדם רבה עליו :] There ſeems to be no Connection be-tween theſe Clauſes; and for this Reaſon, I imagine, becauſe they are Parts of different Verſes. The firſt ought to be connected with the preceding Verſe, and rendered thus — BECAUSE THERE IS A SEA-SON AND AN ESTABLISHED ORDER FOR EVERY PURPOSE, or PURSUIT; and the latter Clauſe thus --- BUT THE MISERY OF MAN IS GREAT UPON HIM, BECAUSE HE KNOWETH NOT THAT WHICH SHALL BE &c.

V. 12.

V. 12. — *yet surely I know that it shall be well with them that fear God, which fear before him.* כי גם יודע אני אשר יהיה טוב ליראי האלהים אשר יראו מלפניו:] The latter Clause ought I think to be rendered — WHO REVERENCE HIM: for מלפני preceded by the Verb ירא is only an expletive Sign of the Accusative Case : or thus, WHO STAND IN AWE OF HIS PRESENCE, as Jer. V. 22.

CHAP. IX.

V. 1. — *the righteous, and the wise, and their Works* are *in the Hand of God : no Man knoweth Love, or Hatred by all that is before them.* הצדיקים והחכמים ועבריהם ביד האלהים גם אהבה וגם שנאה אין יודע האדם הכל לפניהם:] Rather — THE RIGHTEOUS, AND THE WISE, AND THEIR HOUSHOLDS are IN THE HAND OF GOD ; but MEN KNOW NOT by ALL that is BEFORE THEM EITHER LOVE OR HATRED : *i.e.* "It is impossible for Men to determine by God's "Dispensations of Prosperity or Adversity, whether he love, or do not "love, them who are apparently righteous and wise." From this Circumstance, among others, one might be led to conclude that God's equal Administration of temporal good and evil in the Jewish Commonwealth was at an End, which is generally supposed not to have happened till about the Time of the Babylonish Captivity. For David says expressly that *he* NEVER *saw the righteous forsaken, nor his Seed begging Bread.* P. XXXVII. 25.

V. 3. — *and after that,* they go *to the dead.* ואחריו אל המתים] Rather --- AND PURSUETH THEM TO THE DEAD, *viz.* the Madness just before mentioned.

V. 5. —— *but the dead know not any Thing, neither have they any more a Reward;* והמתים אינם יודעים מאומה — ואין עוד להם שכר] The whole of what is here said from V. 1. to the End of V. 10. I consider as intended to set forth the Principles of *Epicureans* ; (for their System prevailed among the Jews, as well as the Greeks ;) for the Immortality of the Soul seems here to be denied, and at V. 7. an Exhortation begins to the Pursuit of all Manner of sensual Gratifications.

V. 8 *Let thy Garments be always white;*—בכל עת יהיו בגדיך לבנים] *White Clothes* are not only the pleasantest in a warm Country, as was Palestine, but also the most expensive ; as they cannot be worn so long as those of other Colours; Luxury is therefore here combined with Cost. V. 9.

V. 9. Live joyfully with the Wife whom thou lovest all the Days of the Life of thy Vanity, which he hath given thee under the Sun, all the Days of thy Vanity. ראה חיים עם אשה אשר אהבת כל ימי היי הבלך : אשר נתן לך תחת השמש כל ימי הבלך] As none of the ancient Verſions acknowledge the laſt Clauſe, it is probable that it is repeated from the former Part by Miſtake. I would therefore omit it, and render --- ENJOY LIFE (i. e. *indulge*) WITH THE WIFE WHOM THOU LOVEST ALL THE DAYS OF THY VAIN LIFE, WHICH IS GIVEN THEE UNDER THE SUN. The Senſualiſt, in order to paſs over no Incentive to ſtimulate the Paſſions, ſeems here to recommend *Poly-gamy*; for, by recommending *a favourite Wife*, he inſinuates that the Perſon he ſpoke to had *other Wives*, or *Concubines*; a Practice but too much countenanced by Solomon himſelf, and all the opulent in every Part of the Eaſt.

V. 10. Whatſoever thy Hand findeth to do, do it with thy Might : כל אשר תמצא ידך לעשות בכחך עשה] That is, " If there be any " other Means of pleaſing the Senſes not before enumerated that thou " canſt think of, fail not to have Recourſe to it :" *for there is no Work, nor Device, nor Knowledge, nor Wiſdom in the Grave whither thou goeſt, i. e.* (according to the ſame Syſtem) after this Life the Body moulders into Duſt, and the Soul is annihilated.

V. 11. I returned, and ſaw &c.] *Qu.* does it not ſeem that the Author would here be underſtood as giving an Account of a Progreſs he had made in different Parts, and exhibiting the ſeveral ſtriking Characters he had met with in his Tour?

V. 17. The Words of wiſe Men are heard in Quiet, more than the Cry of him that ruleth among fools. דברי הכמים בנחת נשמעים מזעקת מושל בכסילים :] Rather — THE WORDS OF THE WISE OUGHT TO BE HEARD &c. as Mal. I. 6. *A Son honoureth his Father*, for OUGHT TO HONOUR.

V. 18. —— but one Sinner deſtroyeth much good. וחוטא אחד יאבד טובה הרבה :] Rather --- BUT ONE THAT ERRETH in Judg-ment &c. So חטא ſignifies, Job. V. 24.

CHAP. X.

V. 1. Dead Flies cauſe the Ointment of the Apothecary to ſend forth a ſtinking Savour : זבובי מות יבאיש יביע שמן רוקח] Rather ——
DEAD

DEAD FLIES CAUSE A STINKING SAVOUR, and PUTRIFY THE OINTMENT OF THE APOTHECARY; as in the old Verſion. The original Reading was probably יבאישו ויביע‎.

*** HERE the Author, having finiſhed his Excurſion in Queſt of the leading Characters, which have always diſgraced human Nature in all luxurious States, throws off the Maſk, appears in his own Perſon, and from hence to the Cloſe of the Book inculcates grave and ſerious Maxims, ſuggeſting proper Antidotes againſt the Poiſon of ſome of the foregoing Tenets.

V. 11. *Surely the Serpent will bite without Enchantment ; and a Babbler is no better.* [אם ישך הנחש בלוא לחש — ואין יתרון לבעל הלשון:‎] There ſeems to be no ſort of Connection between theſe two Clauſes, as they are tranſlated in our Verſion. The Verſe ought to be rendered ---IF THE SERPENT BITE NOTWITHSTANDING THE ENCHANTMENT, SURELY there is NO ADVANTAGE iɲ AN ENCHANTER: for the *Exigentia loci* thus fixes the Senſe of הלשון לבעל‎; or הלשון‎, by a Tranſpoſition of Letters, may be a Miſtake for להשון‎, as יבחר‎ for יהבר‎ in the laſt Ch. V. 4. The LXX, Aquila, and the Syriac, ſeem to have had this latter Reading in their Texts.

V. 12. — *but the Lips of a fool will ſwallow up himſelf.* ושפחורת‎ [כסיל תבלענו:‎] Rather— WILL DESTROY HIM: thus בלע‎ is rendered in other Places.

V. 15. *The Labour of the fooliſh wearieth every one of them :* עמל‎ [הכסילים תיגענו‎] Rather— WEARIETH HIM ; as in the old Verſion. — *becauſe he knoweth not how to go to the City.* אשר לא ידע ללכת‎ [אל עיר :‎] Rather— WHO KNOWETH NOT (or cannot prevail upoɲ himſelf to take the Trouble to learn) HOW &c. The Phraſe, *how to go to the City,* ſeems to be proverbial, and to denote *a Thing eaſy and obvious.*

V. 16. — *and thy Princes eat in the Morning.* [ושריך בבקר יאכלו :‎] Rather — FEAST &c. for the next Verſe ſhews that this is the Senſe ; and that thoſe Feaſts were attended with Exceſs both in eating and drinking.

V. 20. — *for a Bird of the Air ſhall carry the Voice* כי עיף השמים‎ [יוליך את הקול‎] The repreſenting Fame as endowed with Wings is a fine poetical Image. So Virgil, *Æn.* IV. v. 175.
—— *mox ſeſe attollit in auras* &c.

CHAP.

Chap. XI.

V. 1. *Caſt thy Bread upon the Waters:* — שלח להמך על פני המים] Some Critics underſtand this enigmatical Expreſſion as a Direction to ſow one's Seed in a moiſt Soil: but if that be good Huſbandry, it is not however ſuitable to the Context. The old Verſion ſeems to give the true Meaning, *viz.* " Be liberal to the poor; and though it ſeem " to thee as a Thing ventured on the Sea, yet it ſhall bring thee Profit."

V. 3. *If the Clouds be full of Rain, they empty* themſelves *upon the Earth:* — אם ימלאו העבים—גשם על הארץ יריקו] Rather — IF THE CLOUDS BE FULL, THEY POUR DOWN THE RAIN UPON THE EARTH. This ſeems to intimate, " that the rich ought to dif- " tribute out of their Abundance to the poor." In the ſame Senſe the next Sentence ought, I think, to be underſtood, viz. *where the Tree falleth, there it ſhall be,* i. e. " where a Favour has been conferred, " there it remains, or is not ſoon forgotten."

V. 4. *He that obſerveth the Wind ſhall not ſow &c.* שמר רוח לא יזרע—וגו"] This I apprehend is not to be confined to the mere Let- ter, but to be underſtood as a general Caution againſt Procraſtination.

V. 8. *But if a Man live many Years, and* rejoice in them all: כי אם שנים הרבה יחיה האדם בכלם ישמח] This Verſe, like the next, ought, I think, to be conſtrued as an Irony — BUT IF A MAN LIVE MANY YEARS, LET HIM REJOICE IN THEM ALL.

———*yet let him remember the Days of Darkneſs; for they ſhall be many. All that cometh is Vanity.* ויזכר את ימי ההשך כי הרבה יהיו כל שבא הבל:] Rather, I think — BUT LET HIM REMEMBER THE DAYS OF DARKNESS, THAT THEY ARE MANY, and that ALL THAT COMETH is VANITY.

V. 9. ———*and let thy Heart cheer thee in the Days of thy Youth.*] Theſe Words בימי בחורותיך ought, I think, to be here rendered — IN THY CHOICEST DAYS, particularly as thoſe Words, *in thy Youth,* immediately precede.

Chap. XII.

V. 1. —*while the evil Days come not* — עד אשר לא יבאו ימי הרעה] Rather --- BEFORE THE EVIL DAYS COME; for that is the Force of theſe three Particles thus united.

V. 4.

V. 4. — *and he shall rise up at the Voice of the Bird* — ויקום לקול הצפור] As there is no Antecedent to the Relative in the Text; it would, I think, be best either to supply — AND a Man WILL RISE UP; or construe the Verb imperfonally, *viz.* AND ONE RISETH UP AT THE SINGING OF THE BIRD.

— *and all the Daughters of Musick* — כל בנות השיר] Or — THE WOMEN SINGERS.

V. 5. —— *and the Almond Tree shall flourish:* וינאץ השקד] All Critics agree that this Passage relates to the Infirmities of old Age: but how the Phrase —*the Almond Tree shall flourish* — can possibly imply that " their Heads shall be as white as the Blossoms of an Almond " Tree," as it is explained in the Margin of our old Version, I cannot conceive. No Language I believe can justify such a Figure: neither is it true that the Blossoms of an Almond Tree are white. I would therefore render these Words --- AND HE THAT IS WAKEFUL SHALL BE CONTEMNED; for it is well known that old People sleep little; and that, on account of their Infirmities, they are too often the Sport of the inconsiderate.

—— *and the Grashopper shall be a Burden,* ויסתבל החגב] This Expression is as unintelligible as the preceding one. Jerom had long since affirmed that חגב signified *the Ankle* as well as *a Locust*; and it is evident that this Word in Arabic is used for *the Thigh*: wherefore I would thus translate the Text, with the Chaldee —— AND THE ANKLE SHALL BE A BURDEN TO ITSELF; or unable to support the Burden of the Body.

V. 6. *Or ever the Silver Cord be loosed;* — עד אשר לא ירתק חבל הכסף] By this Figure must, I think, be meant *the Spinal Marrow.*

—— *or the golden Bowl be broken:* — ותרץ גלת הזהב] That is, I imagine, " Before the Head is reduced to a mere empty Scull," not unlike then in Colour to Gold, or in Form to a Bowl.

— *or the Pitcher be broken at the Fountain:* —ותשבר כד על המבוע] Perhaps — " Before the Circulation of the Blood be stopped at the " Heart."

—— *or the Wheel broken at the Cistern.* ונרץ הגלגל אל הבור:] Possibly — " Before the general Dissolution of the whole Mass, Solids " and Fluids."

V. 7. —— *and the Spirit shall return unto God who gave it.* והרוח תשוב אל האלהים אשר נתנה:] Here the Author takes Care that no

O o

one

one might be misled by what had been asserted by those who supposed the Soul became extinct on it's Separation from the Body.

V. 10. — *and* that which was *written* was *upright,* even *the Words of Truth.* וכתוב ישר דברי אמת :] I read with the Syriac and Vulgate וכתב, and construe ישר adverbially, or supply the Preposition ב, thus --- AND HE WROTE PROPERLY THE WORDS OF TRUTH.

V. 11. *The Words of the wise* are *as Goads, and as Nails fastened* by *the Masters of Assemblies,* which *are given from one Shepherd.* דברי [חכמים כדרבנות וכמשמרות נטועים בעלי אספות נתנו מרעה אחד : Rather --- THE WORDS OF THE WISE are AS GOADS, OR AS NAILS that are FASTENED: THE COLLECTORS of them WERE APPOINTED BY ONE SHEPHERD. By Shepherd in this Place our Translators understood *God* to be meant. He is indeed called *the Shepherd of Israel:* but by this Expression Solomon seems to point out himself; for this Title is more than once given to Kings, Isa. XLIV. 28. Ezek. XXXIV. 23. and we know of no other King before him, who collected Proverbs.

CRITICAL REMARKS

ON THE CANTICLES,

OR

THE SONG OF SOLOMON.

CHAPTER I.

VERSE 3. *Because of the Savour of thy good Ointments, thy Name* is as *Ointment poured forth:* [שמן תורק שמך — לריח שמניך טובים Rather --- THY NAME IS AN OINTMENT POURED FORTH, LIKE THE SAVOUR OF THY GOOD OINTMENTS. Thus ל is used, Joſh. VII. 5. 1 Sam. XXV. 37. &c.

V. 4. *Draw me, we will run after thee:* [משכני אחריך נרוצה All the ancient Verſions ſeem to have had theſe Words in their Text, *viz.* בריח שמניך ; for they all add here—*on account of thine Ointments.*

V. 9. *I have compared thee, O my Love, to a Company of Horſes in Pharaoh's Chariots.* [לססתי ברכבי פרעה דמיתיך רעיתי :] The Word לססתי occurs nowhere in SS. in this Form. The ancient Verſions conſider it as the ſingular or plural Feminine with the Aſſix: but I think it may not improperly be conſtrued *as ſpecial* with our Verſion, and of the Maſculine Gender, as if it were written fully, לסוסותים. The Compariſon of a beautiful Woman to a Set of Horſes harneſſed in a Chariot may perhaps appear uncouth to the refined Manners of this Age. But let it be remembered that the Greek and Latin Poets frequently compare the ſame Object to *an Heifer*, a Creature far infe-

rior

rior in refpect to the Comelinefs and Elegance of it's Form : thus Lycophron calls Hellen, Αλεξ. V. 102. (See Potter's Notes.)

Και την ανυμφον ΠΟΡΤΙΝ ——

So V. 857. Εν ειτι ΠΟΡΤΙΣ οςχατον τωξει θεα.

Ovid alfo diftinguifhes her by this Appellation, *Epift. ad Parid.*

Graja JUVENCA *venit, quæ te, patriamque, domumque*
Perdat : Io prohibe ; Graja JUVENCA *venit.*

Nor let it be thought that this Name was given only to *Women of bad Fame* ; and that for this Reafon Io was fuppofed by the Poets to be metamorphofed into *a Cow.* For Sophocles defcribes ευωπις αξρα, *a beautiful, delicate* Virgin,

—— ως ΠΟΡΤΙΣ εςημα· *Trach.* V. 532, 539.

And Euripides calls Polyxena ΜΟΣΧΟΣ, Hecuba, V. 526.

Σκιρτημα ΜΟΣΧΟΥ της καθεξοντες χεροιν.

So Pindar, *Pyth.* Od. IV. v. 253.

Μια ΒΟΥΣ Κρηθει τε ματηρ.

And Horace in like Manner calls a young Woman JUVENCA, *Lib.* II. *Od.* V. and in another Place compares her to A MARE, *Lib.* III. *Od.* II.

Quæ, velut latis EQUA *trima campis,*
Ludit exultim, metuitque tangi,
Nuptiarum expers, et adhuc protervo
Cruda marito.

V. 10. *Thy Cheeks are comely with Rows of* Jewels, *thy Neck with Chains of* Gold. : נאוו לחייך בתורים צוארך בחרוזים] Rather, I think --- THY CHEEKS ARE COMELY WITH ORNAMENTS, THY NECK WITH NECKLACES.

C H A P. II.

V. 7. —*that ye ftir not up, nor awake* my *Love,* אם תעירו ואם תעוררו את האהבה [האהבה being here emphatical wants not the Pronoun : I would therefore render --- NOR AWAKE THAT BELOVED ONE.

V. 8. *The Voice of my beloved!* קול־ דודי] This Place would be more intelligible, were we to fupply, as in the old Verfion —— " It is " *the Voice.*"

V. 11. *For lo, the Winter is paſt, the Rain is over, and gone.* כי הנה
[הסתו עבר — הגשם חלף הלך לו:] The Aſyndeton, as it is in the
Text, would I think be more poetical — THE RAIN IS OVER, IT IS
GONE. So Ch. V. 6.

V. 17. *Until the Day break, and the Shadows flee away:* —— שיפוח
[היום ונסו הצללים] Rather — UNTIL THE DAY BE SPENT &c.
literally, *be out of Breath:* that this is the Senſe is very clear from
the next Clauſe, for in the Abſence of the Sun there is no Shadow;
and, as this Hemiſtic ought to make Part of the foregoing Verſe, it is
farther evident, that it is in *the Day* Time, not in the Night, that *the
beloved* there mentioned *feedeth among the Lillies.* The ſame holds in
reſpect to Ch. IV. 5, 6.

—— *turn my beloved, and be thou like a Roe,* —— [סב דמה לך דודי לצבי]
That is, Come to me with the Swiftneſs of a Roe from thy lurking
Places; V. 14.

CHAP. III.

V. 4. *It was but a little that I paſſed from them, but I found him*
&c. [כמעט שעברתי מהם —— עד שמצאתי וגו"] The old Verſion
ſeems preferable here --- WHEN I HAD PASSED A LITTLE FROM
THEM, THEN I FOUND HIM &c.

V. 10. —— *the Midſt thereof being paved with Love;* [תוכו רצוף האבה]
Rather — BEING WARMED WITH LOVE: for רצף ſignifies *to heat* or
bake with Coals, 1 Kings XIX. 6. and *a live Coal,* Iſa. VI. 6.

CHAP. IV.

V. 3. —— *thy Temples 'are like a Piece of Pomegranate within thy*
Locks. [כפלח הרמון רקתך מבעד לצמתך:] Rather — THY CHEEKS
are LIKE A PIECE OF POMEGRANATE ABOUT THY LOCKS.
The Word רקה occurs nowhere elſe, except Judg. IV. 21, 22, 26. in
which Places it ſignifies that Part of *the Temple that borders upon the
Cheek:* but here it can, I imagine, ſignify nothing beſides *the Cheek:*
for it cannot be pretended that *red Temples* are a Beauty. The Cheeks
are compared to *a Piece* of this Fruit, becauſe the Pomegranate, when
whole, is of a dull Colour; but, when cut up, of a lively beautiful
Vermilion. *Modeſty* and *Ingenuouſneſs* are called by this Name in Arabic, *viz.* رقة.

V. 9.

V. 9. — *thou haſt raviſhed my Heart with one of thine Eyes,* לבבתני באחד מעיניך] The Maſſora reads באחת; which Reading ſeems preferable, and ought to be rendered either AT ONCE, as Prov. XXVIII. 18. or ALTOGETHER, as Jer. X. 8. thus — THOU HAST RAVISHED MY HEART AT ONCE (or, ALTOGETHER) WITH THINE EYES.

V. 15. *A Fountain of Gardens, a Well of living Waters, and Streams from Lebanon.*] In our preſent Verſion this Verſe is unconnected with the Context, and hard to be underſtood. In the old Verſion it is all expreſſed by the Vocative Caſe : but I think it would be better to ſupply, *Thou art &c.*

CHAP. V.

V. 5. *I roſe up to open to my beloved, and my Hands dropped* with *Myrrh, and my Fingers* with *ſweet-ſmelling Myrrh, upon the Handles of the Lock.* — קמתי אני לפתח לדודי — וידי נטפו מור ואצבעתי מור עבר כפרת המנעול:] This ſeems to allude to a Cuſtom, which prevailed in ancient Times, of adorning the Door of a new married Couple with Garlands, and of perfuming it with odoriferous Eſſences. Thus Lucretius, *Lib.* IV. v. 1120.

> *At lachrymans excluſus amator limina ſæpe*
> *Floribus et ſertis operit, poſteſque ſuperbos*
> *Ungit amaracino, et foribus miſer oſcula figit.*

V. 11. *His Head is as the moſt fine Gold, his Locks are buſhy,* and *black as a Raven.* : ראשו כתם פז — קוצותיו תלתלים שחרות כערב] Though the Ancients prized *the golden* or *flaxen Locks,* (which they called χρυσῃ, whence χρυσοκομος) this cannot be the Senſe here, as they are ſaid to be *black.* This doubtleſs alludes to the Cuſtom that prevailed among them of uſing a Powder of that Colour, or Ornaments of Gold in their Locks ; which Philoſtratus calls ηλιωσαι κομη ; and Eunapius uſes almoſt the ſame Words as Solomon, *viz.* Αι κομαι μελαντεραι τε και ηλιωσαι κατηχοντο. So likewiſe Anacreon, where he gives the Painter Directions how to paint his Miſtreſs, ſays,

> Λιπαρας κομας ποιησον,
> Τα μεν ενδοθεν μελαινας,
> Τα δ' ες ακρον ηλιωτας.

And ſoon after,

> Γραφε μοι τριχας το πρωτον
> Απαλας τε και μελαινας· *Epig.* XXVIII.

·V. 12. *His Eyes* are *as the Eyes of Doves by the Rivers of Waters, washed with Milk,* and *fitly set.* — רחצות — עיניו כיונים על אפיקי מים [בחלב ישבות על מלאת: Rather — His Eyes are as the Eyes of Doves, which are NEAR STREAMS OF WATER, ARE WASHED WITH MILK, and DWELL IN PLENTY. Our Tranflators make · the whole Verfe to have reference to the Eyes: but furely this is a Miftake. The Comparifon ceafes after the Mention of the Dove's Eyes, which are beautiful; the other three Claufes relate only to that Bird, whofe Eyes may be fuppofed to fparkle more than ufual, when fhe is near the Water, either to drink or wafh herfelf. The Expreffion, *wafhed with Milk,* implies *a white Dove*; perhaps the more prized on that account; and the Words, *dwelling in Plenty,* are added to denote her *Plumpnefs,* which contributes to her Beauty.

V. 13. *His Cheeks* are *as a Bed of Spices,* as *fweet Flowers: his Lips* like *Lillies, dropping fweet-fmelling Myrrh.* — לחי כערוגת הבשם [מגדלות מרקחים שפתותיו—שושנים נטפות מור עבר: Thus I think ought the Hemiftics to be divided, and rendered — His CHEEKS are AS BEDS OF SPICES; HIS LIPS AS PERFUMED WREATHS, AS LIL-LIES DROPPING SWEET-SMELLING MYRRH.

CHAP. VI.

V. 4. *Thou* art *beautiful, O my Love,* as *Tirzah, comely as Jerufa-lem, terrible as* an Army *with Banners.* — נאוה — יפה את רעיתי כתרצה [כירושלם אימה כנדגלות: The latter Claufe both here and V. 10. does not feem to be of a Piece with the reft of the Verfe, in either Place. The Defign in both Places is to give an Idea of a beautiful and amiable Woman: but the Quality of *terrible,* and the Comparifon *to an Army with Banners,* can only fuit a Bellona or an Amazon. I would therefore render it --- MAJESTIC (*creating Awe*) AS STAN-DARDS. She is compared to Tirzah, a Town in the Tribe of Ephraim, the Capital not only of that Diftrict, but of all the circumjacent Coun-try before Samaria was built. It is fuppofed to have had that Name from it's Pleafantnefs.

V. 13. *Return, return, O Shulamite* —— שובי שובי השולמית] Qu. is not this Proper Name formed from that of *Solomon* with the femi-nine Termination, as אישה *a Woman* from איש *a Man*; and might it not be rendered --- THOU WIFE OF SOLOMON?

CHAP.

V. 5. — *and the Hair of thine Head like Purple,* —— ודלת ראשך
כארגמן] This Word occurs only in this Place; and has no Connection with any known Root in Hebrew. I wonder therefore our Translators would give it the Signification of *Hair*, as no Hairs are ever of that Colour, or can with Propriety be compared to it. This Word muſt mean ſomething which is *about the Head*: and why ſhould it not as well ſignify A FILLET, or BANDAGE? Now דליל in Chaldee is *Filum tenue, Filamentum, Peniculamentum*. Inſtead of the כ in כארגמן I would read ב, and render — AND THE BANDAGE OF THINE HEAD IS OF PURPLE: which Colour anciently was appropriated to Princes and Magiſtrates.

—— *the King is held in the Galleries.* מלך אסור ברהטים :] In the old Verſion theſe Words are thus rendered — *the King is tied in the Rafters* or *Galleries*, meaning "that he delighteth to come near thee, "and to be in thy Company." But this Senſe (ſuch as it is) is quite unconnected with the Context. I would therefore borrow a Signification of רהט from the Arabic, and render — THE KING IS CAPTIVATED BY THINE ATTIRE; for رهط is a ſort of Apron tied round the Waiſt. An anonymous ancient Greek Interpreter reads here —— και η ᾳραξιτυπτις σε ως πορφυρα βασιλεως περιδεδεμενη ειλημασι — *and thy Dreſs is like the Purple of a King tied about with Bandages.* See Montfaucon's Hexapla.

V. 8. — *and the Smell of thy Noſe like Apples:* וריח אפך כתפוחים :] Rather, I think — LIKE ORANGES, or PEACHES; for تفاح ſignifies either of theſe Fruits, which have a fragrant Smell; whereas in general *Apples* have ſcarcely any Smell, except after they have been kept ſome time, and then it is far from being agreeable.

V. 9. — *cauſing the Lips of thoſe that are aſleep to ſpeak.* דובב שפתי
ישנים :] All the ancient Verſions ſeem to have read here ושנים : and as דובב occurs nowhere elſe, the Arabic may help us to determine it's Signification; which is *To move gently, to creep, to flow ſoftly.* And as the Subject of the Paſſage relates to Wine going down the Throat aright, nothing can be more pertinent in this Place than the Arabic Senſe, or than the Lection adopted by all the Verſions. I would therefore render the Text thus --- MOVING GENTLY THROUGH THE

LIPS

Lips and Teeth. This all know is commonly the Cafe of good Wines. The only Ground on which the Verb רבב has the Senfe of *fpeaking* given to it is, that רבה fignifies *a Rumour.*

Chap. VIII.

V. 2. *I would lead thee*, and *bring thee into my Mother's Houfe*, who *would inftruct me:* — אנהגך אביאך אל בית אמי תלמדני] The LXX, Syriac, Arabic, and Ethiopic Verfions feem to have read (inftead of the laft Word, תלמדני) ואל הדר ילדני; for they all render —— *I would lead thee, and bring thee into my Mother's Houfe,* and into the Chamber of her who bore me.

V. 5. *Who is this that cometh up from the Wildernefs, leaning upon her beloved?*] This Interrogation, inftead of being contained in a Parenthefis, ought to make a diftinct Verfe; as it is neither put in the Mouth of the Bridegroom, nor the Bride. The Speakers are probably the Virgins who attended upon this Occafion.

—— *I raifed thee up under the Apple Tree: there thy Mother brought thee forth;* — תחת התפוח עוררתיך — שמה חבלתך אמך] The Bride-groom having fuggefted to the Bride that he once awaked her from her Sleep under a Tree, feems to take Occafion to remind her, that under that very Tree her Mother had been feized with the Pangs of Childbirth : a Circumftance which cannot be introduced with Propriety but in fuch a Poem as a Paftoral. So Virgil, *Ecl.* VIII. v. 37.

> *Sepibus in noftris parvam te rofcida mala*
> *(Dux ego vefter eram) vidi cum Matre legentem &c.*
> *Ut vidi, ut perii, ut me malus abftulit error!*

Which is an Imitation of Theocritus, ΕΙΔΥΛ. β. 82.

> Χως ιδον, ως εμανην, ως μοι πει θυμος ιαφθη
> Δειλαιας ——

Martial alfo takes Notice of a fimilar Circumftance, *Lib.* VI. *Epig.* LXIV.

> —————— *Dum prandia portat aranti,*
> *Hirfuta peperit rubicunda fub ilice conjux.*

V. 6. — *which hath a moft vehement Flame.* שלהבתיה:] This Word is fuppofed to be compounded of the relative Particle ש, להב *a Flame*, and יה *God:* but I think that להבתי is only the plural Termi-

nation

nation with the feminine Affix; and I would render it —— WHICH
INFLAME HER.

V. 9. *If she be a Wall, we will build upon her a Palace of Silver:*
אם חומה היא נבנה עליה טירת כסף] By this ftrong oriental Phrafe
I apprehend no more is meant, than fimply to fay, that, if fhe be fit to
be married, we ought to feek out a fuitable Hufband for her.

UPON THE WHOLE, this Poem feems to be of a mixt
Nature between the Dramatic and the Paftoral. The Unities of Time,
Place, and Characters are not fo ftrictly obferved as in later Compofitions
of either Kind. There are Traces of feven different Days; during
which Interval the Marriage Feftival lafted among the Jews : fee Gen.
XXIX. 27. Judg. XIV. 12. The Scene fometimes reprefents the Country, fometimes the City, &c. And Solomon appears at Times in his
own real Character, prefently after in that of a Shepherd, then reaf-
fumes his own again. The *Dramatis Perfonæ*, befides the Bridegroom
and Bride, are the Watchmen, or fuch Perfons as are occafionally met
with on the Road, and a Chorus of Maidens, Attendants on the Bride.
The Language is fometimes lofty and fpirited; fometimes only fuitable to Shepherds. Many of the Words, occurring in no other Place,
cannot have their precife Senfe eafily afcertained : neither can we always fee the Juftnefs of all the Comparifons; which probably proceeds
from our Ignorance, not only of the Terms, but of the Manners,
and other Circumftances.

THIS Poem is generally confidered as an *Epithalamium* compofed
by Solomon on his Marriage with the Daughter of Pharaoh, the King
of Egypt. And this appears to me to be the only Point of View in
which it ought to be confidered. In refpect to the myftical Senfe which
it is fuppofed to contain, I muft frankly acknowledge, that I cannot
perceive the leaft Foundation for it. This Notion I fuppofe was originally derived from the *Targum*, and adopted foon after by fome of
the Fathers, who, with more Piety than Judgment, thought that, as
St. Paul compares the Union of Chrift with his Church to a Marriage,
this Poem ought alfo to be interpreted with reference to the fame Subject. But how is it confiftent with this Idea, that neither the Name
of God, nor of Chrift, ever occurs in it? that there is not one religious or moral Sentiment to be found? that it is not once either quoted,
or moft diftantly alluded to, in any Part of the Sacred Writings? on
which account perhaps it is not directed to be read in our Churches.

We

We find alfo, that thofe who attempt to trace the Allegory in every Part are foon loft in an inextricable Labyrinth.

But I feem already to hear it objected, that it is great Prefumption to venture to diffent from an Opinion, which has been eftablifhed for near twenty Centuries, and has been abetted by great, good, and learned Men during all that long Interval; and that this novel Opinion may tend to weaken the Foundation of the Church of Chrift. To this I reply, that mere Length of Time is but a fandy Foundation for the Bafis of Truth to reft upon; that all it can in Reafon pretend to is, to teach us Caution before we quit eftablifhed Opinions: but furely it ought not to preclude us from making due Inquiries, and ufing our rational Powers; or, upon due Conviction of former Errors, from publicly detecting them. In regard to any fuppofed Inconvenience accruing to the Chriftian Religion, I really fee none. On the contrary, as it is fo well eftablifhed *on the fure Word of Prophecy*, which *Thrones, Principalities, and Powers*, cannot prevail againft, it appears to me more for the Intereft of that Religion to quit an untenable Poft, than to expofe it to the Affault of Enemies, who muft inevitably foon become Mafters of it.

F I N I S.

ADVERTISEMENT.

T HE Author firſt intended to have ſubjoined to the preceding Sheets his Remarks *on the Prophets:* but, being indiſpenſably obliged to be abſent from the Univerſity for ſome Time, finds himſelf under a Neceſſity of poſtponing the Publication to another Opportunity.

www.ingramcontent.com/pod-product-compliance
Lightning Source LLC
Chambersburg PA
CBHW031402270326
41929CB00010BA/1289